12^{95}

INVESTIGATIVE REPORTING

INVESTIGATIVE REPORTING

From Courthouse to White House

Clark R. Mollenhoff
Washington and Lee University

Macmillan Publishing Co., Inc.
New York
Collier Macmillan Publishers
London

Macmillan Publishing Co., Inc.
866 Third Avenue, New York, New York 10022

Collier Macmillan Canada, Ltd.

Library of Congress Cataloging in Publication Data

Mollenhoff, Clark R
  Investigative reporting.

  Bibliography: p.
  Includes index.
  1. Reporters and reporting. 2. Government and
the press. I. Title.
PN4781.M57   070.4'3   79-25672
ISBN 0-02-381870-0

Printing: 1 2 3 4 5 6 7 8   Year: 1 2 3 4 5 6 7

FOREWORD

Educator James Bryant Conant once wrote: "Each honest calling, each walk of life, has its own elite, its own aristocracy based on excellence of performance."

Conant was describing, in his own inimitable way, what we call leaders. One such aristocrat is Clark Mollenhoff, the undisputed doyen of investigative reporting in America. It is about time that Mollenhoff did a book on the thing he does best; and this is it.

Investigative reporting is subject to definition. It is the reporting, through one's own work product and initiative, matters of importance which some person or group want to keep secret.

The three basic elements are that the investigation be the work of the reporter, not the work of others that he is reporting; that the subject of the story involves something that is important for his or her readers to know; and that others are attempting to hide the truth of these matters from the people.

Certainly the United States government wanted to keep the Pentagon Papers secret. When portions of these papers were published by the *New York Times*, the *Boston Globe*, and the *Washington Post*, these papers performed an outstanding public service. The subject matter was also important. But it was not investigative reporting because the facts and conclusions that made the Pentagon Papers important were the result of the government's own investigation, not an investigation conducted by those newspapers.

Watergate, on the other hand, was a classic example of investigative reporting. From the President down, some of the most powerful people in the government were determined to keep the secrets of Watergate. *Washington Post* reporters Bob Woodward and Carl Bernstein led the rest of the nation's press in baring the facts of Watergate. Woodward and Bernstein were not reporting the results of someone else's investigation. They conducted their own, doggedly trudging from source to document to source for nearly two years until they forced the truth into the open.

The same can be said for Pam Zeckman and her fellow reporters on the *Chicago Sun Times*, who in 1979 opened a Chicago saloon called The Mirage Bar and worked for nearly a year recording the corruption of the local officials who systematically preyed upon the city's bar and restaurant owners. That this project did not win a Pulitzer Prize when it was clearly the best piece of investigative reporting done that year, is less a comment on the project than it was on the domination of the Pulitzer board by *Washington Post* editor Benjamin Bradlee.

Watergate and The Mirage Bar are perfect illustrations of investigative reporting. President Nixon did not want the people to know how his administration tried to hide the facts of Watergate. Grafting Chicago officials did not want the people to know that they were extortionists. In each case, there were facts that a person or a group of persons were trying to keep secret. The secret involved important matters. And in each instance, the reporters used their own initiative and work product to uncover these secrets and reveal them to the people.

Mollenhoff is right when he says there is nothing mysterious about investigative reporting. But, I think he is being charitable when he says that the average intelligent, inquisitive person can become a fine investigative reporter. Competent, perhaps, but the really good investigative reporter is, as the late Louis Armstrong used to say: "A real special breed of cat." Not a better breed, but certainly a special breed.

Virtually all of America's top investigative reporters share, in one degree or another, the following traits: desire, drive, judgment, determination, persistence, imagination, integrity, a sense of organization, and a basic jugular instinct.

Some of these traits need no explanation, others do. Judgment, for example, is one of the most important attributes, yet the most elusive of definition. It is the ability to correctly estimate the nature, scope, and importance of a story and then to report and write it in a professional way. Extremes are avoided; passion is controlled; conduct is guarded.

Another trait that needs more definition is organization. I refer to a person with a methodical mind. Most investigations are exercises in logic. Facts pile upon each other in such a way that they lead to a valid conclusion. Some people are capable of thinking in logical progressions, others think in emotional terms. The organized mind plans investigations; the organized mind breaks down complex subjects into easily understood segments. This type of person is capable of setting a goal and then reaching it by the most logically direct path.

The word imagination also has a special meaning in talking about good investigative reports. By imagination, I mean an ability to perceive patterns from facts and events and then to apply those patterns in furthering the investigation. This is better known as seeing the forest when others see only trees. There is also a second definition: the ability to apply new, imaginative solutions to reporting and story problems.

The final attribute which I think needs further explanation is sense of the jugular. This hardly means bloodthirsty. It means the ability to cut through extraneous facts and go directly to the heart of the matter. Too many investigative reporters get bogged down in facts and lose sight of their planned goals. Too many others get intrigued with collateral information developed during the course of an investigation and drift off the main highway onto meandering side roads that move further and further away from their original destinations. A reporter with a jugular sense is undeterred by extraneous facts or the blandishments of collateral information. He or she moves unswervingly to the planned goal.

Add to these traits the ability of the reporter to stay cool under fire not only during the reporting and writing process, but also the inevitable personal attacks, libel suits, and second-guessing that follow most successful investigative projects.

Clark Mollenhoff has all of these attributes. So does Pam Zeckman of the *Chicago Sun Times*. Dick Cady of the *Indianapolis Star*, Jerry O'Neill of the *Boston Globe*, Jack Nelson of the *Los Angeles Times*, Gene Miller of the *Miami Herald*, Jerry Uhrhammer of the *Eugene* (Ore.) *Register-Guard*, Harry Jones of the *Kansas City Star*, Bruce Locklin of the *Bergen* (N.J.) *Record*, Jack Taylor of the *Daily Oklahoman* and some 40 other reporters in this country who have given investigative reporting most of its current credibility.

A universal hallmark of these reporters is durability in their chosen field. There are many reporters in this country who have done fine investigative stories, a number of them Pulitzer prize winners. But there are only a few who stand the test of time, who do consistently fine investigative stories of local, regional, or national importance. These are the names mentioned when knowledgeable people discuss investigative reporting, whether it be in Washington, D.C. or Duluth, Minnesota.

Most of these reporters are what we call naturals. They take to investigative reporting as instinctively as ducks take to water. Many of them never attended journalism school. The rest of them had no journalism school courses in investigative reporting when they were in college. They evolved into investigative reporting on a full or part time basis because it was the thing they felt most comfortable doing, and, because they felt comfortable doing it, they did it better than anyone else.

I do not mean by this that someone who isn't a natural cannot become a competent investigative reporter. Increased concentration on the techniques of investigative reporting in the nation's journalism schools, increased general awareness of the importance of investigative reporting, and the increased body of knowledge being delivered to the craft by such professional groups as Investigative Reporters and Editors, have combined to present all reporters with programs and guidelines that they can employ to attain competence in the investigative reporting field.

Because good sources are as vital to investigative reporting as solid documentation, investigative reporters spend long hours developing and cultivating sources. Because these sources are frequently at the fulcrum of newsworthy events, the good investigative reporter frequently is a newspaper's best source of exclusive stories. While these exclusive source stories are not within the definition of investigative reporting, they are just as vital to a newspaper and bring it just as much—and sometimes more—national recognition.

The good investigative reporter can be a newspaper's most valuable asset. One solid story carried on the front pages of the nation's newspapers and quoted on radio and television with attribution to the paper that broke the story, is worth more in recognition than the entire annual budget of the average newspaper's promotion department. Prize recognition of these stories is worth even more.

There are many otherwise ordinary papers that have been transformed by the consistently outstanding work of one or several reporters into nationally recognized press institutions. Consider, for example, the *St. Louis Post Dispatch*, for many years one of America's great newspapers. Ted Link was virtually the last in an unbroken chain of great reporters who worked for the *Dispatch*. We must ask ourselves: Has the *Post Dispatch* become a second-rate newspaper in recent years, because it no longer has a Ted Link? Or has the attitude of the newspaper management changed so radically in recent years that it is no longer possible for the paper to have someone like Ted Link? The *Des Moines Register*, a good state newspaper for many years, became a national entity while Clark Mollenhoff was in its national bureau. Now that Mollenhoff is no longer there, the *Register* is once again just another good state newspaper. Who would hear of the *Daily Oklahoman* nationally, if it were not for Jack Taylor, the *Indianapolis Star* if it were not for Dick Cady, the *Bergen Record*, if it were not for Bruce Locklin, and so on.

I naturally except such papers as the *New York Times* and the *Los Angeles Times*, which have become institutions in themselves. And I recognize that with editors like Jim Hoge on the *Chicago Sun Times* and Tom Winship, Bob Healey and Jack Driscoll on the *Boston Globe*, some newspapers create the kind of exciting atmosphere that breeds and attracts the best investigative reporters. But the editors of many newspapers should realize that it is only a small handful of reporters—many of them investigative—that have earned them their national reputations over the years.

Of all these, Clark Mollenhoff is perhaps the most enduring. Like most of this country's top investigative reporters, Mollenhoff never carried the formal title. He was always a beat reporter, whether it was in the Polk County (Iowa) courthouse, the Iowa State House or his newspaper's Washington bureau. He was one of those natural investigative reporters that just seem to pop on the scene once in awhile. He found injustice where other reporters didn't bother to look; he searched for patterns; he questioned relentlessly; he developed key sources; and he regularly did investigative stories from his routine news beats.

Mollenhoff solidly established his credentials as an investigative reporter in Des Moines long before he went to Washington. This is a fact that many young investigative reporters should keep in mind. Some are so convinced that they can only make their mark nationally in Washington, D.C., that they overlook the fact that most of the nation's best known investigative reporters made their reputations in their own home towns and continue to work in those localities.

Through the years, however, one unique trait has .set Clark Mollenhoff apart from his working colleagues. That has been his ability to reduce and abstract the basic rules that we all follow more or less instinctively as investigative reporters.

On countless occasions an editor or a younger reporter has asked me: "Why are you doing———this way?" Occasionally I have been able to give a reasonable response. But, more often I have not, at least, not on the spot. The reason, I think, is that our minds act very much like computers. In my case, the computer has been storing experimental factors for some 30 years and my actions and reactions to events are automatically triggered by these factors without consciously being translated into rules. If I sit down for an hour or so and reflect on the why of a particular action, I can usually come up at least with an operating premise.

But Clark Mollenhoff has an almost casual ability to translate act into premise, premise into guideline and guideline into precept. Usually he is unerringly accurate when he does so.

Mollenhoff's few detractors translate his tendency to speak in precepts as pomposity. But as a close friend and associate of nearly 20 years, I know it as something else. Precepts are generally more accurate and informative than illustrations which may only vaguely approximate the ideas we wish to convey. Mollenhoff is simply using a faculty that the rest of us wish we had.

There is something else about Clark Mollenhoff. He really cares. He has a passion for his craft and he desperately wants to pass on intact what we have learned to a new generation of reporters. As such, he does not easily tolerate inaccuracy, sloth, or less than total commitment. He has spent long years abstracting rules from the best that we have done and the best that he has done and he offers it to the next generation on a silver platter.

That is what makes this book so important. It will take its place along side the late Paul Williams' *Investigative Reporting and Editing"* as the textbook that will most influence the nature and quality of investigative reporting for the next twenty years.

It is more, however, than a textbook for journalists, investigators, and those interested in learning how to probe the innards of government. It is, in a sense, the autobiography of the finest investigative reporter of our time.

Clark Mollenhoff's life is his work. *Investigative Reporting* is a fascinating account of that work, skillfully written in such a way that it serves as a ready-reference guide for investigative reporting of everything from the local police precinct to the White House.

As we read, we learn, step-by-step what to look for, how to overcome problems, what checklists to follow, what roads to take, and what paths to avoid.

I am still convinced that the best investigative reporters are born, not made. But if any single book can make the difference, this one will.

Bob Greene, *Newsday*

PREFACE

This book is an effort to explore my own experience and the experiences of other newsmen for lessons that will have some universal application in public service journalism and for students of government, history, or political science. Looking back on nearly 40 years of experience on the front line of what we now know as investigative reporting, there were few total successes where exposure of wrong brought swift action to correct the wrong. There were many partial successes in which government officials or others made some moves designed to give the impression they were righting the wrong, when in fact they were engaging in further deceptive posturing to fool the public.

There were also many failures where dishonest officials, arrogant in their power to control investigation and prosecution machinery, simply refused to do anything to correct the injustices while further abusing their power with efforts to retaliate against those truthful individuals who had helped in exposing them to the press.

Often, I learned more from the partial successes and the failures than I did from the quick successes that required little courage and no persistence. It is seldom the courage and persistence of one reporter that prevails, but it is the courage and persistence of the majority of individuals who make up an entire organization, and the moral support and encouragement from colleagues in long fights against entrenched power.

I would like to pay specific tribute to Frank Eyerly, the longtime managing editor of the *Des Moines Register*; Herbert D. Kelly, Ray Wright and Charles Reynolds, news editors of the *Des Moines Register*; Alan Hoschar, and John Zug, city editors of the *Des Moines Register,* and George Mills, the chief political writer for the *Des Moines Register*. Their professional advice, their guidance, their encouragement, and their dedication to honest government and honest journalism were vital to my own confidence that pursuit of the full story was worth the risk.

Also, I was fortunate to work for Richard L. Wilson, the long-time Washington Bureau Chief for the Cowles organization, and to be associated with a group of fine reporters in the Cowles Washington Bureau. I learned from each of them. I would pay special tribute to Wilbur Elston, Fletcher Knebel, Jack Wilson, Nat Finney, and Marr McGaffin as having been particularly helpful and encouraging at crucial times during my first years in Washington.

My historic perspective on the problems of mismanagement and corruption was improved immeasurably through association with Louis M. Lyons, Curator of the Nieman Foundation at Harvard, through the discussions with the other eleven Nieman fellows in the 1949-50 year, and by attending the classes of some of the finest professors then teaching at Harvard.

I worked closely with Dr. Arthur Hanford who taught a course in State Government, and through conversations in and out of class gained a broader knowledge of various forms of city, county, and state government. From Professor Frederick Merk, a great teacher on the westward movement in American history; and from Professor Arthur M. Schlesinger, Sr., who lectured on the social and cultural development of the United States, I learned important lessons on past scandals and the various reform movements. Through Professor John Black and J. Kenneth Galbraith I learned the history of the agriculture problems and government programs and a smattering of agricultural economics. I received my first indoctrination into what was being taught about public administration from Professor Merle Fainsod, who also taught a course that dealt with the operation of the bureaucracy in the Soviet Union. Professor McGeorge Bundy, who had just completed a biography on Army Secretary Henry L. Stimson, gave me my first close examination of the making of American foreign policy.

Under the direction of Professor Theodore Morrison, of the English Department, our class of Nieman Fellows spent months on the research and writing of a special edition of Nieman Reports dealing with the things that were (and are) wrong with the newspaper business and newspapers. Those frank discussions were an enlightening experience for a young newsman who had spent his entire career on one newspaper in a monopoly newspaper town, and isolated from the problems of other news rooms.

I was among the youngest members of my Nieman class and I learned much from the more experienced newsmen in my class. They ranged from John McCormally, a precocious 26-year-old editorial writer from the *Emporia* (Kansas) *Gazette*, to Max R. Hall, a 39-year-old labor reporter for the Associated Press in Washington,

D.C. Others were: Robert H. Fleming, 38, a political reporter for the *Milwaukee Journal*; Richard J. Wallace, 38, a political and editorial writer for the *Memphis Press-Scimitar*; William German, 37, head of the copy desk on the *San Francisco Chronicle*; Donald J. Gonzales, 31, a diplomatic correspondent for the United Press; Murrey Marder, 29, who covered the State Department for the *Washington Post*; William M. Stucky, 29, city editor for the *Lexington* (Kentucky) *Leader*; Hays Gorey, 28, city editor of the *Salt Lake Tribune*; John L. Hulteng, 28, an editorial writer for the *Providence Journal,* and Melvin S. Wax, an assistant news editor and feature writer for the *Rutland* (Vermont) *Herald.*

That association and the experiences we shared during the 1949–50 Nieman year were invaluable as a preparation for becoming a Washington reporter in 1950.

C.R.M

CONTENTS

1 The Free Press—Lifeline of
Democracy   1
The Purpose of Investigative
Reporting   2
The Pitfalls in Investigative
Reporting   4

2 The Investigative Journalist—Talents,
Techniques, and Traits in Summary   8
Necessary Techniques   9
Traits, Inborn or Acquired   11
Mollenhoff Primer   13

3 The Use of Records and
Procedures   21
Reading 1:
Drunken Driving Fix   25
A Valuable Learning Experience   38
Student Work Project Suggestion   39

4 Dealing with Vice and Payoffs   40
Problems in enforcement of
Victimless Crime Laws   40
Reading 2:
The Payoff Story   45
Student Work Project Suggestion   49

5 Police and Court Patterns   51
The Value of Routine   51
Types of Experience   53
Student Work Project Suggestion   58

6 Exposure of Corruption: Part I   59
The Solid Wall   59
Reading 3:
Black Market Cars   61
Lessons from Failure   63
Student Work Project Suggestion   63

7 Exposure of Corruption: Part II   64
Reformers   64
Reading 4:
Paul Walters, Reformer   66
Student Work Project Suggestion   70

8 Polk County Fraud Report   71
The "Hard" Interview   71
Value of an Adversary Interview   72
Who Covers a Story   73
Reading 5:
Interview with Elmer Croft   74
Student Work Project Suggestion   77

9 Polk County Frauds—The Importance
of Follow Through   78
Exposure of Corruption
Is Not Enough   78
A Dishonest Grand Juror   80
Choice of a Judge   81
Choice of a Prosecutor   82
Need for Nonpartisan Attitude   82
Student Work Project Suggestion   83

10 Polk County Fraud Trials   84
A Source of Future Story Leads   84
Evidence from Witnesses   87
Student Work Project Suggestion   91

11 The Polk County Jail   92
Criticism of Cooperative
Officials   92

Reading 6:
No Escape Intended   95
Results of Exposing Laxity   98
Student Work Project Suggestion   99

12   Lessons from Elmer Croft   100
Dealing with Informants   100
Fraud Outside Polk County   103
Student Work Project Suggestion   105

13   Lessons in the Politics of
Prosecution   106
The State Intervenes   106
The Grand Jury Investigation   109
Reversals Owing to
Political Pressure   111
Politically Partisan Courts
A Serious Problem   112
Student Work Project Suggestion   113

14   Payoff Probe Problems   114
The Effect of Politics on a
Criminal Prosecution   114
The Effect on Politics of the
Prosecution   117
Student Work Project Suggestion   119

15   Polk County Lesson on
Government   120
Management of Government
Property   120
Conflicts of Interest   124
Reading 7:
Real Estate Dealings   125
Student Work Project Suggestion   128

16   Assessment of Secrecy   129
Assessments and Real Value   129
Secret Reappraisal Exposed   131
Exposure of Conflict of Interest   133

News Stories Encourage
Clean Government   134
Student Work Project Suggestion   135

17 Investigating at the Iowa Capitol   136
A Dream Assignment   136
Reading 8:
Lew Farrell and the Alcohol
Tax Unit   138
Reading 9:
The P-60 Scandal   142
Student Work Project Suggestion   145

18 Washington, D.C.—Downey Rice
and Senator Kefauver   147
Introduction to the
Washington Scene   147
The Kefauver Crime Committee   150
A System Develops   155
Student Work Project Suggestion   155

19 Congressional Springboard   156
Sources—Members of Congress   156
Reading 10:
Defense Contract Bungling   162
Valuable Lessons   166
Student Work Project Suggestion   167

20 National News of Local Interest   168
A Reluctant Investigator   168
Future Repercussions   171
Student Work Project Suggestion   172

21 It Is the Follow Through
That Counts   176
The Dangers Inherent in
Secrecy Provisions   176
Cooperative Effort   176

Reading 11:
Attack on the Secrecy Blanket   180
A Reporter's Contributions to
Secrecy Reform   182
Student Work Project Suggestion   184

22   The Importance of Justice   185
Need for Press Coverage   185
Saving and Using Printed Stories   187
Reporter's Hours   188
Reading 12:
Truman Administration Scandals   189
Lessons Learned   193
Student Work Project Suggestion   193

23   Learning about Labor Rackets   194
Reporting on an
Unfamiliar Problem   194
Covering the Investigation   199
Press Scrutiny has Important
Effects   202
Student Work Project Suggestion   203

24   A Claim of Security Risk   204
The Problem of "Security Risk"   204
A Reporter Must Be Cautious   205
Careful Preparation   205
Reading 13:
The Ladejinsky Case   209
Rewards of Persistence   215
Student Work Project Suggestion   215

25   The Big Labor Racket Inquiry   217
Local Aspects   217
The National Scene   218
The McClellan Committee
Investigation   223
Young Men and Taylor's System   227
Student Work Project Suggestion   229

for Nov. 12

26 The Regulatory Agencies and the
White House 230

An Insidious Form of
Corruption 230

Executive Privilege Used to
Defend Corruption 233

A Quiet But Thorough
Investigator 233

Involvement of the Press 237

Reading 14:
Sherman Adams and the CAB 239

A Pileup of Pressure Will Break
Through Privilege 243

Student Work Project Suggestion 245

27 The Agriculture Department and
Billie Sol Estes 246

Fraud in Unlikely Places 247

A Giant Scandal 248

The Scandal Dies
With a Whimper 256

Student Work Project Suggestion 258

28 Pentagon Bungling 259

Signs of Bungling or
Corruption 259

A Series of Frauds 261

The "McNamara Monarchy" 263

The Press Fails in Dealing
With the Pentagon 265

Reading 15:
The Flying Edsel—TFX-111 269

Student Work Project Suggestion 278

29 Exposing Bobby Baker and LBJ 280

Reading 16:
Too Much Money 280

Reporting on the
Bobby Baker Story 290

Student Work Project Suggestion 293

30 Coping with LBJ's Coverup 294

A Dramatic Change 294

Attempts to Protect the
Baker Investigation 296

Johnson Moves Against the
Investigation 297

A Partial Success 303

Student Work Project Suggestion 303

31 Probing Commodity Market Scandals—
A Classic Investigation 305

A Different Kind of Investigation 305

A Team Effort 311

Looking for Clues and Following Them 316

Student Work Project Suggestion 317

32 Watergate and the Aftermath 318

The Role of the Press 318

Reading 17:
Reporter's View 321

Student Work Project Suggestion 338

33 The Arizona Project 339

Founding the Investigative Reporters and
Editors (IRE) Group 339

First Project of the IRE 340

Lessons from the Arizona Project 344

Reading 18:
Blueprint for Investigation 347

Student Work Project Suggestion 349

34 The Continuing Problem and
Opportunity 350

The Press—Faults, Virtues, and
Opportunities 350

Recent Softness in Investigative
Reporting 352

The Need for an Honest, Dedicated, and
Respected Press 354

report on
for
Mon
Dec. 7

The Seven Basic Rules   357
The Profits in Ethical Practice   360

Appendix:
Checklist for Investigative Reporters   361
The County or City Board of Supervisors,
Commissioners, or Councilmen   361
Some Common Evils Found in
Local Government   363
The City or County Auditor   364
The Sheriff's Office and
Police Department   365
Office of the Clerk of Court   365
The Recorder's Office   367
The School System   368
The Highway Department   368
The Tax Assessor   368
City or County Health Department   368
A Full Personnel Probe   369

Suggested Reading List   370

Index   373

INVESTIGATIVE
REPORTING

1 THE FREE PRESS—LIFELINE OF DEMOCRACY

This book is written to demonstrate to students and young journalists that any reasonably intelligent individual can become a competent investigative reporter or editor through hard work, the application of a few simple rules, learning to research basic government records, and applying systematic and logical research techniques. This book is not a blueprint for a quick climb to the top. It is intended to be a guide for gaining the depth experience necessary to understand the problems of corruption and mismanagement and, in time, to gain confidence in your own ability to analyze government operations in a solid and responsible manner. We will be dealing with the analysis of government functions from the viewpoint of the investigative reporter or editor. However, it is my belief that the same talents essential to fast acquisition of the facts, the history of a problem, and the law concerning it can be equally beneficial to any position in government or business.

I will apply the rules expounded in this book to the news business because I believe that solid and responsible investigative reporting can be the answer to most of the problems the press faces today from a skeptical public. An understanding of the basic tools, talents, and traits of good investigative journalism will permit newspapers to establish workable standards for aggressive and fair pursuit of mismanagement and corruption in government. These standards are equally applicable in dealing with local, state, or federal government.

This book follows an autobiographical pattern because I know my own story best. I can deal more frankly and surely with my own limitations and experiences at various stages than I can with the experiences of others. My research into the techniques of a wide range of successful investigative reporters, however, has convinced me that there are a few common threads that ran through the careers of Jacob Riis, Lincoln Steffens, Ida Tarbell, Ray Stannard Baker, Paul Y. Anderson, Ted Link, George Bliss, Jack Nelson, and Robert W. Greene. All were without formal training in reporting. All were angered at injustice. All were determined to do something about it. All went about the job with a thoughtful tenacity and a determination to learn all the relevant facts and the laws and procedures related to the subjects of their inquiries.

Reading one book will not make the student an experienced investigative reporter, but I believe that anyone who reads this book carefully, completes the exercises diligently, and applies some common sense will be equipped to take the first step—a simple investigation of corruption or mismanagement in government involving record research.

THE PURPOSE OF INVESTIGATIVE REPORTING

The survival of the American democracy is to a large degree contingent upon whether the American people understand the problems of their society. Only if the press can establish and maintain a large and effective corps of truly professional nonpartisan investigative reporters and editors, can these problems be defined. These men and women must have high standards to test their work, and they must be consistently honest, responsible, fair, and nonpartisan in their attitudes. The tyranny of the press is no more conducive to democracy than the tyranny of politicians.

The efforts to be consistently honest, fair, and nonpartisan must extend to the publisher and top editors and should not be confined to the reporters and the working editors. It makes no difference how knowledgeable and balanced a reporter is, his best work can be weakened or destroyed by a superficial, ignorant, or dishonest editor or publisher.

What Needs Investigation

As the annual cost of the United States government soars above the $500 billion figure, voters are becoming more and more dependent upon the press to tell them what they must know about the operation of the government. It has become the public relations policy of various administrations to push so-called "reforms" of welfare programs, defense spending, and the various regulator agencies to make them "more responsive to the public." It takes a knowledgeable, hard working, objective, and nonpartisan reporter to analyze these so-called "reforms" in a manner that distinguishes between an administration's political posturing and genuine efforts to correct bad procedures and wasteful and corrupt practices.

"Reforms" and new procedures are not the only things that must be scrutinized. A key to good government operations is usually in the hands of the selected official who makes the appointments. Knowledgeable and honest top officials can make even a bad system perform reasonably well. However, officials who are dishonest or of questionable competency can corrupt and undermine a good governmental system in a few months.

Information provided by official sources must also be examined. The adequacy of the job being done by a newspaper cannot be determined by measuring the daily news hole (the space allocated to news) and making an analysis of how much space was given to stories dealing with local, state, federal, or foreign affairs. It is possible to devote the entire news hole to a coverage of government and still do an inadequate superficial job if the material presented consists of routine government announcements and a sprinkling of cute and off-beat features.

Reprinting all of the government handouts may perform one sort of service for the public, but the mass of verbiage will leave the majority of the people ill-equipped to ask necessary questions. Newspaper stories should contain a challenge made possible by record research and historic perspective. A knowledgeable reporter can use the facts available in the established record to put the spotlight on the inevitable oversimplifications, distortions, and outright misrepresentations that are a part of standard procedures in many politically oriented government press offices.

The Difficulties Involved

The inexperienced reporter may be misled by clever government gimmickry and, in turn, mislead his editors and the public. Or, an experienced reporter who lacks independence or is fearful of the partisanship or biases of his editors or publisher may parrot the government line until he receives firm instructions to the contrary.

Government officials who feel they will be held accountable by challenges from an honest experienced reporter will be cautious in the claims they make and the "reforms" they push. However, those officials who feel they are dealing with reporters who can be misled or hand fed will engage in the maximum in oversimplifications and deceptions that they can use without being held up to ridicule.

Although most large daily newspapers have several reporters and editors with some experience on investigations of local, state, or federal government, the quality is spotty. Only a handful of these reporters and editors have had the opportunity to gain a depth understanding of government records, intergovernmental operations, and the law of evidence so that they qualify for classification as well-rounded professional investigative reporters and editors. And, among those who have the tools and talents to plan and execute a newspaper investigation, only a few have had the encouragement to be truly nonpartisan in their approach to evidence of mismanagement or corruption in government.

I believe that an overwhelming majority of the experienced investigative reporters and working editors want to operate in a nonpartisan and nonideological manner, but many bow to the pressures of management (publishers and top editors) to slant stories politically or ideologically or to meet the whims, personal persuasions, or prejudices of a dominant editor or publisher. It is so easy for a reporter to bend to the whims and prejudices of an editor or publisher. It is so difficult to oppose, or even remain neutral, if management whims are accompanied by an arrogant desire to demonstrate personal power or political clout.

Among the best and most experienced investigative reporters, there is an acute awareness that it is a precarious profession and that a publisher's personal whim or an editor's partisanship for a political pal can outweigh the importance of any number of direct witnesses and any amount of heavily documented corroboration. That is the major barrier to a true professionalism in the newspaper business.

No amount of formal education and study can teach you how to cope with superiors who are politically partisan, dishonest, superficial, or expedient in their news judgments. Fortunately, a great many editors and publishers are basically honest in their initial motivations and can be moved from preconceived viewpoints by hard facts, consistent objectivity, and conscientious hard work.

THE PITFALLS IN INVESTIGATIVE REPORTING

The attacks on the press for irresponsibility, partisanship, and dishonesty come from the right, the left, and from thoughtful middle-of-the-road political thinkers. Admissions of vulnerability of the press come from reporters, editors and publishers, and from such thoughtful press observers as Charles Seib, the ombudsman for *The Washington Post,* and James C. Thomson, Jr., Curator of the Nieman Foundation for Journalism at Harvard University.

Thomson summed up the widespread criticism of the values and behavior of news organizations in the January 1978 Poynter Essay for Indiana University in saying: "The breadth and intensity of the concern [about press ethics] seems new. Public officials, lay citizens, and practitioners all now have strong views on what's wrong—much less often, on what's right—with the press and its practices. And in the process one indispensable protector of First Amendment press freedom, a climate of public understanding of the media's proper role, may well be in jeopardy." It is my belief that sound investigative reporting is needed to restore the public faith in the credibility of the press, and to make the press a more reliable and more effective monitor of the problems of government.

Although there are many fine examples of sound and effective investigative reporting, there is too much superficial and sensational trash that passes for investigative reporting. In the wake of Watergate, there is an understandable desire to emulate some of the very fine investigative reporting on that scandalous affair; however one must recognize that Watergate included reporting that was irresponsible, superficial, and filled with inexcusable errors. Examples of irresponsible, superficial and occasionally sleazy reporting were used by the political friends of President Richard Nixon in an effort to discredit the generally sound work that was being done in exposing the crimes and abuses of power by the Nixon White House.

Since the resignation of Richard Nixon in August 1974, there has been an effort by a highly competitive press to find "another Watergate." Editors and publishers see *The Washington Post* as the model, and do not discriminate between the admirable things *The Post* did and the superficiality and irresponsibility of some of the editing decisions.

Confidential Sources

Journalism students and some working reporters envy the sensational financial success of Bob Woodward and Carl Bernstein and see a "Deep Throat" source[1] as the sure swift route to the top of the newspaper business. They do not recognize that it was the persistent search of records and tireless interviewing of dozens of witnesses that was the strength of the Woodward and Bernstein contribution to the Watergate story. On the contrary, any real reliance on the mysterious and sketchy nods and grunts from "Deep Throat" for corroboration was risky, based upon superficial analysis, and probably irresponsible unless the editors knew more about that

---

[1] Deep Throat was the name Woodward and Bernstein used to identify a highly confidential inside source they used to corroborate information they had received from other sources outside the Nixon White House.

mystery figure than we have been told. The "Deep Throat" source provided Bob Woodward with "the second source" his editors demanded, and it was an interesting and intriguing gimmick for promotion of the book "The President's Men," and the motion picture.

Although investigative reporters must rely to some degree upon so-called "confidential sources," every really experienced investigative reporter knows that a great amount of malicious misinformation is peddled, even by high officials of the federal government when they are talking "on a confidential basis." All of us must deal with confidential sources in our efforts to expose mismanagement and corruption in government, business, or labor. Nonetheless even a co-conspirator in a crime must be supported by a net of sworn testimony and firm documentation if he is to be believed in court.

If we are really trying to get to the truth, rather than find bare justification for a story, we learn that few informants are totally reliable even though they may believe they are giving us the full truth. Frequently they will expand on what they know from direct conversations and observations because they believe it is probably true—and they know it is what the reporter wants to hear. A witness who is totally reliable on one subject may be deceptive and misleading where his own interests or those of his family members are involved or where he has reason to dislike the person involved in the alleged corruption or mismanagement.

Editors must keep this very human problem in mind in judging the confidential source of a reporter who has firmly concluded what the truth is but produces only an extremely mysterious confidential source as his corroboration. Unless there is some real and overwhelming problem on the timing of a story, the editor should insist upon a delay to learn the general qualifications of the source, to consult the newspaper's lawyer, and to seek documentation and corroboration. An editor must do this even with the experienced reporter who will not tell the name of the source. To do otherwise because of an edition deadline is superficial rationalization for starting down a path of hazardous irresponsibility. There are only a few publishers, editors, or reporters who would knowingly engage in irresponsible and unsound journalistic practices, but there are many who get into the habit of making split-second decisions to make a deadline on routine news judgment matters.

Lulled into a sense of confidence, and in many cases overconfidence, these same editors may fail to make a distinction between a routine and a difficult situation that requires a tighter standard.

Having carelessly stumbled into erroneous decisions, publishers, editors, and reporters too often defend the indefensible and in the process destroy any semblance of credibility that remains. It is against this background of questionable performance that Nieman Curator Thomson has warned: "American journalism and its guardian angel, the First Amendment, are a unique national asset in the contemporary world. Unless both journalists and citizens learn to appreciate the rarity, fragility and value of the Fourth Estate, it may well go the way of too many other formerly free presses in other nations."

2 THE INVESTIGATIVE JOURNALIST— TALENTS, TECHNIQUES AND TRAITS IN SUMMARY

Great talent for communication is useless in a reporter unless that communication carries an important message against the corruption and mismanagement that can destroy the fabric of government and our public institutions. Priority must be placed on developing aggressive but responsible reporters with depth knowledge of government and balanced judgment. They must be encouraged to live by high ethical standards and to be nonpartisan and objective.

The talents, techniques, and traits described are ideal goals to be sought in perfecting investigative reporting. Probably they are unattainable in their entirety by any one person or small group. Investigative reporting is a constant learning experience as newsmen seek answers to questions that are always just a little different, even when the overall patterns follow the same general outlines.

It is never too late for the reporter or editor to embark on a systematic effort to acquire the talents, techniques, and traits of the investigative journalist. It is well to remember that Lincoln Steffens, Jacob Riis, Ida Tarbell, and Paul Y. Anderson had no formal training, not even in journalism, when they took their first steps on highly successful careers as investigative reporters. Some people are born with an instinct for investigative reporting; many will acquire some or many of the traits by trial and error. It is important to remember that all of the attributes of a fine investigative reporter are attainable by the average, intelligent, inquisitive person. All that is really necessary is an interest in establishing the responsibility for the inevitable malfunctioning of government agencies that wastes tax money, causes injustices, and creates a climate for corruption.

NECESSARY TECHNIQUES

A list of the techniques the investigative reporter or editor needs to be fully effective with a minimum degree of vulnerability is as follows:

1. A general familiarity with various forms of governmental organization and operations at the city, county, state, and federal levels, and the ability to analyze basic problems of conflicts of interest, mismanagement or corruption.

2. A general familiarity with the laws dealing with the operation of tax collection and general revenue-raising functions, assessments, the budget making process, and the laws enacted for the purpose of guaranteeing honesty and fairness in the collection and disbursement of government money. Also, a general familiarity with the ways in which these legal safeguards are circumvented.

3. A specific familiarity with the basic records required under state law to be kept on births, deaths, marriages, divorces, police arrests and summonses, motor vehicle registrations, land transfers, and mortgages.

4. A specific knowledge of the Freedom of Information Laws and policies on local, state, and national levels, and especially the laws, regulations, and practices relative to open public meetings and the availability of records of these meetings.

5. A general working knowledge of court systems and of records available in criminal and civil matters as well as such judicial processes as the probate of wills and the juvenile and traffic courts.

6. A specific knowledge of the jurisdiction and responsibilities of city, county, state, and federal investigators and prosecutors and an understanding of the chain of responsibility in the event of malfunctioning or coverup in the investigation or prosecution process.

7. A general working knowledge of the meaning of due process of law as it relates to procedures and the availability of relevant witnesses and documents and the application of

these procedures in the courts and in various regulatory and administrative agency decisions.

8. General familiarity with the operation of Congress and the state legislatures with emphasis on their legislative, appropriation, and investigative functions and proceedings, especially concerning the jurisdiction and functions of the investigating committee with oversight jurisdiction.

9. General familiarity with the Congressional Record and the records and acts of state legislatures as a research tool and specific familiarity with the hearing records and reports available through various committees and commissions.

10. General knowledge of election laws and election procedures at all levels and of the process for obtaining access to election records and voting lists.

11. General familiarity with the investigations and operations of the General Accounting Office (GAO), the reports filed by GAO, and the manner in which these reports can serve as authoritative background on problems of corruption or mismanagement in federal agencies as well as city, county, and state operations that receive federal funds. This knowledge of the GAO should include an understanding of how GAO investigations can be launched and how to carry out a thorough research of what GAO information may be available in any specific field.

12. Depth background in the history of government scandals and the role of investigative reporting in unearthing and spotlighting these scandals from the days of Lincoln Steffens and the muckrakers at the turn of the century, through the Teapot Dome scandals, through Watergate and Robert Green's great team job of the Arizona crime project.

13. Wide reading on successful and unsuccessful investigations by newspapers on local, state, and federal levels to learn the nuts and bolts of analysis, planning, and strategy to have the best possible assurance of obtaining and preserving key testimony or documents.

14. A depth knowledge and balanced understanding of the "free press–fair trial" problem to minimize the possibility of irresponsible or highly controversial actions that can jeopardize the prosecution of a case, the rights of the accused, or cloud the public understanding of the issues.

15. A depth understanding of the law and practices relative to confidential informants to minimize the dangers for the informant and the reporter and to avoid irrelevant side

disputes in which the newspaper may be viewed as irresponsible or engaged in an obstruction of justice.

16. A general understanding of the rules of evidence in criminal and civil trials, and the general knowledge of when there may be problems of admissibility of important evidence in a libel trial while protecting the identity of a confidential informant.

TRAITS, INBORN OR ACQUIRED

The most important trait that the investigative reporter or editor must have is personal integrity, and this must be coupled with balanced judgment as to how much truth his publishers and his readers can accept and assimilate at any one time. If he has real personal integrity it will follow that he will have objectivity, tenacity, a sense of morality, and compassion in his pursuit of all facts essential to establishing substantial truth.

More specifically, the motivation for the investigative reporter must include:

1. A controlled sense of outrage at injustice, unfairness, or corruption in the operations of government agencies or private institutions and the general knowledge to pinpoint the specific injustice or crimes.

2. A deep understanding that the best chance for success is in a fair and ethical investigation devoid of political partisanship. Any actions by the reporter or the newspaper that are illegal, politically partisan, or even unfair by generally accepted standards can undercut or destroy a valid journalistic inquiry. The investigative reporter must believe that it pays to be honest and ethical and know that any illegality or dishonesty is dangerous for the reporter, the newspaper, and the cause in which they are interested.

3. A real conviction that an honest, direct, and balanced approach is best in dealing with sources and investigative subjects and is the only way to assure continuing successful investigations. This must include an understanding that sources and the public will be disillusioned if the reporter or newspaper misuses the power of the press and intentionally distorts the picture or engages in superficial sensationalism.

4. Patience and confidence that an honest, persistent, and systematic inquiry will eventually unearth the full truth or establish the official responsibility for a coverup of mismanagement, corruption, or other malfunctioning of government or private institutions.

5. The compassion to stand back periodically from the story and view the participants in human terms, to try to step into the shoes of each of the participants, and to ask yourself if you have been fair in your dealings with your confidential sources, your public sources, and with the person or persons who have been the subject of your critical inquiry.

6. The courage to admit that you were wrong on fact or perspective and to take the steps necessary to correct the record immediately when there has been a significant distortion that reflects adversely on anyone.

I am sure that there will be many in the news business who will say that the standards I suggest are too idealistic and cannot be met in the real world of journalistic competition for the news story and for the buck. I do not believe they are. I do understand the real world of investigative reporting and competed successfully for more than 35 years. More than 25 years of that competition was in Washington, D.C.—perhaps the most competitive news city in the world.

In that quarter of a century I saw many scoop artists who blazed momentarily with the light of superficial sensationalism. Most of them faded as they were found to be superficial, untrustworthy, or downright dishonest and partisan in their reporting. I saw a handful of aggressive but responsible reporters, with depth understanding of government operations and balanced judgment who were consistently in the forefront of investigations. Most of them remained active as reporters or were graduated to Washington Bureau Chief or editor responsibilities where experience and influence was beneficial to their organizations, to the newspaper profession, and to the nation.

I do not harbor the hope that any amount of discussion or pleading can turn the newspaper business into the fully effective government oversight mechanism that I suggest, but I do believe that the news business should strive for those specific idealistic goals. And, I believe that, unless there is more concerted effort than has been apparent in the past few years, a disillusioned public will permit and even encourage the politicians to limit sharply the First Amendment rights.

As I view it, there is no alternative to seeking higher journalistic performance standards. Those who do not move seriously and steadily toward honest and responsible investigative reporting could be the weight that destroys the freedom of the press as we know it today.

MOLLENHOFF PRIMER

The best route to becoming an investigative reporter or editor is through a first-rate journalism education with a major in journalism plus the study of government, politics, history, and business administration. Ideally, this academic training under qualified professors would be followed by experience on a newspaper investigation team of well-rounded professionals who are backed by a dedicated editor and publisher who also had some personal experience in newspaper investigation.

Since that ideal route is rarely available, I believe it is essential to develop a primer on investigative reporting so newsmen with no experience, or even those with a wide variety of experiences, can put it all together for themselves. I intend this primer to be a useful guide to the totally inexperienced as well as a helpful reminder to those at all levels on the experience ladder. It is to be remembered that investigative reporting is a constant learning experience, and that those of us with 10, 20, 30, or 40 years of experience in this precarious profession are learning new things and new techniques on every new project we tackle.

In addition to the nuts and bolts guidelines, I hope that this primer will bolster the confidence of middle level reporters and editors by demonstrating that it does not take a superhuman intellect or a superhuman effort to bring success. I believe despite many frustrations inherent in the profession, hard work and systematic methods can and will pay off with successful and satisfying results.

1. *It is possible for the complete novice to learn to do record research and interviews on simple projects that are the first steps toward becoming an experienced reporter or editor.* The list of those who started with no formal training is an impressive reminder of what can be done with simple common sense, dedication to principle, work and follow-through. Most arrest records are public and available at police headquarters or at the local sheriff's office. Court dockets on civil and criminal litigations are also open to any person at the courthouse where the case was tried. The county courthouse holds records on land title transfers as well, and these can be obtained by any citizen who asks for grantor-grantee indexes. The employees of the offices where the records are kept are able to explain what they mean.

The land transfer records (found in grantor and grantee indexes) are usually found in the local county courthouse, but many large cities have their own record of real estate ownership and transfers.

Arrest information is a matter of public record under the laws, regulations or codified customs in most states. Usually the laws or regulations set out those things that must be made public immediately after the arrest. This includes the name of the defendant, his age, his address, the time and place of the arrest, the name of the arresting officer or officers and the specific charge filed. If these records are not made available during normal office hours the law and the regulations should be scrutinized.

Although I was a student at Drake University Law School when I did my first police and courthouse investigations for the *Des Moines Register,* my law studies were of less importance at that stage than was my earlier reading of the experiences of Lincoln Steffens as a police reporter in New York City before the turn of the century.[1]

Over a period of more than 35 years, my conversations with hundreds of investigative reporters from Maine to California and from Anchorage to Miami has reinforced my own view of the soundness of the lessons Lincoln Steffens provides for systematic exploration of government problems and for dealing with the wide range of sources from crooks to reformers. What I learned at the Des Moines city hall, and police station and the Polk County Courthouse, Ed Guthman was learning in Seattle, Bill Lambert and Wally Turner were learning in Portland, Gerard O'Neill was learning in Boston, Gene Miller was learning in Miami, Pam Zekman was learning in Chicago, and Jack Taylor was learning in Oklahoma City.

2. *It is not necessary to wait for an editor to assign you to an investigative project to take your first steps in this field.* Small investigative projects can be developed by individual initiative on the fringe of routine basic coverage of any government beat from the police station through city hall, the courthouse, the state capitol, or at any federal agency.

Most editors are too busy with the routine mechanics of getting out a daily newspaper to supervise an investigative team or to give more than routine instruction to a novice reporter on an investigative project. Be a self-starter on little projects that entail little risk and that deal with simple record research, thorough legal research, and depth interviews on the routine stories that are a part of your basic assignment.

A young reporter would do well to check whether purchasing procedures actually do comply with the law. Usually the law

---

[1] Read *The Autobiography of Lincoln Steffens,* Part II, Chapter I. "I Became A Reporter"; Chapter IV, "The Police"; Chapter V, "Clubs, Clubbers, and Clubbed"; and Chapter VI, "Dr. Parkhurst's Vice Crusade."

concerning government bidding is published for the use of the civil service employees; obtain it and read it. Then ask questions about how these laws and regulations are followed in practice.

This will permit you to develop corroborative evidence to support the tips you may have received or the suspicions you may have. Your editor is less likely to reject projects that are supported by documentary evidence and research that shows him the solid framework of a story he can use with minimum risk and no waste of time. Almost every editor is interested in being a promoter of solid investigative reporting if you can demonstrate that it can be done cautiously and within a framework that puts no additional strain on financial or manpower resources.

3. *Do a sound job of accurate depth reporting on the routine stories on your beat. Keep an attentive eye on the details of government procedures, whether these involve the administration of justice, the purchase of supplies and equipment, the award of contracts, or the handling of personnel matters.* Procedures that stray from legal requirements or sound business methods open loopholes for frauds, mismanagement, and political favoritism.

If you do a reliable job on the routine stories on your beat, at the police station, the city hall, or local courthouse, your editor will have greater confidence in you in situations where that confidence may be crucial to the success or failure of an investigation. There is no easy way to establish your reputation for integrity, reliability, and credibility. It can be done only by willing and energetic work on the boring detail of routine stories over a period of months and years. In addition, this routine can gain for you the depth knowledge of the detailed manner in which the government agencies are supposed to perform. Only through this knowledge can the reporter be fully equipped to detect deviations from the norm that are the red flags signaling improper or illegal activities.

4. *Remember that the foundation stone for effective investigative reporting is the dull, often boring, routine of repetitious record-checking chores at a police station, a city hall, or a courthouse.* It is not enough to review these records casually a few times to be generally familiar with their contents. The reporter must be so familiar with the records and procedures that he knows from specific experience or from "educated instinct" that certain records are available, where they are kept, and what kind of information they contain.

My first stories dealing with the fixing of drunken driving cases in Polk County, Iowa (Chapter 3) were a product of routine checking of the disposition of these cases on the Des Moines Municipal Court dockets and in the Polk County Grand Jury reports. My experiences were much the same as those of Lincoln Steffens in New York City in the 1890s and the experiences of Paul Y. Anderson in St. Louis two decades later. They were essentially the same kind of local record checking done by Jack Nelson in Atlanta, Ed Guthman in Seattle, John Seigenthaler in Nashville, George Bliss in Chicago, Bob Greene in New Jersey and on Long Island, Bob Woodward in Montgomery County, Maryland, and Carl Bernstein in Washington, D.C.

5. *It is not necessary—and it may even be unwise—to inform your editor of your suspicions of mismanagement or corruption until you have made your first exploratory moves on record research or routine interviews.* Your editor is a busy man and may react in a negative way if you go to him with unfounded suspicions, wild rumors, or unchecked charges from an informant. You can make your basic record research and exploratory interviews as a normal followup on routine stories. This will give you some idea of the soundness of a tip or the validity of your suspicions or may demonstrate that they are groundless or that your informant is not supported by relevant public records.

I did not mention my tip on the existence of a black market car racket in Des Moines until after I had examined the registration record on a specific new car, establishing that the car had been purchased on a law-enforcement priority and that the car title had been transferred a few days later to a well-known bootlegger. (Chapter 5 deals with the nuts and bolts of this relatively simple but tedious investigation.) When you have established corroboration in interviews and are armed with documents, it is time enough in most cases to seek the advice and suggestion of your editor or others in the news room.

6. *Develop a simple but accurate method of keeping records on an investigation that assures ready access to the material and preservation of the material.* Although complex team investigations and the more complicated investigations done by a single reporter often require elaborate record keeping systems, it is possible to develop relatively simple methods that will assure preservation of notes and records.

Most investigations that a novice reporter will embark upon in a police station or courthouse do not require the elaborate coding and cross-filing system that Robert W. Greene, of *Newsday*, set up. This was necessary for handling the Investigative Reporters and Editors (I.R.E.) group's complex investigation of Arizona government, following the assassination of Arizona Republic reporter Don Bolles in 1976. Nor can the individual reporter expect to set up the detailed investigative files that Jack Taylor has established as the full-time investigative reporter for the *Daily Oklahoman* in Oklahoma City. The Arizona Project involved thousands of people and millions of details essential to showing the influence of organized crime on the government and business of that area. Taylor's files detailed hundreds of people and dozens of insurance companies involved in the mismanagement and corruption of the multibillion-dollar Central States, Southeast, Southwest Teamsters pension and welfare funds.

I found it possible to keep adequate records on the corruption of local law enforcement in a small pocket notebook carried for the special purpose of keeping this important information separated from my routine police and courthouse story material. In addition, I arranged for the newspaper photographer to take pictures of key court dockets and police records when I had reason to believe that they might be altered or destroyed.

7. *Learn how to analyze a problem of bad government in order to set minimum as well as maximum goals of achievement for an investigative project.* The maximum goal is often the development of first-hand evidence of felony crimes involving payoffs and political favoritism that will result in convictions of the guilty parties and an effective reform. However, it is rarely possible for a newspaper to develop evidence of felony crimes, even when such evidence exists. For the most part, newspapers must be satisfied if they are able to develop sufficient evidence of wrongdoing to force government officials to initiate the investigations and prosecutions that are within their jurisdiction.

Most instances of mismanagement or corruption in government involve a wide range of improprieties in addition to a number of crimes, ranging from misdemeanors to serious felonies, including fraud, bribery, perjury, and income tax evasion. The reporter and editor should analyze each situation for the whole range of conflicts of interest, violations of ethical codes, and breaches of standards and guidelines that may exist. It is unfair as well as a tactical error to charge violation of the most serious nature in the first story unless solid evidence of every element of the crime exists.

It is much better to emphasize only that charge which is supported fully by the evidence and to mention, in proper perspective, the possibility of greater crimes and improprieties. It is preferable to have a small- or medium-sized crime sustained by evidence and official action than it is to overcharge in the first instance and be forced to apologize or back down.

8. *Do not feel compelled to wait until solid evidence of the maximum felony crime you are seeking to establish is in your possession before doing your first story.* Although there may be story

situations that require waiting for solid evidence of the most serious felony, this is not often the case. There is no rule that will fit every situation as to when to proceed with a story of corruption in government. The possibility of a libel suit being filed is always present, and the potential for the filing of a libel action is always a matter of the individual judgments of lawyers.

Frequently a solid story charging only minor improprieties or crimes can be a tool for forcing action by official investigators or prosecutors. In other cases, a solid story of conflicts of interest or minor improprieties will create controversy within the ranks of those responsible for mismanagement or corruption and will cause key figures to give public explanations to the press or to turn state's evidence in prosecutions.

I had experience with this in dealing with liquor and gambling payoffs in Des Moines, and Elmer Croft, who felt he was "the goat," became the key witness in the Polk County fraud trials (Chapters 7 through 16). There were many instances of aggressive reporting that caused conspirators to give testimony in the investigations and prosecutions of the Teamsters Union officials. The squeeze that developed on White House Counsel John W. Dean III was crucial to the unwinding of the Watergate scandal in the Nixon White House (Chapter 32—Watergate and The Aftermath).

9. *Although the proper interviewing technique will vary with the circumstances, it is usually best to assume a simple inquisitive stand that seeks fact and explanation while avoiding personal antagonism.* It may occasionally be wise strategy to play ignorant, but it is never an advantage to *be* ignorant about the facts, the specific terminology, or the relevant law when interviewing a subject. There is no excuse in crucial interviews for failing to examine in advance all relevant public records and the public testimony and documents that may be related to the subject to be discussed. Also, it is usually relatively simple to review the laws and ethical codes related to the specific public office.

State laws usually set out the details of the duties and responsibilities as well as the compensation of city, county, and state officials. Also, many states have ethical codes in the laws, in the rules and regulations adopted by various local government bodies, or in the executive orders of the governor or attorney general. These laws and ethical codes are available through the office of the state attorney general, the county prosecutor, or in any courthouse library.

Usually it is not necessary and may be unwise to express agreement with the subject of the interview on opinions he may express while he is explaining and rationalizing his questionable activities. The challenges to the person being interviewed on facts, law, or opinions should be with a purpose and should be done in a manner designed to achieve that purpose. There should be no tone of personal outrage at even the most outrageous, and no chuckle of amusement that can be misinterpreted as an expression of approval or an indication that you find dishonesty to be either smart or amusing. Do not correct the errors of fact or laws that the person may make unless there is some point you wish to establish that will cause him or her to be more frank in later answers on important questions.

10. *The investigative reporter should exercise extreme care in his dealings with police, government investigators, and prosecutors.* Although the investigative reporter has an interest in proper investigations and prosecutions of the wrongdoing that he exposes, he should avoid being an arm of law enforcement or otherwise compromising his independence.

A degree of cooperation is mutually beneficial when the investigative reporter is dealing with honest law enforcement officials; however, he must avoid any relationship that amounts to a political conspiracy. The reporter must recognize that even the highly motivated policeman or prosecutor will make mistakes and will overstep the bounds of propriety from time to time, so the balanced investigative reporter must be free and independent enough to expose those excesses to demonstrate his objectivity. Further, the investigative reporter must recognize the fact that most law enforcement people will have responsibilities to a political organization or to a political figure that will be inconsistent with the standards of objectivity the press should seek to maintain. Abuse of police powers by selective law enforcement and obstruction of justice are common crimes from the county courthouse to the White House Counsel's office.

Retaining this independence was a problem for Lincoln Steffens and Jacob Riis in dealing with New York Police Commissioner Teddy Roosevelt, and it was my problem in dealing with County Attorney Carroll Switzer and Sheriff Howard Reppert in Polk County in 1947 and 1948. (See Chapters 11, on the Polk County Jail, and 12, on the problems of dealing with Elmer Croft.)

There is no brief rule on the proper stance in dealing with government investigators and prosecutors, and it will be necessary for each reporter to review that relationship constantly with a highly critical eye to determine any danger of losing independence. If the reporter feels any pressure to refrain from legitimate and justified criticism of the tactics of law enforcement officials, the relationship should probably be reassessed as I did constantly through the entire three-year ordeal of the Polk County fraud investigations.

3 THE USE OF RECORDS AND PROCEDURES

Even an inexperienced reporter can, by meticulous research of police and court records, establish evidence of a sophisticated grand jury fix. It is vital to consult with persons who are knowledgeable on the operation of the criminal justice system, for it is necessary to understand the way the system should operate in order to recognize telltale deviations.

In those cases where a reporter is burdened with the routine chores in covering a courthouse, it is usually possible to find a few spare minutes to review the disposition of some specific category of cases (such as drunken driving) to determine if a sample of the cases represents even-handed justice. From a standpoint of organization of the project, the information from the court record should be jotted down in a special pocket notebook that is convenient to carry and avoids the problem of getting the work product mixed with the routine daily stories.

THE USE OF RECORDS AND PROCEDURES

It is impossible to overemphasize the importance of basic knowledge of police and court records and procedures. If you learn records and criminal court procedures thoroughly in one state it will be sufficient to carry you through investigations in any state. Although the terminology on crimes and the official names of the various courts of original jurisdiction for misdemeanors, indictable misdemeanors, and felony crimes will vary slightly from state to state, the framework will be basically the same. Public dockets are available on all criminal and civil court proceedings in the office of the Clerk of the Court.

It is essential to know the details and routine of regular proceedings before it is possible to spot and understand the slight irregularities that may usually signal laxity or evidence of corruption.

Since those who specialize in the corruption of the administration of justice for either payoffs or political favoritism are often knowledgeable lawyers, they leave few clear tracks of their work in "fixing" the police, the prosecutors, or the courts. Thus the first hint of a "fixed" system may be a seemingly insignificant change in the manner in which certain types of cases are handled. Spend a few days in court watching preliminary hearings and trials and you will learn the normal pattern. Ask questions if you do not understand a process. Check the docket to see how it is recorded.

Although a system for "fixing" criminal cases may involve any type of cases, those most subject to systematic tampering are those involving illegal liquor, gambling, and/or prostitution, where organized crime sinks its tentacles into the administration of justice. Serious traffic offenses are often the subject of "the fix" when conviction means mandatory suspension of a driver's permit. Charges of drunken driving are often subject to "a fix" system because this crime frequently involves prominent politicians and businessmen and even an occasional publisher, editor, or police reporter.

Police and court records have been important at least from the time when Lincoln Steffens, Ida Tarbell, Upton Sinclair and Ray Stannard Baker were engaged in their muckraking exploits at the turn of the century. Basic police and court records were important when the Teapot Dome and other scandals of the Harding Administration were being pursued by the *St. Louis Post Dispatch* in the 1920s, and as such great reporters as Ted link, of the *Post Dispatch;* John Strohmeyer, then of the *Providence Journal;* Ed Lahey, of the *Chicago Daily News;* Chet Potter, of the *Pittsburgh Press,* and others made their mark with the cooperation and assistance of Senator Estes Kefauver's investigations of organized crime in 1950 and 1951.

Detailed knowledge of police and court records was important to the band of investigative reporters who exposed a significant section of the labor racketeering in local papers even before Senator John L. McClellan (Dem., Ark.) and his Chief Counsel Robert F. Kennedy made it a major national news story with public televised hearings in 1957, 1958, and 1959.

In Tennessee, John Seigenthaler dug into the police and court records on his own and later had the expert help of Investigator LaVern Duffy of the McClellan Committee. In Oregon a couple of reporters for the *Portland Oregonian,* Wallace Turner and William Lambert, used basic police and court record irregularities to expose Teamster links with local political figures in a "fix" system that covered liquor, gambling and prostitution.

In Washington, Edwin O. Guthman and Paul Stapleton, of the *Seattle Times,* used police and court records as well as land records to report the first indications of the corruption of Dave Beck's Teamsters. Harold Brislin, in Scranton, Pennsylvania, was scouring the police and court records for payoffs and political fixes in labor racket bombings.

Although it is helpful to have an experienced criminal trial lawyer to explain the police and court records and procedures in a particular state, there are usually police or court clerks who are equally familiar with the system and the quirks of the system in any state. The records required and the procedures of the federal courts are governed by federal law and specific court procedures and will follow the same basic patterns as state courts.

I learned about police and court records and procedures gradually and without specific depth instruction except as individual policemen and court clerks would answer my questions on a piecemeal basis over a period of months. Since I was a totally inexperienced cub reporter, my experience in reporting on the irregularities in the handling of drunken driving cases is particularly instructive to the student or to the reporter or editor with limited experience with actual direct coverage of police and courts (see Reading 1).

Normally, the records of arrests should be available to any citizen at police headquarters or at the sheriff's office. These basic arrest cards (or sheets) state the name of the defendant (or defendants), his age, his address, his occupation, where he was arrested, the time of the arrest, the name of the arresting officer or officers, and the name of the specific charge filed. If these records are not made available during regular office hours, it is probably a violation of a state law, state procedural code, or common law custom.

City, county, state, and federal courts keep criminal, civil, and special litigation dockets that are public and available for examination by any person. Usually they are kept in the Office of the Clerk of Court and can be examined during normal working hours. The employees in most Clerk's offices are cordial and helpful in explaining these records to the novice, but there are many offices where employees are rude and irritable with persons they do not know to be part of the local establishment.

In the first reading, which follows, the student should take note of the following points. These, or similar "signposts" should be sought out in later readings, even though no detailed list may be provided.

1. If the novice reporter is surprised or shocked by comments of officials or associates as to how government is run, he should make cautious inquiry to determine whether the suggestions of waste, injustice, or crime are serious commentary or were made in jest. Trust your instinct, but test it.

2. Once convinced that the comment was a serious one, the reporter should make discrete inquiry to determine if others in positions of authority have knowledge of the malpractices and whether the evidence indicates long-term corruption or a single incident of favoritism that may be justified by unusual circumstances.

3. Examine all available public records to determine if they corroborate the verbal information on malpractices.

4. Do not be discouraged by the fears or cautions of informants, editors, or publishers.

5. If possible find a source or direct witness with specific knowledge of the malpractices.

6. Records of such exploratory investigation must be kept completely separate from day-to-day notes on other stories.

7. Record hard facts from police arrest cards (or sheets) and from the court dockets in the Office of the Clerk of Court. This should include the names of *all* people involved, the precise times and dates, and details of the incident involved.

8. Try to obtain an explanation from those implicated in the malpractices to determine whether they have a plausible story for unusual handling of their official duties.

9. If possible obtain authoritative opinions from "outside" sources who are believed likely to be impartial in assessing the probability of a seeming malpractice.

10. Try to avoid involving informants in inadvertent illegalities or otherwise jeopardizing their job security by police involvement in a dispute.

11. While taking great care not to smear an innocent person, be on guard against permitting "sympathy" or "understanding" to obscure the evils of any real malpractice.

12. The best laid plans of mice and men "gang aft a-gley." If one device fails, another may succeed in part. At least the malpractice is kept in the public eye.

13. Plain luck can play an important role, but most "luck" is a result of keeping one's eyes and ears open and in following up systematically on every lead.

Reading 1: Drunken Driving Fix

The irregular manner in which drunken driving charges were handled in Des Moines, Iowa, in the early 1940s represented the clearest indication of favoritism in law enforcement and systematic fixing of cases. Dick Spry, a veteran police and court reporter for the *Des Moines Register,* commented on "the fix" and "the reports of payoffs" in a casual manner as he took me through the routine of records in the building that housed the Des Moines police department and the Des Moines Municipal Court.

Although I was a freshman in the Drake University Law School at the time, I was a most inexperienced cub reporter and more than a little naive about the operation of the police and the courts, and it was somewhat of a shock to me when Dick Spry commented casually about "a fix" and "payoffs" on drunken driving cases (see point 1 in list). However, it was no great secret around the police station and the municipal court that "a fix system" was in operation. Over a period of months Spry's off-hand comment was confirmed by others who were in an even better position to observe direct and circumstantial evidence that certain law firms could get their clients off by arrangements with the Polk County Attorney's Office and with cooperation from a few of the municipal court judges and with a policy of noninterference from key judges in the Polk County District Court.

In answer to my questions, Spry explained that it was the newspaper's policy to report the basic details of all arrests for drunken driving and to follow the progress of the cases through arraignment, preliminary hearing in municipal court, through the Polk County Grand Jury, and through trial in the Polk County District Court.

Spry said that, although dozens of cases of drunken driving were filed in Polk County every year, only a few ever went to trial in Polk County District Court. The system for "fixing" a case involved interminable continuances in municipal court and eventual dismissal through cooperation of a pliable municipal judge and compassionate prosecutor at a time it was believed "the heat was off" on the case. Prosecutors and judges did not like to dismiss such serious charges as drunken driving "when the heat was on," Spry explained. The "heat" he spoke of was generated by the fact that arresting officers often were adamant in following up a charge of drunken driving to try to thwart the "fix system."

The veteran reporter said that there would be "a pretty good story" if a reporter could develop solid evidence of payoffs and a fix, but that the evidence would be difficult to acquire because the prosecutors, courts, and police hierarchy were all a part of the same Republican political machine. Spry said that he simply reported what took place on the police and court record because it was "the safe way" and "besides the desk never gives me enough time" to do the work necessary to pursue a case effectively.

Over a period of months, I heard confirmation of Spry's views from police patrolmen who were angered at a fix and were willing to point to the public record and to give their own off-the-record opinion that there had been a payoff of $400 or $500. The usual unverified rumors were that the payoffs went to someone in the office of the then County Attorney Francis Kuble, and that the money was used variously as a political fund and for small cash payments to police, prosecutors, and judges who were involved in an active or passive manner. (See point 2.)

In cases where a prominent citizen was "sloppy drunk" when arrested at the wheel of his car, there was usually a lot of grumbling by the arresting officer and his closest associates, but all were careful to avoid discussion of specific details in the presence of a reporter. Police patrolmen were at the lowest rung of the police ladder and they were mindful of the fact that it could wreck their careers to be identified as the source of a story that embarrassed the judges, the city prosecutors, or the Polk County Attorney. The chief of police and the police department heads held their posts through political connections, and even the honest ones did not want to be caught encouraging patrolmen to break up "the fix system."

I tried to encourage various police patrolmen to give me specific information on the operation of the fix system. Most of them were fearful of being identified as an informant, and would only point to the police record of the arrest, with the witnesses, and the court record details which were usually sparse. (See point 3.)

Lawyers for persons charged with drunken driving usually avoid a preliminary open hearing in municipal court in which the arresting officer would testify on the facts and circumstances of the arrest and other witnesses would be called to establish, through blood tests, that the defendant was indeed operating a motor vehicle while intoxicated.

Although the Constitution guarantees a defendant a speedy trial, there is no requirement that he accept a speedy trial. Delay was the name of the game so the public and the witnesses might forget the incident, particularly in cases involving a wreck and personal injury or property damage or both. Usually after interminable continuances on the municipal court docket, all duly recorded and reported, the defense lawyer would "waive" his right to a preliminary hearing, and the drunken driving charge would be sent to the

Polk County Grand Jury where the evidence would be heard behind closed doors—an ideal place for an effective fix.

The grand jury deliberation takes place in secret in a tradition that bars the grand jurors from engaging in public discussion of the witnesses they have heard and the documents examined. Usually the members of a grand jury are not lawyers. In addition, although they are supposed to be outstanding citizens of the community, this is no assurance of any particular competence in the gathering of facts or the analysis of the facts or the law. The grand jurors usually rely upon the prosecutor to decide what witnesses will be heard, to decide for the most part the pattern of questioning, and to decide what documentation will be presented. Grand jurors usually rely upon the prosecutor's office for their legal opinions, and ask for and receive recommendations upon whether an indictment should be returned or a case "ignored" by voting to reject an indictment.

In the hands of an honest even-handed prosecutor, grand jury secrecy protects the innocent from being smeared by unfounded charges. In the hands of a dishonest or political prosecutor, the grand jury is the ideal forum for fixing a case in a manner that makes it unlikely there will be evidence available to the press or the public of the details of the fix.

Months of work in following a few specific cases on the court record convinced me that grand jury manipulation was the major method for fixing drunken driving (as well as a good many other cases involving gambling and illegal liquor charges). Disillusioned police patrolmen, and in a few cases a police sergeant, lieutenant, or captain, told me of instances in which they appeared before the grand jury and the prosecutor did not ask them all of the relevant questions to make a prima facie case of crime. In some instances key supporting witnesses were not called, or the expert witnesses from the state bureau of criminal investigation were not questioned about blood tests that showed conclusively that the arrested man was intoxicated.

The reports from these police indicated that, although the prosecutors produced all, or substantially all, of the evidence, it was done in such a fashion as to minimize the impact on the grand jurors. Witnesses on a drunken driving case were called with several days and even weeks intervening, so that the grand jurors had to rely upon the prosecutor for a summary of what earlier witnesses had testified. Police, including veteran traffic Lieutenant John P. Gill, urged me to expose the fix system, but even as they prodded me to pursue the subject aggressively, they were understandably reluctant to take a public part in exposing the fix system. Lieutenant Gill, a former

Marine, knew the bureaucracy of the Des Moines Police Department, understood the deep seated corruption, and wanted to oppose it as effectively as he could without jeopardizing his own future promotions. I understand his position now better than I did then. (See point 4.)

The newspaper was also understandably cautious in embarking upon any all-out assault on a system that included to some degree the hierarchy of the police department, the city prosecutor's office, the county attorney's office, and important judges on both the municipal and district courts. However, on individual cases I was urged to get as much detail from the public record as was possible and as a matter of routine to seek explanations from the county attorney or one of his key assistants on the disposition of all drunken driving cases.

As long as the police were reluctant to cooperate, the editors felt our alternatives were sharply limited. The fact that the cases we believed were "fixed" often involved prominent businessmen or professional men made the subject particularly sensitive because the newspaper did not wish to give the appearance that it was engaged in a vendetta against any individual among the dozens and hundreds who had been charged with drunken driving.

I was restive and not at all content with those decisions at the time, although I have since concluded that all of us were so inexperienced in investigative reporting that the judgments to go slow were the proper decisions. We were facing an able, entrenched machine that was even more corrupt than we suspected at that time, and any unsound story that left us vulnerable might have been pounced upon with devastating results. The loose political alliance included the most active city and county political figures, and the large number of honest officials were the kind who did not want to become involved in controversy unless it was something they could not avoid. I was irritated and occasionally angry at the manner in which they ignored evidence of malfeasance and corruption in the administration of justice. Since then, I have learned that nonaction by the honest majority is the major reason a small actively corrupt group can prevail, using payoffs to the venal and implied threats to the weak, and usually silent, honest majority.

The effective lever had to come from outside of Des Moines and Polk County, and the Iowa Governor and Iowa Attorney General, both Republicans, could not be expected to reach aggressively into Polk County to the embarrassment of the powerful Polk County Republican organization. However, the outside lever I needed emerged in the person of Iowa State Highway Patrolman Napoleon Bonaparte Wilson, an independent and aggressive former Marine boxer. In news stories we referred to him as N. B. (Mike) Wilson as he built a legend for tough traffic law enforcement in his area—the major highways east of Des Moines. (See point 5.)

Mike Wilson was outraged at the manner in which drunken driving cases were being handled by the county attorney in Polk County. When he arrested someone on a moving traffic violation, he took pride in his ability to gather the evidence and testify without fear or favoritism whether the defendant was a local farmer, a prominent businessman or politician, or an Iowa celebrity. Mike Wilson was precisely the right kind of man to challenge the Polk County ring that was fixing drunken driving charges. He was not under the jurisdiction of Chief of Police Floyd Hartzer, whose ties with the bootlegging and gambling fraternity were well known, or Polk County Sheriff Vane B. Overturff, a key figure in the Polk County Republican political machine.

Although Wilson's superiors on the Iowa Highway Patrol did not encourage his independent forays in jousting with local police, prosecutors, and the courts, there wasn't much they could do about it. Mike Wilson was meticulous in the way he gathered and preserved evidence, came across on the witness stand as a cool, objective, and balanced law enforcement official, and knew how far he could go as the honest and independent cop without totally infuriating his superiors. As long as he was provably right on sound law enforcement principles, he was not vulnerable even in those cases where his superior would have preferred that he not push the issue.

Mike Wilson became my ally in a relationship that proved to be mutually beneficial. Although I was generally knowledgeable about law enforcement and court procedures by the time we met, he had the kind of depth experience to know, to understand, and to explain the subtle irregularities in cases that indicated the "fix" was taking place. He was also an experienced hand in testifying before county grand juries, was aware of the details of how his cases were handled, and remembered the important details on other cases from his discussions with other Iowa Highway patrolmen as well as with local police and prosecutors.

For months before our meeting, Mike Wilson had been doing what he could to fight the "fix" by making as complete a record as he could on all charges filed in Polk County. In those cases where his observations of a driver extended from one county into another, and where he had a choice of where the charge would be filed, Mike Wilson filed in the counties adjoining Polk County where his experience demonstrated there was a much better chance of conviction.

From Mike Wilson and John Gill, I learned to distinguish between the overtly crooked political police and those who were involved in a passive manner because they believed they had little choice if they wished to continue in their jobs. I learned to distinguish between Assistant County Attorney General Earl C. Ryan, who was not a part of the fix but was aware of the contacts among the police and the courts, and others in the County Attorney's office who were actively engaged in unusual or irregular procedures.

Prior to meeting Mike Wilson, I had started my own statistical research of the Municipal Court Clerk's Office for the kind of statistical record to demonstrate there was an unusual number of drunken driving cases being dismissed—and under peculiar circumstances. City Editor Herb Kelly and Assistant City Editor Al Hoschar approved the idea, but were operating with a short staff and could give me no special time to compile the record. It was necessary to squeeze in 15 or 20 minutes a day to go back over the record for I was routinely responsible for news developments at the municipal court, federal court, and Polk County courthouse. Fortunately the driving cases were easy to spot in leafing through the docket because of the large handwritten letters O.M.V.I. scrawled near the top on the right hand side of the page. Those letters stood for "operating a motor vehicle while intoxicated."

I carried a separate notebook for compiling those records, and noted nearly all details from the date the case was filed until it was dismissed or transferred to the Polk County District Court docket for prosecution. (See point 6.) The statistics from the record confirmed my own casual observations and the opinions of concerned lawyers, the angry honest policemen, and the honest prosecutors who disliked what was taking place but felt powerless to take any effective action against the power of the system. I took note of the names of the arresting officer, the prosecutors, the defense attorneys, and the judges. (See point 7.) I kept more information than I needed on the dates and number of continuances in the skillfully planned delays in these cases and mused over the legal saying that "justice delayed is justice denied."

I wrote my little stories on the statistics indicating that more than 75 per cent of the drunken driving cases were dismissed. In some instances I included the facts in a few specific cases in which recitation of the chronology of events established that the dismissals had taken place under the most unusual circumstances. Occasionally, I was able to get a paragraph or two into those stories quoting an angry policeman, a concerned lawyer, or an ambitious political figure stating that "a fix" was feared. However, since this was an unflattering reflection upon the honesty of the county attorney, the judge, and the defense lawyer, it was done with extreme caution. More often than not those paragraphs were cut from my copy.

Although Managing Editor Frank Eyerly, City Editor Herb Kelly, and Assistant City Editor Alan Hoschar encouraged my digging and shared my concern, they were still cautious. At that time the Polk County Republican machine was so strong within the state party that it could frighten a governor or state attorney general who had some responsibility to intervene when it was apparent that local law enforcement was either weak and ineffective or corrupt.

In most instances when we were writing an even mildly critical story we would contact the then County Attorney Francis Kuble to get his explanation of the low percentage of drunken driving convictions. (See point 8.) Although he often made himself available for comment, on those occasions when he saw me he was most gracious and said he was eager to answer all of my questions "because it was obvious" that I "did not understand the situation." In a friendly manner, he would explain that he was just as concerned as any citizen about the crime of drunken driving and that if he had his way there would be a great many more serve time in jail for this offense. However, he was "only the county attorney" and that he could do little if a municipal judge believed that a case should be dismissed.

The county attorney said he could do little or nothing about the large number of cases that were dismissed "because the grand jury refused to indict." Kuble explained that the grand jury was made up of average citizens, and that they were often skeptical of the testimony of police officers and sympathetic with the plight of prominent citizens or others who were arrested with liquor on their breath. Some of the police and highway patrolmen were engaged in vicious vendettas against innocent citizens and this came across in their testimony, Kuble explained. This made the grand jurors wary of the testimony of a policeman unless he was well corroborated with witnesses, documents, or the physical facts in a collision or blood tests.

Although Kuble was articulate and convincing in his general arguments, these did not provide answers to the private opinions of Dean Leland Forrest, of the Drake University Law School, and his own Assistant County Attorney Earl C. Ryan. (See point 9.) Dean Forrest, one of my professors at the Drake Law School, had served as an assistant county attorney several years earlier and had given me an explanation of the normal grand jury procedures. He pointed out the manner in which cases could be "fixed" in the secrecy of the grand jury chamber through an inadequate job of questioning key witnesses, failure to present corroborating evidence, or through extended delays in the production of evidence of blood tests and conclusively established drunkenness. Dean Forrest provided the general picture and commented upon what other prominent lawyers had told him about present grand jury practices.

Assistant County Attorney Ryan was a neighbor and a friend, and he was honest. He was not asked to do anything but prosecute in a straight manner, but he was aware of "the possibility of hanky-panky" in the unusual way in which some drunken driving cases were handled. He was also aware that some cases, which would normally have been assigned to him, were assigned to another prosecutor with a more pliable outlook on the responsibility of government prosecution.

With information from Dean Forrest, the off-the-record discussions with Earl Ryan, and my various conversations with policemen, I was not persuaded by Kuble's glib explanations. The generalities dealing with police vendettas and the sympathy of grand jurors for drinking citizens did not explain the deliberate manipulation in at least a few cases. But, I was not free to use the specific information I had been given in confidence by Dean Forrest, Ryan, and various policemen and state highway patrolmen. It was regarded as illegal for the prosecutors or grand jurors to reveal specific actions within the grand jury chamber. However, Dean Forrest and Ryan had found no ethical problem in spelling out the general way that evidence was taken from their own experience or their educated guesses mixed with reasonably reliable second-hand information from other lawyers.

There is no legal or ethical problem in police officers giving reporters an accurate factual account of the circumstances surrounding an arrest, a list of the witnesses they have submitted to the prosecutors, or the fact that a state blood test supported their conclusion on the condition of the man arrested. However, police departments and prosecutors try to discourage detailed discussion of the evidence before the trial on grounds that it might hamper the prosecution or make an important witness a target for challenges to his credibility.

Against this background, I felt constrained by confidentiality as well as tactics to avoid specifics in my questioning that might give the County Attorney an indication of my informants in the police department and in his own office. I was particularly anxious to avoid anything that might identify Earl Ryan as a helpful source, for Earl Ryan needed the job as an assistant county attorney. (See point 10.)

Also, Ryan's cooperation was in a manner not unfriendly to County Attorney Kuble, whom he regarded as a basically able and honest man who was the victim of his own political ambitions within the Republican Party. Although he accepted the existence of "the fix" in cases in Kuble's office, Ryan said he believed Kuble was not benefiting financially from the arrangement and was not an active party in most cases. The real political power was in others, including one highly political judge, Ryan said. Most of the several assistant county attorneys were men chosen by the Republican machine and imposed upon Kuble because he was "a good soldier."

Without indicating specific information from within the grand jury, I asked Kuble about general reports that important witnesses were not taken before the grand jury. He said he could not discuss specific cases because he did not handle most of the grand jury presentations but left them to his assistants. In a general way Kuble explained that the decision on which witnesses to call before a grand jury was a matter of judgment left to the assistant county attorney in charge of specific cases. Kuble acknowledged there were complaints from a few law enforcement officers about withholding witnesses and testimony, including tests on the alcoholic content of blood. He said that he had received explanations from his assistants that convinced him that these represented misunderstandings and differing legal judgments. Not all corroborative witnesses were called because much of this testimony was simply cumulative. However, blood test evidence was presented to the grand jury in all cases, although on occasion, the assistant county attorney would simply inform the grand jury that a blood test existed that indicated alcoholic content above the level establishing intoxication.

When I pointed out the statistics indicating that about 75 per cent of the drunken driving arrests in Polk County were dismissed, Kuble had an explanation that on the surface seemed plausible. He explained that the lopsided statistics on dismissals of drunken driving charges in Polk County were a result of a generally lenient attitude on the part of citizens of Des Moines. It reflected itself in the reluctance of grand jurors to vote for indictments and in an overly sympathetic attitude of petit jurors who refused to vote for convictions in the few cases that went to trial.

Kuble was quite persuasive, for there was some grain of truth in what he said. He told me that he would like to do something about it but that the county attorney was burdened with work and could only do so much in trying to change public attitudes on such matters as drunken driving, bootlegging, gambling and other crimes of that type. He cited the failure of the national prohibition laws in the 1920s as the most significant evidence supporting his view that it was really the fault of the public.

He had convinced himself, as most prosecutors in his position did, that he was doing the best practical job of enforcing the laws. His arguments did not square with the evidence and informed opinions I had heard of a systematic fixing system, but my evidence was largely circumstantial and involved only a handful of cases. It was easy to see that he might rationalize that the arranged leniency he knew about involved only a small percentage of the cases, and he was really not condoning crime or obstructing justice. Kuble could view himself as a compassionate politician who simply helped iron out troubles for prominent businessmen or others represented by prominent lawyers.

After my talks with Kuble I concluded that my friend Earl Ryan might be right in judging him the victim of a political machine system he could not fight. Whether he had tried to fight the system, I did not know; those disagreements would take place behind closed doors in sharp or subtle confrontations with hinted threats of political opposition and whispered hints of future political support for higher office. (See point 11.)

As a reporter, however, I could not condone or excuse miscarriages of justice or "the fix" nor overlook a kinky politician's failure to carry out his responsibilities to enforce the law honestly and fairly. I kept my eyes and ears open for possibilities of getting more conclusive evidence of "the fix" into the public domain and into stories in *The Des Moines Register.* As more and more facts emerged, we would get closer to the whole truth; Kuble would be given full opportunity to make his explanations in newspapers.

With my friend Highway Patrolman Mike Wilson, I hit upon a strategy that could be used to point up the fact that solid drunken driving cases were being rejected by the grand jury. Wilson was to select some particularly outrageous case of dismissal where there was no question of overwhelming evidence of the two simple elements of drunken driving:

1. That the defendant was driving the car at the time and place charged.
2. That the defendant was intoxicated in the opinion of expert and inexpert witnesses and according to the blood tests from the state chemical laboratory.

The fact that a case had been ignored by the grand jury did not bar the arresting officer from filing the same charge again. Only the finding of acquittal by the petit jurors, or dismissal by a judge of the Polk County District Court would create the double jeopardy bar to refiling the charge. However, if the charge was refiled it would probably go the same route to secret dismissal without even a public preliminary hearing in municipal court or in a justice of peace court, since drunken driving was an indictable misdemeanor. The way to force an open hearing in municipal court was to file two or more simple misdemeanor charges so that there would be no way the prosecutor could take the case into a secret grand jury for disposition.

Wilson was to select a case in which he could file a simple charge of drunkenness with a state blood test to support his own observations and the opinions of others that the driver was drunk. Also, he would file a charge of reckless driving, driving on the wrong side of the road, failure to yield the right-of-way, or other appropriate traffic charge where there would be several witnesses to the fact that the defendant was driving. It would be ideal if the incident involved an accident, and if the defendant made admission statements in the presence of others that he was indeed the driver of the car.

With public hearings in municipal court on two such misdemeanors, it would be possible to demonstrate in a series of hearings the absurdity of the rejection of the drunken driving charge by the grand jury. It might not provide absolute proof as to who "fixed" the case or, indeed, even that the case was fixed. However, it would provide an open forum in which almost anything could happen if the defendant decided to take the stand in his own defense and the judge was properly mindful of press coverage of his every ruling and wary of being viewed as part of "a fix."

Certainly, this procedure would permit full exploration of all of the evidence relative to the charge that the man was intoxicated, and the testimony of the state laboratory chemist as to whether he had been questioned before the grand jury, when that questioning had taken place, and which assistant county attorney had been in charge of the grand jury presentation. Also, it put the prosecutor in the position of being required to produce all relevant evidence that the defendant was driving the car in a hazardous manner and in violation of traffic laws, plus those admissions against interest that the man may have made in the presence of the arresting officer, the jailer or other booking officer, and any other witnesses to the arrest or accident.

On August 4, 1943, Mike Wilson filed charges of intoxication, reckless driving, and driving on the wrong side of the road against a 40-year-old Des Moines businessman in protest against dismissal of a drunken driving charge by the grand jury. We felt this would set the stage for at least a partial exposure of "the fix" system, and Mike Wilson commented briefly and cautiously in explaining his reason for filing the charges. However, the exposure was not destined to take place so easily. (See point 12.)

A former prosecutor and an active local political figure went into municipal court and arranged with a pliable city prosecutor to enter a plea of guilty to driving on the wrong side of the road if the other charges of reckless driving and intoxication were dropped. A judge, who was either implicated or was asleep at the switch, accepted the plea and fined the businessman $10 for driving on the wrong side of the road. This maneuver frustrated the Mike Wilson strategy to demonstrate in an open hearing the depth of evidence on the two elements of the crime of drunken driving and to dramatize the absurdity of the county attorney's handling of this category of cases. But, the incident stirred public opinion and centered the criticism on the prosecutor who handled the case and tried to justify his actions. It also brought the judge a great deal of unwanted attention and left the general impression that he was incompetent, senile, or a crook.

That case was but the first of several efforts by Mike Wilson and other law enforcement officers to bring dismissed drunken driving charges into open hearings by filing misdemeanor charges of drunkenness and reckless driving. Those few cases kept the public issue boiling and created a condition in which fewer drunken driving cases were dismissed because those with responsibility for the fix system did not wish to take further chances of being singled out publicly as an active part of the fix.

In the aftermath of those stories of the circumstantial evidence of the fix, I stumbled into a story of a Grinnell, Iowa, businessman who said a payment of money to a city prosecutor had paved the way for his release from jail a few hours after he was arrested on a charge of driving while intoxicated on December 2, 1943. (See point 13.) The whole incident might have gone without notice if Highway Patrolman Mike Wilson had not made a routine inquiry of the Grinnell restaurant owner to determine whether his driver's license should be revoked. Faced with an inquiry by Mike Wilson, the Grinnell man explained in detail why he believed that the drunken driving case "had been taken care of" by the city prosecutor. He had told Iowa Highway Patrolman Mike Wilson he was arrested at 5:30 P.M. and that a city attorney had come to the jail between 6 and 7 P.M. and arranged his release on bond within two hours for $50.

The Grinnell man confirmed the story to me and answered additional questions to clarify the situation further. He had not been permitted to make a telephone call to his family or his personal lawyer nor had he asked for a lawyer.

Miraculously the city prosecutor had come to the city jail cell block, asked for him by name, chatted with him about the charge, and asked him if he wanted to get out of jail. The city prosecutor told him that for $50 he could arrange to have a judge come down for a quick arraignment and he could be on his way that evening.

The Grinnell man, distressed over spending Christmas night in jail, agreed to the deal. A short time later Municipal Judge Charles S. Cooter was at the jail to hear his plea of not guilty, to set a $400 bond, and to sign a writ of habeas corpus requiring Police Captain C. A. Dunagan to release him from jail. It was all completed before 9 P.M., the Grinnell man said, and the city prosecutor told him to be on his way and "to forget about" the drunk driving charge for the moment.

When questioned, the errant city prosecutor became tangled in two or three explanations of why he appeared at the jail, and he also told conflicting stories as to whether he was representing the city or the Grinnell man when he gained access to the cell block in the city jail. The incident provided an interesting series of stories about the peculiar circumstances under which one drunken driving case was handled. The Grinnell man claimed the payment of $50 was made in cash, but the city prosecutor, after initially acknowledging to me that he received the money, denied receiving any cash.

The county attorney's office promised a complete investigation of the city prosecutor and then pulled down the usual curtain of silence that so often is a prelude to a whitewash. It was unrealistic to expect a county attorney's office that was involved in questionable handling of drunk driving cases to conduct a thorough investigation of an errant city prosecutor who was accused of a penny-ante fix of the same type of case.

It was a frustrating and yet enlightening experience with the processes of local law enforcement and the courts. Initially, we had naively hoped that the ring involved in the fixing of drunken driving cases would resent the poaching on their territory by the city prosecutor and aggressively move to investigate and prosecute. However, in short order it became apparent that a coverup was in process, and that the city prosecutor was either a part of the fix or knew enough about the fix system that he was regarded as too hot to investigate.

The stonewalling started behind sanctimonious pronouncements about the tradition of secrecy involving grand jury investigations and the presumptions of innocence of public officials accused of crimes. Since both arguments were generally valid, we felt obliged to print those plausible explanations even though we believed there was a criminal obstruction of justice involving top officials of the police department, some persons in the county attorney's office, and some members of the judiciary.

Although the corrupt misuse of the grand jury was exposed to our readers, we were unable to establish the criminal culpability to the point that we could force the officials to prosecute those responsible.

On the plus side, the officials were discredited, the county attorney had to announce that the facts warranted an investigation, and a few minor officials lost their jobs. As far as we could tell the fixing of drunken driving cases in the grand jury was ended for a few months, at least until after I left the newspaper for a two-year hitch in the Navy. When I returned the fixers were at it again and bolder than ever.

For the time, we were outwitted and outlasted on this investigative effort. The grand jury secrecy permitted the county attorney to conduct his investigation behind closed doors, and to drag his investigation on for weeks and months. The newspaper might have broken this fix by hiring professional criminal investigators and lawyers to press the case, but even then it might have been difficult to force prosecutions where local police, the sheriff's office, the county attorney's office, and the local judiciary were all involved in various aspects of the obstructions of justice. Few publishers or editors are willing to take on such an expensive undertaking in the face of such long odds.

A VALUABLE LEARNING EXPERIENCE

Over a period of several months of dealing with the handling of drunken driving cases, I learned many important lessons about law enforcement, about the judiciary, about the grand jury system, and about reporting.

First, I learned that although the grand jury's secret processes could serve a useful purpose in protecting the innocent and the key informant from the wrath of the underworld, the secrecy also permitted a corrupt prosecutor and his associates to hide their abuses of power and obstructions of justice.

Second, I learned how corrupt misuse of a secret grand jury could be effectively exposed through meticulous search of the public records, coupled with systematic interviewing of those persons with direct knowledge of the cases under study.

Third, I learned that it is almost always possible to find some honest officials with specific knowledge or general expertise that will be helpful in understanding the problem and in dealing with it in news stories.

Fourth, I learned that even in a corrupt system involving police, the prosecutors, and the courts there will be a few honest people who know the facts. These people will be willing to cooperate on a confidential basis if they are certain they are dealing with a reporter who is responsible and has the integrity and skill to give a source effective protection.

Fifth, I learned that even when the public record, the direct testimony of key witnesses, and common sense indicate that a fix ring is in operation, it is difficult or impossible to get an effective investigation when the fixers control the prosecutor's office and the criminal court.

All of these lessons were to be repeated over and over and reinforced many times during the nine-year span in which I reported on local and state government in Iowa for the *Des Moines Register.*

STUDENT WORK PROJECT SUGGESTION

1. Do a ten-page analysis of the local criminal justice system on misdemeanor and felony crimes. Take each type of crime from the arrest, through the booking and bond procedures, the arraignment, the preliminary hearing, the trial, and the appeals. Go into the details on these procedures thoroughly enough so that you could recognize the deviations and irregularities that might indicate a "fixed case."

2. Do a study of the handling and disposition of drunken driving cases in your home county with an eye to determining whether these cases are being handled with an even-handed justice or if political influence or corruption might be a factor in the conviction rate or the types of sentences being imposed by the courts.

4   DEALING WITH VICE AND PAYOFFS

Selective law enforcement usually indicates political favoritism or a vice payoff system. It invariably involves corruption or compromise of the police, prosecution, and the courts in varying degrees. It is relatively easy to detect symptoms, but it is difficult to prove the passage of money for the favored treatment. New York City had the problem when Theodore Roosevelt was the police commissioner in the 1890s, at the time of the Lexow Legislative Committee investigation. It was a problem in the 1920s. Senator Kefauver's Crime Committee exposed it in the 1950s, and some version of it will remain to be uncovered by reporters in the year 2000.

My experience at the Des Moines police station in the 1940s will almost certainly be duplicated by reporters who emerge from journalism education in the year 2000 and later, and they will recognize the evidence if they read carefully of my experiences.

The reporter must realize that a newspaper is limited as far as gathering evidence for actual prosecution of crimes and corruption. As indicated in the Primer (Chapter 2), newspapers, in most cases, must be satisfied if they are able to force government officials to initiate investigations and prosecutions.

PROBLEMS IN ENFORCEMENT OF VICTIMLESS CRIME LAWS

The policing authority over crimes of vice—illegal liquor, gambling, and sex—has always been a major governmental problem. Unless there is some radical change in human nature, the enforcement, nonenforcement, and selective enforcement of vice laws will always present a difficult situation for police and for newspaper reporters and editors.

In his autobiography, Lincoln Steffens wrote of Teddy Roosevelt's problems with enforcement of vice laws (now known as victimless crime laws) when he was a crusading police commissioner in New York City just before the turn of the century. In the ordeal of Police Captain Schmittberger, Steffens dealt with the realities of the operations of a naive payoff collector or bag man. Steffens referred to Schmittberger as "an honest policeman" because he did not steal from the payoffs he collected, turned all of the money over to his superiors, and when the pinch was on turned states evidence that assisted in the prosecution and conviction of his superiors.

In his classic series of magazine articles on corruption in local and state government, Steffens dealt with every possible aspect of the problem of crusading against local graft. Unfortunately, as a 17-year-old college freshman, I did not grasp the universality of the lessons Lincoln Steffens was teaching. However, a general awareness of Lincoln Steffens' experiences was helpful when I started work as a police and court reporter for the *Des Moines Register* in 1941 and 1942.

Pressures on a Young Reporter

In the first days and weeks at the Des Moines municipal court and police building, I was fascinated at my first contacts with police, judges, and various functionaries of the courts. I was in awe of my own situation as an inexperienced 20-year-old reporter. The chief of police, a large and distinguished looking grey-haired man in his midfifties, referred to me as "Mr. Mollenhoff." Even more flattering was the fact that, within a few weeks, three of the four municipal court judges referred to me by my first name and complimented me on my two-, three-, or four-paragraph stories on rather routine matters that had taken place in their courts. It was heady business.

I was awed by the court officials who seemed to know precisely what they were doing on very complex legal matters and who were willing to drop other chores to explain the bewildering details of court cases. I wondered if I would ever know and understand even the most routine technicalities about arrest procedures, court arraignments, preliminary hearings in municipal court, the grand jury process, and the trials in the Polk County District Court.

Because there was so much routine to learn, it was weeks before I even had time to ask myself whether there were opportunities for stories like those Lincoln Steffens and his zealous reporter reformer colleague, Jacob Riis, discovered. I thought, with a feeling of regret, that there was no apparent evidence of rampant graft and corruption involving police and courts. I actually envied Lincoln Steffens the opportunity he had with the irrepressible Teddy Roosevelt and the crusading Dr. Charles H. Parkhurst in the exposure of misdoing in government in the late 1890s.

Clark R. Mollenhoff, police and court reporter, Des Moines Register. Flow charts for misdemeanor, indictable misdemeanor and felony crimes in Des Moines and Polk County, Iowa.

Misdemeanor—*Drunk* or *Petty Crimes*	Indictable Misdemeanor—*O.M.V.I.*	Felonies—*Burglary, Larceny* or *Murder*
Arrest—jailed and searched. ↓	Arrest—jailed and searched. ↓	Arrest—jailed and searched. ↓
Arraigned—plea of guilty or not guilty. Bond set by municipal judge. Trial date set. Defendant makes bond or stays in jail. ↓	Arraigned, etc.—plea of guilty or not guilty and bond set pending a preliminary hearing in municipal court. Or defendant waives preliminary hearing and case goes to Polk County Grand Jury. ↓	Arraigned, etc.—plea of guilty or not guilty and bond set pending a preliminary hearing in municipal court. Or defendant waives preliminary hearing and case goes to Polk County Grand Jury. ↓
Trial before municipal judge. ↓	Preliminary hearing in municipal court. Charge dismissed or the judge finds that evidence is insufficient to send the case to the grand jury. ↓	Preliminary hearing in municipal court. Charge dismissed or the judge finds that evidence is insufficient to send the case to the grand jury. ↓
Guilty or not guilty. ↓	Polk County Grand Jury. Secret proceedings and return of "no true bill" with case dismissed or "true bill" which means indictment. ↓	Polk County Grand Jury. Secret proceedings and return of "no true bill" with case dismissed or "true bill" which means indictment. ↓
Fined up to $100 or given jail term of up to 90 days. ↓	Trial set after arraignment in Polk County District Court and new bond posted. ↓	Trial set after arraignment in Polk County District Court and new bond posted. ↓
Final appeals taken to the Polk County District Court.		

Misdemeanor—*Drunk* or *Petty Crimes*	Indictable Misdemeanor—*O.M.V.I.*	Felonies—*Burglary, Larceny* or *Murder*
	Trial before judge or before a jury. Verdict of guilty or not guilty. Fine and jail term by Iowa law. ↓	Trial before judge or before a jury. Verdict of guilty or not guilty. The maximum fines and jail terms are set by Iowa law. ↓
	Appeals of guilty verdicts go to the Iowa Supreme Court. ↓	Appeals to the Iowa Supreme Court. ↓
	Appeals to the U.S. Supreme Court must be on a constitutional issue.	Appeals to the U.S. Supreme Court must be on a constitutional issue.

Hints of Corruption

Events moved in an orderly and quiet fashion at the municipal court and police station. Officials were friendly and helpful. Thus, I assumed they were honest. However, in addition to my routine work of examining all civil and criminal cases filed in the municipal court, I set about the business of making charts on the normal flow pattern of various categories of crimes—misdemeanors, indictable misdemeanors, and felonies. In a short time, I was able to observe bits of evidence that showed hints of ugly activity beneath the surface serenity. There was corruption of law enforcement, which permitted open violation of the state liquor laws in Des Moines and Polk County.

At that time liquor was sold legally only through Iowa State liquor stores. It was illegal to have any hard liquor in any public place, and there was a specific law that made it a crime to have liquor in any tavern where beer was legally sold. Yet liquor was being sold openly in more than 200 beer taverns in Polk County, and each of these taverns had taken the precaution of obtaining a federal liquor license. Many paid federal liquor floor taxes to assure that federal liquor officials had no reason to move in on the bars that were violating Iowa state law.

Police and Newspaper Policy

These law violations were taking place with the approval of the Polk County Sheriff, the Polk County Attorney, and the Des Moines police and City Council. Furthermore, the Des Moines Chamber of Commerce approved because the businessmen "wanted an open town." *The Des Moines Register* company also condoned the arrangement by a policy of "not crusading" against this massive disregard for state law "because it was good for business" and attracted conventions.

Other reporters and *Register* City Editor Herb Kelly explained that *The Register* did not want actively to oppose open liquor sales even when they violated state law. It was a policy that was laid down above the level of Managing Editor Frank Eyerly, who was the operational boss for *The Register* and *The Tribune.* However, if reporters came across evidence of payoffs to police, the sheriff, or any other city or county official, Kelly said those facts could be reported in a straight and objective manner. The same noncrusading, straight approach was to be applied to those cases in which the violators of the liquor laws also violated closing hours or tried to expand the vice operations to include gambling and prostitution.

Selective Law Enforcement

The situation created a condition in which there was an open invitation to misuse the unwritten code further because of the lucrative return. There was also a temptation for individual policemen to develop their own little rackets in shaking down the liquor law violators for payoffs to avoid wildcat raids. These individual shakedown rackets were hard to control because the police department found it difficult to discipline a policeman for arresting a tavern operator because he violated the law by keeping liquor on the premises.

In Des Moines the police department tried to stop the unauthorized shakedown by individual uniformed police. It established a small vice squad of plainclothes detectives who specialized in answering complaints to the police department where liquor, gambling, or prostitution was involved. It took only the most casual examination by a novice reporter to demonstrate that the small vice squad was usually made up of pliable and slightly kinky policemen who would engage in the pattern of selective liquor law enforcement dictated by the safety commissioner and approved by the city council.

Even before a few honest policemen told me of the payoffs, I had observed the criminal court docket at the municipal court and had concluded that Des Moines was not "an open city" with regard to liquor law enforcement but a city of "selective law enforcement." Week after week there would be raids on beer taverns, usually by the vice squad, and charges would be filed in municipal court of "keeping liquor where beer is sold" or failing to observe the 2 A.M. closing hour for taverns.

The obvious question was: Why were these few taverns singled out for raids in a city and county in which more than 200 establishments were violating the same laws? The answer came in time by questioning those who were singled out for the selective arrests for liquor law violations and by talking to the arresting officers. Those who were arrested were bitter, for they were, in most cases, doing nothing different than the other tavern operators who sold liquor openly. Some complained that they had balked at higher payoffs and that the vice squad had "cracked down" to put some teeth in the payoff apparatus. They were intentionally vague about past payoffs and said frankly that they didn't expect the newspapers to be able to do anything effective. The vice squad members usually refused to comment on the record, but would hint darkly that the arrested tavern owner catered to juveniles, was violating closing hours, permitted gambling, or let prostitutes hustle customers at his bar.

It was difficult to determine what the truth was in the jungle of selective law enforcement. It was only rarely that I was able to get into print the vague hints of payoffs that surfaced, even though it was open talk among the uniformed police that the vice squad was made up of bag men for the safety commissioner. The court record indicated that even some of the judges were a part of the system when cases were dismissed on technical grounds for those who hired the right lawyers or got in line with the payoff system.

The *Register's* noncrusading policy precluded me from taking the time necessary to follow up the evidence of payoffs. However, City Editor Kelly and Managing Editor Eyerly encouraged me to find out all I could about the system while covering the routine of four municipal court judges, the police station, and six judges in the Polk County District Court.

Reading 2: The Payoff Story

Political campaigns for city and county office routinely brought charges of payoffs and corruption in city and county law enforcement and provided the opportunity to question incumbent politicians about how they were handling liquor law enforcement. Since city officials could not admit they permitted wholesale violation of the liquor laws, the Des Moines Safety Commissioner usually noted that there were "a few bad spots" but that on the whole he ran "a pretty clean town." It was just such a routine questioning of Safety Commissioner Clarence (Chink) Koenigsberger that led to my first front page payoff story and an interesting personal confrontation with three of the local bootleggers.

It was common knowledge that Al Rosenberg, operator of Mommie's Place, paid no attention to the 2 A.M. closing hours and continued to sell liquor as long as there were customers to buy it. Likewise, Johnnie Critelli's Place on Harding Road paid no attention to closing hours and served liquor and spaghetti to lure customers after most places closed at 2 A.M. Alphonse (Babe) Bisignano operated Babe's on Sixth Avenue as one of the town's finest supper clubs, but there were slot machines in the restrooms and also in the adjoining Jungle Club. Although the supper club operated with a reasonable regard for closing hours, the Jungle Club operated as long as there were customers.

When I questioned Chink Koenigsberger about his law enforcement record, the amiable cleaning supply store owner commented that it was "a pretty clean town" and that he was going to run for a second term. Koenigsberger said he was sorry to hear of the dismissal of a recent liquor case against Johnnie Critelli and said Critelli's Harding Road tavern was among "three or four bad places in town." He named Babe's at 417½ Sixth Avenue, and Mommie's, at 216 Fourth Avenue, as the other "bad places." It was a rather routine interview, but it came at a time when there had been news stories dealing with law violations at those three well-known watering places.

The response from the tavern owners was immediate, dramatic, and direct. Although it had its tense moments, it ended with a series of stories that rocked Koenigsberger and his fund raisers and killed his chances for reelection.

I was at the police station the next day going about the routine of checking records when a bondsman called me to say "there are some fellows in a car who want to see you." Since I was at the police station, I gave no thought to my safety and bounced down the steps to the car. The back door was opened, and Johnnie Critelli motioned for me to get in. As I did I was shoved from the rear and I sprawled on the back seat. As the car sped away, I noted that the other two men in the car were Babe Bisignano and Al Rosenberg. All had scowls on their faces.

"You went too far this time, Mollenhoff," Critelli growled.

"What's this all about?" I asked in genuine confusion, since my personal relationships with all three had been generally pleasant even though I had written numerous news stories about their various problems with police and the courts.

Bisignano responded, "It was the story in this morning's *Register.* You said we had 'bad places.' "

I sat silently while Babe declared that he had "the finest supper club in Iowa—Babe's is a credit to Des Moines."

It was immediately apparent that he resented his high class place being called a "bad place" and lumped with such lower class joints as Mommie's and Critelli's.

Critelli cut in with a rambling complaint that the *Des Moines Register* was in a conspiracy with Koenigsberger and others to defeat him in his plans to be a candidate for Safety Commissioner. Critelli, frequently arrested and often convicted on bootlegging and other charges, later ran unsuccessfully for Des Moines Safety Commissioner on the slogan, "Be Honest With Yourself. Vote for Johnnie Critelli." He was the one candidate who admitted he would run an open town "because that is what the taxpayers want." His perception of what the taxpayers wanted was far wide of the mark, and he received only a handful of votes after an expensive campaign that included a free dance at the huge Tromar Ballroom attended by several thousand.

However, during the ride across town I was not really concentrating upon what Babe or Critelli or Al Rosenberg were saying. Irate as they seemed, it was unlikely that they would kill me; that would only compound their problems. Babe was a former heavyweight wrestler and Johnnie Critelli was also a large man, and it was possible that they might beat me up. I couldn't imagine owlish little Al Rosenberg even getting in a sneak punch from the side. His major physical accomplishment was a swift dumping of the liquor pitcher when police raided his place.

As I viewed it, I had little to gain in trying to escape as the car traveled slowly through downtown traffic. There seemed little danger of permanent injury if I stayed with them, and there was the possibility of a great story if they even tried to assault me. I was not surprised when they drove to John Critelli's Harding Road place where they took me into a back room for serious discussions. Rosenberg contributed little to the discussion except to offer a word of encouragement to Babe or Critelli in their rambling critical comments about Koenigsberger, the *Des Moines Register* and my audacity in calling their establishments "bad places."

"I didn't call your places 'bad,' " I interrupted Babe. "I was quoting what Koenigsberger was saying about the law enforcement conditions."

"He's got his guts talking that way after taking our money," Babe shouted. Critelli added, "And we have to buy all of our cleaning supplies from his lousy place."

They also told me that Koenigsberger had taken cash payoffs from all three of them. I pointed out that I had not known of the payoffs to Koenigsberger or I would not have written my story in the manner I did.

Critelli countered, "Everybody knows he's been demanding and taking payoffs, but you won't write it." Babe added, "You don't have guts enough to write it even now that we've told you."

I replied that I didn't think any of them "had the guts" to stand behind his payoff allegation in a sworn statement. I asked Babe if he or Critelli would give me such a statement in his own handwriting. "I promise you there will be a big story about your payoffs to Koenigsberger."

It was at this point that Al Rosenberg, without offering to write a statement on the payoffs, urged Babe or Critelli to give me a written statement. Critelli first blustered a willingness to write a statement about payments made to a Koenigsberger campaign manager, but then he backed away on grounds that he had some pending problems in court and such a statement might complicate matters. Babe also drew back from an offer to put it in writing on the grounds that he had some present problems over 96 cases of whisky the federal government had seized for unpaid floor tax. It was little Al Rosenberg who finally wrote a two-page statement on payoff demands he said had been made by Koenigsberger's campaign manager.

With the statement in my hand, Bisignano and Rosenberg drove me to the *Des Moines Register* and *Tribune* building and Bisignano escorted me to the city desk to assure City Editor Kelly of the authenticity of the written statement.

The story appeared on the front page of the *Des Moines Register* on November 27, 1943, under the headline:

TAVERN MAN
SAYS PAY-OFF
WAS SOUGHT

It recounted Rosenberg's charge that a campaign worker for Koenigsberger had asked him to pay $100 a week for protection against police raids and that the Koenigsberger representative had also asked him to make a $1000 contribution to Koenigsberger's campaign expenses after the 1942 city election. Rosenberg, Critelli, and Bisignano were quoted as having been pressured to buy products from the Des Moines Sanitary and Supply Company, which was owned by Koenigsberger.

I quoted Rosenberg as saying he knew Koenigsberger's campaign was on in earnest "because members of the (police) liquor bureau have been visiting my place nightly. I was raided shortly after the election, and was told to see one of the managers of Koenigsberger's campaign if I wanted to get things straightened out," Rosenberg added.

Koenigsberger's campaign manager denied the Rosenberg charge, and Rosenberg acknowledged that he had dealt with another man, and named him. The man denied the charges, and the battle of charges and counter charges followed.

An investigation was launched by the police and by the county attorney's office, but it was apparent it was a whitewash and coverup from the outset. To have the needed push for an effective investigation, the newspaper would have had to put a good deal more time and money into the probe than it was willing to do at that time. However, the story did have the impact of knocking Koenigsberger out of the safety commissioner job. Unfortunately, by that time all of the crooked police and others with vested liquor interests had switched their bets to another horse.

Although I had never had reason for doubting the truth of the original payoff statements made by Rosenberg, Critelli, and Bisignano, they did back down on some of their allegations in the face of pressure by local prosecutors and a fixed court system. They knew they could not afford the kind of full and uncontrolled investigation that was needed. In the uneasy months that followed the first payoff story, I saw at first hand the manner in which an entrenched political machine can bring pressure against the direct witnesses. I learned how unreliable witnesses can be when they are, in fact, co-conspirators in law violations and when turning state's evidence challenges the investigation and prosecution establishment.

When I had the written statement from Rosenberg in hand, I believed I had wrapped up a payoff case, but I saw it drift away because of laxity in the investigation and pressures on key witnesses. I realized why Herb Kelly and Frank Eyerly had insisted upon a lower key approach to the payoff story than I believed was warranted by a written statement and general corroboration from two others who had initially said they were direct witnesses to payoffs to Koenigsberger. There were to be more payoff stories later, and the frustrations of that first experience were then of value.

STUDENT WORK PROJECT SUGGESTION

Trace the movement of the most recent liquor and gambling law violations in your area from the arrest through disposition. Note the types of reports and records kept on each movement of the case through the police department and the courts.

5 POLICE AND COURT PATTERNS

It is impossible to say too often that repetition of routine record research is the key to an instinctive understanding of where evidence can be found to document an investigative project or to test the credibility of an informant. The reporter's instinctive reaction is improved by saturation with knowledge of a wide range of records available in a police station, a city hall, or a county courthouse. Thus the years spent on police stories and covering the local civil and criminal courts is invaluable, provided the reporter has an inquisitive eye and an ear tuned to the complaints of victims of injustice. There are always honest and knowledgeable people to help with the story if you ask the right questions and can be trusted to keep confidences.

THE VALUE OF ROUTINE

By 1944 I had nearly three years of experience in observation, analysis, and reporting on local government in Des Moines and Polk County. Although there had been a few successful forays into the exposure of corruption and payoffs, much of the work had been the routine of reporting arrests, court arraignments, trials, and sentencing.

I was saturated with the routine of searching local records in Des Moines. I had learned that Iowa law required every Iowa county to keep similar records on court proceedings, land records, births, marriages, divorces, and deaths. Although I had not had the need to test it yet, I knew that every state in the United States required essentially the same types of records as I had examined in Polk County. With the exception of juvenile court records and a few other records, they were all public and subject to examination during working hours by any lawyer, citizen, or newspaper reporter.

My basic responsibilities included:

1. The daily routine of examining the arrest cards at the captain's desk in the police station and interviewing the arresting officers when there was anything unusual about a case. In addition, I made it a practice to touch base with a few of the policemen who would tip me off if they knew of anything the chief's office was trying to hide.

2. Municipal court where I endured the monotony of combing every case on the civil or criminal dockets for the little irregularities in the record that might signify "a fix" or a special political arrangement.

3. The Polk County District Court building where I had the responsibility for examining every marriage license application, every divorce petition filed, every entry on the probate docket, and every petition filed in civil or criminal cases.

After the first year I no longer needed to ask the clerk of court or his subordinates to explain what the various docket entries meant or the meaning of the legalese in the various petitions and answers. I no longer needed to ask if the bail bond on a drunken driving case was unusually high or unusually low or if the fines or jail terms were particularly light or stiff. I had followed the routine of hundreds of cases of burglary, robbery, rape, and miscellaneous assault charges, from simple assaults in a family fuss to brutal aggravated beatings that left the victim on the edge of death.

I had learned what Lincoln Steffens meant when he said that he and Jacob Riis, the great reformer reporter, could create what seemed to be a crime wave at any time by simply reporting the details of the brutal crime that took place any day in any major city. On any dull day a story could be generated by making some additional inquiries into the circumstances of any arrest, for these ranged from simple assault through aggravated assault to first degree murder. There was always an angle worth pursuing for the city desk.

I knew good policemen, who took their jobs seriously and enforced the law with steady, even-handed justice for even the worst criminal. With a few exceptions I discovered such men were passed by on the promotion lists. Promotion was for the slick political cops, who would do what their crooked bosses told them to do and then provide and stick with an artful fabrication to cover up evidence of police brutality, corruption, or simple mismanagement.

On a few occasions I was present when police used a nightstick to work over a poor black or a green farmhand who had simply protested that they had not started an altercation on a street or in one of the East Side bars. It was common knowledge that one squad car team periodically provoked the curvacious red-haired Katy O'Brien into assaulting them so they could throw her in jail for being drunk. They then undressed her and put her in the padded cell on the thesis that she was so enraged she might hurt herself.

Sometimes I wrote the stories. Often I did not because crusading was discouraged unless it was done with a lighter touch than I could use.

Although I believe it is possible for an intelligent reporter to become properly informed about courts and police in a shorter span than three years, I do not regret having been kept in that kind of work for a somewhat longer period. I have since concluded that the repetitious work with records was the most useful learning experience of my early career in investigative journalism. It was the foundation upon which everything else was constructed. Even if I had not been a law student at Drake University in that period of time, I would have observed and absorbed enough of the law of evidence to know a prima facie case when I saw one and to recognize "a fixed" case for a prestigious law firm or for a political friend.

TYPES OF EXPERIENCE

Initially, I had known little of the courts except what I had seen in the movies. Prior to covering the Des Moines Municipal Court, I had observed only one hour of a trial in the Hamilton County courthouse in Webster City and had been a witness in one automobile damage suit.

Court Experience

In the first months I was covering the courts I often wished I had been initiated into the court system in some small county seat town where there was but one judge, fewer cases filed, and time to examine each case more thoroughly. After a time I concluded that the Des Moines Municipal Court was the ideal size for learning the system. There were four judges, each with his own distinctive personal approach to justice. I was forced to deal with a wide variety of civil and criminal litigation that required diligent work. It forced me to read hundreds of complaints and cross complaints, and to move swiftly through the routine of the pleadings down to the specific acts, specific dates, and specific damages in civil suits. I was required to check and double check dozens of criminal cases each week and to learn the importance of being precisely accurate in stories written from the public record.

At first, it was necessary to ask a torrent of questions on procedures of the employees in the clerk's office, the judges, and the prosecutors. As time went on and I began to report more and more on irregularities and outright fixes, my questions had to become more selective. I had learned that some employees of the clerk's office were programmed to tell the judges of any special inquiry I was making on any of their cases. This spy-on-the-reporter system included engaging me in conversations to get a glimpse of the docket number when I had intentionally taken the docket to an isolated place on the counter to take notes.

Most of the time I found it an amusing game and only occasionally an irritant. There was little the officials could do to cover their tracks on any really significant irregularity in the record, short of tearing out a page in the permanent docket. And that was most unlikely. The bound permanent records had consecutively numbered pages, so that it would be impossible to conceal the fact that a page was missing. A missing page would constitute evidence of a serious and obvious destruction of a court record and would be a criminal offense.

Although I had not yet explored all of the intricacies of tax collecting, land appraisals, budgeting, payroll padding, and equipment control that I later dealt with, I was familiar with the search of land title, with marriage, divorce, and probate records, and the general system for approving and paying county bills.

Corruption in the Police Force

Although there were many basically decent and honest people in the courts, in the county and city office, and in the police department, most of these people were not strong enough or independent enough to speak out. They would whisper tips of wrongdoing and shiver at the thought of being identified as my informant. One technique used to conceal corruption was periodically to appoint aggressively honest police as a facade. Although these men were given the title of Chief of Police, Assistant Chief of Police, or Head of the Vice Squad, they were usually immobilized by experienced and corrupt inspectors and captains who were kept in the actual day-to-day operational positions and were subject to the control and suggestions of Floyd Hartzer. Hartzer was the real power in the police department in most administrations.

A former official of the Des Moines Teamsters Union, Hartzer used his union connections as a political power base for advancement in the police department. It is my recollection that he had a civil service rating as a captain of police shortly after I started covering the police department. Later he became head of the vice squad in a corrupt administration. For a time he served as chief of police and attained the permanent civil service rank of assistant chief of police. Although civil service police were supposed to avoid politics, Hartzer was recognized as a political force and as a bag man for payoffs from prostitutes, gamblers, and liquor law violators. Floyd Hartzer was the man to see to get an appointment to the Des Moines police department because of his connections with the civil service commission and the skillful rigging of appointments and promotions. This power prevailed even when he was out of favor with the incumbent safety commissioner.

One drawback to the use of records as a guide to police efficiency is that raids and arrests may be threats or punishments rather than attempts to enforce the law. In Des Moines, Iowa, in the 1941-44 period, the police raids on the gambling and illegal liquor places were seldom an indication of reform. It was more likely to be selective law enforcement to force a protection payoff or a manifestation of one of the feuding factions within the police department warring on the racketeering friends of another faction. Thus, the statistics on vice arrests were worthless as indicators of the moral climate of the community, the local government officials, or the police department.

The Way Corruption Spreads

Better indicators of the moral and ethical standards of police and public officials are their after-hour companions and their personal friends. Floyd Hartzer's personal friends were the racketeers, the teamster crowd, and the political dealers on the police department. For example, Captain C. A. Dunagan was a friend and supporter of Alphonse (Babe Carnera) Bisignano, operator of a supper club and bar where liquor was dispensed illegally and slot machines purred out their illegal tune in the rest rooms and in the Jungle Club. Inspector Paul Castelline, chief of detectives, spent his off-hours in the company of Chicago mobster Luigi Fratto, who came to Des Moines under the name of Lew Farrell in the early 1940s. It was never explained whether Castelline had known Farrell before he came to Des Moines, reportedly on the lam from a gambling charge in Wisconsin.

Farrell was the Iowa representative for Canadian Ace beer, which was put out by the old Manhattan Brewing Company, the Capone mob-dominated Chicago firm. Farrell, who took Cherry Nose Gioe's place in Des Moines, had been arrested in Chicago on assault and extortion charges. He was picked up for questioning by the

Des Moines police department the first week he was in town on orders of Inspector Jack Brophy, but was released a short time later without charges and in a few weeks was the bosom companion of Detective Chief Castelline. I had met the dapper little gunman in Babe's restaurant when I was talking to Bisignano. Farrell came up, called me by my first name and introduced himself as Lew Farrell, representing Canadian Ace beer.

The conversation indicated he knew all about me—my full schedule in the Drake University Law School while playing two varsity sports and working a 40-hour week as a police and court reporter for the *Des Moines Register.* "You're working too hard," he said with sympathy dripping from his voice. "You don't want to kill yourself off. You ought to take a little time off to have a little fun—see some of the sights in Chicago, St. Louis, or Kansas City."

"Even if I could work it into my schedule, I couldn't afford to travel," I said innocently.

He promptly put his own interpretation on my frank admission that I couldn't afford such luxuries, and suggested that he would be pleased "to take you on a swing of the Big Time, and it won't cost you a cent." Momentarily caught up in the vision of an expense-paid trip to Chicago, St. Louis, and Kansas City, I replied, "that sounds like fun."

Immediately Farrell started to bubble with plans for a trip. His enthusiasm made me wonder why this suave little beer distributor was so interested in my background and my health. Why was he making this generous offer to provide me with a vacation in the first 15 minutes of our first meeting at a nightclub bar? The obvious answer was that he wanted something from me and probably wanted to get me indebted to him for some future use.

Rather than reject the idea bluntly, I said I had a full schedule that wouldn't make it possible to think of a trip for months. I even thanked him for the offer and said it sounded like a good idea, but in my own mind I knew I would never accept Farrell's hospitality. I realized that one swinging trip with that mobster would have destroyed my career as an independent reporter.

A few months later, the comments of another Des Moines night club figure demonstrated the bad impression one gives by accepting even small favors from people who operate outside the law. It was rather common practice at that time for reporters and editors of both *The Register* and our sister paper *The Tribune* to accept free drinks and an occasional free meal from the owners of the bars that sold liquor illegally. "Nothing wrong with accepting a free drink or two," one editor had commented. "Dave is just a generous guy who likes newspaper people. It would be awkward to turn down his hospitality." I had accepted "free drinks, compliments of the house" myself when in the places with older reporters and editors.

However, when a *Des Moines Tribune* columnist wrote a factually accurate but critical story about one of the local bootleg joints, the owner was furious. When I met him on the street the man was seething with anger at the *Tribune* columnist. "How does Gordy think he can get by with writing this crap about me after eating my steak and drinking my booze?" the bar owner fumed. "He accepts my hospitality and then he writes bad stories about my place. Ain't you newspaper guys got any ethics?"

I believed that the *Des Moines Tribune* columnist was an honest newspaper man, but I saw that the nightclub operator had a point. He felt he had bought the reporter with a few drinks and a few steaks and resented the "betrayal." It was an incident that I recalled often in later years when there were unusual offers of hospitality and generosity from political figures, labor leaders, or Washington lobbyists.[1]

I concluded that acceptance of any gifts or meals by reporters was a threat to some degree against their independence. No matter how other reporters and editors operated, I decided with regard to my own conduct, that I would lean over backwards to avoid encroachments upon my independence. Mobster Lew Farrell's overly generous offer, would soon have become a club to be held over me or a sample "carrot" to lead the "ass" further into corruption.

Threats and Promises

There were equally important lessons from dealing with Floyd Hartzer, the power behind much police department corruption and coverup. When I had occasion to question Hartzer about evidence of police corruption and payoffs, he would often launch into a series of vulgar four letter expletives and end it with the comment, "now put that in your family newspaper." There was no way I could clean up his comment for a family newspaper in that puritanic day, and Hartzer knew it was an effective device for stonewalling. In other instances, Hartzer would counsel me like a father, suggesting that I be "a good reporter like Rider and Guy," the veteran police reporters

---

[1] Senator Paul Douglas, an Illinois Democrat, had adopted a rule of accepting no more than he could eat or drink at one sitting in an effort to set some standard when congressional ethics were under fire in the early 1950s in connection with scandals in the Reconstruction Finance Corporation. The good senator from Illinois theorized that he didn't know any senator or congressman who could be bought for one meal and one drink. Even as he set that standard, however, he noted that if the one meal and drink with one lobbyist became a pattern it could amount to a compromising situation.

for the *Register* and the *Tribune* who were usually closer to the police and the politicians than to the city desks. They had to be prodded sharply before they would write anything even mildly critical of the police or public officials.

"Your stories aren't really going to change anything," Hartzer would comment. "Your city editor will have his front page story, you will have your little by-line, we'll close the joints down for a few days, and then it will be right back as it was before you wrote your story. Your bosses want an open town, and they won't let you follow up even if your city editor wants you to." Hartzer said this in a not unkindly way. "Get wise. For your own good, don't be a stinking troublemaker. Troublemakers don't get any place on the police department, and they don't get any place in the newspaper business."

It was obvious that Chief of Police Hartzer, so much like the corrupt policeman in the *Autobiography of Lincoln Steffens,* had never read of the Lexow police investigations and Teddy Roosevelt's smashing of police corruption in New York. It was unlikely that Hartzer had even heard of Lincoln Steffens and his forays against police and government corruption in a dozen cities at the turn of the century. I felt no obligation to enlighten him on the subject of the techniques of Lincoln Steffens.

The young reporter must avoid accepting favors that can limit his independence. Often the efforts to compromise a newsman are more subtle than those efforts of the corrupt police, the bootleggers, and the gamblers in Des Moines in the 1940s, but the motivation is the same and probably always will be. In national government affairs and politics the efforts to buy newsmen also exist, but it is more often that the temptation is a social engagement or a "good" news story.

STUDENT WORK PROJECT SUGGESTION

Analyze the responsibility for vice law enforcement in your city or county. Is there a special vice squad or is the responsibility on the chief of police or one of his assistants? Do an analysis of the background of the individual or the squad members who are responsible for vice law enforcement. The review of the background of these officials should include a survey of real property records and criminal and civil court dockets.

6 EXPOSURE OF CORRUPTION: PART I

THE SOLID WALL

To break the arrogant stonewalling silence of a corrupt local machine that controls police, prosecution, and the courts, it is essential for the newsman to form a loose alliance with a strong civic-minded individual or organization. That working relationship must be properly restricted to lawful methods and proper aims that are not vulnerable to inevitable counterattacks. Jacob Riis and Lincoln Steffens worked with the Reverend Dr. Charles Parkhurst and his little knot of reformers in New York in the 1890s. Steffens also managed to locate equally helpful reformers in St. Louis, Minneapolis, Chicago, Pittsburgh, and Philadelphia. Paul Y. Anderson alligned himself with two United States senators in his years of persistent crusading to break the Teapot Dome scandals. In my own experience in exposing local, state, and federal scandals, I have always been able to find someone who was willing to work with me to expose corrupt government officials and to seek reform.

When the investigation, prosecution and judicial arms of local government are under the control of one political machine for any extended period of time, it is likely that almost all parts of the political machine are corrupt, seriously compromised, or are paralyzed by fear at the mere thought of challenging the power structure. Such a situation presents a most severe test for an investigation-minded reporter or editor. Success against such odds requires cooperation and help from a strong civic-minded person or organization.

The Republican Party Machine

That was the kind of powerful Republican machine control that existed in Polk County, Iowa, in April 1946, when I returned from service in the Navy to resume work as a reporter for the *Des Moines Register*. Pieces of the corrupt operation had surfaced from time to time in the stories of police payoffs that were never pursued by the county attorney, the fixing of drunken driving cases in which nearly all had a part (see Reading 1), or in the aborted prosecution of the black market in new cars purchased on sheriff's office priorities (see Reading 3). The boss, or bosses, of the machine always persuaded or coerced local officials to join ranks in a conspiracy of silence against the press until the evidence of corruption had been buried in a controlled grand jury investigation.

When the machine bosses were deadly serious, the usually talkative police would suddenly say "no comment" and explain they had been ordered to remain silent because of the sensitivity of the investigation. The sheriff, the county attorney, and the municipal and district court judges likewise declined comment and often issued orders barring witnesses from talking to the press.

The Official Coverup

Having dealt with such a conspiracy of silence on a number of occasions, I realized why Lincoln Steffens and Teddy Roosevelt had relied so heavily upon the outside crusading zeal of the Reverend Dr. Charles H. Parkhurst in fighting corruption in Tammany Hall in New York. A spokesman for a reform group who is not a part of the local government establishment can put government mismanagement and corruption in perspective by his comments. He can raise questions about the decisions of the official investigators. He can put various facts together and draw the logical conclusions that provide new angles for keeping a story alive.

Several unsuccessful attempts to stir a depth investigation of circumstances and charges of payoffs demonstrated to me that it was not enough to expose the evidence indicating corruption. The major problem for the reporter and editor was in keeping public attention on the evidence that had surfaced and on the lack of an effective followup of that evidence by officials with the responsibility to investigate.

The Des Moines police department was masterful in its management of the coverup. The minute that any charge surfaced indicating police corruption, the police department seized control of the investigation of the charges of misdoing. In this manner the police investigators could have access to all evidence and the identity of all witnesses. They could minimize the damage from exposure by burying evidence, by failing to conduct key interviews, or by conducting such interviews in a superficial manner.

Reading 3: Black Market Cars

It was the prodding of Des Moines Police Lieutenant John P. Gill that initiated my first investigation involving the workings of the federal bureaucracy and the Office of Price Administration (OPA). In his usual blunt way Gill accused me of being "just another lazy reporter."

"For a while I thought you were going to be different, but I can see already that you are just like the other gutless and dead-assed police reporters we've had around here," he said with feigned sarcasm.

I smarted under the insult and responded, "What do you mean?"

"Why don't you just use your eyes and a little imagination and you'll see what I mean," Gill replied. "Do I have to take you and lead you by the hand?"

"What is it I've missed?" I asked eagerly, as he had expected, and he responded with just enough facts to titillate my imagination.

"Haven't you noticed the Babe (Bisignano) driving around in that new Pontiac?" he said. "Did you ever ask yourself how a bootlegger (night club operator) gets one of those priority slips to buy a new car?"

That was all I needed. I could check the automobile registration records at the Polk County courthouse the next day, but I pressed to find out how much more Gill knew on Babe's new car. In fact, I had been unaware that Bisignano even had a new car. Had I noticed it, I would probably have failed to ask the pertinent question as to how a night club operator could obtain a new car in the spring of 1943 when federal law required a certification that the buyer was a law enforcement official, physician, or other person who "contributed to the war effort or public welfare."

Gill said he had not checked the records but had been told that Bisignano had purchased the car from a deputy sheriff a few days after the deputy had purchased it on the representation that it would be used for law enforcement work. From past experience, I knew that Gill was usually precisely right. At the Polk County courthouse I found this was no exception. The registration records disclosed that the Pontiac Chieftain had been purchased by Deputy Sheriff Roy Holbrook on April 16, 1943, from Schooler Motor Company. The card was inscribed with "Sheriff's Office." Five days later on April 21, 1943, the Pontiac was transferred to Bisignano.

One case might make a few paragraphs for the paper, but not a significant story. Having traced the Bisignano Pontiac with ease, I was determined to see how many quick transfers there had been in Polk County and to learn how widespread was the black market in cars since OPA regulations had been enacted. The examination of each registration for quick transfers took no more than two or three hurried glances at the face of the card, but there were more than 50,000 automobile registrations in Polk County. This work was in addition to my regular court and police coverage and necessitated visits to the motor vehicle registration office at night.

After spending two or three nights trying to do the job alone, I enlisted the help of another reporter, Elise Shane, and together we examined every automobile registration in the county. We turned up more than 30 quick transfers of title that appeared suspicious, and it was no surprise that a number of them were managed through Polk County Sheriff's Office priorities. Whether Sheriff Vane B. Overturff knew of this misuse of law enforcement priorities or not, he was going to have some explaining to do.

At the OPA office, the chief counsel told me there was no arrangement through which a new car could be legally purchased by a night club operator and that willfull circumvention of the laws and regulations could be a federal crime. The OPA counsel also indicated that a number of quick transfers were under investigation at that time, but he declined to identify any of the suspected black market cases. My story on Bisignano's purchase of a new Pontiac through a sheriff's office priority was thus accompanied by the revelation that the OPA office was involved in a broad probe of quick purchases and resale of a dozen cars in Polk County.

Some months later a federal grand jury in Davenport indicted Elmer G. Croft, a Des Moines garage operator, on charges of violating OPA regulations with regard to the sale of two automobiles. Croft was a convicted automobile thief who operated a garage near the Polk County jail and was official custodian of the automobile fleet of Sheriff Vane B. Overturff. He was also a friend of Sheriff Overturff. Sheriff Overturff claimed he knew nothing about the misuse of the law enforcement priority by Croft and Deputy Sheriff Roy Holbrook, but he permitted Croft to continue as official custodian of the sheriff's office cars.

Although Bisignano bought the new Pontiac on a questionable deal and retained the car, he was not indicted because he had made no false representation to the federal government but was only the beneficiary of the misuse of sheriff's office priorities by others.

Twenty days after the federal indictment was returned against Croft it was dismissed on the motion of United States District Attorney Maurice F. Donegan who refused to comment on why he had asked that the Croft indictment be dismissed.

LESSONS FROM FAILURE

In that brief experience with the Office of Price Administration and the black market cars, I learned of the difficulty of prodding the sainted Federal Bureau of Investigation to get off its tail to conduct small fraud investigations. I also learned that Croft, convicted operator of a sophisticated car theft ring, had developed the kind of political connections that could cause a United States District Attorney to drop a case. I was to learn a great deal more about Croft in the years after I returned from Navy service, and I was to become deeply involved in the three-year ordeal of the Polk County fraud investigations and trials.

It was a routine record research of motor vehicle registrations that documented our stories and forced prosecution. It was laxity in following up those developments that made it possible for the cases to be dismissed without a reasonable explanation.

STUDENT WORK PROJECT SUGGESTION

Examine the accessibility of motor vehicle registrations records in your city or county, and write a brief paper explaining whether you could do the research on quick transfers that was possible in Polk County in 1943. A rash of privacy acts (federal and state) has resulted in closing automobile registrations to the press and the public in recent years. Explain the impact of those laws on record research in your community.

7 EXPOSURE OF CORRUPTION: PART II

REFORMERS

A spokesman for a reform group can counter police and political coverups by pushing the thesis that no governmental unit should be trusted to do a thorough investigation involving the actions of its own officials or members. The spokesman for the reform group can forcefully point up the vulnerability of the police investigation of the police, stressing the lack of proper questioning of key witnesses or the failure to obtain important documented evidence expeditiously. Such a spokesman has more "clout" than a young, idealistic reporter.

Civic Action

When I returned to the newspaper after two years of Navy service, I found that Paul W. Walters and B. J. Powers, two Des Moines lawyers, had formed a Civic Action Committee to fight corruption in local government. Working with Basil Grossnickle, a township constable, they had engineered a series of raids on some of the most notorious night clubs where there was open and flagrant disregard for the laws against gambling as well as the laws prohibiting the sale of liquor by the drink.

Initially, Walters and Powers were concerned mainly about the evil of payoffs and selective law enforcement policies by Sheriff Vane B. Overturff and by various Des Moines Safety Commissioners. But, in the summer of 1945, they received a tip that Elmer G. Croft appeared to be involved in defrauding the county of thousands of dollars by submitting false bills for automobile repairs, tires, and tubes for the county's welfare department cars.

Implications of Fraud

The tip came from J. F. (Bill) Baillie, the Republican county treasurer. Baillie was shocked at the evidence that the Republican supervisors and the auditor might be involved in a conspiracy with Croft. Powerless to raise the question directly because he had no investigative power, Baillie knew that an effective investigation could only be done from the outside because of the involvement of the sheriff and the county attorney's office.

Walters hired a former county employee to compile a list of the bills filed by Croft in the auditor's office and to examine the payments made to Sheriff Overturff and his 49 deputies. The results were startling. The county welfare department had paid for hundreds of tires and tubes for the seven welfare department cars, and the repair bills were beyond reason. On the face of them the mileage claims by the sheriff's office were excessive and some were probably false. Walters immediately had the county records photographed so that the proof of the frauds could not be destroyed.

Official Inaction

Walters and Powers took their evidence to County Attorney Francis Kuble and asked for the kind of full-scale grand jury investigation the facts warranted. A distressed County Attorney Kuble stalled, refused to act, and within a few weeks died of a heart attack. Vernon Seeburger was the man named to complete Kuble's term. Walters and Powers were hopeful for more success with him; however, the promised cooperation was slow in coming against the power of the Republican organization in Polk County and in the Iowa capitol.

Walters also sought the cooperation and support of the Des Moines Taxpayers Association, but was told that his reform would be resented by many of the most influential members, who had a stake in keeping the Republican machine in control. The results were even worse when Walters went to the Polk County Republican chairman to plead for help in cleaning up the Polk County courthouse. He was told bluntly: "If a yellow dog was running on the Republican ticket I would feel it was necessary to support the whole ticket." Walters' appeal for a Republican housecleaning was met with the argument that the people Walters wanted ousted—Sheriff Overturff and three members of the board of supervisors—were the strength of the Republican machine in Polk County and had the support of the Republican Polk County district judges.

When it becomes plain that the local authorities whose job it is to clean up corruption are unwilling to act, it becomes necessary to expose the evil to the public. Walters went to the Des Moines Register and Tribune executives where he was informed that "we are not a crusading newspaper," but "will report what you do and what you say" about corruption and mismanagement in local government.

I first met Paul Walters in the spring of 1946, and I soon knew he would be for me what the Reverend Dr. Charles H. Parkhurst was to Lincoln Steffens. We were to be comrades for reform for three exciting and fruitful years of exposure of corruption and mismanagement at the Des Moines City Hall, the Polk County Courthouse and at the Iowa Capitol. We shared the joys of small and large victories and the disappointments and disillusionments when some men in whom we believed bent to the pressures of political expediency or sold out for personal financial gain.

Reading 4: Paul Walters, Reformer

Paul Walters was a disheveled looking man of about 50, with thinning light brown hair that seemed to be patted down rather than combed. He wore dark baggy suits, steel-rimmed glasses and always seemed to be chomping on a soggy cigar. I had not known Paul Walters before 1946, although I had seen his name on petitions I had reviewed in the Polk County Clerk's Office. I heard mention in the newsroom of Walters and the Civic Action Committee as a group of wide-eyed reformers. Walters, who belonged to a temperance league, was said to be opposed to drinking liquor. The establishment Republican political figures and corrupt elements in the city government spoke of Walters as "a temperance nut" who didn't drink whisky and was trying to make it impossible for anyone else to drink whisky. Still another element contended that Walters wasn't sincere about the temperance bit, that it was only a device to gain public office for himself and Basil Grossnickle so they could take over the liquor and gambling payoffs.

When I finally got to meet Walters he said he had read many of my stories on payoffs, black markets, and the "fixing" of court cases. This could have been flattery and I still couldn't be entirely certain about his total motivation. I told him frankly of the two views I had heard about him and asked him to spell out his motivations for getting into the thankless task of trying to reform the city and county government.

"Young man," he said with a warm twinkle in his eye, "it's probably about the same as yours. I got tired of the corruption and payoffs, and decided to try to do something about it."

Walters admitted he did not drink liquor and felt that "it never does anyone any good," but said he was "not a zealot" who would try to interfere with others who wished to drink legally. He said he was more concerned with the "selective enforcement" of liquor and gambling laws because that was an outrage that inevitably was accompanied by payoffs by racketeers and led to the destruction of sound law enforcement. Once the underworld makes payoffs to the police or sheriff's office to sell illegal liquor, they have a club with which to control them. There is little to stop the racketeers from sneaking in gambling and narcotics. "When law enforcement is compromised by payoffs, there is no drawing the line," Walters said. "There can be no honest law enforcement when the top police have been compromised by payoffs." Walters expressed interest in some follow through on Babe Bisignano, Lew Farrell, and Elmer Croft and in breaking up their influences at the police station and the sheriff's office. The war years had been good to all three, despite some minor setbacks.

Lew Farrell, the Chicago mob's representative in Des Moines, had been so open-handed in his generosity to local causes that he had been rewarded with the distinction of a life membership in the Des Moines Junior Chamber of Commerce. Farrell had developed a close companionship with Chief of Detectives Paul Castelline. He was on a first-name basis with many young Des Moines businessmen and politicians, who were unaware that the dapper and generous beer distributor was Luigi Fratto, former gunman for the Chicago mob. In addition to his energetic work for the Des Moines Junior Chamber of Commerce, Farrell was courting the daughter of a politically prominent Italian family, was attending St. Anthony's Catholic Church, and was hobnobbing with judges. Farrell had also developed sufficient local political clout to be confident he could get federal government approval for a beer wholesaler's permit for the Canadian Ace distributorship in Iowa.

The war years had also been good to Alphonse (Babe Carnera) Bisignano. The Babe, a close friend and associate of Farrell, had become a millionaire with income from slot machines and from selling illegal whisky to the Women's Army Auxiliary Corps (WAAC) recruits who flocked to his bars and restaurants from nearby Fort Des Moines WAAC training post.

A few months before I had been discharged from the Navy, Grossnickle and his raiding constables had conducted a surprise raid on Babe's tavern and supper club, seized nearly 100 bottles of liquor, and filed criminal charges against Babe and two employees. The raid was planned by Walters and Grossnickle to set the stage for Grossnickle's effort to defeat the incumbent, Sheriff Vane B.

Overturff, for the Republican nomination in the June 1946 primary.

That raid on Babe's place dramatized the selective law enforcement in Polk County and stirred public interest in Grossnickle's candidacy, but it fell short by 2000 votes of upsetting Overturff in the primary. Walters had hoped to capture the sheriff's office and the county attorney's office so that he and his Civic Action Committee could get deeper and more effective investigations into the frauds and corruption in the Des Moines city government as well as in the Polk County courthouse.

It was after the June 1946 primary that I developed my closest ties with Paul Walters. Although I understood the importance of the selective law enforcement issue very well from the outset, it was from Paul Walters that I learned the mechanics of the frauds being perpetrated on the taxpayers of Polk County, Iowa, through double billing and false billing processes. Walters explained how Elmer G. Croft, operator of the Modern Motor Service garage, was ripping off thousands of dollars from the county welfare department by billing the county for tires, tubes, and motors that were never installed in welfare cars and for repairs that were never performed. Walters had made his own brief examination of the large number of tires and tubes purchased for seven cars, decided there were substantial provable frauds, and then hired a former county employee to do a more thorough job of probing the record.

It was not apparent on the surface whether the county auditor and the county board of supervisors were implicated in the frauds, but on each of the fraudulent billings was the signature of the auditor or his assistant and the signatures of three of the five members of the board of supervisors. The general charges made by Walters of mismanagement and fraud caused the state auditor's office to initiate a formal investigation of spending in Polk County, Iowa, in the summer of 1946. This investigation acquainted me with the state accountants and their examination of county spending, particularly those payments made to Croft's Modern Motor Service.

The state examiners were nonpolitical professionals, who were willing to be helpful. They explained the audit procedures and problems, without revealing their findings prior to completion of their work and the final report. They also answered my questions about the technical requirements of the law in the payment of county bills and the general civil and criminal responsibility of those involved in willful fraud or in negligence that resulted in the loss of county funds.

The procedures established under the law and regulations were for the purpose of centering responsibility for all expenditures of county funds to minimize the possibility of the county paying for goods or services that were not received. The process required the signature of county officials to show' that equipment or materials purchased were actually received. It was also required that at least three of the five members of the Polk County Board of Supervisors approve the purchases. The county auditor was required to sign his name, indicating that he had examined the documentation and that all of the paperwork was in order.

A casual observation of this system established that the key safeguards against fraud had been abandoned in the case of Croft's bills. The county welfare director signed Croft's claims for payment for dozens of tires and tubes and for a wide variety of repairs without having actual knowledge that the goods had been delivered or the car repairs done. Croft's bills then went to the board of supervisor's office, for the signatures of three members approving the repairs or purchases, and then were deposited with County Auditor L. O. Lindstrum. The paperwork was checked superficially in the county auditor's office, and the number of the claim was added to a list to be approved *en masse* at the next official meeting of the board of supervisors.

If it could be established that Croft's bills were false bills and that the goods were not actually delivered, all of the members of the board of supervisors and the welfare director and the county auditor would have some criminal or civil responsibility for the fraud. Initially, Walters said, he did not know whether all of the county officials were engaged in willful fraud or whether they were guilty of gross negligence in trusting Croft to deliver the tires and tubes and make the repairs on the county cars. He declared that, in the light of Croft's background, including the conviction for automobile theft, all of the Polk County officials should have been wary in dealing with him.

I wrote up my research on the records of tire and tube deliveries in an effort to get a story in print before the November election and was assured by the state examiners that my figures were in general agreement with their own findings. However, City Editor Hoschar rejected the story for two reasons. First, the newspapers had already carried some stories on the charges made by Paul Walters, and it wished to avoid any aggressive reporting in the middle of a political campaign. More important was the fact that the Iowa State Auditor's Office was engaged in an official examination of Polk County spending. Publication of this report was due before the end of the year. If, for any reason, the state auditor's office tried to suppress or water down the report of the examiners, then the *Register* would want to do its own probe on why a critical report was not released. My story would be part of that probe.

Although it was not the approach I would have taken at the time, the results were satisfactory. Democrats were elected as sheriff and county attorney and the Republican state auditor felt compelled to release the critical audit report with few, if any, changes. Election of Carroll O. Switzer, an aggressive young Democrat, as county attorney was the key to stopping any possibility of covering up the whole Polk County fraud story. Election of Howard Reppert, a tough and independent Democrat, as sheriff gave Switzer the kind of investigative help he needed to carry on formidable in-depth investigations on a dozen fronts. Although Walters had not thrown his support behind the Democratic candidates after he was unsuccessful in ousting Overturff in the primary, the corruption he had exposed was instrumental in their success. Election of Reppert and Switzer was no assurance of good government, but it could be a step in the direction of cleaning up the festering corruption.

STUDENT WORK PROJECT SUGGESTION

Write a detailed analysis of the legal procedures for the purchase and verification of delivery of automobiles and tires in your city or county government. Are the procedures being followed closely? Would it be possible to defraud the local government by false billing in your city or county?

8 POLK COUNTY FRAUD REPORT

The reporter can make his own breaks by thoroughly researching the background of individuals who are the subjects of official reports on government corruption. Such interviews, although sometimes hard to obtain, can provide opportunities for taking initiatives that would not be apparent to others. The official report is only the beginning. Detailed knowledge of the fraudulent activity and the background of a key figure can produce stories that will force prosecutors to carry out their legal responsibilities.

THE "HARD" INTERVIEW

A month after the 1946 election, Iowa State Auditor Chet Akers released the official examiner's report on Polk County expenditures. The report confirmed, as I knew it would, that Elmer Croft's billings had averaged about $2500 a year on each of the seven county welfare department cars. Those Chevrolets had cost less than $2000 each when new and the repair costs were outrageous by any standard.

Events concerning the state auditor's office were reported by Cy C. Clifton, the very Republican political writer for the *Register*. Slightly miffed that I was not covering the main story on the report, I decided to see what I could do in my jurisdiction by interviewing the Polk County supervisors who were charged with "willful neglect," and Croft who was charged with making the questionable and probably fraudulent billings. I felt well prepared to question any of the public officials or Croft because I had followed the investigation closely through its development in the Walters speeches, my conversations with the state examiners, and my own examination of the records and the law.

Preparation for an Unwelcome Interview

After talking to some of the board members and obtaining their expected denials of wrongdoing, I decided to walk over to Croft's Modern Motor Service garage rather than call him on the telephone. I knew he would not welcome me. In addition I called City Editor Al Hoschar to ask for a photographer to accompany me for safety sake as well as for a possible picture of Croft. Croft had a reputation for a quarrelsome disposition, and I knew he resented my stories on his black market car activities.

As I waited for photographer John Nagel at the west door of the courthouse, I reviewed the relevant facts for the Croft interview and jotted down three or four questions I believed essential. State Examiner Carl Nimrod's report showed that an average of $2553.24 was spent on each of the seven welfare cars serviced by Croft. But even more astounding than the overall cost figures was the fact, that, in 1945, $4,411.46 was spent for 186 tires and 227 tubes for the seven welfare cars. It averaged out that each of the seven cars had 32 and 3/7 tubes and 26 and 4/7 tires in the one-year period.

VALUE OF AN ADVERSARY INTERVIEW

It was a highly significant interview (see Reading 5) and through it I established a relationship with Croft that was to serve me well through more than three tumultuous years of Polk County fraud trials in which he was to be a central figure. The importance of trying for the hard interview, even when one expects to meet a stone wall of silence or a bitter antagonism, was reinforced. I had been genuinely interested in hearing his side of the story and in learning the manner in which he rationalized and justified his actions.

Croft, as many in his circumstances would, did not consider himself as bad as his coconspirators. He had convinced himself that he had been sucked into unethical and illegal acts by others. He felt that he was being made "the fall guy" for those who profited most from the frauds on the county treasury. Probably Croft was motivated to give the interview by a desire to express these considerations. He may also have believed that he could use me and a story in the *Des Moines Register* to throw a tremor into the ranks of his coconspirators. I did not resent being used in this fashion as long as I was not making unjustified and unsupported charges against others.

In this case, my conscience was clear. The charges against Croft and the supervisors were made in an official state report, and the supervisors either chose to remain silent or to issue broad general denials without addressing themselves to the specific charges. They had continued to do business with Elmer Croft and his Modern Motor Service long after Paul Walters had gone to them personally with his suspicions about the Croft bills. The supervisors and the sheriff were aware of Croft's conviction as an auto thief and of his indictment for blackmarketing cars obtained on a sheriff's office priorities.

WHO COVERS A STORY

Within 24 hours of the state report on Polk County financial affairs, Assistant County Attorney Edwin S. Thayer took the chief audit examiner, Carl Nimrod, before the Polk County Grand Jury for two hours of testimony. He also announced that Paul Walters would be called for testimony on the next Monday, and said he hoped to have some indictments before the grand jury term expired three weeks later on December 31, 1946.

I was enthusiastic, contemplating several months of fraud in investigations with a new Democratic county attorney and sheriff. I remembered the stories Lincoln Steffens had done on the Lexow police investigation in New York and saw myself in the same situation.

However, hard work is not always rewarded. The *Des Moines Register* editors also saw a flow of important and sensitive stories from the Polk County courthouse, and they thought I was too inexperienced for the job. I got a pat on the back for the "fine job" I had done so far but was told that someone with more experience could better handle the heavy workload expected. I argued that my knowledge of the people and the transactions was better than anyone else in the newsroom, but my objections were futile. I was resigned to being moved from the Polk County courthouse to general assignment when, suddenly, the city editor told me the shift had been cancelled. They would, after all, give me a chance at covering the fraud indictments and trials that were expected.

Judge Each Assignment on Its Merits

Later I learned that an older and more experienced reporter had turned down the Polk County courthouse assignment. He had equated assignment to the courthouse as a step back in his career because he had covered it briefly as a cub reporter when the courthouse and police station were regarded as assignments for beginners. He did not see the opportunity I saw for a successful expose.

Although I had been assigned to the police station and courthouse for most of my four years as a *Register* reporter, I did not regard it as dull and I certainly did not believe I knew all there was to know about court coverage. At the time my coverage of the courts had been limited to brief one-, two-, or three-day trials on traffic charges, misdemeanors, or uncomplicated felonies. However, in the next three years I was to be saturated with experience in covering complicated conspiracy fraud trials, which involved a coconspirator's testimony and a network of corroborative evidence. Those trials also provided an excellent understanding of how government is supposed to perform and how a combination of venality and laxity can make it vulnerable to massive frauds.

Reading 5: Interview with Elmer Croft

I had never been in Croft's garage so John Nagel, the photographer, and I entered cautiously, and looked around to get our bearings in the dark, dirty, and oily cavern. Our eyes had barely adjusted when the beefy 250-pound figure of Croft emerged from the shadows. He had a long steel tire iron grasped firmly in the grimy hand that emerged from the even grimier heavy sweater he was wearing.

"You son-of-a-bitch," Croft said to me, "haven't you caused enough trouble already? Get the hell out of here before I break your head." He advanced menacingly, and Nagel hastily prepared to take his picture. He whirled toward Nagel. "No pictures, God damn it, or I'll break your camera and your head."

"Elmer, you're just going to make things worse," I warned.

Croft stopped, but continued to castigate me, Paul Walters, Basil Grossnickle, and the *Des Moines Register* as the source of his troubles. He said he didn't have anything to say to me because "the paper would twist it." Also, he added that he expected criminal charges might be filed against him.

"I don't want to talk to you about the state auditor's report unless you want to discuss it," I said, adding that I respected his right to remain silent on any allegations of crime. What I wanted was to go over the background of his prior conviction as head of an auto theft ring and the federal indictment for conducting a blackmarket in cars in 1943 and 1944. "I just want to get your side of some of those earlier problems," I suggested. "I don't want to get into your present problems any further than you want to go. I respect your constitutional right not to testify against yourself."

Croft was now calming down, and the affable Nagel pretended he was unconcerned about the story and only wanted to make a good picture of Croft that would show how handsome he was. "Why don't you comb your hair and wipe that grease off your face?" Nagel suggested, appealing to the vanity of the darkly handsome 45-year-old garage operator who, we had heard, was dating a pretty young dark-haired secretary in the courthouse.

Croft, insisting that he didn't want his picture taken, shifted his tire iron to his left hand and reached into his pocket for a comb.

Nagel, a born psychologist, commented he had heard Croft was "one of the best mechanics in the state," and asked if he could bring his car in the next time it needed to be fixed.

By this time, most of Croft's anger had disappeared, and he was in a mood that would permit me to go into his past troubles with a basically soft and nonaccusatory line of questions. I reinforced my own position with laudatory comments about his service in France during World War I, his "great mechanical ability" and the "many problems" that had plagued his life.

Croft related that he enlisted in the Army at 14 years of age and served in the infantry in France where he was wounded twice and gassed three times. It was consistent with what I had been told by others who had searched his service record and the records of his court trial in 1933. Concerning his 1933 conviction for auto theft, Croft said he "took the blame" to protect others. He indicated vaguely that some important Des Moines police were involved in the auto theft ring.

"I wouldn't do it again," he said, implying he did not intend to sit quietly in prison while public officials went free.

Lapsing into a brief comment on the state auditor's report, Croft said he thought an effort was being made to "make me the goat for the whole thing." He declared that the so-called "excessive money" he had received for repairing county cars had been "at OPA (federal price ceiling) prices and at union wages." "What better could I give the county?" he asked. "I've been checked by the OPA and they said everything is O.K." Croft said he had "documentary evidence" to back up his claim that an attempt was being made to put the responsibility on him for matters where he was not at fault.

We moved to the crowded little office in a loft in the garage where he ruffled through the papers on the desk for the "documentation" which he held in his hand but did not show us.

The indictment in 1944 for illegal sale of rationed automobiles was another case in which he said he was being made "a goat" to save the reputations of some "big people." Croft hinted that the United States Attorney's Office had moved to dismiss that indictment only after he threatened to implicate the "big people" and hired a politically influential attorney. The indictment was dismissed in April 1944 by United States District Judge Charles A. Dewey on the motion of United States District Attorney Maurice Donegan, who refused to give any explanation. One of the cars involved in the Croft indictment was purchased on a sheriff's office priority and within a few weeks sold to tavern operator Alphonse (Babe) Bisignano (see Reading 3).

Initially, Croft remained silent on the charges by the state auditor that he could not account for some ten new car motors, radios, first aid kits, spotlights, tires, and tubes bought for the seven welfare cars. However, after being warmed up by his previous answers, he volunteered that he had receipts for two checks he had paid to the county for $525.20 and $296 which he contended were inadvertent overcharges he had made. Although the checks had been written in the last two weeks, Croft insisted that the state audit did not cause him to refund the money.

"I was going to do it all along, but I talked to [Supervisor Charles E.] Parmenter and he told me not to bother about paying it until they figured what I owed them" Croft said.

In his effort to appear to make a clean breast of his problem, Croft revealed something we had not known. He said that only a week earlier he paid $6700 to the state treasurer as sales tax and income tax he had failed to pay from October 1, 1941, to June 30, 1946. He said he was delinquent only $5000 in taxes but had a penalty of $1700. Regarding the back state taxes, Croft conceded that the state examiners "caught me up on it because I did all my banking by check." He admitted he had made "a lot of money" but said, "It's all been legal." He explained that his bookkeeping was careless in some respects because he had often told customers, particularly on large purchases, to "just forget the tax." Although he had settled accounts with the state government, Croft said he still had to settle with the federal government.

Having pried about as far as he was willing to go in areas outside of the audit report, I turned back to the audit report figures on tires and tubes. I told Croft that, even if his explanations on repairs of the welfare cars were accurate, there still remained some unbelievable purchases of tires and tubes. I asked him if he believed the public or a jury would buy the story that each of the seven welfare cars had used an average of more than 26 tires and 32 tubes during a one-year period. With straight-faced earnestness Croft insisted that the tires and tubes were actually used on 18 cars, which had included some cars in the sheriff's fleet. "They were of synthetic rubber," Croft said. "In one case just a little over a week ago I put six tires on a car in one day. I put four new tires on it in the morning. Two of those synthetic tires blew out before night and had to be replaced."

"Did the supervisors have knowledge of these unusual tire and tube replacements?" I asked.

He replied obliquely that he "didn't make any unnecessary repairs" and "had not replaced any tires or tubes without an okay from someone on the board."

When I had finished about an hour of questioning and learned a good deal more than I needed or wanted to know about the deprivation in Croft's early life, I signaled Nagel that I was through and he took two or three pictures of Croft in the office. Croft did not protest the pictures until Nagel made an effort to get him to pose with the tire iron in his hand. Croft said he didn't want the public to get the impression that he was a man who would use a tire iron on a reporter. He apologized for having the tire iron in his hand, and said he hoped I realized he had been working on a tire and would not make reference to it in my story.

I decided to go along with his request on the tire iron incident because, in fact, he had given me an interview with some insight into what might be ahead if the Polk County Grand Jury indicted Croft in connection with the welfare car bills. Croft had said he was not going to be "a goat" another time.

STUDENT WORK PROJECT SUGGESTION

Examine the state law relative to the responsibility of the state government to audit and discipline various county and city officials. Write a paper explaining the procedures in your state if county frauds should be exposed by a local newspaper and county officials and local prosecutors fail to initiate an investigation through a grand jury or otherwise.

9 POLK COUNTY FRAUDS—THE IMPORTANCE OF THE FOLLOW THROUGH

Official reports exposing part of the evidence of corruption can be the end of the story unless reporters and editors understand the need to keep the newspaper's spotlight on the operations of the prosecution machinery. Obstruction of justice is an ever-present problem when dealing with a crooked political machine. The exposure of government corruption for a news story is a meaningless gesture unless there is an effective follow-through to convict those guilty of crime and to correct the system. In fact, the exposure alone may be counterproductive in that it results in a public display of the success of an arrogant and corrupt machine.

EXPOSURE OF CORRUPTION IS NOT ENOUGH

There had been no effective follow-through on my exposures of bits of corruption in Polk County between 1941 and 1944, and the corrupters had continued in control with confidence that the *Des Moines Register* did not have the know-how and persistence to force depth investigations and effective prosecutions. I do not know where the full fault was but must admit that my own naivety was a part of it. Initially I believed, as did some of my superiors, that bringing the evidence of corruption to light was the end of our responsibility and that public opinion would force prosecution and reform.

It is important for the investigative reporter or editor to remember that exposing government corruption is just the first step

78

in the battle for good government. If the grand jury is fixed, as it frequently is, there will be no indictments returned against crooked politicians which is a victory for the dishonest officials. It is also a setback for those officials and groups who have taken considerable personal risk in the hope that the crooks would be caught and punished. Even if indictments are returned, a corrupt machine can destroy the possibility of successful prosecution through assignment of an inadequate prosecutor, through the wily actions and rulings of a corrupt partisan judge, or through skillful and corrupt control over the petit jury panel members.

Although we were naively unaware of it at the time, the corrupt Republican machine enjoyed a tight control over investigations, prosecutions, the grand jury, the local courts, the jury commission, and the selection of petit jury panels. This did not mean that all, or even a majority, of the Republican officials in Polk County were corrupt. It simply meant that all officials were dependent to some degree upon the support of the Republican political machine and would be likely to bend to the extreme partisan political pressures in a government fraud case involving one of their team members.

The Roles of the Jury Commission and Jury Board

An understanding of the mechanics of investigation and prosecution must include the details of the system for selecting grand jurors if you are to assure yourself that there is no political tampering. The election of a Democratic sheriff and a Democratic county attorney in 1946 did not change the Republican control over the Polk County district judges who, in turn, controlled the membership of the Polk County Jury Commission.

I did not understand, and I know there was no one else at the *Des Moines Register* who understood, the importance of the three-member county jury commission until January 1947. We had never had occasion before that time to question the mechanics of how the grand jury and petit jury panels were selected. We were amazed to find that the Polk County Jury Commission was composed of two people who were long-time Republican party functionaries and one man who had operated a gambling club illegally in downtown Des Moines.

Democratic County Attorney Switzer and Paul Walters commented privately on the difficulty of getting a strong and non-partisan grand jury from a list of 150 persons named by such a partisan jury commission. From those 150 names a jury board selected at random the names of the 12 persons who would serve as grand jurors for a two-year period. The jury board consisted of the county auditor, the county clerk, and the county recorder. In this case they were all Republicans and highly partisan in their defense of the integrity of the Republican supervisors.

It took no genius to see how dishonest political figures might manipulate such a system for the benefit of Republican crooks, but we needed something more concrete than our suppositions and fears of a grand jury fix. Since the petit jury panels were named by the same partisan jury commission, it was safe to assume that the same partisan bias might infect the petit jury panels that would be sitting in judgment on the criminal indictments returned by the prior grand jury.

A DISHONEST GRAND JUROR

In the first week of January 1947, County Attorney Switzer received evidence that Norman Strayer, a Republican member of a recently impaneled grand jury, had offered "to take care of" a traffic case involving a death. Strayer, a 54-year-old former Des Moines policeman, was eventually found guilty of contempt of court and was ousted from the grand jury. During the trial it was established that Strayer had approached a truck driver, had taken the truck driver to a tavern, and had said he could "take care of" his manslaughter case pending in the grand jury by getting two or three other members to vote against indictment. Although no amount of money was mentioned, the illegality and impropriety of Strayer's acts were a clear demonstration of the way the grand jury might be fixed by unscrupulous or political grand jurors.

Strayer's background demonstrated that he should never have been named to the grand jury panel in the first place. He had been fired in the late 1920s from the Des Moines police force after wrecking a new Cadillac emergency car while intoxicated. He was convicted of driving while intoxicated in 1934 and had been arrested in 1937 on another drunk driving charge after a 70-mile-an-hour chase by police. Strayer stopped only after the police opened fire on his speeding car.

Although Strayer was sentenced to six months in jail on the 1937 charge, a lenient judge paroled him from jail after serving only ten days so he could "tend his farm." Despite that record, Strayer served as a constable and justice of the peace in his home township and was a diligent worker for Republican causes. I reported in the *Register* on Norman Strayer's background and political connection in the kind of detail that made it clear that he was not a proper person for grand jury service, and would not have been selected if he had not been regarded as a loyal Republican chore boy.

The conviction of Norman Strayer for offering to fix a grand jury case provided County Attorney Switzer with the opportunity to point up the seriousness of corruption of the grand jury system, the jury system, and the courts. "If the honesty of the grand jury is to be questioned by the public, all justice will flounder and fall down," Switzer said in his argument to the court for severe punishment. "You and I, or any of us here, may have our lives before that grand jury and we must have confidence in that body."

When District Judge Russell Jordan fined Strayer only $50, it was another demonstration of the softness of the Polk County District Court Republicans toward political team members caught red-handed tampering with the administration of justice. Although Switzer did not publicly criticize the light penalty Strayer received, he and Paul Walters commented privately that it was indicative of the attitude that could be expected from the partisan Republican judges toward the Republican officials involved in the fraud indictments.

CHOICE OF A JUDGE

The Republican judges had jointly signed a political advertisement in the newspaper expressing their belief in the integrity of the entire Republican county slate, and Switzer and Walters said this seemed sufficient grounds to ask that they disqualify themselves from presiding at the Polk County fraud trials. However, before Switzer or Walters could file a motion asking the Republican judges to disqualify themselves, the judges voluntarily requested that the Iowa Supreme Court name "an outside judge" to preside at the fraud trials.

Aware of the close political links between the Polk County District Judges and the Iowa Supreme Court Judges, both Switzer and Walters were wary that a highly partisan judge would be imported to do the dirty work of dismissing the charges or handling the trials in such a politically biased manner that conviction would be impossible. When the judge was named I examined the *Des Moines Register* files and found that this same judge had been previously appointed as an "outside judge" in Polk County when another matter had been considered too sensitive for the Polk County judges to handle. He had dismissed the cases after some highly questionable rulings. I reviewed those old rulings, talked to Paul Walters about my conclusions, and wrote a low-key story about the earlier appearance of this "outside judge" in Polk County. As a result of my story the judge voluntarily asked that his name be withdrawn from consideration.

The Iowa State Supreme Court then assigned District Judge John Schaupp, a 56-year-old Republican from Fort Dodge, to hear the Polk County fraud trials. The newspaper files disclosed no questionable or highly partisan political activity by Judge Schaupp, and questioning lawyers I knew in the area indicated he was a man with a reputation for impeccable integrity among Democrats as well as Republicans.

I interviewed Judge Schaupp in his chambers when he arrived in Des Moines for the trial of Elmer G. Croft. I was impressed with his frank answers and his sincere desire to do a fair job on the politically sensitive trials. Although one highly political Polk County District Judge tried to take Judge Schaupp to lunch and otherwise socialize with him, Judge Schaupp avoided any but the most formal and proper contacts with the Polk County judges and was a pillar of nonpartisan rectitude throughout the trials.

CHOICE OF A PROSECUTOR

To keep the prosecution from being regarded as a partisan Democratic venture, County Attorney Switzer gave up his initial plan to handle the prosecutions personally in the court. Although Switzer had good general credentials as a lawyer, he had virtually no experience in criminal prosecution. Also weighing against him was his past partisan political campaigning, and his obvious interest in using the prosecutions of Polk County Republicans as a stepping stone to the governor's office. It would have made him highly vulnerable to charges of political prosecution. To avoid this, Switzer yielded to the suggestions of Paul Walters and assigned veteran Republican prosecutor Edwin S. Thayer the job of presenting the evidence and arguing the case in court.

Thayer was a life-long Republican and had more than 30 years experience in criminal and civil courts. He had handled the presentation of evidence to the Polk County Grand Jury in December 1946 that resulted in the indictment of Elmer G. Croft, County Welfare Director H. H. Thompson, Board Chairman W. H. Cotton, and Board Member Charles Parmenter. In communication with Walters, Thayer had expressed firm views on the justification of the indictments and had indicated he would be available to handle the prosecutions.

NEED FOR NONPARTISAN ATTITUDE

That was the politically charged scene in Polk County in January 1947 when United States District Judge Schaupp started selecting the jury for the trial of Elmer Croft. For the next two years, I was kept busy with the coverage of more than a half dozen fraud trials, with continuing new investigations and indictments. From that experience I learned, in depth, lessons about the politics of prosecutions of government frauds, the importance of having a nonpartisan prosecutor, and the value of a truly impartial judge who is aware that his rulings must be perceived as being nonpartisan as well as fair.

Also, in dealing with Democratic County Attorney Switzer and his assistants, I learned that partisan political goals can distort the thinking of basically decent officials and that a newsman must be constantly aware of the temptation of political prosecutors to cut corners and to rationalize unfair tactics or double standards in their decisions as to which cases merit prosecution.

In review I have concluded that day-to-day coverage of every facet of criminal trials of public officials provides numerous advantages. It is the only way a reporter or editor can gain a full understanding and full confidence in weighing the testimony and evidence that is so vital in any probe of governmental corruption. It is a helpful measure in ensuring that the public can judge the fairness of the trials. It is a curb on the officials involved in the trials that may prevent either political prosecution or political favoritism.

STUDENT WORK PROJECT SUGGESTION

Write a paper on the system for selecting grand jurors and petit jurors in your state. Who has the responsibility for selecting the commission or other group that suggests names for the grand jury panel? Is the grand jury named by random selection, or are they named by a judge? How is the foreman named or selected? What is the proper legal relationship between the state prosecutor and the grand jury? Is the letter of the law followed in the selection and operation of the grand juries in your county?

10 POLK COUNTY FRAUD TRIALS

The focus of a fraud trial is on a specific crime, but for the perceptive reporter that narrow focus is only the start. It is inevitable that evidence will be produced and testimony given pointing to laxity and corruption that encompass other parts of the political and governmental machinery.

A trial centering on frauds in one department will often expose evidence indicating frauds in other departments. It also exposes irregularities indicative of waste and mismanagement in other government offices similar to those involved in the criminal charges. These solid leads to other stories should be followed up aggressively to force the prosecutors to do a thorough investigation. Although it is vital to keep the focus of attention on the specific defendants and the specific charges of fraud in any individual case, it is also important constantly to review the testimony of the key witnesses for admissions of laxity and bad practices as well as admissions of varying degrees of complicity in the frauds. It is also profitable to review and scrutinize carefully all documents introduced into the trial record.

A SOURCE OF FUTURE STORY LEADS

Buried in the record of the trial will probably be evidence of gross neglect and minor venality by public officials who were not named as defendants. An intelligent and logical followup on this evidence will often uncover still more pockets of corruption or mismanagement in other local government agencies. During the trial of Elmer G. Croft, in late January and early February 1947, I learned to jot down memorandums of possible leads to follow at the conclusion of the trial or at those points in the trial where there is interminable haggling over technical problems.

Croft's Trial

The trial of Croft centered on the manner in which he defrauded the county by double billing and false billing on a wide range of parts and repairs for Polk County Welfare Department cars. Through the testimony of State Examiner Carl Nimrod and Paul Walters, it was established that, in the period between 1943 and the end of 1946, Croft had billed the county for 10 motors, 346 tires, 401 tubes, 17 heaters and defrosters, 26 transmission jobs, 58 brake relining jobs, and 100 new brake drums for the seven cars. Although Croft contended that he had actually delivered all this equipment, his story was made ludicrous by the very numbers of tires, tubes, and brake drums. Because automobile motors have serial numbers, the prosecution was able to establish that all seven cars still had their original motors.

Croft's defense was a preposterous effort to confuse the jury. He said he had lost his records in two fires and had to reconstruct from memory. He said the "women drivers" in the welfare department were responsible for the heavy wear on the welfare cars. He also contended that he was the innocent victim of a political plot by Attorneys Paul W. Walters and B. J. Powers to oust the Republican supervisors and Sheriff Vane B. Overturff in order to put their friend, Basil Grossnickle, in office.

On February 8, 1947, the jury found Croft guilty of the charge of obtaining money from Polk County under false pretenses. The stage was set for prosecution of Board Chairman Cotton and other public officials, and the return of still more indictments against two other supervisors, Sheriff Overturff, and his top deputies.

Implication of Fraud Concerning Polk County Home

One aspect of the fraud charge against Croft did not involve the welfare cars but dealt with fraudulent payments for the repair of a smokestack at the Polk County Home. A steeplejack, Roy Franklin, testified that he had not dealt with county officials but only through Croft in handling a repair job costing the county $2553. The steeplejack admitted that Croft paid him $1000, but he said he had never seen or signed the bills totaling $2553 that Croft had submitted to the county auditor for payment. A handwriting expert testified that Croft had signed the steeplejack's name on the bills submitted to the auditor's office for payment.

The testimony by the handwriting expert on Croft's forgery contradicted the deputy auditor's sworn statement that the steeplejack had appeared personally and signed the smokestack bills.

This evidence established the gross negligence of County Auditor L. O. (Louey) Lindstrom and his chief deputy, Monty St. John, in connection with the approval of Croft's fraudulent bills. The auditor's office employees had apparently abdicated their public responsibility rather than have a nasty disagreement with the politically powerful members of the Polk County Board of Supervisors who were coconspirators and beneficiaries of Croft's frauds.

Thompson's Trial

H. H. Thompson, the Polk County Welfare Director, was the second person to go to trial on the fraud charges involving the seven welfare cars. Although he had signed his approval of the requisitions, he said he was only following the orders of Board Chairman Cotton when he signed the bills as "a routine" matter and made no investigation to see if the goods were delivered.

When Judge John Schaupp sentenced Croft to a seven-year prison term, County Attorney Switzer and Sheriff Reppert made further overtures to Croft to try to get him to testify against Thompson, Cotton, and Parmenter. Croft, still confident that the Polk County Republican machine would save him from prison, rejected suggestions that he cooperate with the prosecution until after the Thompson trial was concluded.

With only the paper record against him, Thompson convinced the jury that he signed auto repair bills without checking them "on orders from Supervisor W. H. Cotton." The prosecution was unable to trace to Thompson any of the benefits of the fraud money that Croft had received. The jury acquitted Thompson of the willful participation in the Croft frauds after five ballots and five hours of deliberation. The first ballot had found four of the jurors voting not guilty, two guilty, and six undecided. The second ballot was 8 to 4 for acquittal.

Other Implications of Fraud

Thompson's successful defense resulted in the newspaper giving much closer scrutiny to the procedures under which the county approved requisitions and paid for equipment and repairs. We found an incredible amount of sloppiness in the way records were kept on equipment purchased, and we discovered that none of the Polk County offices kept a reliable inventory on equipment ranging from typewriters to road graders.

There were reports that one of the rackets in the county involved the purchase and sale of road equipment. We were told that new road equipment was purchased when old road equipment was still serviceable and that used equipment was traded in for substantially less than its market value with cash payments to the supervisors. Examination of the county records indicated that it was likely this happened, but County Attorney Switzer and Sheriff Reppert had their hands full with other investigations involving the Polk County Home for the elderly and the Polk County Juvenile Home. Evidence indicated that everything from the sale and resale of registered Holstein cows at the Polk County Home to the purchase of food and bed clothing for the juvenile home had some racket connected with it involving kickbacks to the county supervisors or to other key county employees.

EVIDENCE FROM WITNESSES

The acquittal of Thompson, the welfare director, made County Attorney Switzer less optimistic about First Assistant Ed Thayer getting further convictions without testimony from Croft. Croft, convicted but free on bond, had not agreed to testify at the time the jury was being selected for the trial of former Polk County Board Chairman W. H. Cotton, and it appeared that H. H. Thompson might be a key witness for the prosecution.

A Hostile Witness

Thompson had not volunteered to testify, and would be a hostile witness, but in defending his own laxity he had laid the blame on Cotton. In his opening statement, Thayer had told the court that Thompson would testify that he signed requisitions for seven motors and seven transmissions with no knowledge that the goods were delivered. "He will testify he protested to Cotton concerning the signing of the statement and that Cotton ordered him to sign them," Thayer said.

Cotton's defense lawyers objected to Thayer's use of Thompson as a credible witness on ground that, only a month earlier, Thayer had contended that Thompson was lying about his knowledge of the Croft frauds. Cotton's name was signed to hundreds of Croft's bills, but the defense centered on establishing that the Polk County Board of Supervisors approved 8000 to 10,000 bills a year and that "it is not possible to thumb through those claims and pass on them."

Although Switzer and Paul Walters knew that Cotton had been warned a number of times about Croft's false bills, and had continued to do business with Croft, they were also aware that Cotton had skillful defense lawyers who might be able to confuse the issue if the prosecution depended too much upon the Cotton signatures linking him to Croft's frauds. What they needed was Thompson's testimony about his protest to Cotton on the Croft bills. They also needed testimony from Croft that would link Cotton to direct knowledge of the frauds, and, in addition, they needed to demonstrate the manner in which the County Board Chairman had benefited from those frauds.

Cooperating Witnesses

Midway in the Cotton trial, I learned that Croft had disappeared and that he had mortgaged five of the seven county-owned welfare cars and five other cars to procure a $10,000 loan from the First National Bank of West Des Moines. In seeking the $10,000 loan, Croft had claimed to own the five county cars he described in the mortgage as well as a 1946 Pontiac actually registered to Supervisor Charles Parmenter. When questioned, Parmenter declared that "Croft never had title to my car and the mortgage is no good." Parmenter and the other board members said they had never given Croft the authority to mortgage the county cars.

An intense search for Croft was launched by the bank, the bondsman, and Sheriff Reppert as the prosecution was winding up its case in the fraud trial of Cotton. Tired of running and determined not to be "the goat" again, Croft called Sheriff Reppert from Kansas City, Missouri, and agreed to take a train to Fort Madison, Iowa, to meet Reppert at the prison there as an alternative to having Reppert seek his extradition as a fugitive from justice. Croft surrendered to Sheriff Reppert on Friday, March 28, 1947, and agreed to turn state's evidence. The following Monday, Judge Schaupp overruled a defense motion to bar Croft's testimony and the stage was set for dramatic inside testimony on the Polk County frauds.

A Problem in Credibility

Reporting on Croft's inside testimony about his dealings with Cotton and other county officials taught me my first depth lesson on why the law required extensive corroboration when a coconspirator, such as Croft, agreed to testify against other defendants. It was apparent why Croft would not be believed unless there was corroboration. It was too likely that he might make up a story out of spite or for the purpose of getting a lighter sentence than he might otherwise have received. Croft was a convicted car thief and had been convicted of fraud against the county by an overwhelming mass of solid documentary evidence and direct testimony. He had told the biggest, blackest lies in his own defense and had, with a straight face, told the jury he had delivered 346 tires, 401 tubes, and 10 new motors for the seven welfare cars in a two-year period.

How could the prosecution make Croft's testimony believable in the face of the assault that Cotton's lawyers could make on Croft because of the lies he had told in his own case? How could I believe Croft? How could Ed Thayer, Paul Walters, or Sheriff Reppert believe anything Croft said?

Establishing Credibility

In the first place, Croft would have to admit that the story he told in his own defense was a false story. Walters said, "Reppert and Thayer are going to have to insist that he stick with the truth in his present testimony regardless of how it hurts him personally, and that his story be supported by the documents or the testimony of other witnesses on nearly every point. It should be emphasized to Croft that he must not embellish the story in any respect for making a better case against Cotton or any others," Walters stressed. "Any exaggeration or embellishment will be likely to backfire against the prosecution."

What I learned from Walters and Ed Thayer in handling Croft was a valuable lesson to me in dealing with informants. Walters and Thayer continually stressed that witnesses should avoid any distortions, embellishments, or exaggerations and that they should stick as closely as possible to facts and events that could be corroborated by other witnesses or by documents. Also, in dealing with an informant of highly questionable background, it is always wise to have a reliable witness present to avoid having the informant charge later that you coached him or put words in his mouth. Further, it is wise to avoid any promises of lighter treatment in connection with the truthful testimony. Promises of immunity or any relaxation of prosecution can be embarrassing to the prosecution or the newspaper reporter who engages in such conversations.

Corroboration Pays Off

In the Cotton trial, the large number of tires, tubes, and motors made it obvious that the Croft bills were, in fact, fraudulent. Cotton's signature approving these bills linked him to those specific fraudulent bills, and his refusal to stop doing business with Croft, after being warned, was corroboration for Croft's testimony that Cotton was a knowing part of the frauds.

Croft's story that he had contributed $4000 to Cotton's primary election campaign in 1946 was pretty much a case of Croft's word against Cotton's word. However, Croft's testimony that he paid rent-a-car bills for Cotton's election campaign was supported by the records of two rental car agencies. There were also garage records and shipping records to support Croft's story that some tires the county paid for were put on Cotton's personal car, whereas others were shipped to Kansas to Cotton's daughter for use on her personal car.

The jury took only two ballots to convict Cotton of obtaining money by false pretenses. The initial ballot, after several hours of reviewing the documents and testimony, was 11 to 1 for conviction.

With heavily corroborated testimony by Croft, the conviction of Supervisor Charles E. Parmenter was almost automatic. Croft testified he gave Parmenter "between $14,000 and $15,000 in 1946 from money obtained on fictitious claims." The prosecution used more than 40 witnesses to introduce bills and to corroborate Croft's associations with Parmenter.

Among those corroborating Croft's testimony was an Ankeny, Iowa contractor who testified that a four-car garage constructed on Parmenter's farm was paid for by checks from Elmer Croft. Also, a jewelry store owner testified that Croft paid $2116 for two diamond rings for Parmenter. Croft said he used the money from the false claims for items for Parmenter, including a $1600 Pontiac car, new clothing, $674 worth of flowers, male hormone pills costing $72, and a $380 dental bill for Parmenter's girlfriend.

Parmenter, 52, still a member of the Polk County Board of Supervisors, was found guilty of obtaining money by false pretenses. The jury's verdict was on the third ballot, with ten for conviction on the first ballot, and 11 for conviction on the second ballot.

County Attorney Carroll O. Switzer ruled that the conviction of fraud meant automatic ouster for Parmenter from his post as a supervisor. By this time, the Polk County grand jury investigation was in full swing and, with the aid of Croft's testimony, indicted Parmenter for a second time and returned indictments against Supervisor Roy J. Hild and Supervisor Ben B. Dewey.

The trial and conviction of Hild in December 1947 followed the same pattern as the trials of Cotton and Parmenter, even though the Hild trial was held in Boone, Iowa. Hild's lawyers sought a change of venue on grounds that he could not receive a fair trial in Des Moines because of the wide publicity given the Des Moines trials of Croft, Thompson, Cotton, and Parmenter.

Moreover, despite defense arguments that Croft was "an admitted liar, perjurer and a thief," the Boone County jury found

Hild guilty on the third ballot, because of adequate corroboration of Croft's evidence.

STUDENT WORK PROJECT SUGGESTION

1. Write a step by step analysis of a criminal fraud trial from the arraignment, through the opening statements by the prosecutor and defense lawyer, to the testimony of prosecution and defense witnesses. Conclude with the arguments to the jury and the verdict. Explain in detail the types of motions and actions by the court that can change this sequence or terminate the trial before a jury verdict.

2. Why does the law require firm corroboration for the testimony of a coconspirator? What should this chapter teach newsmen about the hazards of dealing with confidential informants?

11 THE POLK COUNTY JAIL

The reporter's loose alliance with law enforcement officials to bring down a corrupt political machine must not blind him to the errors and misjudgments of those with whom he is cooperating. Maintaining an independent and critical posture may be difficult, but it is essential to retaining public credibility. In Des Moines the county attorney and the sheriff were doing a generally honest job of investigating and prosecuting frauds against the county, but the sheriff was careless in his relationship with two local racket figures and with a key government witness in the fraud trials. The partisan political desire of the county attorney to protect the sheriff compromised the actions of both to some degree, and this could not be overlooked. A reporter must maintain an independent posture so he can freely investigate and criticize even those he is working with on some matters. This independence is vital to doing a balanced job of investigative reporting and maintaining credibility with the public.

CRITICISM OF COOPERATIVE OFFICIALS

One of the major hazards for the investigative reporter or editor in exposing crime and corruption in government is the problem of keeping a safe distance from the public officials with whom he deals. The newsman must depend to a large degree upon public officials to do the followup investigations and prosecutions resulting from his stories. However, he must not let his cooperative work with investigators or prosecutors compromise his objectivity. A reporter should never permit himself to develop the kind of close personal friendship that would bar him from writing critically about any law enforcement officials.

A Gregarious Sheriff

Sheriff Reppert was a big, gregarious, good-natured owner of a truckline before becoming Polk County Sheriff in January 1947. The balding, six-foot four-inch Reppert was a political accident if there ever was one. He had permitted the Democrats to put his name on the ballot as their candidate for sheriff, and never dreamed that he would be elected. Reppert gave no campaign speeches and appeared at only two Democratic rallies, where he simply smiled and waved at the crowd. He was elected because of the effectiveness of Paul Walters and the Civic Action Committee in their criticism of the incumbent Republican sheriff, Vane B. Overturff.

But, Reppert was pleased with his victory, and was determined to have a good time being sheriff. One of his first acts after the election was the purchase of an ivory handled revolver and holster, a gold sheriff's badge with a diamond in the center, and a large white felt hat. The big guy with the wide smile was like a child with a new toy. Paul Walters and I became concerned that he might carelessly become involved in scandal because of a good-natured naivety. However, Reppert's genial and outgoing personality was also an asset. He persuaded Elmer Croft to give himself up to serve his prison term on the fraud charge. In a low-pressure manner he convinced Croft he should cooperate with the prosecution against the Republican county officials. In addition, he was a good businessman. He organized the office with top deputies who were responsible, honest, tough, and frank enough to tell Reppert when they thought he was engaged in actions that might draw political criticism.

Hints of Carelessness

Although Walters had been opposed to Sheriff Overturff, he did not endorse Reppert because of reports that Reppert was friendly with two of Polk County's leading bootleggers and gamblers. Walters did not have evidence of any close friendship with the two men, but there was a reliable report that Reppert had been seen with each on at least one occasion. I had only talked with Reppert on a few occasions before his election so I did not know him well. After the election, however, I asked him, in a casual way, about his relationship with the two racket figures.

Reppert said he had known both men for years because he had done some trucking for them, and volunteered the information that one of his truck drivers had reported that the material shipped on one occasion had been gambling equipment. Reppert insisted he had no advance knowledge that his truck was being hired to haul gambling equipment, but he admitted frankly he wasn't sure it would have made any difference at the time because he was "a live and let live businessman" with no particular sensitivity about hauling gambling machines or equipment.

With respect to the period before the election, Reppert said he met with the racketeers "out of curiosity." He had been curious as to what they wanted to talk about and was a little disappointed that "they were only feeling me out." I suggested to Reppert that in the eyes of others such meetings might appear "to be deals," and now that he was sheriff he should keep that in mind.

Although Reppert's answers seemed frank enough, I reserved judgment. Even if he was completely innocent, naive curiosity of that nature was not a plus quality in a sheriff. He might innocently fumble his way into a situation that would be an embarrassment and a setback for the Polk County fraud trials.

Implications of Favoritism

Sheriff Reppert's gregarious personality and his curiosity led him to fraternize with the prisoners in the county jail. He would spend hours at the jail talking with them and listening with amusement to the tales they told of their lives of crime. From time to time, Reppert's talks with Croft brought forth revelations that the county attorney's office found merit in pursuing. Reppert felt this justified some special concessions for Croft and other prisoners he liked.

Walters and I became concerned over reports that Reppert's efforts to be accommodating to Croft had included arrangements for Croft's girl friend to visit him in the comfort of a new visitor's lounge and without benefit of a chaperon. We knew that the woman made periodic visits to the jail to see Croft, but we were unable to learn anything concrete about what took place within the jail lounge. Genuinely concerned about the special accommodations accorded Croft, we did not want to raise the issue directly with Reppert until such time as we were certain of all our facts.

It was the contention of Switzer and Reppert that the Republicans were trying to get Croft sent to Fort Madison penitentiary where a Republican warden and Republican control would be used to try to persuade Croft to recant his testimony against the Republican officials in Polk County. This might be true, but Paul Walters and I were concerned that County Attorney Switzer's fast blooming interest in the Democratic gubernatorial nomination was upsetting his judgment in handling Croft. Switzer and Reppert had already told Walters and me privately that Croft had provided them with leads on Republican scandals at the state capitol involving the sale of used cars. They planned to develop those cases in 1948, at the time Switzer would launch his campaign for governor.

I certainly believed that every bit of evidence of fraud should be pursued, even to the state capitol, but I also believed that Switzer's political ambitions were beginning to influence his judgment. His desire to be away from Des Moines for speeches was starting to interfere with the operations of his office. Although Paul Walters and I had been treated as friends of the prosecution throughout the first nine months of 1947, that status was shaken by an incident that occurred at the Polk County jail involving nightclub operator Peter A. Rand. The Rand incident served notice on Switzer and Reppert that they too would be subject to criticism if they did not handle their responsibilities in an even-handed manner.

Reading 6: No Escape Intended

While scouting for information on Croft's special accommodations, I came across reports that Peter A. Rand, jailed for one year on a gambling charge, had been leaving the jail on weekends for visits with his wife at home. Rand, owner and operator of the Mainliner club, had found ways to get out of jail periodically in the six months since he started his term.

A Polk County District Court judge had permitted him to go to the Mayo Clinic, at Rochester, Minn., for "poor health" reasons. County Attorney Switzer and Sheriff Reppert had approved the order for Rand's visit to the Mayo Clinic, but we had reports that the "ailing" Pete Rand had been cavorting at lake resorts in Minnesota. Only a short time after Rand's return from the Mayo Clinic and his Minnesota outing, he made application to Iowa Governor Robert D. Blue, a Republican, for executive clemency. Sheriff Reppert had written a letter supporting Rand's request. Reppert said Rand had been a good prisoner, had worked hard in the jail garden and as a jail cook, and was also suffering from poor health.

Although we both liked Reppert personally, Walters and I were beginning to have our doubts as to whether he was telling the truth about his relationship with Rand when we heard the reports of Rand's weekly nocturnal visits to his home. Walters, Grossnickle, and two township constables watched the Polk County jail for two weekends. They saw Rand slip out of the jail, walk rapidly down an alley, and get into a long black Cadillac driven by a woman. They then followed the car, which was registered to Pete's wife. It made a loop around the business section, and then turned South on Seventh Street in the direction of the Rand home.

Walters kept me posted on Grossnickle's surveillance, which indicated that this was a weekly event scheduled for every Saturday at about 7:30 P.M. Grossnickle told Walters the Rand car was not parked in the Rand driveway, but in an adjoining drive. Pete and his wife would walk across the backyard, enter a back door, and remain there as long as two or three hours. They would then come out, get in the car, and drive to a point near the jail to drop Pete.

In mid-September Walters confided to me that Grossnickle was thinking of arresting Rand and charging him with conspiracy to escape jail. "I don't know what Reppert or Switzer know about this," Walters said. "It may be that Rand has made some deal with the jailer, but, whatever the circumstances, they're foolish and are asking for a scandal." He also cautioned me not to tell Reppert or Switzer about Rand's home visits until we could confront them with solid evidence. Although the man leaving the jail was a short, fat man who looked like Rand, although the woman was driving a car registered to Gladys Rand, and although they drove to the Rand home, we had to have more positive identification.

I did not tell anyone at the *Register* about the Rand home visits either because I didn't want gossip in the newsroom to tip off Rand or Reppert. On Saturday, October 11, I told the city editor I would be working on a special project, swore him to secrecy, and gave him our general game plan for what could be a sensational story on laxity at the jail.

Shortly after 6 P.M. on Saturday night, Walters and I met with Basil Grossnickle who had two constables in his car, and who indicated that there were still more constables in another car. We planned to watch for Pete Rand to leave the jail, then take off directly for the Rand home to post a watch on the driveway. Another car was to tail the Rand car to the home, and, as soon as Rand and his wife were in the house, Grossnickle and another man would be waiting to close in to make the arrest. At that point Walters and I were to drive back to the jail, and I was to ask the jailer for permission to speak to Pete Rand. If Rand was not produced immediately, I would call Reppert.

It was shortly after 7:30 P.M. when Rand walked out of the jail. Walters and I drove immediately to a point a short distance from the Rand driveway. Instead of cruising around the block once or twice as was usual, the Rand's Cadillac wheeled into the adjoining driveway on the first pass. Grossnickle and Bill Rice, a furnace installation man, were waiting for Rand in his back yard. As Rand got out of the car Grossnickle flashed a light in his face and declared he was under arrest.

From Walters' car we heard the shouts, followed by the sound of running figures. Then we heard Grossnickle fire one warning shot in the air. Walters and I drove quickly to the jail. While I went inside to ask the jailer for Pete Rand, Walters saw to it that constables were posted as sentries a half block away at the Polk County courthouse to block Rand from entering the jail through the tunnel from the courthouse.

Jailer Art Wright told me Rand was in his cell and that 8 P.M. was too late for prisoners to have visitors. I told him I had information that Rand was not in jail, and I was there to see if he could be produced. A nervous Art Wright reiterated his assurance that Rand was in his cell, but there was no confidence in his demeanor as I asked for a telephone to call Sheriff Reppert. I was unable to reach the sheriff but did reach Chief Deputy Jack Rawles to tell him we believed Rand was out of jail. Rawles contacted Reppert, who arrived at the jail to state emphatically that he had not authorized Rand's visit home.

"I didn't have any idea what was going on," Reppert said. "You can bet it won't happen again."

At 11:30 P.M. two deputies brought Rand to the jail explaining they had found him walking in south Des Moines in the direction of the jail.

Rand, who was serving as the jail cook and had "trusty" status, told me from his jail cell, "I was baking a marble cake and just went to get some cream of tartar. I went home to get it because I couldn't get cream of tartar anywhere else at that time of night. My wife took me home in the car so I wouldn't be gone long," Rand said. "I was just going to get the cream of tartar and go right back to jail."

Rand said he ran away from Grossnickle because he didn't recognize him. "I thought he might be a robber or gangster or something, and I pushed my wife toward my brother's house and started running. I heard a shot, or shots, and I just kept on running. I didn't know who it was." He added that he came and went frequently as a trusty at the jail, and he declared that some other trusties came and went more freely than he did.

Jailer Art Wright confirmed that he had let Rand out of the jail "to get some cream of tartar." However Deputy Sheriff Wilbur Hildreth said a search of the jail kitchen disclosed that there was a box of cream of tartar on the shelf. After questioning jail employees for two hours, Sheriff Reppert fired jailer Art Wright and requested County Attorney Carroll Switzer to initiate a grand jury investigation of Pete Rand's night out. Reppert said that it was completely "wrong" for Rand to have been let out of jail and blamed it on lax policies that had been established in the years before he was sheriff. Nonetheless Grossnickle filed a charge of conspiracy against Rand, Mrs. Rand, and "persons unknown" for unlawfully aiding a prisoner to escape from custody at the county jail.

RESULTS OF EXPOSING LAXITY

Paul Walters, Grossnickle, and I were among the witnesses called before the Polk County Grand Jury in its probe of any criminal responsibility for Pete Rand's night out. The grand jury found that neither Rand, his wife, nor jailer Art Wright had any criminal responsibility because Rand did not intend to escape from jail, and was indeed in "trusty" status as the chief jail cook. However, the grand jury recommended that the sheriff should put a stop to such freedom for jail trusties, permitting no absences from the jail except in the custody of a deputy. It was also suggested that there should be a jail register for keeping a record of the prisoners who left the jail for any purpose, when they left, and the name of the person responsible for the prisoner's custody.

The grand jury report had all of the earmarks of a Democratic-controlled whitewash of laxity for special prisoners at the Polk County jail. But the Pete Rand incident served the purpose of notifying Sheriff Reppert and County Attorney Switzer that Walters and I would hold them to the same standards as other public officials in Des Moines and Polk County. Also, the Pete Rand incident demonstrated that, although we were in general agreement with the Democrats on the Polk County fraud prosecutions of Republicans, we did not intend to overlook or cover up any abuses of power by the Democrats.

Deputy Sheriff Wilbur Hildreth told me at the time that he believed the Pete Rand incident had been a good thing for Reppert and Switzer. It jarred them into realizing that they should treat Elmer Croft with less favoritism. They suddenly recognized that, if Croft were caught in a questionable visit outside or inside the jail, it could disrupt the remaining Polk County fraud trials and perhaps upset the convictions that had been won to that point.

Unfortunately political friends and lawyers for the Polk County Republican machine wasted little time in grasping the Rand incident to try to discredit the Democrats, create chaos and political confusion, and further cloud investigations and prosecutions of government corruption. It was difficult for the public to keep a clear perspective on Republican corruption at a time when the Democrats had, through foolishness, made themselves vulnerable to criticism for the laxity at the Polk County jail.

It was disturbing to me that the clean-broom Democrats had become, to some degree, corrupt in so short a time, even as they were exposing Republican corruption. A few months earlier I would have sworn that the new reform-minded Democrats would not be so stupid or careless in the exercise of power as they appeared in the Rand incident. It taught me, while constantly hoping and praying for the best, always to be prepared for disillusionment with regard to public officials—a vital lesson.

STUDENT WORK PROJECT SUGGESTION

Examine the security practices at the local city or county jail. Are the prisoners allowed to have visitors? Are there any special privileges for any category of prisoners such as trusty? Are there any individual prisoners who receive special accommodations? Write a paper on the handling of prisoners at the local city or county jail and describe any conditions that you consider might be special accommodations.

12 LESSONS FROM ELMER CROFT

Reporters and law enforcement officials must deal cautiously with informants, particularly those who have been coconspirators in crimes. Such confidential informants may turn against you in a matter of hours if it is to their advantage to do so. It is wise to have witnesses present when dealing with informants to preclude a disastrous turn of events. In addition, various pressures by friends and lawyers for political defendants and the carelessness of a prosecutor or sheriff can create grave doubts with regard to the credibility of a key witness.

DEALING WITH INFORMANTS

Investigative reporters and editors must exercise extreme care in dealing with informants and must make every reasonable effort to seek corroboration before using the informant's testimony. This is particularly true when the informant is a coconspirator in crime, a person with a criminal record, or generally of questionable credibility. Reporters and editors must be aware that government investigators and prosecutors are engaged in a precarious undertaking when they establish any relationship with informers. There is, of course, a great temptation to develop a close relationship with a helpful informant. It is always wise, however, to keep in mind that most informants are of value because they are turning on former coconspirators. There is no way of being sure that they will not turn on their new "friends" if it is to their advantage and if the new "friends" have any degree of vulnerability in dealing with them.

Maneuvers Around a "Friendly" Witness

This point was drilled home to me in 1948 when Elmer G. Croft, key government witness in the Polk County fraud trials, became hostile to the prosecution and flew into a courtroom rage in the middle of an important fraud trial. Croft had been a docile and cooperative government witness in the trials of Supervisors W. H. Cotton, Charles Parmenter, and Roy Hild. He had been helpful to First Assistant County Attorney Edwin S. Thayer in giving important grand jury testimony, which had resulted in the indictment of Supervisor Ben B. Dewey, former Sheriff Vane B. Overturff, and several of Overturff's deputies. Croft was now to be the most important single witness in the retrial of former Welfare Director H. H. Thompson, who had been acquitted in his first trial.

The Pete Rand incident at the Polk County jail (see Reading 6) established that some prisoners had received favored treatment and gave credibility to reports that Sheriff Reppert had permitted Croft to have relations with his girl friend in the jail lounge. Defense lawyers for the indicted Republicans made the general complaint that Croft was "a trained seal" for Democratic County Attorney Carroll Switzer. They claimed that Croft was being prompted to give testimony to push prosecutions of Republicans in a manner that would be helpful to Switzer's ambitions to be governor of Iowa.

Immediately after the conviction of Supervisor Hild, the defense lawyers petitioned the Polk County District Court to force the return of Croft to Fort Madison penitentiary until his testimony was required for the next trial. The interest of the Republican state officials in returning Croft to the penitentiary to break up his cooperation with Polk County Democrats was obvious. Croft had told me and others that there were frauds in the sale of cars by the State of Iowa, and he had indicated that several state officials had benefited from these frauds. It was known that Switzer was gearing up for investigations and prosecutions of some unnamed Republican state officials in 1948—an election year.

It was in that setting that Polk County District Judge C. Edwin Moore, the most influential Republican judge in Polk County, entered an order that Croft be returned to Fort Madison penitentiary. The order was entered on January 9, 1948, over the objections of County Attorney Switzer, who contended that he needed Croft in the Polk County jail for convenience in consulting and preparing for the upcoming fraud trials. Switzer protested that Judge Moore, a part of the Republican Polk County machine, should not be permitted to rule on any matter related to the conduct of the fraud trials. However, Judge Moore ruled that the return of Croft to prison was not directly related to the Polk County fraud trials; thus, it was not necessary to appoint a judge from outside Polk County to decide Croft's disposition.

"Friendly" Witness Turns Hostile

It was nearly two months later when I next saw Croft. He was being returned to the Polk County jail for preparation for the retrial of former Welfare Director Thompson. Croft's former jovial mood was missing when he appeared in court on March 3, 1948 for his appearance in the retrial of Thompson. He did not give me his usual friendly smile, but simply nodded and looked away in a furtive manner.

We all knew there had been efforts by the lawyers for convicted Polk County Republicans to get him to recant his testimony. This Croft had rejected. He was street smart enough to know that if he now stated that he had given false testimony in those trials, he could face a multiplicity of prosecutions by Switzer's office. However, we had heard that, in return for some preferred treatment at the Fort Madison penitentiary, Croft was amenable to softening some of his testimony on his dealings with Polk County officials.

When Assistant County Attorney Thayer put him on the witness stand, he appeared ill at ease and scowled. He was reluctant to answer direct questions on Thompson's knowledge of various fraudulent transactions, even though he talked freely about the role of Supervisors Cotton, Parmenter, and Hild. Apparently the time at the Fort Madison penitentiary had changed Croft. He was evasive throughout the 90 minutes of testimony during which Thayer attempted to establish criminal responsibility by using Croft to identify Thompson's signature on the false claims.

Croft's behavior during his first day on the witness stand was but a prelude to his testimony on the second day when he stated that in 1945 Thompson did not have knowledge that the car repair bills were fraudulent. Croft said, "He wasn't supposed to know anything about them." Croft admitted that he had informed Thompson in 1946 that the car repair bills were fraudulent because "the bills were getting so big." However, Croft claimed that Thompson was not aware that the tire and tube bills were false.

During his third day on the witness stand, Croft flew into a wild rage when Thayer pressed him to answer questions dealing with the cash Croft had given to Thompson and with Thompson's personal use of one of the welfare cars. Croft ignored the admonitions from District Judge Martin Van Oosterhout of Orange City to be quiet and screamed, "Take me out of here." The explosion in the midst of questioning by Thayer left the jurors and spectators stunned. Threats to cite Croft for contempt of court were meaningless because he was already serving a seven-year prison term. Prior to his courtroom tantrum, Croft had written a secret letter to Polk County District Judge C. Edwin Moore in an obvious effort to win favor with

Republicans. In the letter Croft accused Thayer of limiting the questioning to give an erroneous impression to the jury for political purposes and of blocking his effort "to tell all."

Adequate Corroboratory Evidence Prevents Disaster

If Croft staged the courtroom rage and the secret letter to save Thompson, the ploy was a failure. Judge Van Oosterhout sent the jury out of the courtroom after the first few minutes of Croft's rage, and he shielded the segregated jury from other emotional or partisan political developments in the trial. The jury neither saw the stories nor heard any of the newscasts of the Croft blow-up. The remaining days of the trial were calm and on March 16, after four hours of deliberation, the jury convicted Thompson of conspiracy to defraud the county.

That was the end of Croft's usefulness as a prosecution witness. Lawyers for the Republican defendants obtained a wide range of statements from Croft in efforts to upset the convictions of the Republican defendants. However, after extended hearings on a wide range of political issues, Judge Van Oosterhout overruled Thompson's motion for a new trial and sentenced him to a three-year prison term at Fort Madison. Judge Van Oosterhout declared that there was "ample evidence" in the testimony of 46 other witnesses and in county records to uphold the jury verdict that Thompson had knowledge of the Croft frauds and approved repair bills despite that knowledge.

FRAUD OUTSIDE POLK COUNTY

During the hearing on Thompson's motion for a new trial, County Attorney Switzer and Paul Walters, who was now acting as a special assistant county attorney, contended that Warden Percy A. Lainson sought to have Croft returned to Fort Madison penitentiary in January "to protect the boys on the hill." Walters filed an affidavit, taken from Croft in July 1947, in which Croft had related the details of various frauds in car transactions with a number of Iowa State officials, including a Republican United States Senator, a Republican Governor, and a former state car dispatcher. It was the thesis of Walters and Switzer that the Republican state officials had a joint interest in discrediting Croft so they would not be prosecuted.

The Croft affidavit was "hot stuff," involving frauds in the purchase and sale of state cars, in the sale of state gasoline coupons during the rationing period, and in the use of state-purchased gas and oil in political campaigning. It included identification of specific personal cars he had purchased for state officials, details on the amounts of money paid to him, and the sums he claimed to have obtained by filing false bills against the state of Iowa. One glance at the Croft affidavit, made at a time when he was pleasantly disposed to Polk County Democrats, was enough to demonstrate that the Iowa Republicans had a big stake in discrediting Croft as a prosecution witness.

Switzer and Walters attempted to fight back. They gave sworn statements concerning conversations with Warden Lainson at the time Croft first turned state's evidence in the Polk County fraud case. Lainson had sought assurance from them that Croft would be used only against Polk County officials and would not be asked to testify in cases involving state officials.

"I've got to protect those boys on the hill," Lainson was quoted by Walters and Switzer as saying.

Switzer stated that, when he first went to Fort Madison prison to visit Croft, Lainson "asked me whether I was interested in going higher or beyond the Polk County fraud cases and investigating the activities of state figures. He (Lainson) at that time expressed concern to me about the welfare of certain of his superiors in state government and told me I would have his cooperation so long as I did not raise my sights above the Polk County level." Switzer also related, "Mr. Croft told me when he returned to Des Moines after having been sent back to Fort Madison . . . that he was grilled in the warden's office for a period of four hours and that he told them he had given an affidavit to Paul Walters concerning the state situation."

Paul Walters swore in his affidavit that he was present and "overheard Warden Lainson distinctly state to Mr. Switzer that as long as this was a Polk County matter, Switzer would have Lainson's cooperation, but that he did not want to involve the state of Iowa or any of the officials there." Walters also stated that Croft had volunteered to make a statement on the Iowa State officials because he felt "it would be protection to him for the statement to be in existence" and that "he was fearful of what might happen to him if he was returned to Fort Madison."

The Thompson request for a new trial was rejected, but it was merely the first step in a political war between the Democratic county attorney, who was an announced candidate for governor, and the Republicans who ran the Iowa capitol. Bizarre as they seemed on the surface, I was convinced of the general truth of these allegations of prison pressures to save the political hides of state government officials. It was apparent that the Republican officials were involved in a concerted effort to cover up evidence of a variety of small and large frauds.

STUDENT WORK PROJECT SUGGESTION

Write a paper analyzing the lessons that newsmen should learn from Elmer Croft's effort to recant testimony that he had given under oath before a grand jury and in more than one fraud trial. What does it tell us about the importance of corroborating every possible aspect of the testimony of a controversial witness, particularly one who admits to participation in some of the criminal acts?

13 LESSONS IN THE POLITICS OF PROSECUTION

There is an ever-present temptation for prosecutors to permit political aspirations to warp their judgments and to interfere with a sound timetable for investigation and prosecution. Although political advancement is an honorable motivation, it should not be the only motivation or even the dominant motivation for prosecution of political crooks. Political hopes can warp investigative decisions and can jeopardize solid prosecutions on legitimate subjects of inquiry. Reporters and editors should be wary. The desire to develop a new story may blind them to the dangers in premature story breaks.

THE STATE INTERVENES

State courts have a number of legal devices through which they can inject themselves into a prosecution even after the local judges have disqualified themselves from presiding because they have close political ties with the defendants. This happens occasionally when political figures are implicated in fraud, but, when the prosecutor is of the opposing political party, the temptation to interfere is overwhelming. With the conviction of former Welfare Director H. H. Thompson, Polk County Attorney Carroll O. Switzer took full aim at the Republicans holding office in the Iowa capitol. Since Switzer was an announced candidate for the Democratic nomination for governor of Iowa, there was an obvious political motivation that had to be taken into account.

Indictment or conviction of any Republicans at the Iowa state-house, whether elected or appointed, could be harmful to incumbent Governor Robert D. Blue. Governor Blue was a quiet, handsome country lawyer from Eagle Grove, Iowa, with a spotless reputation; however, a number of his appointees had been named by Elmer Croft as implicated in the same kind of frauds that had been taking place in Polk County.

Opening Moves in a Political Prosecution

Croft's courtroom tantrum in the Thompson trial had seriously undermined his value as a prosecution witness; however, Switzer and Paul Walters believed that a solid case could be made against some of the state officials with a minimum of reliance upon Croft's testimony. They were convinced that a prima facie case of fraud could be made from the paper records of purchases and sales of state cars as recorded in the state car dispatcher's office. After combing Croft's affidavit and other records, Switzer's office issued subpoenas calling for the Iowa State car dispatcher's office to deliver to the Polk County Grand Jury all of the mileage claims, repair bills, and other figures on the purchases and sales of all state cars owned from 1940 to 1947.

The issuance of the subpoena was County Attorney Switzer's opening gun in what was to be a full-scale effort to investigate the Republican-held Iowa capitol. Even though Switzer's political motivations were obvious, the Croft affidavit made it essential that the Polk County Attorney follow up serious allegations of fraud at the Iowa capitol in Des Moines, which was under his jurisdiction. It was obvious by this time that Governor Blue and Attorney General Robert L. Larson, also a Republican, were not going to initiate a state investigation of Republican wrongdoing in an election year.

Facts and Allegations

It was a fact that Elmer Croft, convicted car thief, had done business with the state car dispatcher's office and with other state offices from 1940 until he was indicted on the Polk County frauds. There was every reason for Iowa State law enforcement officials and Polk County officials to do a thorough investigation to determine whether records corroborated Croft's allegations. Croft's affidavit also included an allegation that he had done work on the personal cars of agents for the state criminal bureau of investigation and had billed the state of Iowa for the repair bills. Furthermore, he claimed that state agents had brought 18 or 20 state confiscated slot machines to his garage for cleaning and conditioning, and then had "sold them in other parts of the state."

In addition to Croft's assertions of state car frauds, there were separate allegations of wrongdoing. Other sources claimed that Iowa Republican officials had used a revolving fund established to purchase World War II surplus goods, cars, trucks, and other equipment at bargain prices for themselves and for their political friends and relatives.

The car registration records and other records demonstrated that a number of federal war surplus cars were purchased on an Iowa state priority in Kansas City, Mo., and were delivered directly to a used car lot in a northwest Iowa county seat town. Such a transaction had the potential for being prosecutable under federal as well as state law.

Countermoves

Under Iowa law, the Iowa Attorney General can move in on any county attorney and take charge of the investigation or monitor the investigation through the use of a special assistant attorney general. Walters and Switzer believed that the Iowa Republican organization would not take that step because it would smack too much of a coverup and an obstruction of justice. However, he was wrong. Although neither Governor Blue nor Attorney General Larson were directly involved in any of the allegations of wrongdoing, they were under heavy pressure from Polk County Republicans and from some powerful figures in the Iowa Republican organization to move in and supersede Switzer's probe.

Even before the Iowa state car dispatcher's office could respond to the first subpoena, Attorney General Larson asserted his authority to intervene in the Polk County Grand Jury investigation. He notified Switzer, by a hand delivered letter at 7:15 A.M. on the day the state car dispatcher was to appear, that Jens Grothe, a Des Moines Republican lawyer, had been named as special assistant attorney general to assist Switzer's office in the inquiry.

In his letter to Switzer, the Republican Attorney General cited his power to supersede any county attorney, and said he felt it his "duty" to see that the investigation was "complete, fair, and impartial" and "without regard to politics, ambitions, or position." This was a gratuitous slap at Switzer, a Democratic candidate for governor. Switzer slapped back that he had not asked Larson for help and that he had told Larson he would keep him posted on "future developments," but it did no good.

Acting on the authority of Iowa Attorney General Larson, Grothe entered the grand jury with first Assistant County Attorney Ed S. Thayer and took part in the questioning of Walter J. Ruther, a recently appointed car dispatcher who was the official custodian of the past records for that office.

To put the stamp of the court on the Attorney General's intervention, Polk County District Judge C. Edwin Moore called the grand jury into his courtroom with special instruction on the right of Jens Grothe to appear before them as a special assistant to the attorney general.

It was immediately apparent that the Polk County Republicans and the Republicans at the Iowa State capitol were joining forces to control, if not terminate, Switzer's investigations of Croft's allegations of fraud at the Iowa capitol. If Switzer was to be successful in making cases against the Iowa Republican officials, he was going to have to put his whole and undivided attention on the development of sound cases. Decisions would have to be made quickly to subpoena records and bank accounts. Switzer and Thayer said they now had to assume that state officials would be tipped off on the evidence being developed in the grand jury.

THE GRAND JURY INVESTIGATION

The records of the Iowa war surplus commodities board showed that from April 10, 1945, to August 10, 1946, more than $28,000 in war surplus goods was sold to various state officials and their friends. It was an obvious violation of the spirit of the federal law on the disposal of war surplus. That law provided the state government with one of the highest priorities in the purchase of federal surplus. This priority permitted the state government to make purchases after federal government agencies made their purchases but before war veterans had an opportunity to buy.

Records showed that the Iowa war surplus commodities board had used its priority to purchase 31 automobiles in the period immediately after World War II when automobiles were very scarce. In one instance, the 12 automobiles purchased with a state priority and with money from a state revolving fund were driven from a federal war surplus depot in Kansas City, Mo., to a used car dealer in northern Iowa. The 12 cars were sold to the used car dealer for $12,000. In that same time period, the used car dealer had transferred a new car to the executive secretary of the war surplus commodity board.

War surplus goods sold to other Iowa State officials included pillow cases, blankets, towels, shotguns, utility cabinets, brushes, tires, and automobiles. There were no records that those supplies were sold by competitive bidding. The executive director said he had purchased the cars and the supplies with the understanding that they might be bought by the various agencies of the state government. He said that a survey of state government agencies indicated that there was no demand for the cars or the goods. He made them available for purchase by various officials so the state wouldn't lose any money.

Although the sales of cars and tires that were part of the war surplus commodities were worth thousands of dollars, the amount purchased by Governor Robert D. Blue, State Treasurer John M. Grimes, State Auditor Chester B. Akers, and Agriculture Secretary Harry Linn were so insignificant that it would have been ludicrous for Switzer to suggest fraud prosecution. Their purchases were for pillow cases and other small items with prices ranging from $2.60 to $4.25, and it was, at worst, a carelessness that was devoid of any intent to break or bend federal or state law.

The sale of $4582.05 in surplus tires to a Des Moines firm and the sale of 12 war surplus cars to a northwest Iowa used car dealer were a different matter. The federal law on war surplus sales provided that "no surplus property shall be resold or otherwise transferred by the purchaser within one year of the date of purchase without written consent of the disposal agency." There was no written consent for the resale of the surplus cars, the surplus tires, or the sale of seven of the ten war surplus dental chairs purchased by the Iowa war surplus commodity board for the Iowa State Health Department. Those seven chairs were sold to individual dentists who were friends or relatives of various state health department officials.

Politicking by Prosecutor Spells Disaster

County Attorney Switzer's investigation of the state war surplus matter was justified, but his effort to tie the responsibility on Governor Robert D. Blue was politically motivated and without merit. Moreover, with full knowledge of Republican efforts to undermine his investigation, Switzer flitted around Iowa making political speeches that further blurred his image as an objective prosecutor and made him vulnerable to charges of partisan politics. Also, he left the day-to-day strategy to Ed Thayer and other assistant county attorneys. They were frequently at odds on the strategy and were ill-prepared to make important decisions.

The Polk County Grand Jury made its report on the investigation of Iowa statehouse irregularities in late August. Although the grand jury was critical of the loose operation of the state war surplus commodities board in its handling of nearly a half million dollars worth of war surplus, it stated that there was insufficient evidence to warrant indictment of any officer or employee of the state of Iowa.

The manner in which the Republican Attorney General intervened in the investigation was politically partisan and protected some persons who should have been indicted in connection with the sale of war surplus cars and tires. It is possible that Switzer might have been able to develop those cases if he had been in his office tending to business instead of off in the boondocks making political speeches.

REVERSALS OWING TO POLITICAL PRESSURE

In chasing political butterflies Switzer contributed substantially to his own problems in the state war surplus probe. He also made himself less credible and more vulnerable to a political lambasting from a Republican Iowa Supreme Court. On September 23, 1948, the Iowa Supreme Court reversed the fraud conviction of William H. Cotton, the former chairman of the Polk County Board of Supervisors, on grounds of "prejudicial error" on the part of the prosecution. Neither County Attorney Switzer nor First Assistant Ed Thayer had been present to argue the merits of the prosecution case before the Iowa Supreme Court.

The majority opinion written by Justice William L. Bliss, a Republican from Mason City, was a bitter document that had the ring of a defense lawyer's argument to the jury. It referred to Elmer Croft, the key government witness, as "the opposition's seasoned liar," as "a twice-convicted crook," and as a "self-confessed perjurer." "The defendant and other supervisors may have been derelict in the performance of their duties in this matter," Bliss declared. He then highlighted the fact that Cotton "has been active in responsible business positions and activities in Des Moines for many years prior to becoming county supervisor." He noted that "numerous reputable witnesses testified to his (Cotton's) good repute for honesty and fair dealing."

A strongly worded dissenting opinion by Justice W. F. Wennerstrum declared that the seven-member majority of the Iowa Supreme Court had "substituted their judgment for that of the jury and denied the jury their right to pass on, what is in my judgment, a proper record."

The Bliss majority opinion held that the practices and business procedures of the Polk County Supervisors, under which Croft had filed fraudulent claims, had been established by long usage prior to Cotton's election to the county board of supervisors. It was also held to be prejudicial for the prosecution to produce testimony of Attorneys B. J. Powers and Paul W. Walters, of the Civic Action Committee, to establish their meeting with Cotton in which they said they had warned him (Cotton) of Croft's fraudulent bills.

Wennerstrum, in his dissent to the majority, said, "As disclosed by the testimony, Cotton remained silent during most of the recital of the statement of the two witnesses (Powers and Walters). In my judgment, this was the proper matter for the consideration of the jury on the basis of the authorities cited by the majority. It is for the (trial) court to determine as a preliminary question whether the circumstances were such as reasonably to require a party to reply to a statement addressed to him. It was then for the jury to decide whether or not the appellant (Cotton) actually heard and understood the statement."

Privately, Walters and Switzer were critical of the decision as political, and they praised Justice Wennerstrum for having the decency and the courage to break with his Republican colleagues in the forceful dissent that had pointed up the weaknesses of the majority opinion. Walters noted that the majority opinion, written by Justice Bliss, "went too far in its bitter criticism of the prosecution and prosecution witnesses and was too much of an advocate's plea for Cotton." However, they declined comment for the record at that time and said that they could throw more light on the unsoundness of the Iowa Supreme Court decision in the official petition for rehearing.

Thayer went before the Iowa Supreme Court in a petition for rehearing and declared that, if the principles of law stated by the majority opinion prevailed, it will be "impossible to punish public officials who are guilty of corruption. This case affects the interests of all the taxpayers," Thayer argued. "The majority opinion, in effect, overrules many of the former decisions of this court and substitutes principles of law hitherto unrecognized by this court."

POLITICALLY PARTISAN COURTS
A SERIOUS PROBLEM

In his campaign as the Democratic candidate for governor of Iowa, Switzer spoke of the need for "a nonpolitical judiciary if Iowans care to have continued confidence in their courts. Too often, and not through their own wishes, judges are subjected to political pressure," Switzer said in speeches. "Even when they desire to resist this pressure they are unable to do so, because their nomination in the next primary is dependent upon approval of party heads."

The Iowa Supreme Court's action in reversing the Cotton conviction was followed by reversal of the convictions of supervisor

Roy J. Hild and welfare director H. H. Thompson. I had been familiar with personal and political favoritism in the actions of judges of the Municipal Court and the Polk County District Court, but this was my first experience with partisan machine politics in the Supreme Court of Iowa. I was to learn later a great deal more about the impact of power politics in the courts in other states, in the federal district courts, the federal appeals courts and even in the United States Supreme Court.

Although there are many fine objective judges who take their oaths seriously and operate with a high sense of integrity, there are a lot of legal scoundrels on the bench who wheel and deal in politics. Judges are often only politicians in robes. That is the hard reality when it comes to prosecution of politicians or political crimes, and it is a mistake to treat the decisions of judges with too much reverence. It takes the ultimate in independence and integrity for a judge to break completely with his political past. Thus, criticism of judicial opinions is definitely of value. Switzer and Walters said that my stories in the *Des Moines Register,* which quoted extensively from Wennerstrum's decision as a counter to the majority opinion, had made the political nature of the decision clear to any Iowa lawyer who was really interested in being objective in his analysis.

From the Polk County fraud trials I learned a great deal about trial procedures, and the law of evidence—particularly as it dealt with the practical problem of corroborating the testimony of an informant who was, in fact, a coconspirator in the crimes I was seeking to expose.

I also became a great deal more understanding of the feelings of prosecutors who are reluctant to prosecute persons with political connections or with the money to hire the services of politically-connected law firms. It is a long step from a news story that spells out the prima facie case of a fraud or embezzlement of government funds and the making of a criminal case that will withstand all of the normal trial tests as well as run the gauntlet of political pressures.

STUDENT WORK PROJECT SUGGESTION

Do a paper on the responsibility and authority of the attorney general in your state to supersede a county attorney on an investigation if he disagrees with the manner in which an investigation is being handled. Has this procedure been used in your state or your community to take over or direct an investigation? Is it necessary to get a court order for the attorney general to take over a prosecution in your state?

14 PAYOFF PROBE PROBLEMS

Never underestimate the potential destructiveness of a partisan political judiciary when the political machine is pressed into a corner by desperation. Total day-to-day scrutiny of the actions by the prosecutor, defense lawyers, and the judge are essential. A careful analysis of the judicial selection system in your state, county, and city will certainly produce some evidence of political favoritism if not corruption. A part of this analysis should include a depth background article on each of the local and state judges in your circulation area, complete with political connections and property holdings. This material can be supplemented by a careful study of any controversial case any judge may have handled within the last few years.

THE EFFECT OF POLITICS ON A CRIMINAL PROSECUTION

There was no known link between the Iowa Republican officials who fought the Polk County Attorney's investigation of the war surplus commodities board and the Des Moines bootlegging and gambling fraternity. Yet, in the fall of 1948 they found themselves on the same side in opposing the active investigations of Polk County Attorney Carroll Switzer and First Assistant County Attorney Ed Thayer. Even as Switzer and Thayer were continuing investigations of frauds at the Iowa capitol and in Polk County, Thayer was conducting a quiet two-month investigation of payoffs of $100-a-week by Des Moines night clubs for protection on liquor law violations.

The Charges

Switzer and Thayer filed the criminal charges on August 27, 1948, charging that Safety Commissioner Myron J. Bennett unlawfully conspired with six Des Moines tavern operators to accept payoffs from these operators and to violate the city ordinance on the closing hours of beer taverns. Bennett, a 41-year-old radio disc jockey, was charged jointly with Jack Wolfe, owner of a printing company. Conviction on the conspiracy charge carried a mandatory three-year prison term.

Polk County finally had a county attorney who would follow up evidence of vice payoffs. It appeared to be a solid case constructed on the testimony of six night club and tavern operators, various city and county officials, as well as high officials of the Des Moines police department. There were affidavits from the night club operators of the police raid pressures prior to cash payments made to Jack Wolfe, who said he was collecting for Bennett's campaign fund. There was Jack Wolfe's affidavit that he put $500 in cash in Bennett's hand, and that Bennett gave it back to him to pay for campaign printing expenses. Also, there was the sworn statement by Des Moines Mayor Heck Ross that Wolfe had told him and City Solicitor Sid Harvey that he had collected the $500 from Dave Fidler, a night club operator, for Bennett's election campaign.

The Defendant's Counter Attack

However, within a few days of the filing of the county attorney's information and the arraignment of Bennett and Wolfe, the case turned into a political nightmare for Switzer and Thayer. Bennett's lawyers made much of the fact that City Solicitor Harvey said he could not remember Wolfe mentioning the amount of $500 or saying specifically that it was for Bennett. Bennett argued that Thayer's summary of the evidence was false because Thayer had contended that Harvey fully corroborated Mayor Ross's version of Wolfe's conversation. In addition, the audacious Bennett, who continued to conduct two daily radio talk shows, engaged in constant criticism of Switzer and Thayer and belittled the charges filed against him.

When Thayer asked that Bennett be cited for contempt of court because of the broadcast of "scurrilous, malicious, abusive and prejudicial statements," Bennett retaliated by filing three criminal charges against Thayer in municipal court. He charged Thayer with oppression in his official capacity, interference with the administration of justice, and subornation of perjury. The charge of oppression dealt with Thayer's comments to officials of radio station KSO, indicating they could be prosecuted if they did not restrict Bennett in discussing the candidacies of Switzer for governor and Thayer for county attorney.

This controversy was reported straight from the court record, and we avoided the strong temptation to ignore the charges we did not agree with. To avoid a questionable "slant" it is often necessary to write with a repetition of key facts and issues to avoid the distortions of oversimplification.

Although the charges against Thayer were eventually dismissed by Municipal Judge Harry B. Grund, the court hearing on the charges resulted in the county attorney's office being forced to disclose much of the details of the evidence it intended to use in prosecuting Safety Commissioner Bennett and Wolfe. It also revealed minor discrepancies in the testimony of witnesses for the prosecution, and gave the political critics of Switzer and Thayer the opportunity to raise questions about the propriety of swearing out a county attorney's information in the payoff cases when a grand jury was in session.

By the time the charges against Thayer were dismissed as groundless, all of the prosecution witnesses, including city officials and night club operators, were aware of the testimony of others. Thus, defense lawyers were able to develop a divide and conquer strategy. Cooperative witnesses suddenly became hostile. They changed their testimony in minor ways, or became uncertain and vague as to precise conversations.

The Republican Counter Attack

The week before the November election, Polk County District Judge C. Edwin Moore dismissed the criminal charges against Bennett and Wolfe on grounds that the county attorney's information was defective because of "legal technicalities" involving the questioning of witnesses. Judge Moore, already at odds with Switzer and Thayer on the custody of Elmer Croft in the Polk County fraud trials, ruled that Thayer had engaged in an "incorrect" abstracting of the testimony of City Solicitor Harvey and Mayor Ross. He also ruled that it was improper for Deputy Sheriff Wilbur Hildreth to have been present in the county attorney's office during the questioning of witnesses in preparation for the filing of the county attorney's information.

Although Judge Moore offered the Polk County Grand Jury to begin complete investigation of the allegations of payoffs at the earliest possible moment, it was obvious that this could not be done until after the election, if ever, since key witnesses were modifying their original testimony. Simultaneously with the dismissal of the payoff cases, the Polk County Republican organization lambasted Switzer and Thayer for their ineffectiveness as prosecutors and for engaging in "persecution" of Polk County Republican office holders.

Donald Beving, member of a law firm that had defended one of the Republican officials charged with fraud, spoke at a Republican rally. He lauded Judge Moore for his dismissal of the conspiracy charge against Safety Commissioner Bennett. He praised Judge Moore for having the courage to throw out the questionable county attorney's information and to send the case to the Polk County Grand Jury where he said it should have been handled in the first place.

"Polk County has six very fine and honorable judges under the present method of selection," Beving said, and added that Judge Moore is one of the finest judges Polk County has ever had and "is probably one of the finest in the state."

Democratic Response

In return, several Democratic speakers accused Judge Moore of "playing politics" with his rulings in the Des Moines payoff cases. At the conclusion of a rally at the Democratic county head-quarters, the Democrats played a recording of a 1946 campaign speech by Judge Moore in which he had endorsed all of the Republican candidates for office in the face of the fraud charges leveled by Paul Walters of the Civic Action Committee.

Neither Switzer nor Thayer attacked Judge Moore in their political speeches, but Assistant County Attorney Joseph Z. Marks made an indirect attack on the Polk County Republican judges. As a Democratic candidate for state representative from Polk County, Marks said he would introduce legislation to establish a nonpolitical judiciary system in Iowa.

"It is about time we took politics out of the dispensing of justice," Marks told a Democratic rally. "It is hard for a person who does not work directly with the system to realize how vicious it is."

THE EFFECT ON POLITICS OF THE PROSECUTION

Despite the controversy of the payoff investigations and the reversal of the Cotton conviction, Polk County voters gave Ed Thayer a 41,000 to 30,000 victory at the polls. In traditionally Republican Polk County it was a significant demonstration of public support for those who aggressively pursue evidence of government frauds and payoffs. It was also a demonstration that the public can understand the clever manipulations of entrenched machine politicians when the newspapers give the public sufficient details of the frauds, the payoffs, and the rulings of the courts.

Sheriff Reppert had even a slightly larger margin of victory than did Thayer in a Democratic sweep of all major county offices except Treasurer, where Republican J. F. (Bill) Baillie was returned by a discerning electorate. Baillie, who initially tipped off Paul Walters on the Croft frauds, was untouched by the scandals that had disclosed major and minor compromises in nearly all other offices.

Political Intent and Carelessness Spell Defeat

Although the Democratic sweep demonstrated support in Polk County for the aggressive approach to fraud and payoff investigations, County Attorney Carroll Switzer was defeated in his race for governor by William S. Beardsley, the labor-backed Republican candidate. Switzer gave the initial leadership to the Polk County investigations and was generally sound in his judgments, but he had permitted himself to be pushed into an active campaign with politically partisan speeches in the far corners of the state. This made him vulnerable to charges that he was not paying attention to business in the Polk County Attorney's Office, and that he was using it as a stepping stone to higher office. Although Switzer put in long hours to keep on top of the most important matters in his office, it was apparent that Thayer and other assistant county attorneys were doing the actual trial work.

With regard to the existence of frauds in the Iowa war surplus commodities board, Switzer was probably right, but he carelessly overstated the case with regard to the direct involvement of Governor Robert D. Blue and other top state officials. His absence from the office made it possible for the Republican attorney general's office to outmaneuver him relative to some key testimony and documents that could have resulted in two indictments. In the late days of the 1948 campaign, Switzer told me he would probably have been ahead politically if he had stayed in Des Moines and had personally run the county attorney's office in a manner that would have prepared him better to meet the political chicanery of the embattled Republican bosses.

The Effectiveness of Adequate Reportage

The turmoil of the highly charged atmosphere of the 1948 political campaigns demonstrated several dangers: a prosecutor can become engaged in serious investigations on several fronts at the same time so that his effectiveness is reduced; a county attorney's information, used as a short cut to indictment in a politically charged judicial forum, can fail owing to political pressure.

Since there was little substantial precedence for the proper procedures of gathering evidence for a county attorney's information, it was precarious to use that short cut method of initiating criminal charges within the jurisdiction of a judge who was likely to be politically hostile.

Only the willingness of the editors of the *Des Moines Register* to carry long and detailed stories explaining the evidence and the court rulings made it possible to keep the public fully advised of the political nature and background of the investigations, prosecutions, and judicial decisions. Anything less than that total day-to-day press scrutiny of the actions by the prosecutors, the defense lawyers, and the courts could have resulted in a coverage that was lopsided, distorted, or tilted to either side. Superficial newspaper coverage could have destroyed any chance the Democratic reformers had for winning the election in Polk County.

STUDENT WORK PROJECT SUGGESTION

Analyze the details of the handling of a criminal case involving liquor or gambling law violations or involving charges of fraud made against a prominent political figure. Give particular attention to court rulings that dismiss some of the charges or that exclude evidence that the law enforcement officials and prosecutors believe is admissible.

15 POLK COUNTY LESSON ON GOVERNMENT

False billing and double billing practices drained hundreds of thousands of dollars from county funds. A sloppy property inventory system made those frauds possible. It was a result of long-time public and newspaper neglect in failing to recognize flagrant conflicts of interest and serious weaknesses in the management of personnel and property. The problem is present in city, state, and federal government agencies.

One of the classic cases of government scandal involving double billing dealt with the activities of Orville Hodge, a former State Auditor in Illinois. George Theim, a reporter for the *Chicago Daily News,* exposed the Hodge scandal in the mid-1950s and won a Pulitzer Prize for the *Chicago Daily News.* Theim's book *The Hodge Scandal* contains an excellent explanation of the techniques he used in exposing this million-dollar scandal and overcoming the coverup engineered by Hodge and his political friends. The fraud exposed by George Theim followed the same patterns as those I uncovered in Polk County, Iowa, in 1947 and 1948.

MANAGEMENT OF GOVERNMENT PROPERTY

The more than two years of investigations and trials of government corruption and fraud cases in Polk County were illuminating. Although the major focus in each case had to be on the guilt or innocence of the defendant and the adherence to the safeguards that assured each defendant due process of law, there was much to be learned about the machinery of government and the proper manner in which bills and expenditures of government funds are approved and authorized.

The Rubber Stamp

The trials were also instructive to county officials, who wished to avoid the mistakes their colleagues made and thus any possible criminal culpability in the future. When members of the board of supervisors noted how Prosecutor Ed Thayer used the signatures of prior board members to link them to approval of the fraudulent bills filed by Elmer Croft, they authorized the use of a rubber stamp by the county auditor. Under this new procedure, the auditor would place a checkmark by the supervisor's stamped name, and the supervisor would not be required either to sign his name or initial the approved county bills.

When I learned of the use of the rubber stamp, I realized that it would be difficult or impossible for any future prosecutor to establish the personal culpability of any supervisor with any specific fraudulent bill. The fraud trials had drilled home the lesson that the so-called red tape in the approval of government purchases and authorization for the payment of government bills is essential to establish firm responsibility. I went to Paul Walters with my discovery and my conclusion that the rubber stamp had been devised for the specific purpose of avoiding responsibility for fraudulent bills.

Walters agreed with my conclusion as did Thayer, so I wrote a story on the use of the new rubber stamp for county business. There was an immediate uproar over the new procedure. Although Board Chairman Mark Conkling said it was for expediting board meetings and was not intended to protect the present board from fraud responsibilities, the board abandoned its rubber stamp and went back to a system of individual signatures and initials to indicate approval.

That "rubber stamp incident" impressed me with the importance of making a periodic examination of the mechanics of government spending practices while asking three basic questions:

1. Would it be possible to establish the criminal responsibility of the supervisors or other elected or appointed officials for any false billing or double billing?

2. Are the weaknesses in the purchasing system that permit avoidance of responsibility the result of carelessness, or are they a result of a willful policy change?

3. A collateral question raised in my mind by the fraud trials dealt with the accuracy of inventories of equipment purchased by the county government. If automobile motors and

tires were missing, what about typewriters, desks, filing cabinets, and road equipment?

Inventory Systems

My curiosity about the inventory system was stimulated by a conversation with a member of the board of supervisors relative to a new filing case in his office. I commented that the new filing cabinet was the type that I needed for keeping records for my stories, and the supervisor interpreted my comment erroneously as a hint that he give it to me. He remarked that he would like to give me the filing case, but that the fraud investigations made him fearful of being so accommodating at that time.

I quickly assured him that I was not hinting for a gift of county equipment, and tucked the incident away as a reminder to examine the county government inventory system. It had to be thoroughly unreliable if the supervisor believed he could make a gift of a filing cabinet to accommodate the whim of a newspaper reporter. Over a period of weeks, I checked each office on the adequacy of its inventory system and was not surprised to find that there was no adequate inventory of office equipment at all.

At the time of the first fraud indictments, County Auditor L. O. Lindstrum had asked the various departments to supply him with an inventory of equipment. That one-shot inventory was a simple listing of "on hand" equipment by the various departments. It was in no way an effort to determine whether the offices actually had the number of typewriters, desks, filing cabinets, and other equipment that had been purchased for them with tax money over the years. The inventory was left up to the individual officeholders, and only Treasurer J. F. (Bill) Baillie had an up-to-date list, complete with serial numbers of county equipment.

One of those caught off-base by my inventory check was County Attorney Carroll O. Switzer who had a brief, incomplete listing of equipment in a drawer in his desk. This list did not include the serial numbers on the equipment. Also, he had not forwarded a copy of this list to the auditor's office as the county supervisors had requested in a tardy effort to establish a master list that would at least have given the appearance of being businesslike. Switzer admitted his lack of a running inventory was an oversight, but said he could find no notice from the county auditor requesting that he file the equipment list. "It is a great safeguard, and I believe all equipment received should be accounted for," Switzer agreed and suggested that the supervisors take immediate steps to establish a complete running inventory.

Deputy Auditor F. B. St. John said no attempt had been made to keep a listing of serial numbers on equipment in the past because department heads often traded off equipment without going through the board of supervisors for approval. However, it was obvious that such property inventory laxity could have permitted continuing misuse and frauds involving county property. Thus, the supervisor appointed a county inventory director who had the specific responsibility of bringing inventories up to date and keeping them up to date.

Personal Use and Sale of County Property

The laxity in inventory of office equipment extended to the county road equipment, radio equipment for the sheriff's cars, the supplies purchased for the Polk County Juvenile Home and the dairy herd and dairy production at the Polk County Farm. The county farm maintained a dairy herd of 50 Holstein cows. but there was no effective system of accounting for the income by the farm manager. Much of the milk was used at the county home, but part of the production was sold for cash by the farm manager, who claimed the cash was spent on purchases for the county home.

There was great opportunity for unreported profits in the purchase, sale, and trading of blooded cattle for the dairy herd. Registered cattle were bought for high prices with county money, but there were no records of the descriptions of these cattle or the number bought, County Attorney Switzer said. There were unconfirmed reports that the high priced cattle were sold or traded to supervisors or their friends and that the lack of adequate records was intentional.

Switzer's investigation of the handling of the dairy herd was totally frustrated by the lack of records. He also ran into a similar problem with regard to grain sales.

Personnel Management

The same laxity with regard to purchases and inventories that made the county government a sitting duck for Elmer Croft's double billing infected Polk County personnel management. In fact, there was no central management of personnel and no standards for hiring, promotion, firing, vacations, or sick leave. Each elected officer was given total discretion in the hiring of employees, and, although many were conscientious men and women of integrity, there were a good many political hacks with few regular duties.

The five members of the Polk County Board of Supervisors split the patronage on jobs in various ways. Once the split was made, each was permitted almost total discretion in his sphere of activity. That is why former Chairman William H. Cotton was the key figure in the welfare department frauds, and home service workers in the welfare department, hired to go into the homes of the poor, were used for service chores at Chairman Cotton's political parties. Supervisor Roy Hild had major responsibility for the irregularities in the juvenile home, and Parmenter was involved in the false billing for repair work on the Polk County Home smokestack. The irregularities charged against Supervisor Ben B. Dewey centered on the purchase and sale of road equipment, and the illegal construction of a road equipment garage without the bidding that was required under Iowa law.

CONFLICTS OF INTEREST

Supervisor Dewey conducted a lucrative insurance and bonding business that ran parallel to his duties as a supervisor. County records showed that the bulk of the bonding business for beer and cigarette license holders in Polk County was handled by Dewey. The veteran supervisor was listed in state records as the agent for 16 insurance firms. He had signed 26 of the 39 beer bonds approved by the Polk County Board of Supervisors for the 1947–48 year.

Dewey said he had not solicited the beer and cigarette license bond business, but that the people who ran the restaurants and beer places in his district came to him voluntarily. Although each of these bonds, to serve as a guarantee against law violations, had to be approved by the board of supervisors, Dewey said, there was no question about the legality of his dealings.

"I've checked the law on that very close and as long as I don't sell to Polk County I'm safe," Dewey said. "I've never solicited a single bond from one of those people. If they come to me and want to buy a bond I won't turn them down."

A search of the board of supervisors' records disclosed that Supervisor Mark L. Conkling was among those voting approval of Conkling's tailor shop (Glasgow Tailors, Inc.) to supply new French blue uniforms for the patrolmen in the sheriff's office. Because I was working on the story, the board members, including Conkling, voted to rescind the resolution of approval.

There was scarcely an office in the entire county government that did not have some conflict of interest involving personal business, jobs for relatives, or special transactions in the sale of property that benefited friends or relatives. Much of it was small stuff, amounting to a few hundred dollars. At the *Register* we tried to keep a proper perspective as we wrote about little conflicts of interest that amounted to small violations of the law or were handled in a manner which cleverly skirted the law.

Information from Informants

Once the stories started appearing, my telephone was busy with tips on others in the city, county, or state government who were engaged in the same or similar transactions. Some of the informants told me their names, and in some cases I recognized the voices of county employees even when they declined to give me their names. Sometimes the information was general, and it was difficult or impossible to check out. Frequently, however, the informant had precise details on land transfers with the amounts of money and dates. Then it was a simple matter to check the public land records in the auditor's office, the mortgage records in the recorder's office, or the tax records in the treasurer's office.

Reading 7: Real Estate Dealings

In the fall of 1947, I received a report from a nervous informant in the Polk County welfare department that a relative of Jack Winegardner, head of the real estate division, had purchased an old age recipient's five-room home for $1200. It was the first time that I had even known there was a real estate division in the county welfare department.

Upon inquiry, I learned that the real estate division had responsibility for handling the properties of old age pension recipients after their death. These properties were sold by the state after the death of the pensioners, and the money was used to help reimburse the state for the assistance given that person. If there was money left after the state had been paid, the remaining funds would be distributed to the heirs.

My investigation ran into trouble because of tight policies of secrecy that covered all welfare programs. The theory was that the secrecy protected the poor from embarrassment, but it was also often the case that it shielded the welfare administrators from exposure of frauds against the poor funds. My effort to review the old age property sold by the welfare department was frustrated from that end, but I was not discouraged. I went to the auditor's office to check land records for a property purchased by a Winegardner.

A house at 2436 E. Walnut Street had been transferred to a Robert J. Winegardner in December 1946, but it had been transferred from a Russell Casson and not from the estate of an old age pensioner. However, the record disclosed that Russell Casson had purchased the property from the estate of Mr. and Mrs. Gus Eckman in January 1946.

Up to this point I had gone about the business of checking the public records in a quiet manner because I wanted to get as many hard facts from the records as possible before asking any questions of Winegardner or the county supervisors. There seemed to be some conflicts between my informant's claims and the facts. For example, the purchase by Casson seemed at odds with my informant's comment that Winegardner's relative had purchased the property directly from the real estate division of the welfare department, but there was a notation on the deed that "no money changed hands" in the transfer from Casson to Robert Winegardner. Also, my informant indicated that Robert Winegardner had been living in the home for several years. This was at odds with the real estate records indicating transfer to him only a few months earlier, in December 1946.

Initially, I did not know Robert Winegardner was Jack Winegardner's son, and again I did not want to question him until I had all possible facts pinned down with public records. Remembering that I had filed my Navy discharge papers in the office of the Polk County Recorder, I took a chance that Robert Winegardner had been in service and had also filed his military discharge papers and the chance paid off.

Winegardner's Navy discharge papers on file in the recorder's office, disclosed a bonanza of information that I wanted. They revealed that he listed his home address as 2436 E. Walnut St. when he entered service on April 24, 1944, and when he was discharged in November 1946. He was the son of Jack Winegardner, and had been living in the old age pensioner's house at least since April 1944.

The probate record of the estate of Mr. and Mrs. Gus Eckman disclosed that the old age pensioners had died in 1943, and that they were survived by one heir, a niece, Mrs. Clarence Gaard of Blue Earth, Minnesota. The state social welfare department had a $3300 lien against the property as a result of old age payments made to the Eckmans. I called the niece and learned that she had made some inquiry with regard to redeeming the property. She gave up the idea when told that the $3300 lien was more than the $2000 value that Jack Winegardner had placed on the property in the welfare department records.

Records disclosed that early in 1944, before an administrator for the estate had been named, Robert Winegardner and his family moved into the house belonging to the Eckman estate. In April 1944 papers were filed in probate court in which Jack Winegardner, as head of the real estate division, and Welfare Director H. H.

Thompson had recommended a friendly Des Moines attorney as administrator of the Eckman estate. The court and the state welfare department had routinely approved the suggested administrator.

There were only two people who could have properly given Robert Winegardner permission to occupy the Eckman estate house in 1944—the lawyer or the niece. Mrs. Gaard told me she had given no one permission to occupy the property and had received no rent from it. The lawyer said he did not know the Robert Winegardner family was occupying the house until the sale of the property to Russell Casson, who, it turned out, was Jack Winegardner's brother-in-law and an uncle to Robert Winegardner.

At the time I called Casson to learn of his role in the transaction, he volunteered his relationship to the Winegardners but declined further explanation. I asked County Attorney Carroll Switzer if he was aware that the pensioner's property had ended up in the name of the son of the head of the welfare department's real estate division. Switzer said he had some information on the subject and had just assigned Assistant County Attorney Clyde Herring to make inquiry. He did not know the precise status of the investigation.

By this time, Jack Winegardner and Supervisor Mark Conkling, then chairman of the Polk County welfare board, had heard of my inquiries. Conkling moved quickly to remove Winegardner from his post as head of the real estate division. However, he continued him on the payroll as a senior welfare worker under the state merit system. Jack Winegardner said he had "nothing to do with the sale" of the old-age pensioner's property to his son, and retreated behind a stone wall of secrecy on grounds that all welfare department matters were subject to strict rules of confidentiality imposed by the state board of social welfare.

Despite the fact that Jack Winegardner had many friends in county government and on the state board of social welfare, the facts in my stories made it essential that the state initiate an investigation into the sale of the Eckman home. That investigation had to include the circumstances under which Winegardner's son had occupied the house "rent free" for two years before purchasing it at a price that was less than half its market value.

A foot-dragging investigation by the state board of social welfare raised some serious questions in my mind. It certainly appeared they were not too eager to uncover the truth. I wondered how the state was monitoring the 1500 pensioners' homes which were turned over to the state each year. In the 1946-47 fiscal year the sales from these homes totaled more than $1,300,000. If all were handled in the loose manner of the Eckman estate, heirs were being ripped off and the state and federal government were losing money.

The Eckman house was carried on assessment roles at $2130, which was theoretically 60 per cent of its value. In this case it was sold for $1200, and by the time attorneys' fees, court costs and taxes were subtracted, the welfare department received only $379.

The reluctance of the Polk County welfare board and the state department of social welfare to fire Winegardner made me doubly suspicious that such irregular handling of the properties of old age recipients was widespread and that Winegardner had something on the welfare board officials with regard to other transactions. It seemed a great area for further inquiry, but I was already submerged in the detail of dozens of other investigations that were more pressing. Even with maximum prodding from County Attorney Switzer's office, the county board of social welfare had not fired Jack Winegardner two months after the incident. In fact, the board indicated it would take no further legal action with regard to trying to void the sale of the property to Winegardner's son. Supervisor Conkling said that he believed Jack Winegardner's story that he had no part in the property transaction that resulted in his son getting title to the Eckman home.

One of the problems in covering Polk County government in that period was that there were so many minor and major scandals in almost every office that there was too little time to follow each one through to force a satisfactory conclusion. In the case of welfare department irregularities, the county, state, and federal laws and regulations had to be examined and analyzed in an atmosphere that was clouded by vague secrecy policies. Inaction at the county level was blamed on state and federal policies that were often difficult or impossible to pin down.

STUDENT WORK PROJECT SUGGESTION

1. Outline the legal procedures for purchasing equipment and for contracting in the city and county in which you reside. How much of this process is controlled by state law, and how much is left to the discretion of local and county officials?

2. Write a paper explaining in detail the state government procedures and practices with regard to personnel management. Also, analyze the scholastic, political, and experience background of key personnel.

16 ASSESSMENT AND SECRECY

Superficial coverage of assessments and review of assessments is a chronic problem in many areas and contributes to the continuation of inequitable real estate values as a tax base. The problem is compounded when special interest groups are permitted to meet secretly with those responsible for establishing assessment standards.

There are a wide range of irregularities in assessments and assessment revaluations in almost any local governmental unit. It is also inevitable that there will be wide variations in the standards used by various city and county governmental units in setting real property values. A survey of the evaluations of the property of long-time office holders or prominent political or business leaders will give an indication of the extent of the problem in your area. In most states records dealing with assessments and taxes are public. If any aspect of the assessment and real estate tax procedure is secret, that shocking fact is deserving of full exploration in a depth news story.

ASSESSMENTS AND REAL VALUE

In the spring of 1949 the property owners of Polk County received the jolting notice that assessments on farm land and other property outside Des Moines would be increased sharply under the new county assessor law. Glaring inequities under the township appraisal system had resulted in the new law being passed by the Iowa legislature to bring an end to the ridiculous underevaluations in many rural townships.

County Auditor Harold Anderson laid out this general picture on what the new "expert appraisal" system would do:

1. Assessments of homes in the districts surrounding Des Moines would double in some areas.

2. There would be substantial increases in the values of most farmland, and the assessment of farm buildings would be doubled or tripled in most instances.

"I don't believe any tax payer will complain if he knows the appraisal is being done on a fair basis," the county auditor said optimistically. "I believe that most of the property owners whose assessments have been increased realize they have been paying taxes on only about 10 to 30 per cent of the value instead of 60 per cent, as the law provides."

Under the old township assessment system, where close neighbors set the values, there was about $35,000,000 in taxable real property outside of Des Moines. The new values would boost the total by $12,000,000 to $47,000,000, according to Elmer Thulin, the chief deputy assessor. Although the reform of the rural township assessment process was long overdue, opposition by farm groups was to be expected and was exacerbated by the stories about the frauds and conflicts of interest involving the board of supervisors and many present and former county officials. Within a few days after the release of the new assessment figures, a revolt started to shape up among the farmers, with the Polk County Farm Bureau Federation taking a leading role. Examination of the complaints of the protestors demonstrated just how far out of line the assessment had been in the rural areas.

The new land values set by the J. M. Cleminshaw Co., of Cleveland, Ohio, included a few glaring errors. In a few cases, the Cleminshaw firm's employees had placed farm buildings on the wrong farm, for example, but these were rare exceptions. In general, there could be no doubt that the new figures were more realistic than the old evaluations—particularly the valuations placed on farm buildings. Nonetheless, it was the exceptional errors that were being stressed by farmers and their lawyers in contending incompetence. In meetings with the Polk County Board of Supervisors, the farmers were bitterly critical of past "misuse of county funds" and the present "high cost" of county government. In addition to the harangue about too many county employees, the farmers also cited farms in adjoining counties—across the road from Polk County—where farmers paid only half the taxes.

The protests of the farm groups were loud, bitter, and disorganized, but they provided a reason for a close examination of past assessments of Polk County officials and the whole new system for appealing assessments. It turned out that the names of two former county officials were included in the list of 43 protests initially filed in Polk County. Those protests were filed by former

Supervisor Ben B. Dewey and former Sheriff Vane B. Overturff. Records disclosed that the 60 per cent assessment on Dewey's 43-acre farm near Johnston had increased from $960 to $4138— more than 400 per cent. The assessment value on Overturff's two farms near Mitchellville jumped from $10,385 to $14,262—an increase of more than 37 per cent. The old assessment on Dewey's 43-acre farm had been a ridiculous $18 an acre, and the value of two cottages and a corn crib was set at $180.

SECRET REAPPRAISAL EXPOSED

The three members of the board of supervisors from rural districts were eager to appease the protesting farm lobby but did not want to make a public display of their political cowardice. In violation of specific provisions of the new assessment law, they closed the doors of the Polk County board room for discussions with a delegation from the Polk County Farm Bureau federation.

Desperate Measures are Necessary

When my protest of the illegality of such a closed meeting failed to unlock the board room door, I went into a nearby office, climbed out on a second floor ledge, and made my way around the courthouse to an open window in an office off the board room. I slipped in the window of the empty office without being noticed, and sat in a chair near the door to the board room taking notes on the closed meeting. It was only about 10 or 15 minutes later that a secretary discovered my presence.

In answer to the board chairman's order to leave, I cited the law requiring that all assessment matters be handled in public. When I sat tight in the face of his repeated orders to leave, the chairman declared the secret meeting at an end and said he would protest to the editor of the *Des Moines Register*.

That ended the efforts of the Polk County Board of Supervisors to conduct secret meetings on the assessment controversy. However, under heavy lobbying pressure from the Polk County Farm Bureau federation, the five members of the Polk County Board of Assessment and Review, on June 20, announced that they had agreed "on a trial basis" to let the Farm Bureau federation help set land values.

After an unsuccessful effort to meet illegally in a closed session with the Farm Bureau committee at the courthouse, the Board of Assessment and Review adjourned for what they called "a private meeting" at some unspecified place away from the courthouse. A secretary in one of the county offices informed me that the meeting was to take place at the Farm Bureau office in east Des Moines. Accompanied by a photographer, I went there and insisted on covering the discussions because the law specified that all meetings on assessments should be public.

Proof of Secret Meetings

The group disbanded, but I received a call at the office a few hours later to say that they were meeting that night at a farm in Bloomfield township. Again accompanied by a photographer, I drove to a point near the farmhouse. We walked through a corn field to the house and stationed ourselves near an open window until we heard that the discussion did involve lowering the Cleminshaw assessments. Having established that it was indeed an illegal closed meeting on assessments, we went back to the car and drove into the farmyard where several cars were parked. As we got out of the car, all but one light in the house went out.

The woman who came to the door said the men were not there and had not been there. She stuck to her story even when we made comments about the large number of cars in the driveway. As we drove out we were amused by the idea of the Board of Assessment and Review members and their Farm Bureau advisors crouching in the darkened farmhouse. We parked down the road, and a few minutes later saw the men emerge from the house, get into their cars, and drive off in different directions. It was not necessary to follow them any more for the story about their brazen efforts to get around the law on public meetings was confirmed.

As I was writing my story on the "phantom committee" hiding out somewhere in Bloomfield township to consider overthrowing the new assessed value on Polk County farmland, I received a call from an informant on the board that they had met later at still another farmhouse to continue working over the tax lists in the irregular review with the Farm Bureau committee.

The actions of the "phantom committee" subjected it to ridicule, editorial criticism, and threats of ouster. Two days later the members of the Polk County Board of Assessment and Review came out of hiding, and announced that they had no intention of discarding the J. M. Cleminshaw Co. appraisal. The board members also said that all future meetings would be "public" as provided by state law. They claimed the Farm Bureau had proposed a specific formula for lowering the assessments on land and buildings and had suggested that the Polk County Board of Assessment and Review accept recommendations from Farm Bureau appointed committees in each township.

"We've decided to let them make their recommendations, but we are not going to be dictated to by any pressure group," Earl McClannahan, the chairman of the review board, said.

EXPOSURE OF CONFLICT OF INTEREST

Although that ended the secret meetings on the assessment reviews, it did not end the controversies. Serious conflicts of interest continued after McClannahan resigned as chairman.

As McClannahan's successor, the Polk County Board of Supervisors named Raymond Uhl, a Mitchellville, Iowa, lawyer. Research disclosed that Uhl was serving as attorney for 16 of the 39 people protesting the new values in Beaver township. In addition, Uhl had filed a protest on the new valuation of his mother's eight-room house in Mitchellville. It had been assessed at $2136 by the former township assessor, and the Cleminshaw firm had raised the value to $3535—an increase of approximately 65 per cent.

When questioned, Supervisor B. E. (Bill) Newell, who had nominated Uhl, told me he had done so at the recommendation of the resigning chairman McClannahan. Supervisor Newell claimed he did not discover that Uhl was acting as attorney for a protesting group of property owners until after the appointment had been approved. County Attorney Ed Thayer said it would be necessary for Uhl to give up the review board position or withdraw as attorney for the property owners.

"A man cannot be on both sides of the fence," Thayer said.

Uhl countered that he had been paid by the property owners to file their protest, and that he would take no further role in those cases. "I'm an attorney and I know something about ethics," he said. "I know I can't be acting as a judge and representing the people who have complaints."

Another attorney, Hiram Hunn, was not so sensitive to possible conflicts of interest in connection with the assessment problems. Hunn, a Des Moines lawyer, was permanent chairman of the Polk County Assessment Conference as a result of being one of the five members of the Polk County Board of Education. In the middle of the heated assessment dispute, Hunn was named as attorney for the Polk County Taxpayers Association, a group organized outside Des Moines to fight the new higher assessments—and he accepted the position. Hunn said he found "nothing incompatible" in the two positions.

The Polk County Assessment Conference, which Hunn headed, was composed of members of the board of education, the five Polk

County Supervisors, and 13 mayors of the incorporated towns outside of Des Moines. This conference had the joint responsibility of appointing the county assessor and his deputies. Hunn insisted that there were "two main reasons" why the positions were not incompatible:

1. "As lawyer for the taxpayers' association I do not represent individual landowners in tax protest before the board of review or the assessor."
2. "The board of education casts one vote as a whole in deciding conference policy. I am only one member of that board. My position might be incompatible if I had one of the votes, but I am twice removed from direct control over the county assessor or his deputies," Hunn said.

The Des Moines lawyer clung to both positions in the face of a critical *Des Moines Tribune* editorial suggesting that he should resign. It was noted in the editorial that Hunn was, in fact, chairman of the county assessment conference that would choose the new Polk County Assessor and his deputies. "It is not illegal, perhaps, for a person to be in the employ of a special-interest group of taxpayers and at the same time to occupy a highly responsible and influential public office affecting the fairness of property assessments," the editorial said. "But the discreetness of this strikes us as most doubtful."

Over the next month Hiram Hunn filed suit against the Polk County Board of Assessment and Review to reduce the assessed value of farmland for various clients. How the Polk County Board of Assessment and Review would deal with the clients of Hiram Hunn and more than 2000 other protesters against the new higher assessments was the pending business on September 10, 1949, when I left Des Moines for a year of study on a Nieman Fellowship at Harvard University.

NEWS STORIES ENCOURAGE CLEAN GOVERNMENT

Although I was excited about the prospect of spending the 1949–50 academic year at Harvard, it was with some regret that I left the Polk County courthouse and the fascinating problems pending. The controversy over assessments was only the most recent and the most pressing of the problems. There were also the new reorganization of the county school system, the pending fraud indictments against former Sheriff Overturff and several other officials, and the question of whether County Attorney Ed Thayer, Sheriff Howard Reppert, and the new Democratic officeholders would continue the aggressive investigations and prosecutions and open government policies. I knew much depended upon the enthusiasm, diligence, integrity, and mental attitude of the reporters who would be given those assignments in my absence.

Many reporters would want to cover the Polk County courthouse now that it had become "a hot beat," but I knew that some of that number would shy away from the day-to-day work with records that was so important in developing story opportunities. They would not understand that it was the depth knowledge of the law, the background of the individuals, and the details of land descriptions and valuations that made the county budget manipulations or the county assessment disputes the fascinating front page stories of the last three years.

From my courthouse and police reporting experience, I learned that essentially any governmental function can be interesting once you become familiar with all of the nuances of the political struggles involved. But, it is important to understand that you cannot communicate the fascination of those battles to others unless you have thoroughly familiarized yourself with the subject matter, and have the ingenuity to crystallize those controversies into simple examples in clear direct language that can be understood by the average person with no expert knowledge.

STUDENT WORK PROJECT SUGGESTION

Students should be required to do a comprehensive paper on the state law governing assessment for local tax purposes. This paper should include tracing the title of one parcel of real estate back as far as county records exist. The paper should include both the legal description from the land plats and a commonly used description (street address or road location). The paper should include the last evaluation, the taxes paid or due, and the breakdown of tax rate for city, county, school, and other purposes. Students can use these papers for discussion of the fairness of the evaluations and the potential for frauds and inequities in the system.

17 INVESTIGATING AT THE IOWA CAPITAL

The investigative techniques used on county government were equally successful in forays into Iowa State government scandals and the general patterns of corruption were nearly identical. Take particular note of the following points while studying Readings 8 and 9.

1. The steps taken to avoid identification of the confidential sources.
2. The proper use of that source to obtain documentary evidence and leads.
3. The development of the story in a manner that made it unnecessary to make any reference to the confidential sources in the news stories.

A DREAM ASSIGNMENT

When I reported for work at the *Des Moines Register* at the completion of a Nieman year at Harvard University, I fully expected to go back to the Polk County courthouse to put the finishing touches on some pending projects. Instead, City Editor Al Hoschar told me that Managing Editor Frank Eyerly had decided to assign me to investigate state government operations.

I asked him if Eyerly had anything particular in mind, and Hoschar explained, "No. He just wants you to go up there and pry around to see what you can find. Cy Clifton will continue to cover state politics, and Lefty Mills will continue to cover the day-to-day developments. We don't want you to try to turn in a story every day or even every week. Just go up there and try to find out what is being stolen and who is responsible," Hoschar said. "Keep your own hours, and feel free to work with Mills if you need any help."

This was precisely the kind of an assignment I had been dreaming about, but suddenly I felt cold, lost, and a little afraid that I would not be able to produce. I didn't know the territory, and felt I could never top my performance at the courthouse. I didn't say it, but for a few moments I considered asking to go back to the familiar territory of the Polk County courthouse, at least for a few weeks. I knew where a few more "bodies" were buried, which would give a little spark to the routine court business that had to be covered every day.

Blueprint for Investigative Reporting

This would be a real test for my blueprint for investigative reporting. The first step was to learn the territory by studying the Iowa State law that established each department or agency and then, systematically, to become familiar with the services provided, the money expended, and the potential for fraud, favoritism, and conflict of interest.

The easiest and most comfortable way to become acquainted with government agency personnel and operations was to cover the day-to-day operations as I had at the municipal court and the Polk County courthouse. Word of my coming had spread around the Iowa capitol, and everyone was nervously on guard and fearful of being seen talking with me alone. All of the Iowa state officials, from Governor William S. Beardsley to Secretary of Agriculture Clyde Spry, were Republicans. They knew of my work in exposing the Republicans in the Polk County courthouse so they were cool or openly hostile. I longed for the help of a Paul W. Walters.

Remembering the earlier investigation by Switzer of the state car dispatcher's office, I made a routine examination of records and found no apparent irregularities in the way cars were being purchased and sold. Going by the office was enough to stir up the "animals" and let them know my interest in any tips on where the irregularities might be.

I also made a call at the office of the Iowa Liquor Control Commission, to demonstrate an interest in the purchases and prices in that 40 million-dollar-a-year state business. There is nothing like a couple of routine questions by a reporter on the size of the state liquor business or its purchase policies to set tongues wagging.

The Blueprint is Correct

About a month later, Elmer E. Drees, comptroller of the Iowa Liquor Control Commission, called to say he was being fired for disclosing examples of discrimination in liquor buying for the Iowa state stores. Liquor Commission Chairman A. A. Coburn said that the comptroller's post was a political job, and was being abolished

"in the interest of economy." However, Drees, who had been comptroller of the liquor commission for nine years, claimed that his
"fatal mistake" had been a report in which he called the attention
of the commissioners to a recent deviation from the formula that had
been set up to avoid "discrimination and favoritism" in the brands
of liquor purchased by the state.

There had been persistent rumors of political payoffs and
personal payoffs in connection with the brands bought for sale in
the state liquor stores. Although there were periodic political flurries
over these allegations, there had never been a real depth investigation
by the Republican-controlled legislature or by the Republican state
executive committee. The Iowa governor appointed the members
of the liquor commission, but, in recent years, had kept a hands-off
policy to avoid responsibility for controversial actions of the liquor
commission.

I hoped that, with a little persistent prodding for records and the
systematic questioning of all of the responsible officials, I would
be able to force the commission out in the open or force an investigation by the next legislature. It was not to be that easy.

I contacted a friend at the Iowa State Bureau of Criminal Investigation for an opinion as to what kind of new evidence would be
necessary to force a state investigation. He was not encouraging.
Although he agreed that an investigation of the Iowa Liquor Control
Commission was justified, he said that a direct order from the
attorney general or the governor was necessary to authorize an
investigation of a state agency. He thought it highly unlikely that
any Republican officials would open up such an investigation of
Republican appointees. The best hope for any meaningful investigation was to establish facts within the jurisdiction of the federal
liquor tax laws or the Democratic controlled Congress, the state
investigator said and added, "The involvement of any Democrats
in the payoffs or other irregularities could destroy that avenue."

Reading 8: Lew Farrell and the Alcohol Tax Unit

At about the time I was asking questions concerning the liquor
commission, I was asked to meet an agent for the federal Alcohol
Tax Unit (ATU). The agent and his teammate wanted to know what
I knew about Lew Farrell, the Capone mob's man in Des Moines.
Farrell and August J. Randa, one of Farrell's wife's relatives, had
filed an application for a basic federal permit to operate a wholesale
beer distributing warehouse in Des Moines.

The district supervisor in the St. Paul, Minnesota, office had
reviewed Farrell's criminal record, which was under the name of

Luigi Fratto in Chicago, and he was filing a notice that he was con templating denial of the permit. However, Farrell had been able to generate a lot of political support in the Treasury Department in Washington through his Chicago contacts. Therefore, the agents were trying to pull together everything they could on Farrell's record in Des Moines.

They had read my news stories about him being charged with illegal gambling in April 1948, as a result of a gambling raid on the Sports Arcade. Those charges had been dismissed by Polk County District Judge C. Edwin Moore with the approval of County Attorney Carroll Switzer. The agents were interested in anything I could tell them about the evidence, the circumstances, or the political pressures involved in Farrell's gambling case. I told them I would be happy to tell them anything I could, with the exception of the identities of my confidential sources, because I had been concerned and frustrated by Farrell's seeming political clout in both parties and his seeming invulnerability to any meaningful prosecutive effort.

I had been with Assistant County Attorney Clyde E. Herring and sheriff's deputies when they raided the basement gambling place on April 26, 1948. I had seen the deputies seize the records that tied Farrell to the operation of the Sports Arcade, and I had followed every step of the case from the raid through the filing of the county attorney's information against Farrell, Hymie Wiseman, and Al Cramm who were charged with violating gambling laws.

The seized papers included records showing the Sports Arcade paid $756 to the Mid-West-Illinois News Service Co. of Chicago, a nationwide horse racing service formerly operated by James M. Ragen. The bills for this horse race betting service carried Farrell's name, and an Iowa retail sales tax application listed Wiseman and Farrell as partners in the Sports Arcade. Despite this documentary evidence, Farrell denied any ownership or knowledge of the operations of the Sports Arcade.

"I am a close friend and lifelong buddy of Hymie Wiseman, but I am in no way connected with the operation of that place and no one has any proof that I am," Farrell told me. "I am a married man with a couple of children and I have been tending to my beer business . . . . For nine years, as long as I have been in Des Moines, I have had these people trying to link my name with all types of things but there is nothing to any of it . . . I wish people would forget that I happened to grow up in Chicago."

I told the federal ATU agents how the Iowa state tax commission had clamped a secrecy lid on the records of Farrell's application for an Iowa retail sales tax application. They wouldn't give it to me or to the county attorney on the theory that it was "a confidential business record."

The Polk County District judges had refused to sign a subpoena for the state records, which presumably should have contained a retail sales tax application with Farrell's signature. Polk County District Judge Moore held up the county attorney's use of business records seized in the raid because of a defense lawyer's argument that they were "confidential communications."

When County Attorney Switzer and his assistant Joe Marks went to Judge Moore's court to get his signature on the county attorney's information, I was present and witnessed the extreme reluctance of Judge Moore to sign the information. In fact, he did not sign it until after I had said that if he didn't sign it, I was going to want a full explanation of why. It appeared to me at the time that the judge was actually afraid to sign it. He signed it only after asking us to step out of the room while he made a call.

Then the situation became even more peculiar. Although Switzer had been eager and willing to push the prosecution of Farrell on a gambling conspiracy charge in mid-May, a few months later he became the moving party in asking that the charge against Farrell be dismissed on an agreement in which Wiseman, the listed owner of the Sports Arcade, and Al Cramm, an employee, plead guilty to a lesser charge of keeping a gambling house. The agreement was reached on November 17, 1948, a few days after Switzer was defeated by Republican William S. Beardsley in the campaign for Governor of Iowa.

Switzer was tired of being the aggressive prosecutor, and he fell back on the lame excuse that he would not spend public money prosecuting Farrell when it had been predetermined that certain key evidence linking Farrell to the Sports Arcade would not be admissible in the trial before Judge Moore. Switzer said the inadmissible evidence was an application allegedly filed by Farrell and Wiseman, as partners, for a state retail sales tax permit.

"It has been determined that the records of the state tax commission could not be used as evidence," Switzer said.

I explained to the federal ATU agents that I did not know whether Switzer's decision was a result of political pressure from Democrats or was an indication that his defeat had smashed his courage. Whatever the real reason, the mysterious power of Luigi Fratto, also known as Lew Farrell, seemed to be effective with Democratic as well as Republican political figures.

The ATU agents said that Farrell's brazen denial of association with the gambling operations of the Sports Arcade was in line with the false testimony he had given before a hearing officer of the ATU a few years earlier when he had obtained his first federal basic permit to wholesale Canadian Ace beer in Iowa. In that hearing Farrell denied that he had ever been arrested in Chicago, despite the fact that a number of the arrest records showed that the Luigi Fratto arrested listed the same home address and the same age. When faced with his police photograph in one case, Farrell then recalled "a police pickup," but not an arrest.

The hearing examiner said he believed that Farrell had given false and misleading testimony and ruled that, on the question of credibility alone, Farrell should not be given a beer wholesaler permit. The ATU agents explained that there "was some political hanky-panky in Washington." The regional director was overruled, and Farrell got his federal permit.

This was all news to me because it had taken place in a closed hearing in St. Paul. The regional recommendation against granting Farrell the permit was not made public, nor was the Washington decision that overruled the regional supervisor.

However, the fact that Farrell had switched from Canadian Ace to Blatz beer and was going into business with one of his wife's relatives under a new business name, was giving the regional director another chance to review the Farrell record. The two ATU agents were interested in running down every possible vulnerable point in Farrell's background. It was apparent that they believed, as I did, that Farrell's background did not justify approval of a federal permit to wholesale beer. The laws had been written to keep organized crime figures with their mobster competitive tactics out of the wholesale beer business.

The ATU agents titillated my curiosity with the comment that I would be surprised at some of the Des Moines people who had written letters of endorsement in favor of Farrell. Those letters were included in the secret hearing record. Unfortunately, the agents couldn't give me any documentation to support their comments that Farrell had committed perjury in the first hearing, or that Democratic political forces in Washington had forced the permit to be issued to Farrell. The hearing record was secret, and the agents said they could be fired if they were identified as having given me any information from those confidential files. As to the political pressure on the Farrell case, they only knew what was general talk around the agency, but those reports and rumors coincided precisely with what had happened in the case.

Despite the problem of protecting them as sources, my cooperation had paid off. I now knew that Farrell and August J. Randa were seeking a new basic beer wholesaler's permit and that an investigation was in progress in preparation for a hearing. That fact alone was a lead for a new story about Farrell that would justify reviewing his record, his connections, and his charmed life. I had other plans, too. I would make an effort to get the Bureau of Internal Revenue to open up the secret hearing record in which Farrell was apparently guilty of perjury. The way I viewed it, there was no justification for secret hearings on federal beer permits, and it was only a temptation for the agency heads to yield to political influence and pressure as had been done in the Farrell case.

I did not reap what I had sowed until months later, however. Just prior to the time those hearings started in early October 1950, Managing Editor Frank Eyerly told me that I was being transferred to the *Des Moines Register and Tribune's* Washington bureau. I was apparently the only one in the newsroom who had been unaware that my assignment at the Iowa statehouse was largely to give me broader experience for the Washington assignment.

Reading 9: The P-60 Scandal

Another most promising and most interesting investigation that was completed by a colleague involved reports that some prominent Republican politicians had persuaded Clyde Spry, the Iowa Secretary of Agriculture, to approve sale of a highly destructive salt-base antifreeze. The approval of the questionable antifreeze was against the advice of the state chemists, who said it was "excessively corrosive" and could create serious damage to automobile or tractor motors within a few weeks.

A few days after my first tip on this highly explosive story, I received a call from C. E. Miller, a young chemist in the Iowa Department of Agriculture. We arranged to meet secretly away from his office, and I agreed that anything he told me would be in the strictest confidence. He was very worried because he felt political influence was resulting in the approval of a substance that would destroy automobile and tractor motors. He was also fearful of being identified as a dissenter and of being fired from his job.

The young man told me that his superior, Mrs. Esther Johnston, the acting state chemist, was in total agreement with his view and had expressed her opinion in reports to Agriculture Secretary Spry prior to the time he had given approval to Producers Technical Corporation for the sale of P-60, the salt-base antifreeze. It was a shocking example of political influence overriding public interest for the financial profit of friends, but it seemed almost too bad to be true. Also, it included a lot of tests that might be read one way by Miller, but could be interpreted another way by another politically pliable senior chemist.

I asked Miller if it was as lopsided as he indicated. How could Secretary Spry justify approval to his own staff? Miller said that one of three batches of P-60 tested by Iowa State College at Ames, had been described as showing some "merit." The promoters had taken that one test with "merit" and twisted it into justification for overriding the objections of Mrs. Johnston.

Before taking a chance on this story, I wanted to review all the tests and reports by Iowa State. In dealing with technical studies, it is easy to oversimplify and end up in a vulnerable position. Miller understood my position and said he would help me in any way he could.

What I really wanted was a copy of the entire file, and I wanted to get it without Secretary Spry knowing of my interest in P-60. Miller said he had access to the file but could not be caught duplicating any part of it. Also, the file could not be taken out of the office because it was current business, and Spry or someone in his office might request it at any time. I suggested that, if he took the file out late in the afternoon and delivered it to me, I could have it photographed in the newspaper office and back to him within a few hours. This would make it possible to return it to its proper place in the evening, or in time for any early morning requests.

He agreed and I left the timing up to him. The mission was accomplished a week later along with the duplication of some letters and reports that were not in the file at the time of the first delivery. The file was so complete that it was unnecessary to check the public records.

Miller said he had told Mrs. Johnston that he had talked to me, but had not told her I had a duplicate of the office file on P-60. Although I would normally have called her to test her attitude, I deliberately avoided having any discussion with her so she could truthfully state that she had not talked to me or given me any information. My meetings with Miller took place in a quiet residential neighborhood more than a dozen blocks north of the Capitol.

Also, I had carefully avoided any discussions with Miller in any place where there would be any witnesses, except for one brief conversation in the Capitol corridor which was innocuous and he was free to relate it to anyone.

My upcoming transfer to Washington put some time pressure on the development of the P-60 story. However, I had sufficient time to do a quiet background of all of the political figures, businessmen, and chemists who might become involved in the controversy. I drew a brief chronology and a list of the people involved in the various testing. I kept City Editor Al Hoschar advised generally on the progress of the P-60 story, but did not go beyond him because of the inevitable leaks from newsmen to politicians. On the day I was ready to move, I asked Assistant City Editor Dixie Smith to accompany me to Spry's office for the confrontation, and gave him a quick briefing on key points I wanted to be sure to cover.

Although I had checked Spry's schedule to be certain he was in the city, I had not made an appointment. When Smith and I walked into his office, Spry had no idea what was in store for him and was unaware why we wanted to see him. I opened the conversation by saying we had heard some disturbing reports about the approval of a salt-base antifreeze and wanted to go over those reports with him to determine their value.

Spry was uneasy, but tried to appear confident as he acknowledged that he had approved P-60. He said the approval was given on the basis of an Iowa State College test, which demonstrated that P-60 "had merit" and "deserved a field test."

I went through the routine of asking him the name of the firm and the names of the owners and officers of the firm. He acknowledged that they were political friends of his and that one of their number, who was active in Iowa Republican affairs, had been chairman of the Polk County Republican Central Committee.

Spry declared that the promoters of P-60 had added "inhibitors" to stop the natural tendency of the salts to corrode a motor. As he read out of context and selectively from the material he found supportive of the decision to approve licensing of P-60, Secretary Spry said he was sorry he could not show us the entire file because it contained "confidential business secrets."

After letting him proceed with that tactic briefly, to see how much he would falsify the presentation, I stopped him on several incomplete and out-of-context statements to ask him if he was certain of those statements. Then, as he squirmed uneasily, I read from documents in the file on my lap. He grudgingly conceded that his initial comments had been abbreviated and misleading.

I did not identify the documents from which I was reading but merely kept him uneasy and off-balance until he was admitting that two of the Iowa State tests of P-60 had indicated the antifreeze was excessively corrosive. Then, without prompting, he acknowledged that his own chemists had registered strong disapproval of the licensing of P-60, and he was "taking a chance" on the basis of one Iowa State test that indicated P-60 "showed sufficient merit to warrant a field test." He acknowledged that even that report had warned that state approval should not be given until the field tests had been run, and admitted, "A field test has not been run."

"I know I'm sticking my neck out and these boys (the producers) could flood the state with this stuff (P-60), but they've told me they won't," Spry said.

By the time we were through, Spry had admitted all the facts in the file. It was not necessary to quote Mrs. Johnston or Miller in order to demonstrate the shocking misuse of authority. But Spry insisted that he was going to go through with his decision and put the responsibility on Iowa State College chemists. He said the sale of P-60 would be "limited" and would be "the field test" of the product.

The *Des Moines Register* lashed out critically and declared that, "the law of Iowa certainly does not contemplate testing such antifreeze on the general public when state chemists call them unsafe . . . . The state secretary of agriculture has no business permitting even the possibility of this," the editorial said.

A day later, Charles E. Friley, president of Iowa State College, and four Iowa State chemical engineering professors asserted that they did not approve the licensing of P-60 as an antifreeze. President Friley said Secretary Spry had "warped and twisted" the results of the college tests to support his approval.

"The secretary of agriculture and the promoters of this product have disregarded the real meaning of the (college) report, which says clearly that this antifreeze should not be approved for sale," Friley said.

For several days, in the face of sharp and growing criticism, Secretary Spry stubbornly clung to his approval of P-60. Finally, however, he yielded to public uproar and revoked the license for marketing of the salt-base antifreeze. By that time I was on my way to Washington and the story was written by George Mills, the long-time Iowa capitol reporter.

I read the Mills story in Washington with satisfaction. It had been one of the most successful exposés in my career, with total research, full documentation, and corroboration completed without a bobble. The reaction had been almost total public condemnation of Spry's actions, and the revocation of the P-60 license.

STUDENT WORK PROJECT SUGGESTION

Do an analysis of the functioning of any state regulatory agency. First, examine the law establishing the agency and list several specific areas of regulatory responsibility. Then, examine the law relative to the election and appointment of various regulatory officials and the stated qualifications of appointees that are established in the law or in agency rules and guidelines. Is there a specific compliance with the law or guidelines on qualifications of personnel? Interview business executives or individuals, who have been subject to actions by the agency, and listen for evidence of complaints of political favoritism or corruption. Interview the agency head and his key subordinates relative to the complaints or criticisms. Examine the public record for corroboration of the critics or the agency officials.

18 WASHINGTON, D.C.— DOWNEY RICE AND SENATOR KEFAUVER

The first depth experience in dealing with a congressional committee demonstrated the opportunity for effective reporting in proper and cautious cooperation with government investigators. It is essential for the reporter to know how a proper congressional investigation should be conducted to enable him or her to recognize when investigations are being bungled through incompetence, intentional sabotage, or restrictions that make them useless.

Development of a congenial working relationship with a congressional committee chairman or counsel can be important to gain an understanding of what congressional committees are doing, the limits of their jurisdiction, the location of public documents that can be used for story development without quoting the chairman, the counsel, or the congressional hearing record, and problems of government that are beyond the jurisdiction of the committee. If you gain a reputation for being a trustworthy reporter, it will be of benefit in getting tips and documents. Senators and congressmen as well as staff members who receive information of corruption and mismanagement will be willing to communicate information, even concerning matters beyond the jurisdiction of their committees or concerning other probes with which they do not want to be associated.

INTRODUCTION TO THE WASHINGTON SCENE

When I arrived in Washington in late October 1950, it was the second time I had been in the nation's capitol. The first time was a brief one-day visit as a tourist. On that hot June day I visited the Washington bureau of the *Des Moines Register and Tribune*, chatted briefly with Washington Bureau Chief Richard L. Wilson, and went to lunch with Bureau Manager Marr McGaffin.

Although I lacked Washington experience as a reporter, I had certain advantages over other green men. My year at Harvard had given me a chance to study Washington coverage systematically with experienced reporters, editors, and academics. I had studied the *New York Times* and the operation of *Times* Bureau Chief Arthur Krock, and had come to appreciate the work that made him a monument to integrity, independence, and competence in Washington journalism. I recognized that much of Krock's stature was owing to the broad influence of the *New York Times,* but I knew that Richard Wilson had many of the same qualities and had achieved a reputation and standing in Washington far beyond that of reporters for much larger newspapers than the *Des Moines Register and Tribune.*

I had hoped that Dick Wilson would give me some guidance and introduce me to a few of his contacts at the highest levels in Washington, but it was not to be. Wilson was a working bureau chief and he had neither the time nor the inclination to take my hand and lead me through the Washington wilderness. Wilson did his own story every day, plus a Sunday column for the Des Moines and Minneapolis newspapers. He also did periodic articles for *Look* magazine, and a monthly farm column for *Successful Farming* magazine. He didn't even want to review my stories before they went on the wire to Des Moines and Minneapolis.

Wilson let me know that I was on my own and that he believed I would do a good job for the Washington bureau because my coverage of local government scandals in Des Moines demonstrated I was "a self-starter." He was a wise man and he set only a few simple goals for reporters in the Washington bureau. "I like to have the bureau members try to be on the (story) schedule every day and to try to put together some special roundup for Sunday that will be of interest to people in Iowa or Minnesota."

Basic Duties

I was given the responsibility for the Iowa congressional delegation of eight congressmen and two senators. As the junior member of the Washington bureau, I would share with Wilbur Elston, new to Washington from Minneapolis, the chore of assembling the roll call votes each week for all Senators from Iowa, Minnesota, North Dakota, South Dakota, and Wisconsin, as well as the votes of the members of the House from those same states within the circulation area of the *Des Moines Register and Tribune* and the *Minneapolis Star and Tribune.*

Wilson explained that after taking care of the basic responsibility for the Iowa delegation, I was free to cover those areas that most appealed to me but to "try to set a schedule of making two new contacts a week—one for local stories and one for national stories. Setting that pattern will keep you out of the rut of seeing just the same people month after month and will eventually result in a wide range of contacts across the whole government," Wilson pointed out.

"Find something you like to cover, and concentrate on being the best in that field. I think people always do their best when they are doing something they like and are not hemmed in by restrictions," he said. "By the time you get here, you should know what you are doing, and I don't intend to nursemaid any member of the bureau."

Although there were a few times when I missed the direction of a city editor, most of the time I appreciated the freedom. In the first days the goal of turning in a story every day seemed too stringent, particularly when a story I was working on was not coming together fast enough. Dick had said it was not essential to be on the schedule every day, but he indicated he liked to maintain that standard. He was on the schedule every day as a pace setter and an example.

After several panicky evenings when I hurriedly wrote stories that were not yet ready to go, I decided to build a bank of stories that would be appropriate at almost any time for use in an emergency. These were the little feature items about Iowans in Washington, or hard news stories on situations that I knew no one else would be able to touch—stories out of the much-overlooked United States Tax Court, or stories out of the Census Bureau dealing with Iowa and the statistics of livestock and crop production. These are the routine things that a good reporter learns to do with his left hand. My real interest was in becoming expert on Washington investigations and eventually understanding it as well as I understood the Polk County courthouse.

Learning the Ropes

In those first months in Washington, Jack Steele, of the *New York Herald Tribune,* became my role model. Jack Steele and *New York Herald Tribune* Bureau Chief Bert Andrews were constantly scooping the *New York Times* and the Washington newspapers. They were constantly finding new developments on the major investigations of scandals in the Reconstruction Finance Corporation, the Defense Department, the State Department, and other agencies.

The *New York Times* had a great Washington bureau, with experienced and independent reporters on all beats, and yet, Steele and Bert Andrews were constantly beating them to the punch with stories that made it essential to read the *Herald Tribune* in order to have the last word on a story. The Steele stories were frequently reliable indicators of the direction the big investigations would take in the future.

Steele was an energetic, roly poly native of Indiana. He won the Raymond Clapper and National Sigma Delta Chi awards for Washington coverage in 1949 and was on his way to winning the Heywood Broun Award in 1951. Upon analysis, his formula was quite simple: excellent confidential sources in a number of agencies, total integrity in dealing with those sources, a wide range of contacts among congressional and agency investigators, a willingness to work hard studying old transcripts and records, a quick mind, and a highly competitive spirit.

It was apparent in following his stories that he had reliable confidential sources, but he did not carelessly endanger their identity. He knew his subjects thoroughly, and remembered more of the details than most of his competitors. He had done his research in the records of the agencies and congressional hearings. In the method of Lincoln Steffens, I was sure he was working on the basis of tips from staff investigators for congressional committees who wanted certain facts spotlighted. They were willing to point out the public records available for a reporter who would not quote them or otherwise reveal his sources.

THE KEFAUVER CRIME COMMITTEE

Even as I was learning from the exploits of Jack Steele, I was having my own first fruitful experiences in working with congressional investigators. Senator Estes Kefauver, of Tennessee, was involved in his great investigations of organized crime that were to set the stage for his effort to win the Democratic presidential nomination in 1952 and 1956. By the time I arrived in Washington, he had already become a major national headline figure as a result of hearings on crime in Kansas City, Chicago, Florida, Louisiana, and California.

Local crime reporters from coast to coast were having a field day in cooperating with Kefauver's investigators to expose new angles of the power of organized crime in politics, and to spotlight again the many unanswered questions on the crime links with politics. The formula was simple, and the mutual advantages were obvious. In nearly every major city in the United States, and in a good many smaller cities, organized crime had a control and often a stranglehold on the administration of justice through secret political support for prosecutors, sheriffs, and judges. In many areas this control and influence included governors, state legislators, and members of the House and Senate.

Crime reporters for local newspapers could write part of a story, but they also had other information that they could not write because of libel or because of a political partisanship of publishers or editors. Kefauver's lawyers and investigators used the local crime reporters as a basic source of information, and then used the subpoena and hearing processes of the Senate Crime Committee to obtain tax returns and business records that were out of the reach of the newspaper. The Kefauver Crime Committee could also bring public officials and mobsters into a public hearing room and, under oath, ask them questions they would never answer for a newspaper reporter.

Meeting Senator Kefauver

In my first weeks in Washington, I went to see Senator Kefauver in his office in the Old Senate Office Building. I had attended several of the hearings, and saw how a hearing before the Crime Committee could expose the entire Lew Farrell story (see Reading 8) in a manner beyond the scope of any criminal trial. Certainly, Farrell's political punch in the Democratic and Republican party in Iowa would not be effective in stopping Senator Kefauver if the really big mobsters like Tony Accardo, Frank Costello, Jake (Greasy Thumb) Guzik, and the Cook County Democratic machine had failed to stop the crusading Tennessee Democrat.

I introduced myself to Kefauver as a friend and Nieman classmate of Dick Wallace of the *Memphis Press-Scimitar.* The tall Tennessean smiled broadly and commented that he was fond of Wallace and had worked with him in breaking the power of the Boss Crump machine. In short order I spelled out the Lew Farrell problem in Iowa and his connection with the Capone mob in Chicago and the Gargotta brothers in Kansas City. I also called attention to the specific area of federal agency jurisdiction—the federal basic permit to wholesale beer.

Senator Kefauver said he was interested in getting to work soon on a new crime-control package and was limiting new investigations that were simply duplicative of earlier hearings. However, he was interested in hearing more about the issuance of a federal basic permit to wholesale beer despite Farrell's organized crime background in Chicago. It was a specific problem within the jurisdiction of the Alcohol Tax Unit (ATU) and the Internal Revenue Service

(IRS) and indicated improper political influences for organized crime figures at the top of those agencies.

Introduction to Downey Rice

Without making a commitment to conduct an investigation or hold a hearing on the Farrell case, Senator Kefauver arranged for me to talk with Chief Counsel Rudolph Halley and Associate Counsel Downey Rice. Halley talked with me briefly to determine whether I knew precisely what I was talking about. Satisfied that I did, he sent me to see Downey Rice at the old Home Owners Loan Corporation building, a short walk northwest from the Capitol. Halley commented that some reporters came in with few facts and a lot of wild suspicions that wasted the time of the committee investigators.

"When the committee was starting we could afford to do a little time wasting, but we aren't taking on anything new unless it is against a solid background of fact and for a specific reason," Halley explained.

It was my good fortune that Downey Rice was a quick perceptive lawyer-investigator, a master of the swift, effective investigation conducted with a minimum of effort, and had served as an FBI agent in the Des Moines office for a short time. He knew the territory and he was "interested in Luigi Fratto," consistently referring to Farrell by his true name. He saw immediately that the key documents he needed were Farrell's tax returns, the transcript of the closed hearings before the ATU hearing examiner in St. Paul, and copies of the order from Washington that overruled the regional director's initial decision to deny Farrell a basic federal permit to wholesale beer.

While I was in the office he called and requested copies of Farrell's tax returns and the ATU records. He mentioned that he had some vague recollection that Farrell's name had been mentioned at several points in the hearings in either Kansas City or Chicago, and suggested that I might want to read the transcripts of those records. Also, there had been considerable testimony about the Mid-West Illinois News Service Co., which had serviced the Sports Arcade, and the circumstances under which James M. Ragen, former owner of that horseracing wire service had been murdered.

Rice made it clear that our conversations on the Farrell case were off the record, and that I should not quote him or write that an investigation of Farrell was in progress until I had checked back with him or was quoting Chairman Kefauver. When he called me a few days later, he had received Farrell's tax returns and the transcript of the closed hearing before the ATU. Because of my familiarity with Farrell, he allowed me to read a part of the transcript of the closed hearing record so I could help him in his analysis. Properly, he did not let me see Farrell's tax returns.

Later Rice dropped the hint that Farrell's returns showed some gambling income, which directly contradicted Farrell's public denials, and said it would all become public at a hearing. I was very careful to obey his warnings about what could be printed. Rice learned I could be trusted, and the relationship I developed with him in dealing with the Farrell case was the start of a long and pleasant association that wound through important investigations of defense spending and major labor racket investigations. He was a totally reliable source, a wise adviser and a good friend.

Buildup and Delivery of the Story

The story that Lew Farrell was under investigation by the Kefauver Crime Committee was big news in Iowa. However, I sat on the story for several weeks, and then, when I wrote it, I kept it as straightforward and factual as possible, with only minor speculation on the focus of the possible hearings, even though I knew precisely what the record would show.

Over a period of weeks I periodically dropped stories that were gleaned from reading earlier hearings that dealt with Farrell in some minor way. These had been missed by the Associated Press coverage of the earlier hearings in Washington and in other parts of the country. It always pays to go back and review the transcripts of old hearings, particularly those that are staged outside Washington. Local reporters usually focus on some local issue and sometimes overlook important testimony or documents that deal with some national story. Contrariwise, the wire service reporters are so harried to find new story leads on a national story that they often overlook testimony or documents that would be of major significance in Des Moines, Denver, or Memphis.

Even potential big stories are overlooked because the wire service reporters are hurried and do not grasp the political significance of the testimony. In other instances, new testimony or a document may be the long sought piece of evidence of a political payoff or a government contract manipulation that will be recognized only by someone familiar with the details of the case.

Local Impact of the Hearings

By the time Lew Farrell's testimony started on March 24, 1951, I had been able to write a dozen or more stories that put in focus the many lines of questioning the Kefauver Committee might pursue. Farrell made his debut as a crime committee witness on national television, denying gambling income in the face of his own tax returns. He denied he was a part of organized crime, even as he admitted acquaintanceship with organized crime figures in Kansas City, Omaha, St. Louis, and Chicago, and also admitted he had driven to Harlan, Iowa, to help post cash bond when the notorious Gargotta brothers were jailed on a burglary charge.

He winced when he was asked if he had been known as "Cock-eyed Louis" Fratto in Chicago, and he insisted that his links with organized crime were "myths created by some newspapermen." He leaned heavily on his "clean record" in Des Moines, his participation in church affairs, and the lifetime membership he had been given by the Des Moines Junior Chamber of Commerce at a time when one of his friends was president and had relied upon Farrell to finance and organize Junior Chamber dances.

Farrell did not take the Fifth Amendment, but his testimony was so sharply contradicted by the documents that Chairman Kefauver suggested "perjury prosecution." Senator Charles W. Tobey, the ranking Republican on the crime committee, said there was no question in his mind that Farrell was "the Mr. Big in gambling" in Des Moines. "He contradicted himself with his pettifogging," Tobey declared. "He was anything but an honest witness."

Senator Lester Hunt, a Wyoming Democrat, said, "It was perjury without a doubt when he (Farrell) disclaimed knowledge of what was going on at the Sports Arcade when it was apparent from his income tax that he paid for the wire service."

Managing Editor Frank Eyerly was ecstatic over the televised hearing that exposed and discussed so many things that we had not dealt with because of libel problems, including Farrell's close relationship with Chief of Detectives Paul Castelline. Fletcher Knebel, the writer for *Look* magazine in the Washington bureau, and I covered the hearings. I wrote the major news story and Knebel did the color piece. We bought the entire transcript of Farrell's testimony and sent an edited version of it to Eyerly who used it in the *Des Moines Sunday Register.*

Eyerly, an enthusiastic supporter of my investigative efforts, was proud of the role I played in getting Kefauver to focus on the organized crime problem in Des Moines. I had accomplished it in less than five months in Washington. Also, I had laid out plans for a half dozen different investigations. These were all offshoots of the Kefauver crime investigation that indicated serious mismanagement in the Internal Revenue Service, the Department of Justice, and the Defense Department.

A SYSTEM DEVELOPS

I had developed what I believed was going to be a sure-fire system for investigation and follow through with congressional committees. This system evolved from a combination of my own experiences in Polk County, the operations that Jack Steele used so successfully, and my own experiences with the Kefauver Committee and with other congressional investigating committees.

From a standpoint of successful investigations, Washington was actually easier to cover than the Polk County courthouse or the Iowa capitol. A one-party Republican control made it difficult to get effective investigations moving in Polk County and at the Iowa statehouse. Washington was a genuine two-party town, where it was always possible to find senators or congressmen with an interest in pursuing and exposing mismanagement or corruption. Often theirs was a selfish interest for partisan advantage, but I was willing to risk almost any cooperative alliance that would expose wrong-doing in government. For myself, it was just good sense to be non-partisan and nonideological in the investigation of wrongdoing in Washington.

STUDENT WORK PROJECT SUGGESTION

1. Students should obtain the general rules for the operation of House and Senate Committees and should research any special rules that have been adopted to govern the procedures and conduct of permanent or special subcommittees with oversight responsibilities.

2. The student should analyze the rules obtained for project 1 with an eye to the history of investigative abuses that these rules were designed to control. The student should examine how these rules are being implemented. Are they being ignored, watered down, or misused and abused as political barriers to full and fair investigations of influential business or political leaders?

19 CONGRESSIONAL SPRINGBOARD

The reporter's responsibility for state and regional coverage of a congressional delegation is a great opportunity as well as a chore. Proper cooperation with reform-minded senators or congressmen can be the most beneficial relationship possible in the effective exposure of corruption and mismanagement. Caution should be exercised to avoid either a partisan or an ideological conspiracy that interferes with the independence of either the reporter or the legislator.

Although it is best to work with a legislator who is a senior member of the majority party, it is possible to gain valuable assistance from any reasonably honest member of the United States Senate or United States House of Representatives. They all want to appear able and effective in the eyes of the newsmen from their home state. The story of the small Iowa manufacturer's experience with a defense contract (Reading 10) demonstrates how a relatively inexperienced reporter can work with a weak United States Senator to develop documentation for an important local story dealing with Pentagon bungling.

SOURCES—MEMBERS OF CONGRESS

Developing and retaining a wide range of congressional sources is probably the most important thing a Washington newsman can do if he is even remotely interested in effective investigative reporting. On almost any investigative effort, the reporter must have allies in obtaining information that is not readily available from public sources. High-level allies are even more essential in getting the effective congressional investigation necessary to any legislative reform.

The Representatives from Iowa

I analyzed the Iowa congressional delegation in 1951 and found it far from stimulating. Republicans controlled all of the eight congressional seats. Some Republican House members were openly hostile because of my role in exposing the Republican frauds at the Polk County courthouse and at the Iowa capitol. They had heard from prejudiced sources that I was a Democrat, a wild-eyed liberal, and a hatchet man who might try to do them in. I had noticed a cold-eyed aloofness in the attitude of four of the Republican House members and a lack of cooperation on routine stories that was uncharacteristic in most people who have run for political office. The lack of cooperation did not bother me; it simply convinced me that they were wary because they had something to hide. I simply marked them for close examination at the first possible time. Nonetheless it was essential that I develop a working relationship with these men.

Ben Jensen was a big, frank Norwegian, a former lumberyard operator from Exira, Iowa, who had probably been a handsome man in his youth. In the first months in Washington, I went to his office on some routine matter, and he took the opportunity to hit me with a blunt accusation. "Young fella, my friends back in the district tell me you're a wild-eyed liberal Democrat and pretty close to bein' a Communist." Ben started his lecture in a loud voice pointing a finger at me. "They tell me you are always going around trying to upset Republicans, and just generally causin' trouble. The members of the delegation (all Republicans) have had a couple of meetings about you, and we don't like it at all that the *Register* sent you down here." He added that some members of the Republican delegation "are considering writing a protest letter to Gardner Cowles to try to get something done about you."

"I don't know where you are getting your information, but you are all wrong," I protested. "Have I written any story about you or any other member of the delegation that isn't true?" At that point I had only written routine stories on their views on legislation because I had been too much involved with much more interesting research. "I come from a Democratic family, but I'm not registered as a Democrat." I went on. "I have been registered as an Independent because I don't believe a reporter should have any partisan political leanings. I did help expose some Republicans who were stealing tax money. If they were your friends, I'm sorry that you have that kind of friends. Are you troubled because I exposed Clyde Spry (the Iowa Secretary of Agriculture) on the P-60 deal?" I asked. Did you want your farmers to have their trucks and tractors rusting out with that salt-based antifreeze? I know that some Republicans accused me of interfering with the free enterprise system because I exposed P-60."

"No. No." Ben interrupted to say he was not opposed to my P-60 stories or my exposing the Polk County crooks, but he had "heard you went too far sometimes and weren't right on your facts."

I said that I couldn't swear to the total accuracy of all of my stories, although I was unaware of any substantial factual errors and knew of no complaints from any of those I had dealt with except Lew Farrell, Pete Rand, and a few who I hoped he knew were liars. "I've exposed crooks, and I am going to keep on exposing crooks," I went on aggressively because I knew this was safe ground, "and I don't care whether they are Democrats or Republicans, liberals or conservative, or Communists. If you don't like it that's just too damned bad, because I had hoped I could get along with you."

"That's just the way I feel, young fella," Ben interrupted. "You're just the same way I was when I got into politics back in Exira. If you really mean it, we're going to get along okay. You shoot straight with me, and I'll shoot straight with you."

It was the start of a good working relationship with Ben Jensen who was a high-ranking member of the House Appropriations Committee and a well-liked member of the House club. Although he was never of any value as a spearhead on investigations, he was a ready source of reliable confidential information as to what took place in any closed meeting he attended, whether at the White House or in the appropriations committee.

Representative Karl LeCompte was a genial and easy-going publisher of a small newspaper in Corydon, Iowa. Even when the Republican freeze was on, he was pleasant to me and loved to gossip about Iowa political figures. He was a member of the House Administration Committee, and had strong, sincere beliefs that the government should be accountable to the people and the press. He was not energetic, nor was he ever dynamic enough to have been effective if he had been inclined to be a boat rocker. He was honest, was occasionally helpful in obtaining some information that would not have been available to me otherwise, and was always willing to express his disagreement with the Republican leadership.

Representative Thomas E. Martin was the senior member of the Iowa Republican delegation and used his position as "dean of the delegation" to try to impose an oath of secrecy on other Republican members. He tried to instigate a policy of noncooperation with me based upon his information about me from his political lawyer friend in Iowa City. Even as he was trying to get others to write to the publisher of the *Des Moines Register* to make some vague complaint about me being a partisan Democrat, Martin was deceptively friendly. He told me that he would like to tell me about "secret meetings of the delegation" but that the members had decided not to say anything. It was a deception designed to give the impression that he was my friend and champion.

Tom Martin was a member of the House Armed Services Committee and fancied himself as an expert on military tactics as a result of service as a lieutenant in World War I. He had also been an assistant professor of military tactics in a military reserve program at the University of Iowa. He would go into exasperating detail if asked any question involving problems before the House Armed Services Committee, but he wasn't useful for an objective report on any discussion of a military controversy.

In the military area I was fortunate to have cultivated Congressmen from other states. Representative F. Edward Hebert, of Louisiana, and Representative Porter Hardy, of Virginia, were accurate, tough, and willing to challenge the Pentagon bosses—military or civilian—on allegations of "fixed contracts" and military coverups. By contrast, Tom Martin always saw himself as on the inside with the military leaders and ended up defending them regardless of the facts.

Paul Cunningham, who represented Des Moines and Polk County, had practiced law with some of the lawyers for those prosecuted in the Polk County frauds. He did not like me but tried to cover it up with an effusive, friendly welcome every time I appeared in the office. He was quick to offer assistance with information from any agency of government but was ineffective in getting results. His wife, who was on his congressional payroll, was in the office every day. The wife of his administrative assistant was also on the payroll, but during that time nepotism was not illegal.

Representative Charles B. Hoeven, lawyer and president of a savings bank in Alton, Iowa, was a member of the House Agriculture Committee and was most helpful in getting a fast and intelligent summary of the central controversy on agricultural legislation. Although he was initially cool to me, he became a good friend and an excellent source soon after I started writing stories about the Democratic scandals in the Truman Administration. Up to that point, he feared that I might be a Democratic hatchet man.

Perhaps the most useless member of the Iowa delegation, as far as I was concerned, was Representative James Dolliver, an amiable Fort Dodge lawyer. He was middle of the road in his philosophy and was without any deep feelings on any subject. When he was elected to the House, it was because of the reputation of his uncle, the dynamic United States Senator Jonathan P. Dolliver—a giant in Iowa politics from the turn of the century.

Jim Dolliver was an inactive member of the House Judiciary Committee; he rarely knew much about the controversies in that important committee and made no more than token attendance at committee meetings. For several years, he paid close attention to his attendance at House votes, but he was only present at about 35 per cent of the votes in his last disastrous term when he took a month's vacation in Alaska during the busiest part of the session.

The academic of the delegation was Representative Henry O. Talle, a conservative, former professor of economics at Luther College. He was a traditional conservative Republican, a professional Norwegian with close personal ties to the Norwegian Embassy, and a member of the House Banking and Currency Committee. He was of limited value as a source of information on the Banking and Currency Committee, but his office was aggressive in following through on the problems of the farmers and businessmen in his district. He was of help on the details of the problems of business-men in his district, which were often typical of the problems of other Iowa and midwestern businessmen. In this respect his office was useful to me in gaining an understanding of the business problems of the area.

The eighth member of the Iowa Republican delegation was Representative H. R. Gross, who had defeated an incumbent Repub-lican in the 1948 primary. In defeating a well-liked member of the Republican organization, Gross won the bitter enmity of the conservative organization Republicans who considered him to be dangerously liberal. That, of course, did me no harm. Gross, with only a low-ranking position on the Post Office and Civil Service Committee, was a better news source than any of the other Repub-lican members of the Iowa delegation.

A former radio newsman, Gross was not afraid to tackle any members of the Democratic or Republican leadership. He was a fine parliamentarian with the ability to tie up the whole House in order to stop hasty actions on legislation, such as congressional pay boosts, which usually had the backing of both the Democratic and Repub-lican leadership. Gross knew how to get the General Accounting Office (GAO) to do responsible investigative work for him, and he knew the kind of letters to write to the executive branch agencies to raise serious economic and ethical questions that no one else wanted to raise. My relationship with Gross was beneficial from the first months, although it was somewhat cautious until I had tested him. I found him to be equally critical of frauds and mis-management whether in Republican or Democratic administrations.

The Senators from Iowa

On the Senate side, I had a convenient split delegation. Senator Hickenlooper usually followed the Republican leadership position, and Senator Guy Gillette generally followed the lead of the liberal Democrats. It gave me an opportunity to explore both sides of all major national issues, and, through the arguments of Hickenlooper and Gillette, to present Iowa readers with rational arguments on both sides of most issues.

Both Iowa senators were on the Agriculture Committee and the Foreign Relations Committee. Hickenlooper was a former chairman and the ranking Republican member of the Joint Congressional Committee on Atomic Energy, which was much in the news. Although Hickenlooper had come under severe criticism from the *Des Moines Register* editorial page for his controversial efforts to oust David Lilienthal from the chairmanship of the Atomic Energy Commission, he was friendly to me and was a reliable and coopera-tive source on a wide range of political and governmental issues. If a real issue of national security was involved, he was tight-lipped and responsible. However, he was a sharp critic of phony national security to cover up frauds and blunderings by bureaucrats or politicians.

Handsome, silver-haired Guy Gillette looked every inch the statesman senator, but any close examination of his record demon-strated that he was not the forceful far-seeing legislator he seemed to be on first glance. He was a favorite of the *Des Moines Register* editorial page because he usually found some way to do what the *Register* suggested, regardless of his original position.

On issues that were highly controversial with his Iowa constitu-ents, he often equivocated—arguing both sides of the issue right down to the wire on his votes. He often had a speech on one side of an issue, and a last minute vote and speech on the other side. He would answer letters with the copy of the Congressional Record speech or action that coincided with that of his inquiring constituent. However, he managed it all with such convincing sincerity that he ruffled few feathers, except for those with a direct personal interest and a reason for following through.

Gillette's office would make convincing appeals to agencies on behalf of constituents. Because he usually did not call these matters to the attention of the press, he was not required to follow through when the agency gave him and the constituents a clever bureaucratic brushoff. Senator Gillette was not a man seriously to challenge an agency action on behalf of a constituent if he could dodge the issue.

Reading 10: Defense Contract Bungling

Only a few months after I arrived in Washington, I wrote my first story on a problem that a small Iowa manufacturer had taken to Senator Gillette with regard to an obvious injustice on a small defense contract. I did not hear about it from Gillette's office, but from the small businessman, Joseph P. Lawlor, owner and operator of the General Filter Company, of Ames, Iowa.

Lawlor, who was then the mayor of Ames, called me and came to my office in the National Press Building. His complaint was simple. He had been squeezed out of an Air Force contract for 104 mobile water demineralizers although he had been the low bidder and was fully qualified to perform the contract. Lawlor's original bid on the 104 mobile demineralizers was $348,000—more than $61,000 lower than the next lowest bid by the Refinite Corporation, Omaha, Nebraska. He explained that the Air Force arbitrarily tossed out all bids on the contract and negotiated with the Refinite Corporation for a still higher price of $422,000 under a deal where the price could raise to $443,000—nearly $100,000 above Lawlor's bid.

This was my first serious examination of a Defense Department contract controversy, and I could hardly believe Lawlor's story. If he was right on his facts, the Pentagon was virtually throwing away something between $60,000 and $100,000 by ignoring a responsible low bidder. Fortunately, it was a relatively small contract that involved construction of a simple wheeled cart for demineralizers used in treating the water for military aircraft. Lawlor assured me there was no way the Air Force could claim that a sensitive national security issue was involved.

Still disbelieving that such a clear case of discrimination could exist, I questioned Lawlor extensively and asked to examine the documents on the dispute. While examining them, I noted a letter to Senator Gillette. The records checked with Lawlor's account, and he acknowledged that he had asked Senator Gillette's office to make inquiry. He had been advised, by Senator Gillette's office that they would look into the contract problem, but he was asked not to make a public fuss so they could try to settle it quietly. He became dissatisfied with the progress by Gillette's office and called me, he said.

I was now convinced that there must be some element that Lawlor had not disclosed, for I did not believe that Defense Department officials would dare such a brazen and wasteful action in the face of a senatorial inquiry. The Air Force press office routinely confirmed the basic facts related by Lawlor, and the spokesman speculated that there must have been some serious question about Lawlor's ability to perform the contract. I said it seemed possible, but not likely because a water demineralizer was a simple mechanism.

With Lawlor I went over his qualifications to complete the contract, including the training and education of his personnel. To my casual observation they were qualified and probably overqualified from a standpoint of college degrees and work experience. Lawlor assured me there could be no question about this.

At this point I called Cy Farr, secretary and press spokesman for Gillette, to ask him what response Gillette's office had received from the Pentagon. He acknowledged that the office had made inquiry, but said they were proceeding without publicity in the hope they could settle it quietly. I said it appeared to be an outrageous waste of tax money, and that the Air Force was still making excuses indicating Lawlor's firm was not qualified. Senator Gillette should initiate an investigation, haul the Air Force procurement officials before a Senate committee, and grill them in the same manner that Senator Kefauver was using in the crime probe. I suggested the Senate Small Business Committee as the forum, or a subcommittee of the Senate Armed Forces Committee.

Cy Farr agreed that the Senate Small Business Committee was probably the best forum, and said that he would suggest it to Senator Gillette. He called me back a little later to say that Senator Gillette would arrange for Lawlor to explain his case to the Senate Small Business Committee investigators. I envisioned a hearing in which top Air Force officials would be called to explain what seemed to be a raw "fix" that would add more than 45 per cent to the cost of a defense contract.

Instead, on February 12, 1951, Senator Gillette simply accompanied Lawlor to the Senate Small Business Committee staff room where Lawlor repeated the story that he had told me and that Gillette's office already knew. This was a vehicle for putting the whole sordid story together with Lawlor's claim that he was "squeezed out" of a defense contract. I quoted one investigator as saying, "It appears to be a clear-cut case of discrimination. The top Air Force procurement officers are going to be asked to explain this case." The investigator said the Lawlor case was "one of three or four the committee will take up." Also, Senator Gillette said he had personally called the case to the attention of Charles E. Wilson, defense mobilization director.

A few days later, the Air Force reported back to Gillette on what was purported to be an Air Force investigation of the handling of the Lawlor case. Although the report came from the office of Undersecretary of the Air Force John A. McCone, it was obviously superficial and little more than a rewriting of reports from the field offices to parrot weak excuses rather than give responsible explanations. McCone reported to Gillette that unidentified Air Force experts had concluded that the bid by Lawlor's firm was so low he couldn't make money on the contract, that the plant facilities were inadequate, and that the firm lacked sufficient capital.

Under my questioning, Senator Gillette said the Air Force report was not satisfactory and explanations were "inconsistent and unsatisfactory." The genial Iowa Democrat did not really want to quarrel with the Air Force, and the Air Force officials knew that it was easy to give Guy Gillette a snow job without risking trouble.

I called the Air Force for further explanation as to what kind of an investigation had been done, and drew the admission that the Washington officials had simply examined the records submitted by Lt. General Benjamin W. Childlaw, head of the air material command at Wright-Patterson Air Force base. The Air Force said the records were examined by a lieutenant colonel whom they refused to identify, and the report was written for McCone's signature.

During questioning, the spokesman left the room for consultation and returned to say the Washington air force office "has no responsibility in the matter. We simply rewrote a report and submitted it to Senator Gillette," the spokesman said. "The department is taking the stand that it is too busy to investigate (such small contracts) and must depend on reports submitted from the field. "Of course now that the senate is going to investigate this, we'll go into it more thoroughly," the Air Force spokesman added.

The brazen gall of the Air Force irritated me, and I concluded that I never would accept as fact a letter or report simply because it was signed by a high defense department official. It was now obvious that McCone's name was being used to give weight to the report, and that he had no understanding of the facts except probably as explained to him by some unidentified lieutenant colonel.

Under my prodding, the Air Force finally produced a report two months later, on April 13, 1951, in which Air Force Secretary Thomas K. Finletter said the procurement officials were in error in the conclusion that Lawlor's firm did not have adequate facilities or financing to fabricate the Air Force mobile demineralizers. However, the report excused the erring procurement officials for their decision to negotiate rather than take the low bid. The report rationalized that the country was "in a state of emergency," and "the question of whether facilities are adequate is often a difficult question and calls for the exercise of judgment."

The indecisive Senator Gillette let the Small Business Committee investigation be terminated, even though the Air Force indicated it would not reverse itself and award the contract to Lawlor nor direct any disciplinary action against the officials who had admittedly erred. That was the unsatisfactory situation in early May when I received a call from Joe Lawlor.

Lawlor had received a letter from Wright-Patterson, dated after Air Force Secretary Finletter's letter, notifying him that his firm was not qualified to bid on mobile demineralizer contracts. It was another gross blunder, and I immediately called James T. Hill, the general counsel for the Air Force. Hill said there had been no subsequent ruling against Lawlor, that it was another error, and he made an immediate long distance call to Wright-Patterson to correct the blunder. He said he could give no explanation as to why Major Charles W. Atterholt, a contracting officer at Wright-Patterson, would have sent a letter to Lawlor stating that his firm was "not qualified."

Having the Air Force in another tight bind, I pressed for access to the special inspector general's report. This report was the basis of Finletter's letter ruling that Lawlor's firm was qualified and establishing the responsibility for the earlier erroneous ruling.

Hill said the inspector general's report showed no evidence of ulterior motives or corruption on the part of the officials involved in the judgment that Lawlor's plant was not qualified. He reluctantly identified the key official as Albert King, a procurement officer in the Chicago office. Hill said the inspector general's report showed that King used poor judgment in the following ways:

1. King notified Lawlor that his plant facilities were inadequate without going to the plant to inspect those facilities.
2. King arrived at a decision that Lawlor's plant was not adequate after a conversation with procurement officers from Wichita, Kansas, who had never seen the Lawlor plant.
3. Later, King was wrong again in his second judgment that the Ames plant was inadequate after Lawlor insisted that King make an actual inspection of his plant. He was wrong on his facts.

Although Hill admitted there were a large number of errors, he concluded that, since the procurement officers handle great volumes of business, mistakes are to be expected. The procurement officers in the Wichita office who had said Lawlor's firm was inadequate had dealt with the Refinite Corporation of Omaha, and liked to do business with that firm, Hill said.

"The case was full of mistakes," Hill told me. "Thank heaven we don't have many cases that have been handled like this one."

I wondered if Hill, the inspector general, or anyone else in the Air Force knew the number of mistakes, minor favoritisms, and outright frauds that were covered up each year. The Air Force would not have investigated this one if I had not alternately prodded and encouraged Senator Gillette to follow up. Even then it was necessary to make my own investigations of the inadequacies of the Air Force investigations.

For the *Sunday Register* of May 15, 1951, I tried to round up this shocking story of one blunder after another involving the Iowa firm. "This is the story of how badly a defense contract can be bungled by the armed services without resulting in disciplinary action," I wrote as a reminder to myself as much as to my readers. The internal investigations of the Defense Department are often "whitewashes" and "coverups" that fall just short of criminal obstruction of justice.

VALUABLE LESSONS

Even though it was an unsatisfactory conclusion, I learned many important lessons that served me well in later investigations of multimillion and multibillion-dollar defense contracts. I was sharply disappointed in Senator Gillette. However, I mentioned him favorably in my reports in the hope that it would encourage him and other members of the Iowa delegation to be more diligent in their responsibility to police the operations of executive branch agencies.

The experience with Joe Lawlor's contract bidding was important for a realistic view of investigative reporting in Washington. It taught me:

1. Not to be afraid to challenge any decision.
2. Not to accept any self-serving claim that an investigation has been thorough and complete.
3. That a high level official's signature on a letter to Congress does not mean that the official knows or understands the contents of the letter.
4. That there is essentially no limit to the falsifications and deceptions that the Pentagon bureaucracy will stoop in obstructing an inquiry that is embarrassing.

5. That even when proved wrong, the Pentagon bureaucracy will find ways to refuse to award a contract to "a whistle blower."

STUDENT WORK PROJECT SUGGESTION

1. Do a brief background sketch on the two United States Senators from your state and list their committee and subcommittee assignments and other areas of interest. Give an assessment of each of them from the standpoint of the assistance they might give you on investigations of corruption or mismanagement in federal agencies.

2. Do the same kind of analysis of three members of the United States House of Representatives from your region.

20 NATIONAL NEWS OF LOCAL INTEREST

Most investigations must have a local angle to arouse interest but certain people are so newsworthy in themselves that they always make good copy. The various forays of Senator Joseph R. McCarthy, the Wisconsin Republican, were among the biggest news stories in the period when I was breaking in as a Washington reporter. Anyone following congressional investigations was certain to know him, for he was the ranking Republican member of the powerful Senate Permanent Investigations Subcommittee. Later he destroyed himself with his excesses as chairman of that investigations subcommittee.

The simple fact that Senator McCarthy was the center of almost constant controversy made it important to know him and to follow a few of his investigations. Although I was not one of the constant McCarthy watchers and critics, I followed him closely enough to conclude that he was not a sound investigator, that he had a good many irresponsible political opportunists in his entourage, that he was careless about conflicts of interest, and that he was flying too high, and living in a style he could not afford.

A RELUCTANT INVESTIGATOR

Senator Joseph McCarthy's activities became of direct interest to me in 1951 when Senator William Benton, a liberal Democrat from Connecticut, leveled ten charges involving possible illegal, improper, or unethical conduct at him. That investigation fell under the jurisdiction of the Senate Privileges and Elections Subcommittee, which was chaired by Senator Guy M. Gillette, of Iowa. The cautious Iowa Democrat had no stomach for the investigation, but, under the prodding of his Democratic colleagues, he reluctantly permitted the staff lawyers and investigators to study the allegations against McCarthy. Senator Gillette avoided any reference to the progress of the investigation citing propriety, but it was his fear of McCarthy that prompted his reticence.

Paying little but routine attention to Senator Gillette, I kept in close touch with the staff investigators. I knew they were preparing a documented report that would be particularly devastating in detailing questionable financial dealings with the Lustron Corporation, a firm that manufactured prefabricated housing, during a period when McCarthy was chairman of the senate committee on housing legislation.

Senator McCarthy, aware of Senator Gillette's lack of political courage, went on the attack on December 6, 1951, charging that Gillette's subcommittee was "spending tens of thousands of dollars" without authority to investigate his background. He claimed Gillette was using the Benton charges as an excuse to dig up campaign material for the Democrats for the 1952 election. Senator Gillette denied the charge, but his nervousness raised considerable doubt in the staff that the report on Senator Joseph McCarthy would ever be made public.

Nonetheless, the study was completed and corrected, and read and reread, while the staff and Democratic members of the Senate Subcommittee tried to get Senator Gillette to authorize release or even to bring it up for discussion in the subcommittee. Chairman Gillette was obviously afraid that he would be the next subject of Joe McCarthy's venom if he took any step to release it.

Two Reporters are Sometimes Better than One

I had seen a copy of the staff report, and knew that it came down hard on McCarthy for accepting $10,000 for writing a pamphlet on housing for Lustron while he was chairman of a Senate housing committee. My source let me read the report, but would not let me take notes. I was only able to remember a few phrases, certainly not enough to go out on a limb on my own on such a hot story.

I told my friend, Edward J. Milne, Washington correspondent for the *Providence Evening Bulletin* (which had no circulation overlap with the Des Moines newspapers) that the report existed, that I hoped to get another look at it, and suggested that he use some of his New England sources who were close to Senator Benton. I was sure that Benton had a copy of the report or could get one from the staff if he tried. I told him of my own fears that Senator Gillette would delay and delay because of his fear of McCarthy and that the report would never be released.

A few days later, Milne told Senator Benton and a member of his staff that he had heard about the report and of our desire to break the story and force publication so the Senate would not be able to duck its responsibility on the issue. Not long after, Milne received a call from someone on Benton's staff who told him to come up to the office. After brief conversation, he was left alone in the office with the suggestion that, if he was observant, he might find something of interest to him. The report was lying open on the table, Milne told me. He read it, took notes at will, and several hours later put the report back where he had found it and left the office. He did not identify the person who made these arrangements and I did not ask him because we both knew that we might be under subpoena if the story on the report caused the storm we expected.

I checked my sketchy notes and my recollection of what the report contained with the notes Milne had made. We agreed to break the story simultaneously in the *Providence Evening Bulletin* and in the *Des Moines Tribune,* the afternoon newspaper. I would have preferred that we break the story in the *Des Moines Register,* the morning paper that carried the Washington bureau stories most of the time, but Milne wrote for the afternoon paper and had no flexibility.

Results of Publication

Our stories, published in Des Moines and Providence on February 20, caused more of a storm than we had expected. Senator McCarthy and his friends were furious because they believed they had frightened Senator Gillette into inaction. Senator Gillette was furious because McCarthy and some of his supporters believed Gillette, an Iowa senator, was responsible for a "leak" to the leading newspaper in his home state. In this case, the normal deduction that Gillette would leak to an Iowa newspaper was far off base. Indeed, if Senator Gillette had been moved to "leak" the report, it would have been to some reporter far removed from Iowa.

Although the storm died within a few weeks, the pressure mounted on Senator Gillette to take some effective step to find out who had leaked the staff report on McCarthy. He called me to come to his office and was all smiles and persuasiveness as he asked me to tell him who had given me a copy of the report against his instructions. When I said I could not reveal my source, he changed his tone. He said I had embarrassed him as chairman of the committee, that he was suspected of having given me the report, and that he intended to issue a subpoena and take other steps to force me to disclose my source.

However, even as McCarthy was engaging in harassment of Gillette about the "leak" of the report and the lack of progress on finding out the source of the leaks to me and Milne, the Senate, by a 60-0 vote, authorized the Gillette subcommittee to continue with its probe of McCarthy. On April 19, 1952, a subpoena signed by Senator Gillette was served on Eddy Milne to try to force him to reveal the source of the secret staff report. Reportedly, he had also signed a subpoena for me, but had not directed that it be served. Although Milne was actually brought before the subcommittee and refused to testify, there was no action to cite him for contempt, so that matter died. By that time Milne and I had taken an informal poll of sentiment on the five-member Senate Privileges and Elections Subcommittee and its parent, the Senate Rules Committee. We believed that a majority would oppose a citation for contempt.

In mid-May, Chairman Gillette started the hearings on the charges as recommended by the staff report which we had made public. Under the chairmanship of Senator Gillette, the Senate Privileges and Elections Subcommittee investigation of McCarthy fumbled forward in an uncertain manner. It was an election year, and Senator Gillette was under constant attack from Senator McCarthy and Senator Herman Welker, an Idaho Republican who was an outspoken McCarthy supporter on Gillette's committee. On the one hand, Welker charged Gillette with playing politics with the committee while, on the other hand, Democrats were critical of Gillette for delays in the McCarthy investigation.

On September 25, 1952, Senator Gillette submitted his resignation as chairman of the investigation subcommittee to Senator Carl Hayden, the Arizona Democrat who was chairman of the Senate Rules Committee. The Gillette resignation effectively destroyed the McCarthy investigation. However, the stage was set for action on the issues that resulted in the historic censure against McCarthy two years later.

FUTURE REPERCUSSIONS

Senator Ralph Flanders, a pleasant New Hampshire Republican became embroiled in a dispute with McCarthy in early 1954 because he criticized McCarthy's crusades against Communists for taking the nation's attention off of more important business. When McCarthy launched a bitter counterattack, Senator Flanders' attention was directed to the tough documented report written by the Senate Privileges and Elections Subcommittee staff charging McCarthy with improper financial dealings and unethical political behavior. Flanders expressed shock upon reading the two-year-old staff report.

On June 11, 1954, Senator Flanders walked into the Army-McCarthy hearing and handed Senator McCarthy a letter notifying him he intended to attack him in a speech that afternoon. That same afternoon, Flanders filed in the Senate a motion to strip McCarthy of his chairmanships of the Senate Government Operations Committee and of the Permanent Investigations Subcommittee unless he purged himself of the charges of improper financial and political behavior detailed in the staff report of the Senate Elections Subcommittee in 1952.

Journalistic Reflections

Ed Milne and I got a great deal of satisfaction in knowing that our efforts had forced the Gillette committee to publish the report in 1952. At the time we were planning to break our exclusive stories on the report, there was no way that we could have forecast that the report would be a time bomb, lying dormant for more than two years until detonated by a mild-mannered senator who stumbled on to it. Political impact is often a matter of timing, and the reporter who remembers the contents of old and dusty reports can often find ingredients for some new explosive stories when those reports fall into the hands of someone who has a use for them.

I believe that "pack journalism" in Washington is as destructive to real competition as the "pool agreements" and other similar deals among reporters covering local government. However, a certain amount of cooperative team effort can be helpful if the newspapers are not directly competitive, if the goals are generally the same, and if each reporter can provide a specific ingredient whether it is knowledge of a local political situation, details on a local crime ring, or depth background on either the facts or the law.

It is often helpful to have the impact of a story breaking in two or three areas so the wire services will not be able to ignore it. Wire services often ignore significant stories printed in cities outside of Washington and New York. Even the Chicago and Los Angeles newspapers suffer from their remoteness from Washington and New York, and the problem increases as the hometowns of the newspapers become smaller.

STUDENT WORK PROJECT SUGGESTION

Write a paper explaining why sources in Senator Benton's office would be likely to cooperate with a reporter from a Providence newspaper. Explain why it was important to publish a story on the report on Senator McCarthy's involvement in a questionable financial transaction. Also, explain the reason for the arrangement in which Ed Milne was not personally handed the report but was left in a room where it was available to him to use as he saw fit.

21 IT IS THE FOLLOW THROUGH THAT COUNTS

Nearly every major congressional investigation develops some evidence that is outside the direct jurisdiction of that committee. Frequently that evidence and related documents point in the direction of serious corruption and mismanagement that is directly within the jurisdiction of another committee. An aggressive follow through can persuade or prod the committee with direct jurisdiction into taking action.

This chapter illustrates how several reporters were able to use evidence and leads that surfaced in the Kefauver Crime Committee investigation to create pressure for investigations that centered on tax scandals in the Treasury and Justice Departments. By piecing together information from various hearings and executive agency sources, it was possible to establish that there was no justification for the secrecy on tax-exempt institutions and Alcohol Tax Unit hearings and that this excessive secrecy permitted a cover-up of questionable decisions. Depth research on the operation of these Treasury Department agencies made it possible to force reluctant officials to remove the unjustified secrecy on hearings and records. Systematic research on specific cases and persistent questioning of policies from a number of news organizations created the pressure for change.

THE DANGERS INHERENT IN SECRECY PROVISIONS

Senator Estes Kefauver put an end to his Senate crime hearings in 1951 to launch his campaign for the Democratic nomination for President. For a good many reporters the next steps were follow up stories on criminal indictments and prosecutions in state and federal courts. The voluminous hearings and reports on crime in America contained more than colorful yarns about mobsters cavorting with politicians. There were literally dozens of leads on serious problems in the nation's governmental and political institutions that had barely been touched, and there was much solid evidence from which to launch new investigations. Much of that evidence had piled up in the records unnoticed because of the wealth of material the investigators had uncovered.

It can be said that the tax scandal investigations, Justice Department investigations, and labor racket investigations were all off-shoots of the Kefauver crime investigations. Kefauver's crime probe spotlighted the favored treatment that the Bureau of Internal Revenue accorded Tony Accardo, one of the bosses in the Capone mob in Chicago.

The questioning of top federal tax officials by the House Ways and Means Committee in February 1951 was the first opportunity I had to stimulate the followup questioning on how members of the gambling fraternity were able to avoid giving detailed answers to income tax investigators. I went to Representative Tom Martin, an Iowa congressman who was a new member of the House Ways and Means Committee, to suggest a line of questioning for the February 7, 1951, appearance of George L. Schoeneman, Commissioner of Internal Revenue, and Charles Oliphant, the chief counsel for the Bureau of Internal Revenue. Since the line of questions would put the Truman Administration officials on the spot, Republican Tom Martin was willing and even eager to follow my suggestions.

The Iowa congressman told Schoeneman and Oliphant it was hard for him to see how the American people could be asked to pay more and more taxes when evidence indicated such apparent discrimination in the tax collection system. Martin's specific question concerned how Chicago mobsters, Tony Accardo and Jack (Greasy Thumb) Guzik, could defy an internal revenue agent and refuse to give details of their income from gambling rackets.

Schoeneman refused to give a public explanation on the handling of the mob's income tax matters, and Oliphant said the bureau would "stand on a technicality" in the law and would refuse to discuss any income tax matters in public.

Martin noted that the Kefauver records showed that Accardo and Guzik formed a partnership in 1946 and reported $130,000 merely as "other income." The Kefauver records showed that Ned Klein, the tax agent sent to investigate, had written on the bottom of the return: "The partners refused to divulge the source of this income. Insomuch as the partnership reports a substantial amount the correctness of which is impossible to check, it is opined that further investigation is impracticable."

In the face of Schoeneman's continued refusal to discuss the tax returns, Martin said he was sure that they could answer one question without going into executive session: "Have these men (Accardo and Guzik) been required to answer all questions asked by Ned Klein?"

"Every taxpayer must answer all questions for the investigators," Oliphant responded generally, but Martin pressed for a more specific answer. Then Oliphant said that tax agents must ask for a court order if witnesses are unwilling to answer questions.

"Has any court procedure been started?" Martin asked and Oliphant answered, "No."

Because of the blanket secrecy provisions in the Bureau of Internal Revenue, Schoeneman and Oliphant were able to avoid explaining actions that indicated favoritism for racketeers. This stimulated rather than repressed my interest in the subject and also had the same effect on a number of other reporters.

COOPERATIVE EFFORT

The Newsmen

Through the Kefauver crime probes I became acquainted with a large number of local crime reporters across the country, and I developed a mutually beneficial friendship with Ted Link, the great investigative reporter for the *St. Louis Post Dispatch*. Ted Link was an expert on the makeup of the underworld and its operations, particularly in St. Louis, Chicago, and Kansas City with tentacles that stretched to Las Vegas. He was specifically interested in Lew Farrell and his links with the notorious Gargotta brothers who were slain in a northside Democratic club in Kansas City, and in my information on the manner in which the Washington office of the Alcohol Tax Unit (ATU) had overruled a regional director to give Farrell a federal basic beer permit.

Cooperation with Ted Link was totally beneficial, for we were not in competitive circulation areas and we could both gain from periodic consultation. The relationship was of value to both of us throughout investigations and hearings on the Internal Revenue scandals during the Truman administration, the Justice Department scandals of the same era, and the major labor racket investigations of the late 1950s.

The interest that Ted Link and I had in the evidence of political favoritism and corruption in the Bureau of Internal Revenue and the

ATU happened to coincide with the interests of John Strohmeyer, of the *Providence Journal,* and Chester (Chet) Potter, of the *Pittsburgh Press,* both able, tenacious, and aggressive crime reporters. Also, all of our interests overlapped with those of Senator John J. Williams, who was just emerging as a critic of the officials and policies of the Bureau of Internal Revenue.

A Serious, Honest Senator

Senator Williams, a quiet conservative Republican from Delaware, was a member of the Senate Finance Committee and a close friend of Senator Harry F. Byrd, the powerful Virginia Democrat who chaired the Finance Committee and one of its subcommittees. Williams became interested in corruption and mismanagement in the federal tax bureau because of a personal experience involving the mishandling of his income tax payment from his feed and chicken business in Millsboro, Delaware. He received notice that his taxes had not been paid when, in fact, he had cancelled checks establishing the payment of those taxes. In pressing to get this tax matter straightened out, he stumbled into evidence indicating that federal income tax checks were being cashed in an irregular manner that made it possible for tax officials to pocket the money with only a rare chance of discovery.

Unable to get a satisfactory explanation from federal tax officials in Delaware and unable to stimulate any effective action from Washington, Senator Williams concluded that the top level in Washington was incompetent or corrupt or caught in political deals that made it impossible for them to clean house. With help from Senator Byrd, Senator Williams was quietly and methodically running down evidence. However, the Senate speeches he made were overlooked because of his politics, his low-key manner, and his lack of press release ballyhoo. As I read them, I was struck by the careful documentation, the precise analysis and the seriousness of the questions raised.

Individually and jointly, Ted Link, Chet Potter, John Strohmeyer, and I started to work quietly with Senator Williams. He already had his own probes going on evidence of corruption and mismanagement in tax affairs in Delaware, New York, Boston, Kansas City, and St. Louis. He made little public mention of any area except Delaware and New York at the time I dropped in to see him to try to get some follow through on the ATU and the Farrell case.

During our first meetings he was friendly, but cautious, about dealing with reporters he did not know. He was interested in all evidence of corruption of mismanagement at the Bureau of Internal

Revenue and the ATU. He would follow through with inquiries to the Treasury. He would not promise special news breaks on any reply about the questions I asked. If something seemed important enough for comment, he would make his comments on the Senate floor and would provide me with the same statements and documents he provided everyone else. He would make no comment on how he felt about the legality or illegality of any action until he had fully examined it, and then he would make his statement in the Senate.

Toward the end of one of our conversations he explained that exposing mismanagement or corruption at top levels in government was a serious business, and he did not want to harm innocent people, as Senator McCarthy did, by loosely throwing serious allegations. He said he did not wish "to smear" anyone with irresponsible charges and that he believed it better to understate the case at first than to overstate it. He was wary of being quoted by reporters in criticism of public officials, unless he was on the Senate floor, because of the danger of a misquotation, misinterpretation, and a libel action that might be filed by those who would try to stop or discredit him.

A Press Agent Can be Helpful

In the spring of 1951, Senator Williams reviewed the facts in his Senate speeches and discussed the questions that might be raised with Treasury Secretary John M. Snyder and Commissioner of Internal Revenue Schoeneman. Following up the Senate speeches by Senator Williams, I called Schoeneman's office. Schoeneman came on the line, but upon hearing my questions, referred me to Harry Schneider in the Bureau of Internal Revenue press office.

Schneider was a highly professional pressman who was frank and open and not overly protective of the agency or its policies. He rarely tried to give a public relations pitch. If the reporter was not satisfied with his brief explanation, Schneider would usually refer you directly to the man or woman who could answer your question. But, he had not been asked any searching questions on the subject of the corruption charged in the speeches by Senator Williams. As a result, he was not fully informed on the facts and had been getting by with the explanation that, under the Bureau of Internal Revenue internal management controls, the kind of corruption that Senator Williams suggested just could not take place.

When I persisted with specific questions about the precise operation of the internal checks that made corruption impossible, he admitted frankly that he now realized, as a result of my questions, that he didn't completely understand them himself. He volunteered to take me to the "authority on this subject," who would explain it completely. This was Assistant Commissioner Daniel Bolich, who Schneider identified as "a career guy, who knows more about the workings of the system than anyone I know."

Carelessness Leads to Exposure

Dan Bolich was a dapper charmer with a penchant for fancy ties that, I later learned, cost $25—in a period when $25 was an unheard of price for a government official to pay for a tie. Bolich certainly knew the agency. He spelled out the system of investigative checks within the agency that kept regular tax agents from entering into collusion with taxpayers or their lawyers or fraternizing with the agents of the intelligence and inspection divisions.

Top officials recognized that the secrecy on tax matters could provide a breeding ground for corruption, so they had set up a system that made impossible the kind of tax fixing that Senator Williams suggested, Bolich told me. He was so articulate and convincing that, instead of proving innocence, he sold me on the fact that no corruption could exist in the lower levels of the tax service unless there was collusion or neglect at the level of Assistant Commissioner and in the Chief Counsel's office.

It was only a few months later than Dan Bolich stepped down because of ill health. He then resigned just before he was indicted on charges that he had more than $200,000 in unreported income from unknown sources over a period of three or four years. By that time Commissioner Schoeneman had resigned, Counsel Oliphant had been fired because of his financial dealings with a notorious tax fixer, and the investigations of Senator Williams and a House Committee had forced the resignations of the Directors of Internal Revenue in Boston, New York City, San Francisco, and St. Louis.

LOCAL ANGLES ON BIG INVESTIGATIONS

Ted Link's work with Senator Williams was beneficial in exposing the American Lithofold Corporation, its payments to various federal tax officials, and the award of a $3.5 million contract to that firm after it hired Democratic National Chairman William M. Boyle, Jr., as its attorney.

James B. E. Olson, a 56-year-old former supervisor for the ATU, admitted to the House Ways and Means Subcommittee that, while he was with the ATU in 1949, he received $5909 in commission on printing business sales made by American Lithofold to liquor companies under his jurisdiction. American Lithofold also made payments to James P. Finnegan, the former Collector of Internal Revenue in St. Louis, and Joseph D. Nunan, Former Commissioner of Internal Revenue and Former Collector of Internal Revenue in New York.

Chet Potter, of the *Pittsburgh Press,* worked with Senator Williams on the investigation that led to Senate speeches charging that William (Big Bill) Lias, notorious rackets figure from Pennsylvania and Wheeling, West Virginia, had been able to avoid paying more than $2,230,744 in federal income taxes and penalties for several years. It appeared to be the same type of favored treatment as that received by mobsters Accardo, Guzik, and others.

John Strohmeyer, of Providence, in cooperation with Senator Williams followed a local interest in Attorney General J. Howard McGrath, a former governor of Rhode Island, into a series of national and local stories showing evidence of corruption in the Treasury Department and in the tax division of the Justice Department. In cooperation with Ted Link, Strohmeyer exposed some of the first evidence that T. LaMar Caudle, Assistant Attorney General in charge of the tax division, was involved in political decisions to drop tax fraud prosecutions.

Reading 11: Attack on the Secrecy Blanket

While following the general tax scandal story on an almost day-to-day basis and cooperating with Link, Strohmeyer, and Potter, I singled out the secrecy area for special attention. The Internal Revenue laws provided a statutory secrecy blanket for income tax returns, but it was apparent to me that tax officials were stretching this secrecy blanket to cover evidence of mismanagement and corruption in much the same manner that the defense department used "national security" to cover up frauds and favoritism.

There were several areas that were immediately apparent by early 1951, and I made up my mind to attack that unjustified secrecy with the same total energy that I had given to the Polk County courthouse frauds.

The Kefauver report, issued on May 1, 1951, criticized the treasury department for granting Lew Farrell a federal permit to wholesale beer in the face of evidence that he associated with the Capone syndicate. Dwight Avis, chief enforcement officer of the ATU, told the Kefauver committee he expected that Farrell's permit would be revoked.

I intended to press that issue, and also to do what I could to force the ATU to abandon its policy of secret hearings on the federal wholesaler permits. The Kefauver committee had stated that it "could not understand how the Alcohol Tax Unit could grant wholesale permits to such hoodlums" as Farrell and Joe Di Giovanni, a Kansas City liquor distributor.

Various ATU officials had told me privately that the secret hearings were the problem and that there was no justification for secret hearings except to protect the mobsters from public discussion of their record. Downey Rice agreed with me, and so did Senator Kefauver, but Commissioner George Schoeneman and Charles Oliphant defended the closed hearings and the secrecy imposed on settlements regarding violation of the federal liquor laws. "It is easier to obtain settlement if the liquor law violators are assured that the record will be secret," Oliphant stated, a philosophy totally inconsistent with the open criminal and civil court system.

John B. Dunlap, a former collector of internal revenue in east Texas, was named head of the Treasury Department "racket squad" for a war on gangsters. I made an appointment to see him to argue the case for open hearings in the ATU. I pointed to Farrell's record of perjury in the closed hearing that was buried until the Kefauver committee forced the record out in the open. Dunlap said he agreed with me, but that the decision on such policy matters would be left up to Schoeneman. I countered that, if he really wanted to win the war on gangsters, he should insist that the ATU bring the mobsters out in the open in public hearings.

Only a few months later, Schoeneman resigned and Dunlap became the Commissioner of Internal Revenue with the authority to make a meaningful recommendation that the closed hearings be abolished. By that time I had two or three other suggestions for opening up records on the tax case compromises where secrecy had been used as a cover for ridiculous settlements of tax liabilities. I also suggested removing the secrecy that surrounded the list of tax-exempt institutions and their annual reports.

Although the law said that the tax returns filed by individual taxpayers and businesses must be kept secret, there was no reason or logic for extending this secrecy to the names of institutions that had been granted the privilege of tax exemption. As a taxpayer, I wanted the right to examine the list of institutions that were not paying taxes. I wanted to examine the justification for this status and not have it bottled up in a bureaucracy subject to political favoritism or bungling.

Dunlap knew to what I was referring on the tax-exempt institutions as did everyone else down the chain of command at the tax bureau. My stories had pointed up the absurd situation in which the Des Moines University of Lawsonomy was secretly granted tax-exempt status by the federal government. This so-called university had no student body, no faculty, and no purpose except to promote the strange cult of Alfred Lawson, the eccentric originator of the cult of Lawsonomy. Iowa and Polk County had denied his application for tax-exempt status, but the Bureau of Internal Revenue had routinely approved it.

Dunlap initiated an investigation of the tax-exempt status after I wrote stories pointing out how Lawson used this status as a bona fide educational institution to buy war surplus machines at about 5 cents on the dollar. He then sold some of the machines for a profit of approximately $150,000. The school never paid taxes on the profit, and Lawson told a Senate committee that the Des Moines University of Lawsonomy paid all living expenses for him, his wife, and their two small children, including air travel and hotel rooms for a Florida vacation trip.

Initially, the Bureau of Internal Revenue would not acknowledge that the University of Lawsonomy was tax exempt, and claimed that even its application for exemption was secret. By the time Dunlap started the investigation, he was convinced that secrecy on tax-exempt institutions was an invitation to trouble. In the spring of 1952, he lifted the secrecy veil on a number of internal activities. He also withdrew the tax-exempt status of the Des Moines University of Lawsonomy and an associated Humanity Benefactor Foundation. The ATU also revoked Lew Farrell's federal permit to wholesale beer.

With the vocal support of James S. Pope, then executive editor of the *Louisville Courier-Journal,* and the American Society of Newspaper Editors Freedom of Information Committee, I had a near total success in my campaign against excessive corrupting secrecy at the Bureau of Internal Revenue. Dunlap entered orders to:

1. Lift the secrecy surrounding the applications, hearings, and granting of beer and liquor permits.
2. Make public the list of tax-exempt institutions and their applications for tax-exempt status and agree to explain why and how institutions got on the tax-exempt list.
3. Remove the confidential classification given to information regarding the compromise settlements of certain types of federal tax cases.

A REPORTER'S CONTRIBUTIONS TO SECRECY REFORM

For that successful year-long campaign against unreasonable secrecy in the federal internal revenue bureau I was awarded the National

Sigma Delta Chi Award for Washington Correspondence for 1952. I was the runner-up in the competition for the Raymond Clapper Memorial Award. In my second year in Washington I had been able to put together a successful campaign against the power of the racketeers and the power of the bureaucracy. It had actually been easier to bring off a successful investigation in Washington than in Polk County, Iowa.

I had researched and written extensively about specific examples of the corrupting influence of secrecy on the ATU, on tax-exempt institutions, and on the compromises of tax delinquencies for as little as five or ten cents on the dollar. It was necessary to rely upon Senator Williams to reveal most of the favoritism and dishonesty in the secret tax compromises, for most of that information was hidden from the press under the general tax secrecy policies.

Over a period of several months, I pinpointed the specific rules, regulations, and laws that had to be changed to lift the unjustified secrecy and the names and titles of those who had the authority to initiate changes. I also discussed the secrecy problems in detail with key Democratic and Republican members of the congressional committees and subcommittees with jurisdiction over the Treasury Department and the Bureau of Internal Revenue.

Those senators and representatives would control the investigations and the legislation, and it was essential that they understand the seriousness of the problem before they were brainwashed by the bureaucrats and political appointees on the necessity of secrecy. It was necessary to counteract the lobbying of the skillful and corrupt bureaucrats who had a stake in continuing the secret dealings. Unfortunately, some of the senators and congressmen were in league with the crooked agency officials, and it was apparent that they had closed minds.

The discussions served two purposes. One, they gave the reporter a nose count on the crooked or compromised legislators who would oppose lifting the secrecy curtain or any other reform. Two, they served notice on the legislator that a reporter was covering the subject, that he was well informed and not easily brushed off, and that the reporter intended to follow through with a persistence that might expose even a well-hidden payoff or political deal.

Many senators and congressmen are honest and open minded but in need of a clear and specific briefing. Staff members are rarely well informed on the details of cases of corruption and mismanagement. The reporter who does the briefing must have his facts in mind, be able to cite the specific laws and regulations involved in the problem, and explain precisely the new point to be dramatized in a speech, letter, or hearing.

Although many senators and congressmen are intelligent and quick to grasp a new subject, most do not have the time or the inclination to try to piece together laws and facts and then decide upon a politically safe plan of action. They do not want to stick their political necks out on a questionable factual or legal case. They are easily confused when they do not know precisely what they are doing.

Senator John J. Williams was a notable exception. He would take down the facts on the incident of mismanagement or corruption, and he would study them until he knew them thoroughly. Then he would ask for legal opinions from committee staff experts or the agency, or perhaps from the research section of the Library of Congress or the General Accounting Office. Others who consistently followed this type of thorough, but slow, process were Representative John Moss, a liberal California Democrat, Representative H. R. Gross, a conservative Iowa Republican, and Representative Porter Hardy, an independent Virginia Democrat. There were a few dozen others who would do that kind of tough demanding research from time to time, but most were only as knowledgeable as the staff experts they consulted.

It was the follow through that separated the men from the boys in the effectiveness of their Washington reporting. Most of the great investigative reporters were tenacious in the pursuit of all of the facts and answers from all those with official responsibility. From time to time a reporter may be lucky in turning up a good source, unearthing an important document, or stumbling into a significant story. However, there must be systematic study and follow through to achieve any consistency in performance over any extended period of time.

STUDENT WORK PROJECT SUGGESTION

1. Write a paper explaining briefly why it is illogical to extend the secrecy that covers individual and private business tax returns to the so-called tax-exempt institutions.

2. A good working relationship with responsible congressmen is helpful to a reporter. Explain why it was important to work with Senator Williams on tax matters.

22 THE IMPORTANCE OF JUSTICE

The Department of Justice controls investigations and prosecutions, and the Attorney General is often a partisan political figure who will use that power to persecute the opposition party officials and to cover up the crimes of his own political party unless his decisions are given close scrutiny. In many instances only the cooperation of a number of aggressive investigative reporters can develop the full story of the patterns of corruption at the Justice Department.

This chapter illustrates how a relatively small group of reporters can, by persistent follow through on leads, force the Congress to start an official inquiry. This chapter also demonstrates the tremendous importance of gaining the interest and support of an outstanding reporter who is published in Washington or New York with immediate story impact on the White House and Congress as well as the Associated Press and the United Press International. Most government officials have an attention span that is only as long as the press interest. If the reporters are constant and astute observers, the committee members and staffs will be more alert and more penetrating in their questioning and observations.

NEED FOR PRESS COVERAGE

The investigation of the Truman administration tax scandals demonstrated that there were serious problems of mismanagement, if not corruption, at the top in the Treasury Department and in the Department of Justice. It was apparent to Ted Link, Eddy Milne, John Strohmeyer, Ed Edstrom, Chet Potter, and this reporter that the House Ways and Means subcommittee was not going to do a complete investigation of those agencies under its jurisdiction—the Treasury, Bureau of Internal Revenue, and the Alcohol Tax Unit. Certainly,

Chairman Cecil King, a live-and-let-live Democrat from California, was not going to pursue evidence of tax fixes and other scandalous doings in the bowels of the Justice Department.

The establishment of that investigation had been forced upon Speaker Sam Rayburn (Dem., Tex.) and the Democratic leadership by the Senate speeches of Senator John J. Williams, of Delaware, and by the aggressive reporting of the reporters for the *St. Louis Post-Dispatch,* the *Providence Bulletin,* the *Des Moines Register and Tribune,* the *Minneapolis Tribune,* the *Pittsburgh Press,* and the *Washington Star.* Those House tax scandal hearings first gave me an appreciation of the importance of the Washington and New York newspapers, and of the value of great reporters such as Cecil Holland, of the *Washington Star* and C. P. (Peck) Trussell, of the *New York Times.*

These men had major impact on the perspective of the news that flowed out of Washington on the wire services and in all of the Washington newspaper bureaus. The stories by Cecil Holland and Jerry O'Leary, also of the *Washington Star,* on the tax scandals and other equally important investigative hearings were used as a guide by dozens of Washington reporters and the Associated Press and United Press for accuracy of facts or for perspective. I knew, as did all of the fine reporters I worked with on that story, that it was the reporting of Holland in the *Washington Star* that forced Chairman King to push the probe far beyond what he would have done.

A Model Reporter

The Republican members of the King subcommittee would tip Holland off on investigations they believed should be pursued before they raised the question in the committee. As a result he was always fully apprised of the relevant facts and the law even before the issue came up. He did not rely wholly upon the Republican version, but quizzed them at length for holes in their presentation. Holland was completely trustworthy and would not reveal facts in the newspaper or to the Democrats prior to the time the Republicans wished to raise the issue.

However, Chairman King and the other Democrats (even O'Brien and Keogh) trusted Holland to deal with them fairly. He had excellent personal relations with all members of the committee and with all of the members of the staff. They trusted him not to betray confidences of information supplied for background, but they knew he would not cover up for their mistakes or their political chicanery. They respected his knowledge of the facts, and his understanding of the subtleties of the legal decisions in the Treasury or Justice Department that would set the stage for tax fixes.

Chairman King would answer Holland's questions and make documents available to him prior to the time they were entered into the hearing record, with the understanding that Holland's story would not be printed until the document was an official part of the record.

Where the Influence Is

I had learned by that time that the *Des Moines Register* stories had virtually no impact in Washington unless they were picked up by the wire services or were reprinted in the *Washington Star* or the *Washington Post*. The exception was when some member of the Senate or House saw the story and called it to the attention of an investigating subcommittee or commented on it in the House or Senate.

SAVING AND USING PRINTED STORIES

In dealing with the tax scandals, I often had exclusive *Des Moines Register* stories, which I discussed with Cecil Holland. Frequently he wanted them for his own background. From time to time he asked for an extra clipping of the story to take to Chairman King or the subcommittee staff. It was often an ordeal to get that second clipping of a *Des Moines Register* story because the Washington bureau received only two copies of each paper.

Copies and Copying Them

We kept one file copy, and I clipped the other copy for my chronological scrapbook. Sometimes it was necessary to clip the file copy or have the page of the scrapbook copied. Duplication of a scrapbook page was a clumsy business, so I started to make a practice of pasting my most important clippings neatly on legal size sheets of paper for ease in duplication. In this way I could have a copy for my scrapbook and another copy on file for duplication. I also followed the same practice for key stories written by other reporters that were printed in newspapers outside of Washington. I found this process a particularly practical one when I had to demonstrate to committee members, staff members, and other reporters the entire background of a particular investigation.

Keeping Other References

From time to time, a senator or congressman would insert my stories, and the stories of other reporters, in the Congressional Record to demonstrate the need for further investigations or specific legislation. I would then jot down the date and page of the Congressional Record for a ready reference for myself or any other reporter or public official who was interested in reading the complete background of what had been written and by whom. This practice, which I started during the tax scandal investigations in 1951 and 1952, became an automatic part of my system of operation with the reading, clipping, and pasting down between 8 A.M. and 9:30 A.M. when other reporters started drifting into the office and I had to leave for hearings.

REPORTER'S HOURS

Being an effective Washington reporter is not an eight-hour job for five days a week, and none of the Cowles Washington bureau reporters regarded it as such. The clock meant nothing to us, nor did the weekends. As the most inexperienced member of the Washington bureau, I felt compelled to put in two or three hours extra each day. But experienced reporters worked just as hard. Cecil Holland's great performance on the tax scandal investigation would not have been possible if he had been a less diligent worker.

Because he wrote for an afternoon newspaper, Holland's normal hours would have been from 8 A.M. until 5 P.M., unless he had a story that had to be written early in the morning for the first edition of the *Washington Star*. During the tax scandal investigations and hearings, Holland frequently spent the early morning hours writing stories from information he had obtained in interviewing the committee members and the staff the previous evening. He met with the staff after the hearings ended between 5 P.M. and 6:30 P.M. After interviewing the committee members and staff and after obtaining the documents to be used in the next day's hearings, it was necessary for him to study the documents and write a story so it would be ready for release at the moment the documents were entered into the hearing record.

Mechanics

Stories had to be written in a manner that would be open for inserted paragraphs on precise testimony and reactions of the congressmen to the new evidence. While Holland's basic story was being written, it was important that he keep on top of every word of testimony that might amplify or undercut his document in any way. He had to be prepared to leave the hearing room and quickly dictate an accurate insertion into any story.

Holland was a cool master of the mechanics of accurately updating a story. He was also perceptive in noticing the questions that were not answered and the tag ends of testimony that indicated still more scandalous conditions for which subcabinet officials, Cabinet officers, or the White House might be responsible. His stories pointed up those responsibilities, and he or others on the *Washington Star* would follow up with questions at the executive agencies and the White House.

Reading 12: Truman Administration Scandals

Because it was possible to rely upon the accuracy and objectivity of Holland's coverage, Eddy Milne and I frequently left the tax scandal hearings to go down to the Bureau of Internal Revenue, the Treasury Department, or the White House to confront officials directly with questions on their involvement in or knowledge of questionable or illegal actions.

I recall several occasions when we went personally to Secretary of Treasury John Snyder to ask him questions. Although it was easy to get to see a Cabinet officer in 1951, it was not the custom then to agree to a spur-of-the-minute interview with reporters. The technique used was to tell the Treasury press officer that we had some questions we wanted to ask Secretary Snyder and insist we didn't want a press office release. When the PR man balked, we pushed the notion that it was more important for the Secretary to talk to us than for us to talk to him. If the Secretary didn't want to see us, we said that we felt no obligation to reveal the nature of our questions. We would write our critical story and quote the PR man as saying, "the Secretary won't see you."

The Treasury Department was already shaking under the bad publicity of the tax scandals, and neither Secretary Snyder nor his press man wanted more criticism if they could avoid it. We would be ushered into Secretary Snyder's office for direct questioning on the tax scandal. Such meetings might provide an exclusive story on that week's developments, but more important, they provided an opportunity to get the views of the man at the top of the embattled Treasury Department.

During the questioning, it became apparent that Secretary Snyder was not well advised on important details that had been in the newspapers for days and weeks and that he was a victim of the self-serving reports of the bureaucrats who were corrupt or were involved in a cover up for their friends. There were also a few policy matters involving political favoritism that could be traced directly to Secretary Snyder's intervention for his friends, and these political deals now barred him from taking the firm action that was needed. The Bureau of Internal Revenue claimed defensively that they had tried to do a reasonably good job but had been frustrated by the negligence and deals at the Justice Department. Secretary Snyder repeated that message clearly even though he was poorly informed on details.

Thus, Secretary Snyder pronounced general denials and few facts on matters involving his own culpability. Mainly, however, he pointed an accusing finger at Attorney General J. Howard McGrath and T. LaMar Caudle, the head of the Justice Department's tax division. It was easy to point critically at Caudle. In fact, it would have been difficult to defend him because he had fumbled into an admission that he had taken a $5000 fee for selling an airplane for a man with a tax evasion problem. Worse, from a symbolic point of view at that time, Caudle said he had used the money from the plane sale to buy an expensive mink coat for his wife. Cartoonists, editors, and editorial writers had a field day. Caudle was fired by President Truman.

Attorney General McGrath admitted he had authorized Caudle to accept the fee, but insisted he did not know the plane Caudle sold was owned by a man who was under a tax fraud probe. Caudle admitted that former Attorney General Tom Clark, then elevated to the Supreme Court, had been with him as a guest on an airplane flight with a wealthy North Carolina businessman who was under investigation for tax fraud. Justice Clark said he did not know the North Carolina man was under tax investigation or had any other business with the Justice Department. These incidents all pointed to serious laxity, if not worse, at the Justice Department.

Secretary Snyder, in hope of avoiding some criticism, joined those who were pointing at the Justice Department as the real trouble spot. Steeped in all aspects of the tax investigations, Eddy Milne and I knew there was plenty of blame to go around. The negligence and corruption at the Justice Department did not mean that the Treasury was blameless, and I was eager for both departments to be thoroughly investigated. As we wrote our stories on the Snyder interview, I repeated the old adage I had learned from my Mother, "When thieves fall out, just men get their due."

The tax scandal investigation was endangered because Chairman King was trying to bring the curtain down at the earliest moment possible in order to avoid further political damage to the Democrats in the 1952 election year. However, enough fingers had been pointed and enough news stories printed that closing down the tax investigations would not end the exposures.

In early 1952, the Judiciary Committee authorized a subcommittee to investigate the Justice Department. The chairman was

Representative Frank Chelf, a Kentucky Democrat, and the ranking Republican was Representative Kenneth Keating, a New York Republican. Representative Peter A. Rodino, a junior congressman from New Jersey was also a member of that subcommittee. Because Representative Emanuel Celler, an elderly dictatorial New York Democrat, was chairman of the full Judiciary Committee, I had little hope for a real investigation. However, Frank Chelf was an honest and forthright man, and Ken Keating was a shrewd lawyer with a good feel for doing and saying the right things to keep an investigation moving forward.

Also, the committee hired a distinguished Chicago lawyer, Stephen A. Mitchell, as chief counsel and Robert Collier, an able former FBI agent, as the minority counsel. They worked well together. Steve Mitchell was originally a farm boy from Waterloo, Iowa, and, despite years of practice in Chicago, had not lost the capacity to become indignant at mismanagement and frauds in government. Because I worked for the *Des Moines Register,* had Iowa farm work in my background, and was a graduate of the Drake University Law School, we struck up an almost immediate personal friendship.

By this time, Howard McGrath had been fired as Attorney General, and President Truman had nominated United States District Judge James P. McGranery, of Philadelphia, as his successor. Before McGranery was sworn in, Steve Mitchell and some members of the judiciary subcommittee had been involved in several quarrels with Justice Department officials over requests for information on the outside practice of United States District Attorneys, their assistants, and other Justice Department lawyers.

Both Steve Mitchell and Bob Collier were pleased with McGranery's offers of cooperation and with his assurances that, if there was any problem about access to information, they were to come to him. My own initial skepticism was modified as a result of a personal meeting with McGranery in his Justice Department office. This was my first visit with an Attorney General in the impressive Justice Department surroundings, but I was back a number of times over the next months, and I became a friend and admirer of this craggy-faced lawyer. He gave up a lifetime appointment on the federal bench to take on the difficult job of trying to straighten out the Justice Department because President Truman had asked him to do it.

From McGranery I learned that President Truman had been shocked at the extent of the scandals. The initial reports by McGrath to Truman had been sketchy, the problems minimized, and the

Republicans blamed for political prejudice in their criticism. A month after he took office, Attorney General McGranery asked for a full report on "the outside law practice" of each of the United States district attorneys. It was a step preparatory to issuing rules that would bar United States District Attorneys from outside practice. This was an essential first step in combatting the maladministration in the enforcement of federal laws. It went to the heart of the problem by stopping the temptation to take outside income from sources that might compromise judgments on official matters.

The $5000 fee that Caudle received from an airplane sale was only a sample of what might be happening among United States Attorneys as long as they and their assistants could take on private clients in civil litigation. It was possible camouflage for outright bribes, because it is very difficult to determine the value of legal services in any case when there is no relationship between time and legal fees.

The next step was for McGranery to ask for a list of all lawyers with official connections, who had been counsel in cases involving the United States government, whether criminal, civil, or admiralty. The list of lawyers with official connections was not limited to federal employees or former federal employees but was broad enough to include public officials in any branch of the government, federal, state, or municipal. The Attorney General also asked for a "detailed" report on "all cases of bribery and tax evasion and any federal violations which give evidence of criminal conspiracy to aid and abet vice and which suggest the activity of organized crime, whether connected with horse racing, boxing, other sporting events, or gambling, and which indicate a group attitude of disrespect of the federal laws."

Quite properly, Attorney General McGranery said the reports would be confidential, but would be made available to the House Judiciary Subcommittee. I could hardly wait to get my hands on them although I knew Steve Mitchell would not give them to me.

The combination of Mitchell as chief counsel for the investigating subcommittee and McGranery as head of the Justice Department seemed a good one for sweeping reforms in the administration of justice, but it was President Truman's last year in office. Then the nomination of Adlai Stevenson as the Democratic candidate for President brought an end to Steve Mitchell's role as a congressional investigator in August 1952. However, because of the broad news coverage the scandals had received I held strong hopes that the Justice Department might get the housecleaning it needed whether

Adlai Stevenson or General Dwight D. Eisenhower was elected president.

LESSONS LEARNED

I learned much from following the day-to-day hearings on the tax scandal and the Justice Department scandals. I came to understand how important it is to examine all of the detailed maneuvering on a case in order to unravel a really sophisticated fix. I saw how the Justice Department tried to block investigations by Congress by announcing a federal grand jury investigation and then reporting that all key documents were before a grand jury and unavailable to congressional investigators.

Most important, I learned the vital role of the Justice Department in setting the ethical tone across the whole government. The opinions of the Attorney General were only as good as the ethical standards of the occupant of the office. The key point for the reporter to remember is to be properly skeptical of Justice Department legal opinions but to stop short of a destructive cynicism.

I hoped a better era was ahead, but if it wasn't, I felt confident that I had the expertise to cope with essentially any investigative project.

STUDENT WORK PROJECT SUGGESTION

List the highest appointive officials of the Justice Department including the Attorney General, his top aides, the Deputy Attorney General and his top aides, and the Assistant Attorneys General and their chief deputies. How many of these people are political appointees? How many are career Justice Department lawyers? Describe the general area of responsibility of each.

23 LEARNING ABOUT LABOR RACKETS

On first examination the field of labor law appears highly technical and quite complicated, but it is possible with concentrated study to become expert at detecting the dozen or so patterns most common in labor-management rackets. Review of the record of congressional hearings and reports on these patterns should be accompanied by interviews with Labor Department officials, labor union officials, and investigators with background in the labor field. This approach can bring success to any investigation in a specialized field of law.

This chapter demonstrates that a reporter, without experience in labor reporting, can in a matter of weeks become familiar with the law, the history of the law, and the practical political forces at work in an unfamiliar field. The source of story leads came from dissident Teamsters Union members and from employers. The Congressional Record, old hearing records on labor racketeering, and trial court records provided the general framework and background on the problem. This material was supplemented by interviews with lawyers, investigators with experience on specific continuing racketeering cases, and by exchanges of information with other newsmen. The basic facts on frauds and conflicts of interest were relatively easy to establish, but the power of organized labor as the most effective lobby in Washington, made it difficult to get a full effective hearing in even the most outrageous cases.

REPORTING ON AN UNFAMILIAR PROBLEM

The Eisenhower Administration was just taking office in January 1953 when I first found an opportunity to test my ability to do an effective investigation in a field about which I knew virtually nothing. Gideon Seymour, executive editor of the *Minneapolis Star* and *Tribune*, called Washington Bureau Chief Dick Wilson to ask if I could come out to Minneapolis to investigate evidence of labor rackets. Although the jargon of the labor reporters and the labor union people had always been like a foreign language to me, I said I could do it. I recalled that Lincoln Steffens, with no expertise in high finance, engaged in successful investigative forays on Wall Street. Likewise, Upton Sinclair had to start from the ground up to learn the meat packing industry. Certainly, I had been no tax law expert when I had started digging into the tax scandals and the secrecy in the Alcohol Tax Unit.

Obtaining Background

I took an inventory of my knowledge of labor and it wasn't much. I had written a few stories in Des Moines about a fuss by a reform group in Local 90 of the Teamsters Union, but had never understood what it was all about because another reporter covered most of the story. I knew the Teamsters Union had political clout in Des Moines and used it on behalf of a crooked chief of police and a crooked judge. The Kefauver crime committee had touched on the fringe of some labor rackets, but the politically ambitious chairman, Estes Kefauver, balked at tackling corrupt labor, even though he had courageously tackled organized crime and the Democratic political machines in Chicago, New York, Kansas City, and New Orleans.

Downey Rice, the Kefauver counsel who had worked with me on the Lew Farrell case, was chief counsel for a Senate Interstate and Foreign Commerce subcommittee that was investigating the organized crime involvement in the International Longshoremen's Association (ILA) in New Jersey and New York. The chairman of that subcommittee was Senator Charles W. Tobey, the New Hampshire Republican. I had become acquainted with Senator Tobey when he was the bible-thumping ranking Republican member of the Kefauver Crime Committee. I went to them both and asked questions.

To fill a big gap in my knowledge, I read briefly on the history of the Wagner Act, the basic labor law passed by the Roosevelt administration in 1937, and the Taft-Hartley labor law enacted in 1947, which was attacked by organized labor as "a slave labor act." I familiarized myself with the legislative history of the Taft-Hartley Law, specifically with those provisions that required trustees for union pension and insurance funds from labor and management and the requirements that financial reports be filed with the Labor Department.

I learned that prolabor forces in the upper echelons had pulled the teeth on the reporting provision requirements of the Taft-

Hartley Law. Downey Rice reminded me that the Roosevelt and Truman administrations had barred the Federal Bureau of Investigation from initiating inquiries into the actions of labor union leaders unless they were specifically cleared with the Attorney General. This made it virtually impossible to conduct an effective inquiry of a labor leader or a union without notice to the Labor Department and the White House.

On the Scene

In Minneapolis, Gid Seymour told me he had heard stories of serious mismanagement and potential conflicts of interest in the pension and insurance funds of the Teamsters Union and he hoped I would be able to get a congressional investigation started. The *Minneapolis Star* and the *Minneapolis Tribune* had regular labor reporters, but Seymour felt that they were not good investigators and had ideological barriers to writing stories that might reflect badly on labor unions.

During my week in Minneapolis, St. Paul, and Duluth, I spent much time with Sam Romer, the *Minneapolis Tribune* labor reporter. He had a store of knowledge, but it was necessary to choose selectively from it. Sam Romer was a former labor organizer who knew the labor lingo. However, he had a deep-seated bias against all management that made it impossible for him to react normally to labor's crimes. Romer's reaction to obvious "conflicts of interest" in the payment of pension fund fees to labor leaders was a defensive, "Management does that type of thing and worse all the time." Evidence of labor violence evoked the almost automatic response that it was all started by "management goon squads."

Whether or not what Sam Romer said was generally true, it did not justify labor leaders robbing the union funds and the pension and insurance funds of their own members, or using strong-arm tactics against the honest rank-and-file union members who wanted an honest accounting on those funds. As I saw it, Congress had passed laws that made stealing the pension and insurance funds of union members a violation of federal criminal laws. The government had a responsibility to see that those laws were enforced and the funds protected, and Congress had not done enough to call public attention to this serious problem.

Local Sources

In one week in Minnesota I had a cram course on all that was wrong with the Teamsters Union under the leadership of Sidney L.

Brennan, a vice president of the International Brotherhood of Teamsters Chauffers and Warehousemen of America. As I was to learn later, Brennan was only responsible for a part of the problem. A large amount of the terrorism and ruthless misuse of union power could be attributed to the influence of Gerald P. Connelly, who had been pushed into office in a newly created Teamsters local by the influence of Detroit Teamster Boss James R. Hoffa.

Reports from local dissident Teamsters identified Connelly as a Detroit man who was involved as an accessory in an attempted murder in Florida. I was able to confirm this report later through Florida law enforcement authorities. A congressional committee was able to get the reports and affidavits spelling out the allegations of Connelly's role in the gruesome effort to kill, by clubbing, shooting, and drowning, a Black organizer who was suspected of being an informant.

From the lips of dissident Teamsters Union members and the officers of small locals, I heard stories of thievery and terrorism that equalled the stories of the New York and New Jersey waterfront. This was direct evidence from eye witnesses in most instances, and I was able to get corroborative evidence from other witnesses and from documents. In some cases the victims had made their complaints to police or prosecutors only to be ignored. In other cases they said they were afraid to go to the police because the police, the prosecutors, and some of the local judges were regarded as stooges for Teamsters Union officials. Some labor union members had made an effort to go to the press, but labor reporters were assigned to interview them and were uninterested in following up their complaints. In some instances, the labor reporters tried to keep them from taking any steps that would discredit labor.

One officer of a small Teamsters local said that, even if a complaint was made to an honest policeman or prosecutor, the Teamsters had stacked the Hennepin County grand jury. "A spot (on the panel) was reserved for the Teamsters Union most of the time," he said and ticked off the names of Teamsters Union officials who had been on recent grand juries. My check of those lists confirmed his report that Sid Brennan and several other Teamsters officials who were my investigation targets had been on the Hennepin County Grand Jury. It was worth an investigation as to how the grand jury panel could be rigged to accommodate the Teamsters, but this was local government corruption, and I suggested to Seymour that he turn it over to the city desk for a follow-up by local reporters.

My visit to Minneapolis happened to coincide with a testimonial dinner for Sidney Brennan the evening of Wednesday,

January 28, 1953. It gave me the opportunity to hear International Teamster President Dave Beck speak. It also gave me a chance to learn the nature of the crowd that turned out to honor Sid Brennan. Those in attendance ranged from a naive and genial Governor C. Elmer Anderson to Salvatore (Rocky) Lupino, a convicted safecracker and a pal of Teamsters business agent Tony Schullo of Minneapolis Local 638. Mayor Eric Hoyer was there to pose for pictures with Brennan. Other guests included judges, aldermen, Republican and Democratic leaders, and the underworld cronies of the Minneapolis Teamsters bosses.

Some of those present were scarcely friends of Brennan, Connelly, and the other Teamsters bosses. "I've got to get along with the Teamsters," a warehouse and truckline operator told me to justify his presence. "They can be life or death for my business. That union contract is only part of it—it's the interpretation they put on it that can ruin us." An out-of-state Teamster official commented to me, "I don't like Sid Brennan or that racketeer Connelly he associates with. I'm in here because I want to avoid trouble."

Seymour was with me, although executive editors don't usually go on such assignments. He was vitally interested in my investigation, and was busy surveying the room and commenting under his breath on how many of his friends in the business community were swallowing their pride to bow at the throne of the Teamster's power.

The National Scene

In Washington, I talked to Senator Tobey, chairman of the Senate subcommittee that was investigating Waterfront rackets, and received his enthusiastic decision to investigate the Minneapolis Teamsters as soon as the staff completed some tag ends on the waterfront. I had already discussed the Minneapolis Teamsters probe with Counsel Downey Rice and Chief Investigator Francis X. Plant. One of my best informants, William (Bill) Wilson, wealthy owner of the Wilson Trucking System with headquarters in Sioux Falls, South Dakota, had talked to Senator Karl Mundt, a South Dakota Republican, to enlist his support for a Minneapolis Teamsters investigation.

At Seymour's suggestion, I also called on Senator Hubert Humphrey, the liberal Democrat from Minnesota, to determine whether there was any possibility that he would use Democratic political pressure to block a union investigation in his home town. I was surprised to hear Humphrey declare that he had "absolutely no time for Sid Brennan or any of his crowd. I haven't had any help from that Minneapolis Teamsters group since I ran for mayor of Minneapolis," Humphrey said. He volunteered to talk to Senator

Tobey to encourage the investigation and then cited his own unpleasant experiences with the Teamsters when he was mayor. He had quarreled with them over closing down slot machines and refused to appoint several Teamster nominees to the police force.

COVERING THE INVESTIGATION

Story Approach

That cleared away the possible political barriers, and the investigations and hearings seemed a certainty. I talked with Seymour on two possible approaches: I could write a well-documented series on what I had learned about Teamsters rackets. Unfortunately, that raised the possibility that some of our informants might be frightened or even killed. Or, we could wait until the hearings before Senator Tobey's subcommittee in the later summer or fall when the federal government could provide protection for the witnesses who had to be identified.

I believed that an aggressive series was too hazardous because of the political and economic clout of the Teamsters. Although Seymour was enthusiastic and courageous, I was not certain of the intestinal fortitude of editors below him, who would be making day-to-day decisions. I decided it would be best to test the courage and judgment of the *Tribune* editors on a few spot stories from privileged court records before beginning a series of stories that were based only in part on records but relied largely on personal interviews with witnesses who might not stay "hitched" under the tremendous pressure the Teamsters could exert.

One of the testing stories came out of the United States Tax Court records in Washington, D.C., and involved an alleged federal tax deficiency of Minneapolis Teamsters boss, Sid Brennan. Brennan's lawyer in typical Teamsters' fashion complained and hinted vaguely at a law suit with false claims that there were errors in the story and that it defamed Brennan. Without checking with me, the *Tribune* editors ran a front page story of Brennan's lawyer's version in what amounted to an apology. It was a shocking combination of incompetence and cowardice, and, when I protested, the editors explained that they thought my story was in error because the lawyer had been so vehement and firm in his statements and they wanted to get it corrected quickly. Those who had approved the so-called "correction" were not qualified to judge the complaint, as is so often true in such cases.

I took my protest to Seymour, who was not aware of the circumstances of the "correction" and told him that I was not going to push forward against the Teamsters Union and Sid Brennan if this was the kind of support I was going to get. He said he wanted me to stay with the Teamsters investigation, and that he would make certain there was no repetition of the problem with the tax court story. Gid Seymour was a man of his word and there were no more such incidents as long as he was editor. Unfortunately, Seymour suffered a heart attack late that year as a result of a Teamsters strike of the Minneapolis newspapers. He died the next spring—shortly after a congressional hearing in Minneapolis on the Teamsters.

Pushing for a Fair Hearing

The facts in the Minneapolis case were relatively easy to develop from records and interviews, but getting those facts into a hearing was an ordeal. Rice and his team of investigators were ready and well prepared for the hearing when Chairman Tobey died. This elevated Senator John Bricker, a conservative Ohio Republican, to the chairmanship. On paper, Senator Bricker looked like a good man to push a labor investigation, but this didn't take into account his political ties with the corrupt Ohio Teamsters organization. He killed the committee, discharged the investigators, and the Minneapolis hearing appeared dead.

Fortunately, I knew that a House Government Operation Subcommittee headed by Representative Clare Hoffman, a Michigan Republican, was doing some research on the Central State Teamsters pension and welfare fund and the activities of Detroit Teamster boss James R. Hoffa. Chairman Hoffman was an aggressive labor racket investigator and was eager to include the Minneapolis Teamsters officials in hearings he planned for the fall.

With Hoffman's chief investigator Lester P. Condon, I reviewed my own investigation and the information I knew Downey Rice had been able to unearth before the Senate subcommittee was killed. Hoffman had a complicated problem in that the Teamsters Union and its allies had persuaded the members of his House Government Operations Committee to deny him the authority to subpoena records and witnesses for hearings. However, the wily Chairman Hoffman had a plan to get around this roadblock. He had control of the investigators, and arranged to conduct the hearings in a special House Labor Subcommittee headed by Representative Wint Smith, a Kansas Republican. The strategy worked. Several Minneapolis witnesses were subpoened to appear at a hearing in Detroit.

Attempt to Gain National Attention

I went to Detroit for the hearings in November 1953, met Jimmy Hoffa, became acquainted with the Detroit labor scene, and had my first deep look at the frauds and conflicts of interest in the management of Central States pension and insurance fund. My purpose in Detroit was to cover the Minneapolis witnesses, but the evidence produced showed a national story of great significance involving pension and welfare frauds and the corruption of Hoffa and Dave Beck.

Unfortunately, although the Detroit labor reporters covered the local frauds in depth, the news wire services carried only short and superficial stories out of the Detroit hearings. I was amazed that the *Washington Star,* the *Washington Post,* and the *New York Times* also carried only a few paragraphs of superficial copy.

In Washington, I reviewed the transcripts at leisure, and the staff members were willing to answer questions or produce additional documents when they were needed to explain the whole story. I talked to Frank Eyerly, the perceptive managing editor of the *Des Moines Register.* Eyerly grasped the historic importance immediately with a brilliant reference to the pension and welfare fraud investigation being as significant as the insurance investigation by Charles Evans Hughes in 1905. He was enthusiastic about a depth series of articles out of the Detroit hearing record. I pieced them together with other evidence and interviews that gave the series a national scope.

The evidence in the transcripts indicated massive violation of labor laws and criminal laws, state and federal, by union leaders. A series of articles was planned to stress some serious questions: Why wasn't the Labor Department doing something about it? Why wasn't the Justice Department doing something about it? Why weren't the Labor Committees of the House and Senate doing something about it?

At the Justice Department I verified my earlier report from Downey Rice that the FBI was barred from investigations of labor or labor leaders unless they had specific instruction from the White House. At the Labor Department I found a lethargic attitude toward enforcement of criminal laws against labor leaders, and a gross negligence with regard to the inspection of the reports required to be filed under the Taft-Hartley Law. An Assistant Secretary of Labor, Lloyd Mashburn, admitted that the financial reports were not checked for accuracy because the Labor Department did not have any personnel to perform that function.

At the Internal Revenue Services the tax reports of labor unions were subject to the same laxity that the tax bureau accorded to all tax-exempt institutions. Labor union tax matters were virtually never examined or even scrutinized. All these facts were exposed in my stories.

PRESS SCRUTINY HAS IMPORTANT EFFECTS

After the series ran, Representative Clare Hoffman was eager to continue his investigations in Minneapolis. He had found someone who was interested in the investigations and who would put the time and work into a study of the record and get the facts to the public. However, the House Government Operations Committee knocked him out of the chairmanship of the labor investigation and turned it over to Representative George Bender, a Republican from Ohio. Hoffman chided the committee for naming Bender to conduct a "whitewash" of a serious problem.

I went to Bender's office in the Longworth Office Building, told him the facts on the Minneapolis case, and hit him with the direct question: Was he going to preside at a "whitewash"? Bender jumped to his feet in rage. "George Bender has never whitewashed anything in his life, and he isn't going to start now." I mentioned some reports showing that he had Teamsters as political supporters, and he said he had "all kinds of people who support me, but no one has any strings on me." Bender raged about Hoffman and vowed to do a good job. Finally he said, "If you know any good investigators, let me have their names."

I had not expected this opportunity, but I named Downey Rice and Frank Plant, identifying them as former FBI men who knew the business and already had their feet on the ground concerning the Minneapolis Teamsters. Bender was anxious to show me that he meant business and demonstrated it by hiring Rice, Plant, and two men, Stan Fisher and George Martin, who had worked with them on the Minneapolis investigations. My optimism over this news was cut short a few weeks later when I learned that the Democratic members of Bender's subcommittee, influenced in varying degrees by the Teamsters, were threatening to boycott the hearing or to disrupt it.

Because hints of these threats were published, they were never fulfilled. However, when the hearing was finally staged in a courtroom on the third floor of the Federal Courthouse in Minneapolis, the Democratic sabotage did manage to wreck the full potential, because Bender was an incompetent chairman. Representative Hoffman had to explain to Bender how he should rule on various Democratic moves to sidetrack or end the hearings.

The skill of Downey Rice as chief counsel and the solid preparation of his little staff of investigators averted total disaster by making it possible to pour solid documents into the record in addition to the testimony. Because I had lived the investigations, I was able to put together comprehensive stories that accompanied the transcript of the testimony that Gid Seymour arranged to run in the *Minneapolis Tribune*.

Implications for Future Stories

When the hearings were over, Seymour was just as enthusiastic in planning for further work on the labor rackets in Minneapolis. He had suffered a severe heart attack the preceding December as a result of a two-week strike of the *Minneapolis Star* and *Tribune*. He was enraged at labor's abuse of power. The government couldn't shut down the newspapers, but the Teamsters had been able to do it. He invited me out to his home for a Sunday night dinner to discuss future labor racket investigations. He talked like a man who was speaking for the record reviewing the great moments in his life, and he regarded his role in stimulating the Minneapolis labor racket inquiry as one of his finest achievements. A few weeks later he died of another heart attack.

Gid Seymour was gone as the driving force on the labor racket inquiry in Minneapolis, but United States District Attorney George MacKinnon called a special federal grand jury to investigate labor rackets. Working from the hearing transcripts, plus leads from Rice and Plant, MacKinnon was able to indict and convict Sid Brennan, Gene Williams, Jerry Connelly, and several other Teamsters officials.

MacKinnon, a former United States Representative from Minnesota, helped write the Taft-Hartley Law as a member of the House Labor Committee in 1947. He became a good friend and was an honest and reliable news source while he was United States Attorney and also when he was brought into the Justice Department as an expert advisor on labor racket prosecution. He was later named to the United States Court of Appeals in Washington.

Although that first phase of labor racket inquiries fell far short of completion, it served as a great training ground for me and provided the factual background for stimulating other congressional investigations of labor rackets.

STUDENT WORK PROJECT SUGGESTION

Obtain from the Labor Department the latest official report by the division dealing with regulation of employee pension and insurance funds administered under federal law. Examine the latest GAO report evaluating or analyzing the manner in which the Labor Department is policing the administration of various union and union-management pension and insurance funds. Analyze these reports and discuss any continuing problem indicating laxity by the Labor Department or other government agency.

24   A CLAIM OF SECURITY RISK

When a Cabinet official is unresponsive to questions and when the "secrecy" of the government employee security programs is obscuring the facts, it is necessary to take unorthodox steps to bring about conditions that force correction of a grave injustice. A visit to a Cabinet officer's home and persistent questioning of the President was the only avenue open to establish responsibility at the top.

This chapter demonstrates an effective followup on a confidential news tip that moved the controversy over a "security risk" case into public print. Ultimately there was correction of the injustices and a "reform" of a system that did not guarantee due process of law. This case also illustrates the use of public records, challenges to public positions of people and departments, and confrontations with various government officials to force resolution of issues that the Secretary of Agriculture and the President sought to avoid. Note how a reporter can get confirmation of conclusions that a man is not a security risk without asking a direct question of an informant he wishes to protect.

THE PROBLEM OF "SECURITY RISK"

Often the most difficult type of case to investigate and analyze is the one in which a government agency has claimed that a government employee is a "security risk" and that it is not in the best interest of the United States to keep him in the work in which he is expert. This questions the loyalty of the employee to the United States and his right to be judged on his job qualifications. Merely to write that a government agency has found an employee is a security risk can be a severe handicap as this employee seeks any job in the future.

It is also true that the government cannot and should not keep dishonest or disloyal persons on the payroll and must be given a certain reasonable discretion in judging a person a "security risk." This is a most serious and difficult business under any circumstances, but it was particularly difficult in the late 1940s and in the 1950s. Spies and other disloyal persons had been exposed and expedient politicians distorted the problem and influenced the thinking of many basically well motivated persons.

A REPORTER MUST BE CAUTIOUS

It is seldom possible for an individual reporter or even a newspaper to do the depth investigation necessary to make a definitive judgment as to whether a specific government employee is a security risk unless there has been some provable disloyal act or perjury committed on some highly relevant issue. Innocence is even harder to establish. Although occasionally it is possible to prove that an individual has been disloyal, it is difficult to be certain that even a close personal acquaintance will be honest or loyal to his country under all circumstances. When a government agency through its official action, and following an FBI investigation, makes a decision that a government employee is a "security risk," it is difficult to challenge that judgment because the reporter or newspaper cannot usually be certain of access to all of the evidence and recommendations that were in the hands of the agency officials.

That was my basic thinking when the Wolf Ladejinsky security case landed on my desk on Friday, December 17, 1954. The *Des Moines Register's* farm editor, J. S. (Jim) Russell, had been told that Agriculture Secretary Ezra Taft Benson was ousting Ladejinsky as an agricultural attaché on grounds that he did not measure up to the Eisenhower administration's security standards.

Bureau Chief Richard Wilson asked me to "try to run down a story on it" in his usual detached manner and added the comment that "this fellow has some friends out in Des Moines." Dick didn't know Ladejinsky, and neither did I. I had no idea whether the "security risk" label was justified. What I did know was that it was dangerous to challenge such an agency determination because it was impossible to be sure what there might be in the investigative file or report. I was determined not to get into a silly position of defending a real "security risk" and wanted to be sure I did not overdraw conclusions on either side.

CAREFUL PREPARATION

A Congressional Supporter

Wilson said he had been told that Representative Walter Judd, a moderately conservative Republican from Minnesota, was a friend and admirer of Ladejinsky and had failed in his effort to save Ladejinsky from ouster. I know Representative Judd as a sound person and respected his judgment, but I also knew that the best balanced political figures can make mistakes in judgment on family members and long-time friends.

I called Walter Judd to go over his version of the case, and the reasons why he believed he had failed to convince the Eisenhower administration that Ladejinsky was not a security risk. Representative Judd was an early Eisenhower supporter, was a senior member on the House Foreign Affairs Committee, and was recognized as one of those individuals in Congress with clout in the Republican administration. He said he had registered a protest of the decision to oust Ladejinsky with Agriculture Secretary Ezra Taft Benson, and planned a further appeal on Ladejinsky's behalf the next Monday.

"It was a stupid decision," Judd said. "It is as bad as anything Joe McCarthy has ever done. Here is a man (Ladejinsky) who has been a loyal government employee for 19 years, doing great work against the Communists all across Asia, and he is being tossed to the wolves because some of Benson's advisers think he might be a Communist sympathizer. He is a true expert on the kind of land reform programs that are the best tool against Communism. Ladejinsky handled the land reform for General (Douglas) MacArthur in Japan, and I know from my personal knowledge that General MacArthur had a high regard for the work he did. He was the most effective man we had in Asia, because he was a man who knew agriculture and he wasn't afraid to get out and work with the people to show them what to do."

Judd said the Department of Agriculture was apparently barring Ladejinsky, a naturalized citizen, from employment because the 55-year-old agricultural expert had been born in Russia and in 1931 had worked briefly as an interpreter for Amtorg, the Russian trading agency. The Minnesota Republican added that the Agriculture Department official had hinted darkly at "some Communist connection" and suggested that Judd "might be embarrassed" if he pursued his objections.

"This man fled Communist Russia in 1922, and I can't believe he is sympathetic to the Soviet Union," Judd said.

The Agriculture Department's Claim

I called Assistant Secretary of Agriculture Earl Butz who confirmed that Ladejinsky had been notified that he would not be retained in his present position as an agricultural attaché in Japan or in any other position in the agriculture department. However,

Butz contended that the department "was not firing Ladejinsky." There was a technicality involved. Ladejinsky had been employed by the State Department as an agricultural attaché, but the last Congress had passed legislation shifting agricultural attachés from the state department to the agriculture department.

"This is not as if we were firing someone already on the payroll," Butz told me. "This man is not on our payroll, and we have wide discretion in hiring. I think in a case like this Secretary Benson could decline to accept a man because he didn't like the color of his hair."

Then Butz hurriedly said that the comment relative to the right to fire Ladejinsky because of the color of his hair was facetious, and that Secretary Benson had not acted on such a whim. He admitted that Ladejinsky was highly regarded in his professional field, but said he was familiar with the FBI file and he agreed with Secretary Benson.

I commented that Ladejinsky had been an employee of the State Department for 19 years, and had apparently passed that Department's security clearances. "That was under the old Truman administration security program, and Secretary Benson is applying the standards laid down in President Eisenhower's new program," Butz said. He hinted that there might be some material that was not before the Senate Department.

Assistant Secretary Butz was an articulate administration loyalist, and it was apparent that he agreed with the decision and felt confident that it could be defended. Reviewing the whole security file was the only way I could be certain of all elements in the decision. However, the ultimate in secrecy covered these files, theoretically for the protection of the employee. That secrecy was now being used against the employee, and for the protection of those who had judged Ladejinsky a "security risk." They could sit back protected by the secrecy laws, make an adverse decision, and meet each challenge with the taunting retort, "We know something that you don't know and that we can't tell you. If you knew what we know, then you would know we are right."

A Reliable but Confidential Source

The strict secrecy imposed on personnel security files made it dangerous to defend anyone found to be a "security risk," but I believed I had a source who might give me access to the Ladejinsky file. R. W. Scott McLeod, a friend with an Iowa background, was head of the State Department's security program. He was controversial because he was a former administrative assistant to Senator Styles Bridges, a conservative New Hampshire Republican, and was regarded as a friend of Senator Joe McCarthy. By reputation he ran a tough (some said too tough) security program for Secretary of State John Foster Dulles.

Scott McLeod, a former Iowa newspaperman, wasn't talking to many reporters because he had been burned by direct quotations and statements that had been taken out of context, but I could get through to him at any time, even though we had wide areas of disagreement. When he had worked for Senator Bridges, he had accepted the general Republican thesis that the conviction of Alger Hiss for perjury was indicative of widespread Communist penetration of the State Department. However, when he took charge of the security program for Dulles, he found that the reality was somewhat less dramatic. There was some laxity, there was some bureaucratic bungling, and there were some foreign service officers overlooking questionable conduct of other foreign service officers. On the whole, however, he could see no reason for the wholesale housecleaning his Republican friends in Congress wanted.

I was certain that Scott McLeod would shoot straight with me, and I even hoped he might arrange for me to examine Ladejinsky's security file. He agreed to speak to me, but strictly off the record. He did not wish to be caught in a fight between the Agriculture Department and the State Department. Certainly, he did not want to be identified as the source of information that would be an embarassment to a cabinet officer and the Eisenhower administration.

McLeod acknowledged that he had cleared Ladejinsky under the new Eisenhower standards a few months earlier after a personal examination of his file, but he could not permit me to examine the file because it would be a criminal law violation. Although the violation might be in a good cause—saving Ladejinsky's job—he could not risk it. He believed I would keep my source confidential, but pointed out, "I have to be in a position where I can testify truthfully before a congressional committee, or I will be risking my job. There are a lot of people who would like to shoot me down."

McLeod said he could not tell me whether there had been anything added to Ladejinsky's file since it had been sent to the Agriculture Department, but doubted it. However, he noted that this was something he could not state with assurance—it was always possible that some evidence had not surfaced that might create a serious problem. In answer to my questions, McLeod confirmed that the file he examined included the information on Ladejinsky's birth in Russia and his work for the Amtorg trading agency. He also confirmed Judd's assertion that General MacArthur had a high regard for Ladejinsky's work.

The Subject

With essentially all of the basic information in my hands, I called Ladejinsky who had returned to Washington from Japan in October expecting a routine transfer to another assignment. Ladejinsky, who was in his apartment on Fifteenth Street, said he did not want to discuss the case on the telephone and would come to my office in the National Press Building. He said he would answer all my questions, but wanted to appeal to me not to write a news story on his problem.

"Mr. Mollenhoff, you are interested in a sensational news story," Ladejinsky said. "Even if it is favorable, it will be a *cause celebré* for a few days in the press, then you will tire of it and leave me to be destroyed by the bureaucracy. I do not want you to write a story."

"I am going to write a story, with or without your cooperation," I replied. "If I get into a story, I do not drop it after a few days regardless of the obstacles. I intend to stick with this one until there is a satisfactory settlement." I summed up my limited conclusions at that time: "My inclination is to believe that you are the victim of a cruel and stupid decision by the Department of Agriculture, but I am not completely certain of that conclusion and will not be for some time. It is possible that you are a clever Communist operative, and that you have fooled a lot of important people for a long period of time. That is the impression that I get from high officials at the Department of Agriculture."

Ladejinsky said I did not give him any choice but to cooperate in order to demonstrate that he was a loyal citizen. He answered my questions fully from his early life as a farm boy in the Ukraine in Russia through his escape across the Middle East, and finally to his entry into the United States in 1922 without funds. He believed that his own experience in rising from abject poverty to a middle level government job was an achievement of note and felt it was a great advertisement for the United States. As we parted, he made one last plea that I not write his story, restating his fear that his case would be a brief sensation and that he would be abandoned.

Reading 13: The Ladejinsky Case

Without quoting McLeod, I wrote my story with a lead that would point up the problem, but would not take sides: "A sharp controversy was in the making here Friday over Agriculture Secretary Ezra Taft Benson's decision to oust a veteran agricultural expert under the security program." I wrote of Judd's opposition, of McLeod's recent clearance, and of the justifications put forward by

Assistant Secretary Butz. I had tried to reach Benson, but he was unavailable for comment.

The case was an immediate sensation in the world press as well as the national press, for it was evident that Secretary of Agriculture Benson was embracing Senator McCarthy's principles and was destroying the career of a valuable employee. Apparently Benson believed that the United States should be represented abroad by persons who were born and reared in this country.

The *Des Moines Register* lashed out editorially on Monday, December 20, 1954, at "A Shameful Action by Benson." The *Washington Post,* the *Washington Star,* and the *New York Times* were among the newspapers that followed that sharply critical line. News stories flowed in with critical comment from world leaders who had worked with Ladejinsky, but Benson would not back down from his judgment and President Eisenhower and the White House were unwilling to interfere.

Ladejinsky called and said he had "done some checking around," had been told that I would stick with a story, and he wished to give me full cooperation. I wrote a long article for the *Des Moines Register* on why Ladejinsky believed that his own career was the best answer to the Communists.

In the face of threats of a congressional investigation, Secretary Benson on December 22, 1954, released a statement formally branding Ladejinsky a "security risk," but Benson was not available for questioning. The press statement set out the fact that Ladejinsky had sisters in Russia, which made him subject to possible coercion. It set out his work for Amtorg in 1931 and a trip to Russia in 1939 as actions that raised doubts about his loyalty that had to be "resolved in favor of the government."

Milan D. Smith, Benson's administrative assistant, said the statement on Ladejinsky had been prepared by him and others in the department security program, but that it had been read to Benson and "cleared." It was apparent that the Agriculture Department release was intended to cast the worst possible implication on every fact. It erroneously asserted that Ladejinsky had been "an economist" for Amtorg when, in fact, he was employed for a few months as an interpreter. Benson's release also alleged erroneously that Ladejinsky belonged to two Communist-front organizations, on the strength of records showing he was on the mailing list of "The Washington Book Shop" and "The American Committee for Democratic Action." McLeod said that "The Washington Book Shop" was listed as a Communist-front, because the owners held Communist cell meetings in a back room. However, many unsuspecting people bought books there, and so ended up on the mailing list.

A spokesman for Secretary Dulles indicated the State Department did not agree with Benson by asserting that McLeod had cleared Ladejinsky under rules that were as strict as, if not stricter than, those at Agriculture. Then Smith admitted under questioning that the Agriculture Department obtained its information in a review of the State Department file, which McLeod studied before clearing Ladejinsky. In the process of questioning Smith, I drew the further admission that nothing of substance had been added to Ladejinsky's file since it was reviewed at the State Department. Although it was not like a personal review of the file, it gave me the assurance that it was unlikely the Agriculture Department had secret ammunition against Ladejinsky that they would bring up at some later time.

My conversation with Milan Smith, son of a wealthy vegetable packer from Pendleton, Oregon, and a bishop in the Mormon church, convinced me that he was sincere but ignorant in his handling of the Ladejinsky matter. I wanted to talk to Benson to determine just how much of this blundering was Benson's responsibility. Benson was unavailable at the Department on Wednesday. On Thursday morning, December 23, I was told at the office that the Secretary would not be back in the office until after Christmas. The questions would not wait, so I took a taxi to Benson's home.

A pretty dark-haired girl opened the door, greeted me warmly, said that her father was there and that she would get him for me. She did not ask my name, and I did not volunteer it as she went swinging into another room and in a lilting voice said, "Daddy, there is someone here to see you." A few moments later, a smiling Benson emerged to meet his caller. When he saw who it was his jaw dropped, and he said he did not expect me at his home.

I replied that there were some questions on the Ladejinsky case that could not wait and wanted to review his role in the case and his knowledge of it to make certain that I did not do him an injustice.

Benson said he had reviewed the whole file, that the statement prepared by his subordinates had been read to him, and that President Eisenhower had reviewed the Ladejinsky case personally and would back him to the limit.

This was a news story that was explosive and could put President Eisenhower in hot water too, unless Benson knew something I didn't know. I kept a lid on my elation and moved forward with casual questions about President Eisenhower's response and the time and circumstances of Benson's visit with him. This generated some concern in Secretary Benson who said he did not want to be quoted on his conversations with President Eisenhower, but would talk about the details on a background basis to explain why he did not fear the congressional criticism that was swirling around his head.

Benson had gone to the White House on Wednesday to go over the Ladejinsky case with President Eisenhower and to get assurances of Eisenhower's support. On Thursday, he had talked with Secretary of State Dulles, who was irked at the manner in which Ladejinsky had been handled, and won assurance from Secretary Dulles that he would not interfere with the prerogatives of the Secretary of Agriculture to brand Ladejinsky "a security risk." In answer to questions, Benson admitted that President Eisenhower did not have the full Ladejinsky file before him but had relied upon Benson's version of the case against Ladejinsky.

Then I turned to the task of getting Benson's version with some assurance that the terminology and attitude would have been what President Eisenhower had heard. I let him proceed in his own way, without critical questioning and with just enough leading questions to carry him through every part of the most controversial aspects. The result was a picture of an honest but ill-informed Cabinet officer, drawing conclusions he was not qualified to draw, and making decisions that were not justified.

The most disturbing point about it was that President Eisenhower had accepted the version of this Cabinet officer and agreed to back him without hearing any other version of the case. Also, Secretary Dulles had permitted himself to be made a part of the injustice for a political purpose, by agreeing to a pattern of inaction that he knew was wrong.

Benson rejected Walter Judd's assertion that he had done "an injustice" to Ladejinsky. "I've never wanted to do an injustice to any man in my life," Benson said. "I don't think one has been done here. Mr. Ladejinsky just is not our employee, and we decided not to hire him."

He also rejected the suggestion that the department release had put the worst possible interpretation on Ladejinsky's record. "I think everything that was in that statement was justified and more than justified," he said. "I wish I could open the entire file, and then I'm sure there would be no criticism of this case." He said there was material to support the charge that Ladejinsky belonged to two Communist-front organizations. "Much of that material is from FBI reports, and I can't discuss it," Benson said. "I only wish I could."

My copyrighted story on that interview rocked the White House, where it was hoped that Benson's problem would not mar the image of President Eisenhower. It brought even more national and world interest on the subject, and a great deal of competition for newsworthy material developed. I had a difficult time keeping on top of all developments because such innovative hardworking reporters as

Phil Potter, of the *Baltimore Sun,* and William Blair, of the *New York Times,* were assigned to work full time on the story.

Blair, an able reporter with great sources in the Department of Agriculture and Congress, was the most difficult competitor, and it was necessary to work from early morning until late at night to keep from being beat on my own story. Potter was less of a competitive problem because the *Baltimore Sun* did not have a news service, and because he did not normally cover the Agriculture Department.

There were some joint interviews at the Agriculture Department where I welcomed Potter's presence because it kept officials from denying statements when they saw the impact of the stories. This was particularly true when Milan Smith cited antisemitic letters which indicated that Benson's decision was popular with the voters.

It was not a happy holiday season for Benson or for the White House because the barrage of highly critical stories continued to flow and Democratic senators and congressmen were threatening congressional investigations and hearings that could link President Eisenhower to McCarthyism in 1956—an election year. Within a few days, the White House arranged to have Harold Stassen, the head of the Foreign Operations Administration, move in to clear Ladejinsky and to hire him. At the same time, the White House announced that it was doing a sweeping reorganization of its security program to make certain that in any future case the government employee would be given the right of due process of law (notice of charges and a hearing), which had not been accorded to Ladejinsky by Benson before being labeled a "security risk."

It was a clever maneuver to permit the salvage of Ladejinsky's record and to reestablish political tranquility without the necessity of forcing stubborn Secretary Benson to retreat from his unsupported charges. It might have worked except that Agriculture Department officials and supporters of Benson continued to circulate the December 22, 1954, press release as if the charges were firm. After several quiet efforts to get Benson to withdraw those charges, I decided to confront President Eisenhower, in a manner that would dramatize the fact that one arm of his administration was engaging in outrageous smear tactics.

At the February 23, 1955, press conference I asked Mr. Eisenhower a carefully honed question: "Mr. President, in the past you have made it clear that you deplored the fact that certain members of Congress have attacked individuals unjustly on the floor, but you at the same time said that was a matter for Congress to decide . . . for itself. Now, I wonder what steps you would take if it should come to your attention that someone in the executive agency would call an individual a member of a subversive organization when they had no evidence to sustain that and that it was absolutely clear that there was no evidence to sustain it?"

The President replied that like the Supreme Court he did not like to answer long hypothetical questions that he did not understand. "When you bring me facts such as you just now allege and bring them so that I can study them and not answer them in a press conference where I have nothing of any other side except a statement of accusation, then I will give you my opinion, but not now."

"Mr. President," I asked quickly, "is that an invitation to present this . . ."

"You can—if you have any information . . . of wrongdoing," the President answered and opened the way for me to file a two-page letter spelling out the reiteration by Benson of unsupported charges of disloyalty.

"What will the White House do in this case where the Agriculture Department continues to hurl the charge that Ladejinsky was a member of two subversive organizations, when other departments state the charge is untrue?" I summarized at the end of the letter. "What is the general policy of the White House with regard to correcting mistakes if it becomes clear that any executive agency was making charges against an individual that were not substantiated?"

Despite my constant inquiry and the repeated promises of the White House Press Secretary, I did not receive a reply until it became apparent that a Senate subcommittee was going to subpoena Benson and several of his aides to answer questions on the handling of the Ladejinsky case.

On June 21, I received a brief letter from James Hagerty, White House Press Secretary, about the Agriculture Department's false charge that Ladejinsky held "membership in two Communist-front organizations." "I have discussed the matter with the Secretary of Agriculture and he has indicated that the (press) release was probably written a bit too hard," Hagerty wrote on the grudging admission that Benson had finally made. Hagerty's letter said I should "get in touch with the Department of Agriculture for any further discussion of the release." Hagerty also told me the White House was giving Benson a chance "to turn around," but I was advised by others in the White House that Benson had threatened to quit if he wasn't permitted to handle the correction in his own way.

A few days later Benson canceled his decision that Ladejinsky was a "security risk," and voided the press release that erroneously stated he was "a member of two Communist-front organizations." He did it in a letter to Senator Frank Carlson, a Kansas Republican who was the ranking Republican member of the Senate Post Office and Civil Service Committee that was investigating the government's security program.

The *Des Moines Register* and other newspapers applauded the decision with editorials on "A Battle for Freedom Won," and Ladejinsky told the Associated Press in Saigon, South Vietnam, that it was a "belated but happy vindication of the principles of justice and fair play on which American democracy rests." He thanked "the American press and other media of public opinion for illuminating and upholding the larger issues which far transcend the ordeal of a single individual . . . . I have a special debt of gratitude to Clark Mollenhoff, reporter of the *Des Moines Register,* who brought my case to public attention and continued untiringly to cover it in the highest tradition of his profession."

REWARDS OF PERSISTENCE

I was awarded the Heywood Broun Memorial Award, The Raymond Clapper Memorial Award, and my second National Sigma Delta Chi Award for Washington Correspondence for the coverage of the Ladejinsky case. I was told that the Pulitzer awards committee passed over the Ladejinsky case because influential members of that awards jury believed I was too aggressive in my questioning of President Eisenhower.

One of those Pulitzer jurors, later a good friend of mine, said he had believed that I should have pressed the issue with Benson rather than have bothered President Eisenhower with it. When I explained about my unsuccessful quiet efforts to convince the obstinate Benson that he should reverse himself, the Pulitzer committee member said he was sorry he hadn't known it at the time for he had been critical of me.

I learned from this that it is wise to avoid confrontations in the White House press conferences until after all efforts to correct governmental problems at lower levels have failed. Even when a reporter has made reasonable efforts to get reasonable action from an agency, there is always the possibility that a proper followup questioning of the president will be regarded as brash or irresponsible unless great care is given with the precise wording. It is easy for any president to make a reporter look bad in the eyes of the public.

STUDENT WORK PROJECT SUGGESTION

Write a paper explaining and analyzing the present procedures for handling investigations of allegation that a government official is a "security risk." Find the last such case that came to public attention outside of the Central Intelligence Agency (CIA) and the Departments of Defense and State. Give a detailed chronology of the last case involving "security risk" charges that has been brought to a conclusion. Do you feel it was disposed of with even-handed justice?

25 THE BIG LABOR RACKET INQUIRY

Local crime stories are recognized as a national problem only after a number of investigative reporters work together to demonstrate the common threads of labor racketeering, the connections of national crime figures, and the responsibility of various federal agencies and departments to police these crimes. Because of the political power of the Teamsters Union, it was difficult to persuade the labor committees of the House and Senate to do a thorough and effective job of investigating corruption that involved the Teamsters.

It took the combined efforts of many reporters to force the Congress to recognize the enormity of the problem of theft and mismanagement depleting the union insurance and pension funds. Reporters from the western part of the country, the Midwest, the South and the Middle Atlantic states worked together and separately compiling the records that showed similar threads of dishonesty. Those news stories demonstrated that frauds of similar nature were taking place in different regions and that they were not being investigated properly by state or federal authorities. The pension and insurance funds, created for the benefit of union members, were being jeopardized by inadequate laws and by lax enforcement.

The criminal records of union officials were public and available for examination in state and federal courts. The reports on the pension and insurance funds were available at the Labor Department, or through dissident union members who were eager to cooperate with responsible reporters.

LOCAL ASPECTS

The Senate Select Committee on Improper Activities in the Labor or Management Field launched its hearings with testimony from William Lambert and Wallace Turner, the investigative reporters for the *Portland Oregonian.* It was obvious to everyone who heard their testimony on Teamsters racketeering in Oregon and Washington that their great series was based upon meticulous research in local police and court records to corroborate the story of informant James B. Elkins, a Portland racketeer.

Jim Elkins, the committee's chief witness, gave a detailed inside account of how Teamsters representatives tried to impose a monopoly on pinball machines and other coin-operated devices in Portland by picketing any place that used rival machines. I was familiar with the pattern of using Teamsters power and Teamsters pickets because of testimony on similar conditions in Detroit, Cleveland, and Minneapolis.

Lambert and Turner, generally aware that law enforcement was corrupt and compromised in Multnomah County, Oregon, followed the leads of Elkins and other confidential informants inside and outside local government. They contacted my friend, Ed Guthman, of the *Seattle Times,* to get complete information on the identity and connections of Seattle Teamsters who were a part of the union power play that was corrupting local government.

The story they told the committee was a sordid tale of how prostitution, gambling, and liquor racketeering had corrupted or compromised police, prosecutors, courts, and a few Oregon state officials. It was not unlike the conditions I had seen and written about in Polk County ten years earlier. It was what Harold Brislin was writing about in Scranton, Pennsylvania, and what John Seigenthaler, of the *Tennessean,* was unwinding in police and court records in Nashville and Chattanooga.

These were local stories, developed to a large extent by police reporter record research of the type that Ed Guthman had used in Seattle and that I used in Minneapolis. But, great as the local investigative reporting was on union rackets in a dozen or more cities, it did not automatically bring the McClellan labor racket investigation into existence. It was necessary to put together stories of police and political corruption resulting from misuse of union political and economic power to make a national story of great significance. With the help of congressional investigators Downey Rice, Lester Condon, Frank Plant, and William Leece, I recognized the national scope by late 1953.

THE NATIONAL SCENE

Even as I was covering the Dixon-Yates scandal at the Atomic Energy Commission and the Wolf Ladejinsky case in 1954 and

1955, I was pushing various congressional committees to do a big, significant investigation of labor rackets. My focus had broadened from the Minneapolis Teamsters unions into real depth investigation of International Teamsters President Dave Beck and Detroit Teamsters Boss James R. Hoffa.

Hoffa, an international Teamsters vice president, was the second most powerful Teamster leader in the United States dominating the Central States Conference and pushing for power through underworld alliances in California, New York, New Jersey, Tennessee, and Florida. It was assumed he could force Dave Beck out of the presidency when he wanted to do it.

Dave Beck, of Seattle, still maintained a respectable public image with entree to the Eisenhower White House, despite hearings that raised questions about kickbacks in connection with Western Conference insurance. Even if Dave Beck was not personally culpable in connection with the pension and insurance fund thievery, he was responsible for permitting dishonest officials and racketeers to continue in union office. Also, I knew that it was Dave Beck's man Edward Cheyfitz who had pulled the strings to sabotage and kill a half dozen budding investigations of the Teamsters Union in Los Angeles, Seattle, Pittsburgh, Chicago, Kansas City, Detroit, and Minneapolis.

Exchange of Information

At a Nieman Fellows reunion at Harvard University, in June 1954, I had met Ed Guthman, a Pulitzer Prize winning reporter for the *Seattle Times*. Guthman was as fascinated by the Teamsters Union as I was, and he was better acquainted with the details of Dave Beck's operations. "Beck is a crook, but nobody has been able to prove it," Ed Guthman stated emphatically. He had concluded that Beck had too many big political connections to be brought down by a congressional committee.

Guthman filled me in on some of Beck's business connections, which represented likely conflicts of interest, and reviewed stories of how Teamsters goon squads had rampaged in the Seattle area in past years. I filled Guthman in on the activities of Sid Brennan, Jerry Connelly, Jimmy Hoffa, and others who had been the subjects of my investigations and congressional hearings. Guthman and I agreed to a pattern of mutual cooperation which was to pay big dividends in 1956, 1957, and 1958.

In 1954 and 1955, that cooperation amounted to passing information on the abortive investigations of the House Labor subcommittee under Chairman Sam McConnell, a Pennsylvania

Republican, and a Senate Labor Subcommittee that started its investigations under Chairman Irving M. Ives, a liberal New York Republican. Also, Representative George Bender, of Ohio, was pushing ineffective investigations in Cleveland where Louis N. (Babe) Triscaro, a convicted robber was the president of Teamsters Local 436.

Chairman McConnell permitted his chief counsel, Edward McCabe, to hire an expert accountant investigator, Carmine Bellino. He took a few deep investigative bites into the scandals buried in the pension and insurance funds in Dave Beck's own 11-state Western Conference of Teamsters. The hearings in Los Angeles had virtually no press attention, and Guthman was unaware of this foray into the domain of Dave Beck and his top honcho, Frank Brewster, until I brought it to his attention.

Then, Guthman obtained the hearing transcripts and put together a number of stories. Those stories included interviews with Teamsters and explanations of the background that were not available in the hearings. The stories by Guthman gave me a better understanding of some elements of the Western Conference of Teamsters in the same way that my stories and copies of Minneapolis and Detroit Teamsters hearings had given Ed Guthman a greater understanding of the pension and insurance fund problems.

Attempts to Encourage Investigation

In 1955, I talked to Robert F. Kennedy and suggested that the Senate Permanent Investigations Subcommittee should try to investigate the labor racketeers in the Teamsters Union. When he questioned whether the committee had jurisdiction, I noted that the House Government Operations Committee had adopted a theory of jurisdiction based on the evidence that the Justice Department, Internal Revenue Service, and Labor Department were not properly administering and enforcing the criminal and labor laws on union racketeering.

Bob Kennedy was only mildly interested, but he instructed Associate Counsel Paul Kamerick to take down the information on the proposed Teamsters' probe and my theory of the committee's jurisdiction over labor racketeering. I did not know Bob Kennedy well at the time of my first efforts to interest him in a labor racket inquiry, but we became better acquainted as I covered various investigations and hearings of the very active Permanent Investigations Subcommittee. Periodically, I would try to stir his interest and the interest of Chairman John L. McClellan, the conservative Arkansas Democrat.

In the fall of 1955, there was a significant split between Minneapolis Teamsters Boss Sid Brennan and Jerry Connelly, the labor racketeer from Detroit and Miami who Hoffa had sent to Minneapolis in 1952. Brennan, with backing from Dave Beck, had ousted Connelly from his post as a business agent for Teamsters Local 548 in Minneapolis. Then, despite the fact that the entire Minneapolis Teamsters organization backed Brennan, Hoffa arranged to put the convicted labor racketeer back into office. Also, Hoffa was blocking efforts of AFL President George Meany to clean house in the International Brotherhood of Longshoremen (IBL) in Detroit, where a convicted armed robber was directing violence and corruption with Hoffa's backing.

Interview with Hoffa

Those were only a couple of the things I wished to discuss with Hoffa when I called him at the Statler Hotel in Washington the night of November 5, 1955. He was busy at the time, but said he would be glad to see me the next morning at 8:30 in the lobby of the Mayflower.

The Mayflower lobby was crowded with Teamsters business agents and officers the next morning as I waited for Jimmy near the Connecticut Avenue entrance. When Jimmy whipped in the door, 15 minutes late, the effect on Teamsters officials was electrifying. Everyone wanted to talk with the crown prince, and he loved it. He shook hands with them, called most of them by their first names, and thumped some of them on the shoulder with the good-natured roughness of truck drivers.

"Hi ya, poison pen," Jimmy greeted me. He didn't say it critically. It was said with amusement. How naive could I be to think my newspaper and magazine stories could stop Hoffa! When we were seated in the hotel coffee shop, Hoffa advised with a smile, "Why don't you give it up? Nothing will come of it. We're the Teamsters."

Dave Beck tried to hide his moves to kill off government investigations of his union, but Jimmy Hoffa didn't mind saying frankly that the Teamsters were bigger than the government. I started a review of Connelly's thievery and terrorism that had resulted in his conviction for frauds in Minneapolis and was surprised when Hoffa revealed that he had advised Connelly to plead guilty.

"I advised him to cop a plea on that charge and get it over with," Hoffa explained. "I told him there was no need to make a production out of it in court and keep it in the papers for weeks. I figured it would give him a little trouble to start with, but I told him if he'd sweat it out it would soon be forgotten." He said he was not going to start firing union officials for what he called "technical violations of Taft-Hartley."

"In the first place we don't consider it a good law," Hoffa said. "I'd say that 99 percent of the local labor leaders violate it, and most of them don't even know they are in violation."

"What about the membership opposition to Connelly going back on the payroll of Local 548?" I asked.

"I don't believe it," Hoffa snapped. "It is just a couple of guys out there that don't want Connelly back in. Brennan is one of them, and it's strictly a personal matter."

I brought up the reports that Connelly had run out of Florida to escape prosecution for the attempted murder of a Black employee of the Laundry Workers International Union, and Hoffa admitted a role in Connelly's flight.

"We advised him to get out fast," Hoffa said. "Jerry didn't shoot that guy in Florida. He was just unlucky and got connected with a couple of screwballs who did the shooting."

"But won't reinstatement of Connelly damage the labor movement?" I asked.

"I have the philosophy that you never let a fellow down just because he is in a little trouble," Hoffa responded. "Connelly is one of our people. I try to take care of them. Jerry isn't as young as he used to be. He had to run out of Florida. He can't keep on running forever. Sometime you gotta stand and fight. If he doesn't stay in Minneapolis, he'll have to move and it isn't easy to start again."

"Aren't you hurting labor when you keep a convicted labor leader like Connelly in a position of importance?" I asked.

"Who gives a damn what the public thinks as long as the union members think it's okay," he said. "The boys in Minneapolis are going to go along with us. I know. I've talked to a lot of them."

I told him I was going to keep writing stories about Connelly as long as he was kept in power, and I said I thought he and Dave Beck should see the need for taking some drastic action to get their house in order.

"Now look here, Clark," Hoffa said. "They don't pay newspaper reporters enough for you to be giving me the bad time that you've been giving me. Everyone has his price. What's yours?" Hoffa said it cooly and clearly, looking me straight in the eye.

I was uncomfortable for a moment. I wondered if he thought I had been critical of the Teamsters to set up a payoff, or if this was just the normal method of "Hoffa, the direct actionist," that I had heard so much about. My embarrassment gave way to amusement at the guts of this little guy in throwing such a proposition at me. I hadn't said or done a thing at any time in our nearly three years of dealing to indicate anything but the firmest opposition to Teamsters corruption.

"You don't have enough money, Jimmy," I answered with a laugh. It seemed best to treat it as a joke. "Let's get on with the interview."

Hoffa grinned, shrugged with a "well-I-tried-anyway" attitude, and we resumed our discussion of Connelly, other union crooks, the power of the union, and Teamsters jurisdiction. At least he hadn't threatened to have me beaten up as some of my bootlegger and gambler friends in Des Moines had done from time to time.

I related the interview to Bob Kennedy a few days later for his amusement and to demonstrate Hoffa's philosophy. Kennedy smiled and quipped, "Incidentally, what *is* your price?"

"If you're really interested in an answer, it is the same one I gave Hoffa," I answered in the same facetious spirit. Bob repeated that story to Senator John Kennedy a few weeks later in spelling out the arrogant clout of the Teamsters, and Senator Kennedy used it in a magazine article a couple of years later.

THE McCLELLAN COMMITTEE INVESTIGATION

Precipitating Events

In 1956, there were a series of events that made it possible to convince Bob Kennedy and Senator McClellan that they had a responsibility to become involved in the investigations of labor rackets. I had delivered to Bob Kennedy and Chairman McClellan a 13-part series I had written on the Teamsters that appeared in the *Minneapolis Star.* My intensified efforts to demonstrate the Committee's jurisdiction and responsibility were aided by these events:

1. Senator Paul Douglas, the liberal Illinois Democrat, prematurely ended an investigation by a subcommittee of the Senate Labor Committee without touching the festering frauds in the Teamsters Union. Chairman Douglas settled for exposing a million-dollar embezzlement by Eugene (Jimmy) James, the secretary-treasurer of the International Laundry Workers Union.

2. Syndicated Labor Columnist Victor Riesel was the victim of a vicious acid blinding attack at the hands of a Teamsters-connected hit man who was in turn murdered by those who hired him to throw the acid in Riesel's face.

3. Lester Velie, the great crime reporter for *Readers Digest,* wrote a powerful article on Jimmy Hoffa based upon the

various congressional hearings, trial records from court cases, and personal interviews.

4. The *Portland Oregonian* series by Lambert and Turner was published in April 1956, and I delivered a copy to Bob Kennedy to fortify my arguments on the great local investigations that had received no national attention but had established the fact that misuse of union power was a national problem.

5. An investigation of a scandal involving the purchase of millions of dollars worth of military uniforms led the Senate Permanent Investigations Subcommittee to New York and New Jersey mob figures, including Teamsters racketeer John (Johnny Dio) Dioguardi. From this investigation Bob Kennedy saw for himself the insidious corrupting influence of the union-connected mobsters on military buying.

Convincing Arguments

Again Bob Kennedy asked me to spell out the jurisdiction for the Senate Permanent Investigations Subcommittee, and then asked me precisely what the subcommittee could do that others had not done. I told him how a half dozen investigations had been cut off prematurely by the political clout of the Teamsters Union, and of the frustrations of Downey Rice, Frank Plant, Edward McCabe, William Leece, and others. I suggested that he talk to those experienced investigators, and that he consult with ace accountant investigator Carmine Bellino, who was at that time on his staff.

I explained that those investigators could verify everything that I had told him and could also tell him of additional evidence and leads that were in their files at the time their investigations were halted by union pressures. Over a period of months Bob Kennedy talked to all of them, became convinced that the investigation was long overdue, and received Chairman McClellan's authorization to start the research and the field investigations.

Congressional hearing records provided a wealth of material that had not been widely used, and additional material came from frustrated investigators who were pleased with the possibility that their work would be completed. Bob Kennedy said he was going to Seattle and Portland, and asked that I contact Ed Guthman and Turner and Lambert.

Guthman had never heard of Bob Kennedy and was generally suspicious of the motivations of congressional investigators because of Senator Joseph McCarthy's investigations. It was necessary to assure Guthman that Kennedy was honest and would keep confidence and follow through on leads. It is amusing to reflect on that conversation now in the light of the great personal friendship that Kennedy developed with Guthman in later years.

Helping the Committee

In December 1956, when I was doing one of my periodic lectures on investigative reporting at the American Press Institute (API) at Columbia University, I injected a practical suggestion for the 27 reporters in the API seminar. Having reviewed my own frustration in getting action on Polk County courthouse frauds and being aware that many of them had comparable problems, I suggested that they take any labor-related corruption to the McClellan Permanent Investigations Subcommittee. I reviewed how John Strohmeyer, Ted Link, and a dozen or so local crime reporters had cooperated with the Kefauver committee in exposing local corruption, and suggested that a similar opportunity was at hand if they possessed documented union-connected corruption and presented it effectively to Bob Kennedy.

John Seigenthaler, a general assignment reporter for the *Nashville Tennessean,* came up to talk to me during the coffee break. He had been frustrated in efforts to expose Teamsters corruption and a crooked judge who dismissed indictments against local Teamsters and had control of the local grand jury and all criminal cases. I appreciated the difficulty of his problem, having been through a similar situation in Polk County, and suggested that he contact Bob Kennedy, mentioning that the McClellan Subcommittee had some staff members in an office in New York at that time. Although Seigenthaler had a sleepy look about him and talked with a slow Tennessee drawl, the information he recited was precise on key points.

Seigenthaler was an experienced reporter so it was not necessary to explain the mechanics of obtaining police, court, and land records. I emphasized that he develop a chronology of each fixed criminal case from the criminal record, blend it with other relevant information indicating payoffs, and put it together with complete identification of the business and political connections of key figures.

When we assembled after the recess, I made general reference to Seigenthaler's problem and reiterated my suggestions to him with supportive comments from API Consultant Ben Reece, the retired city editor of the *St. Louis Post Dispatch,* and API Director J. Montgomery Curtis, an experienced former city editor with the *Buffalo Evening News.* Reece, a legend in St. Louis where his staff members had won a half dozen Pulitzers, told the reporters they should not pass by this opportunity. He recalled Ted Link's work with the Kefauver Committee and Paul Y. Anderson's great Pulitzer Prize work with the Senate Committee that exposed the Teapot Dome scandals in the 1920s.

Several reporter participants in that API meeting asked me more questions about the upcoming investigation, the specific jurisdiction of the committee, and said they planned to contact Kennedy. However, the most sensational results were obtained by Seigenthaler in Tennessee. He was fortunate because his first contact was with LaVern Duffy, one of the most skillful, resourceful, and thorough staff members. The Tennessee hearing in the late fall of 1957 was one of the most startling after three sensation-packed years. It unveiled a wide range of union and local government corruption and led to the impeachment and conviction of Judge Raulston Schoolfield.

Public and Legislative Gains

During the course of the McClellan investigations, Bob Kennedy and his investigators became personally acquainted with local investigative reporters from Miami to Seattle and from Augusta, Maine, to San Diego, California. The path of Teamsters corruption led to police, sheriffs, and state police; mayors, governors, state legislators, congressmen, senators, cabinet officers, and to the White House door. It included local, state, and federal judges in Michigan, and raised questions about the integrity of state and federal judges in a half dozen other regions.

The favorable press that the McClellan Labor Racket Committee received in conservative as well as liberal newspapers built the image of Senator John Kennedy and Counsel Bob Kennedy as courageous pursuers of labor racketeers. Corrupt labor was equated with the villains Dave Beck, Jimmy Hoffa, Anthony (Tony Pro) Provenzano, and Louis N. (Babe) Triscaro.

These labor racket hearings were drama packed at every stage, and they changed the lives of those government officials, reporters, union officials, and businessmen who had any role in them. The stage was set for the passage of the Landrum-Griffin labor reform act in September 1959, which was Senator Kennedy's only real claim to fame as a legislator in his years in the House and Senate. His leadership role in the passage of the Landrum-Griffin reporting and disclosure act gave him a new standing among his Senate colleagues who had regarded him as an articulate, handsome, and wealthy playboy.

The labor racket hearings provided Bob Kennedy with depth experience in law enforcement problems concerning organized crime and labor, and they provided him with advisors who made it possible for him to be a very effective Attorney General in the area of criminal law enforcement.

The Senate hearings and Bob Kennedy's service as Attorney General resulted in nearly 200 indictments against Teamsters Union officials, their associates in other unions, and the lawyers, accountants, bankers, robbers, and petty racketeers who were a part of the octopus of Teamsters Union power. There were more than 150 convictions up to mid-1965, including Dave Beck and Jimmy Hoffa, both of whom served federal prison terms.

Reporters' Rewards

Wallace Turner and William Lambert were awarded a Pulitzer Prize in 1957 for local reporting for the Portland expose, and I was awarded the Pulitzer Prize for national reporting in 1958 because my stories brought the McClellan labor racket committee into being. My work also won the 1958 National Sigma Delta Chi Public Service Award for the *Des Moines Register* and *Tribune* and the *Minneapolis Star* and *Tribune*. John Harold Brislin, crime reporter for the *Scranton* (Pennsylvania) *Tribune* and *Scrantonian* was awarded a Pulitzer Prize in 1959 for his exposure of union racketeering and its corruption of local government.

The equally fine works of Ed Guthman in Seattle and John Seigenthaler were not singled out for distinction by the Pulitzer Committee, but Guthman had already won a Pulitzer in 1950. However, the work of Seigenthaler, Turner, and Lambert on the labor rackets was an important factor in their selection as Nieman Fellows at Harvard. Seigenthaler went on to become editor and then publisher of the *Nashville Tennessean.* Turner became a West Coast correspondent for the *New York Times.* Lambert worked for more than a decade as a member of the great *Life* magazine investigative team and was personally responsible for the story on questionable financial dealings that led to the resignation of Supreme Court Justice Abe Fortas.

All of the work was basically sound, straight reporting using police and court records, with an aggressive followup of interviews and stories. This is always necessary to keep the pressure on public officials to ensure that they will assume their responsibility for enforcement of the criminal laws. The key attributes were thoroughness and persistence in pushing for answers and actions.

YOUNG MEN AND TAYLOR'S SYSTEM

James Drinkhall, of *Overdrive* magazine, Jonathan Kwitny, of the *Wall Street Journal,* and Jack Taylor of the *Daily Oklahoman,* are a few of the younger group of persistent investigative reporters who are following labor rackets with the same police and court record base. In fact, their work indicates record keeping that is far superior to the records I kept in Des Moines and in my first years in Washington. Jack Taylor's great work on the massive $3.5 billion Central States Teamsters pension and welfare funds was possible because of the complete files he keeps with copies of official documents, court records, and interviews.

Record Keeping

Taylor's system of record keeping is nearly ideal, and is far above the standard that most reporters will find possible or practical. It is not essential to have the private office, the locked closet, and the locked files that Taylor has at the *Oklahoman,* but these ideal conditions have resulted in a work product that is consistently of Pulitzer Prize quality.

Jack Taylor writes extensive memorandums on all conversations with witnesses. He does it immediately after the interview or as soon after the interview as he can find the time to get to a typewriter. He types all key names and the names of business firms in capital letters, and establishes a crossfiling system to call his attention to repeated references to the same people by different witnesses. He takes extensive notes from police records, court records, land title records, and from the state corporation registration records. He then explains these transactions in detailed memorandums for his files. As he is engaged in his record research and interviews, he keeps precise notes on the dates and times of the interviews and on the dockets and page numbers of official records.

When he starts an investigation, Jack Taylor draws up a rough chronology of the major events; as the investigation moves along, he reviews it to see how the records and interviews corroborate or contradict each other. When there are inconsistencies on time or dates he makes a recheck to see if a witness may be confused or if he may be intentionally telling a false story.

Taylor's method is undoubtedly the best way to develop facts and understand complicated financial transactions in the multi-billion-dollar Central States Teamsters insurance manipulations. However, Taylor is the first to say that on many less complicated investigations he would be able to move faster if he did not spend so much time preparing memorandums for his files. Although I was a good deal less systematic in my record-keeping habits, I think Taylor's method is better than my own was. I believe it is better to make the mistake of keeping too many records than to make a mistake in misreading cold notes months after they were taken. Only extensive experience will give a reporter reasonable sureness as to which part of record keeping is important for a specific project, and what is important will vary from case to case. At first it is probably better to err on the side of keeping too much.

When there are several persons working on an investigation, all interviews and records research should be reduced to writing and should be so specific that there can be no possibility of misunderstanding as to what was said or meant. In directing the IRE Arizona Project, Bob Greene demanded written daily reports from the reporters on the widely varying segments of the dragnet on corruption and racketeering involved. Greene personally read all of the memorandums so he would be aware of all the assorted pieces of the puzzle of crime activity and responsibility. That elaborate system is probably impractical and too time consuming for research on small and uncomplicated probes of corruption and mismanagement that make up the bulk of investigative reporting.

STUDENT WORK PROJECT SUGGESTION

Draw up a list of research books for studying the McClellan Labor Racket Subcommittee. What were the exact dates of its hearings and its reports? What was the official name of the subcommittee? Who were the members of the subcommittee in addition to Chairman John L. McClellan, of Arkansas? What legislation was passed as a result of the work of this subcommittee? When was it passed? What legislation has passed since that time that deals with maintaining the integrity of employee pension and insurance funds?

26 THE REGULATORY AGENCIES AND THE WHITE HOUSE

Political favoritism and corruption in the regulatory agencies is often given routine coverage in the trade publications and on the business pages of the nation's newspapers. This insidious corruption, often ignored by the beat reporters and the wire services, is ripe for picking by any diligent investigative reporter, even though he is new to the Washington scene. A limited degree of cooperation by Washington reporters who do not have competitive newspapers gives each of the investigations more impact.

Robert Healy, then a Washington reporter for the *Boston Globe,* and David Kraslow, then a Washington reporter for the *Miami Herald,* demonstrated that intelligent and inquisitive local reporters with good police and court experience can quickly adapt to the Washington scene. By building upon what they knew about local political figures in Massachusetts and Florida they were able in the late 1950's to produce stories with national impact within a few months after being assigned to Washington. They did it by concentrating their attention on the operations of the federal regulatory agencies, most specifically on the Federal Communications Commission. The same thing will work with regard to almost any Washington agency or department at almost any time.

AN INSIDIOUS FORM OF CORRUPTION

For the most part, the coverage of the so-called independent regulatory agencies in Washington is left to the trade press, the Associated Press, and United Press International. This creates a situation in which "conflicts of interests" are ignored or tolerated and where corrupt practices and political favoritism can flourish.

Essentially any of what has been known as "the big six" regulatory agencies was full of insidious corruption and ready for exposure by any diligent investigative reporter.

Difficulties in Dealing with Regulatory Agencies

It would be possible for an experienced reporter to start from the bottom to do an analysis of the standards established in the law and regulations, and the manner in which the various commissions depart from those standards in granting rights by the Federal Communications Commission (FCC), the Civil Aeronautics Board (CAB), the Interstate Commerce Commission (ICC), the Federal Power Commission (FPC), the Federal Trade Commission (FTC) or the Securities and Exchange Commission (SEC). However, it might be months or even years before even an experienced reporter would come across evidence of corruption or conflicts in this manner, although a general analysis in any one regulatory agency might be productive in a few weeks.

The broad analysis of every part of any agency's operation is what a congressional committee with oversight responsibility attempts to do, using an entire staff of technical experts, lawyers, and accountants as well as professional investigators. It is the same type of all-encompassing job of analysis that the General Accounting Office (GAO) tries to do when it is requested by a member of Congress or a congressional committee or subcommittee.

The type of depth investigation is beyond the financial capacity of most newspapers and is certainly beyond the scope of what most reporters could organize, even if they had the time. It would take weeks or months for a reporter to become skillful at charting his way through the bulky open files at the FCC, ICC, FPC, CAB, FTC, or SEC. However, there are short cuts to understanding the operation of any specific independent regulatory agency, and the mechanics of their operations are pretty much the same.

Although the president nominates the members of the regulatory agencies, they are in fact the arms of Congress. They are established to develop expertise in the regulation of various specialized industries. Thus, the FCC has control over broadcast licenses and regulates radio, television, and cable television. The CAB regulates the airline industry; the ICC has jurisdiction over the railroads and the truck lines; and the FPC regulates the interstate power industry. Both the FTC and the SEC have less specialized regulatory functions, and the Commodity Futures Trading Commission (CFTC) (established in 1974) has the responsibility of regulating the trillion-dollar-a-year business in commodity futures trading.

The decisions of these regulatory agencies are worth millions of dollars, and their enforcement or lack of enforcement of the laws can be the difference between federal prison and big profits. For the reporter the problem is much the same as the selective enforcement of liquor laws in Polk County, Iowa.

The "Revolving Door" Syndrome

For all practical purposes, my experience with the regulatory agencies started in 1957, during the time I was doing daily news stories on the labor racket hearing. I had dealt with the general sweep of regulatory agency law at Drake University Law School and had read of the general problems of regulatory agencies while on the Nieman Fellowship at Harvard; however, I was far from having expert knowledge on any single agency.

In general, I was familiar with the views of Supreme Court Justice Oliver Wendell Holmes that all regulatory agencies should be taken apart about every 20 years because in most instances the regulated industry managed to control the regulatory agency. For example, the airline industry executives and lawyers concentrated on the appointments to the CAB and on influencing its personnel and policies, whereas the public and the general press paid little attention to these matters. A movement of personnel, particularly lawyers from the CAB to the airlines and from the airlines to the CAB, created an unhealthy condition from a standpoint of protecting the public interest.

One did not have to be particularly perceptive to see what was called "the revolving door" between the government and the regulated industries, but each administration justified such appointments by the need to gain experienced, competent commissioners. The Senate committees with confirmation hearing authority tended to accept assurances from all appointees that they would not let their past employment influence their decisions in a government regulatory agency. In addition, the regulated industry usually concentrated its lobbying activity and its political contributions on the influential members of the Senate and House committees with oversight authority. This usually made the congressional committees a part of the whole unhealthy setup.

The incestuous relationship that existed between the industry, the regulating agency, and the congressional committee members and staffs made it difficult to stimulate even a superficial investigation unless the newspapers unearthed shocking scandals and pressed demands for a depth inquiry. In a sense even the press was involved. Although the trade press did a knowledgeable and thorough job on the background of all appointments and decisions, they were usually not critical of the regulatory agency or the industry's actions. The trade press was generally a part of the trade establishment, even though I found it to be a reliable guide on actions in the industry. For example, *Broadcasting* magazine was a thorough and reliable reporter of all decisions and actions dealing with radio and television broadcast rights. However, it was never a crusader against the conflicts of interest, political influence peddling, and other shady practices stimulated by the communications bar members.

EXECUTIVE PRIVILEGE USED TO
DEFEND CORRUPTION

In early 1957, the House, at the suggestion of Speaker Sam Rayburn (Dem., Tex.), set up the Legislative Oversight Subcommittee of the House Interstate and Foreign Commerce Committee "to review, study, and examine the execution of the laws by the administrative and independent agencies of the Government." It was an effort to find out if the Eisenhower White House was making illegal contacts and creating unreasonable pressure for business on the regulatory agencies that were designed to look out for the public interest. It was improper, and in most cases illegal, for the White House personnel to tamper with these independent regulatory agencies by asking political favors, bringing pressures, or even making appointments at the agencies for friends when the implication might be political favoritism.

A QUIET BUT THOROUGH INVESTIGATOR

Representative Morgan Moulder, a mild mannered Missouri Democrat, became chairman of the Special Oversight Subcommittee. Dr. Bernard Schwartz, a scholarly New York University law school professor, was hired as chief counsel. Dr. Schwartz, educated at Harvard and Cambridge, had earned a wide reputation as an authority on administrative and constitutional law and had served as a consultant to the Second Hoover Commission in 1954 and 1955. He seemed the safest possible chief counsel and unlikely to do anything to endanger the status quo.

For months Dr. Schwartz went quietly along listening to complaints about the conflicts of interest, the political pressures, and the illegal White House contacts made with various regulatory agencies. Dr. Schwartz was concerned about so-called "ex-parte contacts" that some litigants were making with members of the various commissions. "It is as bad as having one of the parties in a law suit sneak into the chambers of the judges to try to influence his decision in the middle of a trial," Dr. Schwartz told me.

Obstruction of the Investigation

I discussed some incidents with him that I believed merited investigation, and he told me he was having trouble getting access to material he requested. The CAB appeared ready to pull down a secrecy curtain as broad as "executive privilege." Such a claim could have no legal substance for an independent regulatory agency because those agencies were not a part of the executive branch of Government. If the CAB and other regulatory agencies were going to resort to such arrogant and illegal secrecy practices to cover up agency documents, then conditions were probably even worse than I imagined.

Representative John Moss, of California, a leading critic of the executive branch's use of "executive privilege," was shocked at the indications that this illegal doctrine would be extended to the regulatory agencies to block the subcommittee's access to records. In addition to being a member of the Special Legislative Oversight Subcommittee, Representative Moss was chairman of a Government Information Subcommittee and was in the midst of an intensive study of the manner in which government departments and agencies illegally withheld information from the press, the Congress, and even from the General Accounting Office (GAO) auditors and investigators. They did it under distorted and erroneous legal opinions written by politically appointed lawyers, who were often superficial in their knowledge or willfully political in obstructing investigations.

In November 1955, I had testified before the Moss Government Information Subcommittee on the abuse and misuse of "executive privilege" by the Eisenhower administration to hide the evidence of wrongdoing in the Dixon-Yates case, the Wolf Ladejinsky case, and a variety of other instances involving defense and foreign aid scandals. Moss, James S. Pope, executive editor of the Louisville *Courier-Journal,* J. Russell Wiggins, executive editor of the *Washington Post* and *Times Herald,* and Harold L. Cross, special counsel for the American Society of Newspaper Editors, were among those who shared my concern about the use of illegal withholding of evidence in wrongdoing—a criminal obstruction of justice in many instances.

Up to that time, the claim of an arbitrary right to withhold evidence had been restricted to executive branch agencies that were under investigation for possible wrongdoing. There seemed no conceivable legal theory under which the president could seek to impose the "executive privilege" doctrine in behalf of an independent regulatory agency. Yet, in September 1957, CAB Chairman James R. Durfee refused to permit Dr. Schwartz full access to records, documents, and other information pertaining to the functioning of the CAB. Durfee set out the "executive privilege" claim that the material Dr. Schwartz sought was "internal government communications." An irate Dr. Schwartz termed Chairman Durfee's position "completely ridiculous" and suggested that Durfee obtain competent legal counsel.

By this time, the pressure of the investigation was on a number of the regulatory agencies, and it became apparent that many had records they wished to hide from the House subcommittee. The chairmen of the six regulatory agencies met at a luncheon at the University Club in Washington in the last week of September to determine how to handle the inquisitive Dr. Schwartz. Because of the success some government departments were having with the use of "executive privilege" to obstruct access to evidence, some of the chairmen decided they would follow the "executive privilege" road whereas others questioned the soundness of that approach.

Dr. Schwartz was not discouraged, but pressed harder for more information. He persuaded Subcommittee Chairman Moulder to set a hearing date for a showdown with the CAB, and asked that the CAB be prepared to submit a report on "all gifts, honorariums, loans, fees, or other payments," or things of value received by CAB employees from any "person, firms, corporation, association, organization, or group having any interest" in any matter before the CAB.

Argument against "Executive Privilege"

Dr. Schwartz was allowed to examine the public files, but his efforts to obtain files of correspondence with the White House from the regulatory agencies ran into the claim of "executive privilege." In the first months, Dr. Schwartz had been told that Presidential Assistant Sherman Adams and others on the White House staff had been extremely active in their contacts with the regulatory agencies, and he was seeking documentation for these questionable practices in the files of correspondence.

To me the story of the White House cooperation with the regulatory agencies in an illegal coverup of evidence of wrongdoing was as big a story as any evidence that might be exposed concerning improper tampering. Moss and I encouraged Dr. Schwartz to take a strong stand against "executive privilege."

In an exhaustive 72-page "Memorandum of Law," filed on October 17, 1957, Dr. Schwartz exposed the true nature of the "executive privilege" arguments. They all sprang from the idea that "the king can do no wrong."

"In the pretension of those who espouse executive privilege," he wrote, "the infallibility recognized in the king in the days when he was personally sovereign of England has been attributed to the president in our system. The reasoning that supports the doctrine should shock the intelligence, as well as the sense of justice, of those who truly believe in the essentials of representative democracy."

Dr. Schwartz pointed out that the CAB claimed "the authority to screen files and records before they are made available to the subcommittee, with a right to the Board in its discretion to remove any and all documents" that could be considered personal files of Board members or communications within the CAB or with the White House.

"The Civil Aeronautics Board cannot claim privilege with regard to communication between the Board, on the one hand, and the president or other departments and agencies, on the other. Such an assertion of privilege cannot defeat the right of this subcommittee to investigate the relationship between the independent regulatory agencies and the executive branch. . . . 'Executive privilege' is not available to an independent agency like the Civil Aeronautics Board as a possible basis for the withholding of information from Congress. The Civil Aeronautics Board, as the Supreme Court has recognized, is an independent agency whose members are not subject to the removal power of the president. Such a body cannot in any proper sense be characterized as an arm or an eye of the executive. It is instead an arm of the Congress wholly responsible to that body."

He then demolished the argument that the president had the right arbitrarily to withhold evidence from the Congress or the courts: "The doctrine of absolute 'executive privilege' itself is not supported in law. The cases cited by its proponents are not truly relevant on the power of the executive to withhold information from the Congress. On the other hand, there are many decisions squarely rejecting the doctrine, even in courtroom cases. In addition, Dean Wigmore (the leading authority on evidence in this country) flatly repudiates the doctrine."

Although Dr. Schwartz did succeed in eliciting limited promises of cooperation from some officials of the regulatory agencies, most of them dragged their feet and stonewalled. Richard A. Mack, a member of the FCC, wouldn't show investigators many of his records, including the office diary that provided links for his indictment later on charges of having conspired to violate the federal law in connection with the award of a Miami television channel. The lack of cooperation by FCC Commissioner Mack was matched by the resistance at CAB, where Dr. Schwartz was trying to pin down evidence of contacts by Sherman Adams on behalf of Murray Chotiner, a friend of Vice President Richard Nixon who was a lawyer for North American Airlines.

INVOLVEMENT OF THE PRESS

My interest in the regulatory agency investigation was not a result of any local story in Des Moines or Minneapolis or of any particular case in which I had depth knowledge. It was a general interest in details on any and every government coverup that spurred me to ask questions of Dr. Schwartz and Representative Moss about the massive evidence of a conspiracy to hide evidence of wrongdoing. Their answers convinced me there was considerable corruption beneath the surface. However, there were other reporters with specialized knowledge looking into certain aspects of other agencies, particularly for evidence of political influence determining the award of valuable television rights in various cities.

Robert Healy Uses Local Information from Boston

Robert Healy, newly arrived as a Washington correspondent for the *Boston Globe,* and David Kraslow, a recent arrival in the *Miami Herald* Washington bureau, demonstrated what newsmen can accomplish in Washington in a short time by taking a local issue into a national investigation. Healy, an experienced and intelligent local reporter, adapted to Washington quickly by following the story on the controversial award of Channel 5 in Boston to the *Boston Herald-Traveler.* He knew in detail the public file of the Channel 5 dispute, was knowledgeable about all other relevant information that could be obtained from interviews, and was familiar with all of the New England political connections that might have been used in getting the FCC to overrule its examiners.

"Bob Healy knew more about the Channel 5 case than we did," Dr. Schwartz told me in acknowledging that an important part of the subcommittee evidence was produced by following up the leads from Healy. Included in those leads was the data from the telephone company records about long distance telephone calls. Those telephone records in turn were pursued by Subcommittee Investigator Francis X. McLaughlin and produced more evidence of still more political influence peddling.

Bob Healy developed a close working relationship with a few of the members of the Special Legislative Oversight Committee and members of the staff. As he sought information and confirmation from Dr. Schwartz on various angles of the Channel 5 case, Dr. Schwartz was questioning him about what he knew of the background and political connections of local Boston people. In one such conversation, Dr. Schwartz asked Healy what he knew about Bernard Goldfine, a multimillionaire New England industrialist. Although Dr. Schwartz did not relate the full reason for the inquiry, Healy told him what he knew and promised to get more. If the subcommittee was interested in Bernard Goldfine, close friend of Presidential Assistant Sherman Adams, then Healy knew that the *Boston Globe* was interested in finding out all it could about Goldfine.

Healy told Washington Bureau Chief Tom Winship about the Goldfine matter, and contacted the *Boston Globe's* ace courthouse reporter, Joseph Harvey. Harvey's research on land and court records led to an investigation that engaged a number of members of the local staff. The *Boston Globe's* research and stories combined with the investigations of the staff of the House Subcommittee led eventually to the exposure of the infamous Adams-Goldfine scandal and the resignation of Adams for impropriety in contacting the SEC and the FTC on behalf of Goldfine.

It was Bob Healy's first experience with a depth job of investigative reporting, and it gave him the confidence and know-how for great work in defeating the nomination of Francis X. Morrissey, a Kennedy organization political worker, for United States District Judge in Massachusetts. Later, when Healy became executive editor, and Tom Winship, editor, their experience with the realities of investigative reporting and their belief in the importance of newspapers having a strong independent check on government, resulted in the establishment of the now famous "spotlight team" at the *Boston Globe.* The spotlight team has won Pulitzer Prize recognition for the *Boston Globe* on two occasions, and is recognized as one of the best teams in the nation.

Dave Kraslow Scores with a Miami Scandal

Kraslow took depth knowledge of the Miami Channel 10 controversy and parlayed it into an understanding of the FCC's broad picture. His reporting eventually dynamited Richard Mack from his FCC post. Kraslow's work followed what I had come to recognize as the classic lines for depth understanding and effective reporting from Washington.

Dave Kraslow knew the public file on the Miami Channel 10 case, and he knew all there was to know about the background of the issues in other FCC decisions. He added to his own knowledge of Richard Mack in Washington by researching Mack's role as a member of a Florida state regulatory commission in the period before Mack was nominated and confirmed to the FCC.

Use of Trade Publications

I worked with Healy and Kraslow in a cooperation that was only limited by the competitive desire not to be scooped on our own new developments. We admired, and to some degree leaned upon, those reporters who were covering stories for the trade newspapers or magazines. However, we recognized their limitations. Much of the time the best of the trade publication reporters knew precisely what illegalities or practices of questionable propriety were taking place, but they also knew their editors didn't want any boat-rocking stories of wrongdoing that could cause bad feeling in the industry. However, the stories in the trade magazines made apparent, because of the clear presentation of a chronology of events, that there were "conflicts of interest" or other forms of corruption involved. They merely avoided using those terms of derogation to make the story more palatable to their establishment editors. In many cases such stories were able to provide background information or leads that were of value.

Reading 14: Sherman Adams and the CAB

I had information from a confidential source about Presidential Assistant Sherman Adams' contacts with the CAB on behalf of Murray Chotiner, but was fearful of using it. I wanted to wait until Dr. Schwartz had obtained copies of correspondence to corroborate the information from my source, who said he had seen copies of letters the CAB was seeking to hide. The tip that Sherman Adams had written letters to the CAB on behalf of Murray Chotiner's client, North American Airlines, was a possible lead into a big story that would involve the Eisenhower White House. Dr. Schwartz told me the letters were in the subcommittee files, but said he did not believe it would be proper to give those letters to me or to tell me their contents until they were entered into the open hearing record.

All of that changed in late January when Dr. Schwartz, frustrated by the weakness of the subcommittee, insisted that the members get tough and demand full cooperation from the Eisenhower administration and from the regulatory agencies on his long-pending requests for information. Some of the Democrats didn't want to force the issue, and several of the Republicans came out flatly in support of the Eisenhower administration's obstructionist tactics.

At that frustrating point, Dr. Schwartz was persuaded by *New York Times* editors and reporter William Blair that it was his duty and responsibility to leak a staff memorandum for publication in *The New York Times.* It was a lengthy document, setting out the well-settled legal principle that it is improper for members of regulatory agencies to have private talks with litigants when a case is in hearing or in the process of being decided. The Schwartz memorandum also questioned the propriety of the members of regulatory commissions accepting lavish entertainment from executives of the industries they were supposed to regulate.

Tempers flared in the days following the leaked memorandum, and finally, on February 10, 1958, the House subcommittee voted to fire Dr. Schwartz. I called him at home in the early evening of February 10 to inform him of the subcommittee's action and also to tell him that a subpoena was to be issued for him to testify the next morning. At this point he told me he had copies of every important document from the committee files in a trunk and two cardboard boxes. "Someone should have knowledge of what is in these records," he said, "so it will be possible to force the subcommittee to continue hearings." Unless something dramatic was done, he was convinced the investigation would not get off the ground in public hearings.

Dr. Schwartz asked if I wanted the copies of these documents to take to members of Congress who had shown an interest in the problems of the regulatory agencies. I said I could not take possession of documents which might be considered the property of the House subcommittee. In the inflammatory atmosphere that existed, we might both be indicted. However, since the documents were legally in his custody, I suggested that he could take them to the apartment of Senator John J. Williams, the Delaware Republican, and I would be happy to accompany him.

I had talked with Senator Williams of the improper pressures on the regulatory agencies and thought he would take the records. He had fought against tax scandals in the Truman administration, but I regarded him as an objective crusader who would judge things by the same standards even in a Republican administration. I was sure that if he agreed, Senator Williams could use the material to prod the House committee to complete its investigation in the same manner he had urged on the House tax scandal investigations in 1951 and 1952.

Dr. Schwartz said he would be willing to turn the papers over to Senator Williams and explain them to him in detail so I called Senator Williams for agreement and then headed for the Schwartz apartment on Connecticut Avenue. When I arrived, Dr. Schwartz had the trunk and two boxes of documents ready to be loaded into the trunk of my car. Mrs. Schwartz was nervous about her husband's going. I assured her that, for practical political reasons, it was unlikely that the House would take action against Dr. Schwartz for delivering the documents to a United States senator.

At the Mayflower Hotel, we hired a porter to wheel the boxes and the trunk to the apartment of Senator Williams. While we were there Dr. Schwartz received an urgent telephone call from his wife who, I learned later had been called by reporter Jack Anderson. He warned her that Senator Williams, a Republican, might turn the documents over to Sherman Adams at the White House. Because of my long-time relationship with Senator Williams, I knew the fears were groundless; but Mrs. Schwartz was frantic. She made her husband promise to leave the Williams apartment and take the documents with him.

Anderson had suggested that the documents might be taken to Senator Wayne Morse, the Oregon Democrat, and Dr. Schwartz now proposed this to Senator Williams, who did not object. We excused ourselves to go telephone Senator Morse and left Senator Williams alone with the documents so he could review those in which he had an interest. As I was certain he would—for I had previously talked with him about the regulatory agency scandals—Morse assured me he was interested in reviewing any documents Schwartz had available.

On the way to the Morse apartment, we stopped at Drew Pearson's home in Georgetown. Jack Anderson, then Drew Pearson's leading aide, invited himself to accompany us to the Morse apartment. Dr. Schwartz rejected Pearson's attempt to obtain custody of the records on grounds that it might be dangerous and certainly would be difficult to justify to the public.

Senator Morse greeted us calmly and assured us that he wanted the documents because of his official interest in the regulatory agencies, and we left them with him. Now we felt certain we had created a situation in which it would be virtually impossible for the House to avoid going forward with the investigation. The word would move fast that the files had been examined by a leading Democratic senator and by a leading Republican senator. It would create a good many complex problems for any House member inclined to ignore or hide the evidence Dr. Schwartz had accumulated.

Before the Schwartz files were returned to the House subcommittee, Senator Morse read them and with help from Jack Anderson and Drew Pearson made copies of essentially everything that was in the file. Representative Oren Harris, the Arkansas Democrat who was chairman of the House Committee on Interstate and Foreign Commerce, and all of the members of the committee were aware of the possibility that Morse and Senator Williams might have copied some of the documents.

Shortly after the midnight ride with Dr. Schwartz, I came into possession of copies of the two letters from "Sherm" Adams to "Murray" Chotiner my source had mentioned. In the letter, Adams informed "Murray" that he had discussed the North American Airlines case with the acting head of the CAB. This certainly appeared to be one of the prohibited contacts with an official of the CAB during the period when a case was being decided. If Adams had done what he stated he had done in a letter that carried his signature, it was a direct violation of the rules of the CAB. With the letters in my hand from the secret files of the House subcommittee, I was finally able to write my exclusive story on the Adams-Chotiner relations with the CAB.

The story caused a brief furor, and during the February 26, 1958, press conference, I caught President Eisenhower's eye. He recognized me with some reluctance. "Mr. President," I started, "Sherman Adams has written a letter in which he states that he went over the details of a pending Civil Aeronautics Board matter with an acting chairman of the CAB. It is contended up on Capitol Hill, that this was a violation of a CAB rule which states—it is improper that there be any communication, private communication that is, by any private or public person with a member of the CAB, with the examiners of the CAB, or with the staff while the case is pending, except in those matters prescribed by law. I wonder if you could tell us whether you felt Mr. Adams was acting within the proper scope of his authority in this particular matter."

President Eisenhower surprised me by pleading ignorance of news stories that had been on page one for days: "Well, again you are bringing up a thing I have not heard of, but I will say this: there is a number of cases that come under the CAB that the White House must act on. Any time that they refer to have anything to do with the foreign routes that CAB has authorized, or refused to authorize, then the President himself is required to make the final judgment."

The President was confused, as he often was. He was assuming that the case concerned a foreign airline route to which normal rules do not apply. The case about which Adams had written, however, involved a domestic airline, North American Airlines, and I made this clear. My explanation that North American was not a foreign line, but a domestic airline was cut off by the President's cold stare and abrupt comment, "I don't want anything more about that."

There was no opportunity to get in another question, but the record was much clearer to the nation's editorial writers and cartoonists than it was to President Eisenhower. The *St. Louis Post Dispatch,* in a hard-hitting editorial declared: "Whether the President wants it or not, there ought to be 'more about that' at the very next news conference." It was pointed out that in the face of rules that would make Adams' contacts "improper," President Eisenhower had "not only evaded a direct question about whether Mr. Adams' intercession was improper but, having evaded it, told reporter Mollenoff: 'I don't want anything more about that.'"

President Eisenhower was the subject of dozens of critical editorials in the *Washington Post,* the *New York Times,* and many other leading newspapers. The effort to cut me off was symbolic of the efforts of the administration to stop the regulatory agency probe.

A PILEUP OF PRESSURE WILL BREAK THROUGH PRIVILEGE

Although Adams claimed "executive privilege" in avoiding the CAB matter, the *Boston Globe* and Bob Healy were moving after him because of his intervention at the SEC and the FTC for his pal Goldfine on matters that were eventually disastrous for both. The *Boston Globe* was not alone on the Goldfine-Adams relationship. Drew Pearson wrote a column alleging that Goldfine had paid for hotels in New York for Adams and had made gifts to him that included "a vicuna coat and an oriental rug." Sherman Adams was seeing no reporters and White House Press Secretary Jim Hagerty was wisely making no comment.

Blocked at getting to the truth of the Pearson column directly, I decided to stop at the Sherman Adams home just off Rock Creek Park. When Mrs. Rachel Adams came to the door, I politely asked for "Mr. Adams." When she said he was not home, I identified myself as a newspaper reporter and said I wanted "simply to look at the vicuna coat and the oriental rug," so I could describe it to my readers. She met my politeness with an equally polite refusal, saying she was "sorry, but I don't think I should show you the coat without discussing it with Sherman or Mr. Hagerty."

However, that refusal gave me the information I wanted. Mrs. Adams had confirmed the existence of a vicuna coat, and, with more coaxing, she confirmed that it was a gift from Bernard Goldfine. This exclusive story was typical of the types of stories that an innovative reporter can turn up in connection with any national story.

The benefits Adams received from Goldfine were small, but any relationship with the notorious Bernard Goldfine was a source of continued embarrassment to the White House as long as the *Boston Globe* led the pack, describing more of the horrors of Goldfine's legal problems. The embarrassment finally forced Adams to abandon the shield of "executive privilege" in a few areas and come out of the White House into the arena of an open congressional hearing. Although Adams weathered that storm because of mild questioning by most of the committee members, President Eisenhower had to admit that Adams had been "imprudent" in his relationship with Goldfine. However, the President said, "I need him."

When Goldfine appeared before the House committee, he took the Fifth Amendment on questions dealing with evidence of widespread mislabeling of woolen goods, and the failure to file required reports with the SEC. Most devastating was his failure to testify on grounds of self-incrimination about a mysterious $700,000 in cashier's and treasurer's checks he had taken out of his businesses.

Even a million-dollar fortune couldn't save Bernard Goldfine from the disgrace of a federal prison term. He hired the most expensive lawyers and engaged in every conceivable maneuver to stay out of prison, but in the end he lost his freedom and his "friends." Goldfine went to prison on a charge of evading more than $800,000 in federal taxes. He boasted bravely that he would not cooperate with the Justice Department in explaining what he did with the missing $700,000. His health broke while in prison and left him a shattered shell of his former self. Later, the Internal Revenue Service filed liens against his property totaling more than $7,000,000. Because of the *Boston Globe's* cooperation with a congressional committee, the Goldfine magic had lost its potency.

Senator Williams put the pressure on President Eisenhower that finally forced him to request Sherman Adams to resign from his post as the number one assistant to the President.

Although the *Boston Globe* led the way, those of us who were living with the House subcommittee investigation knew that it was not the impact of any one newspaper that forced the hearings. It was also the impact of day-to-day coverage by many newspapers and by a relatively small group of a dozen or so reporters who knew the facts, the law, and the political backgrounds of all of the leading figures in the drama.

For me, the most satisfying aspect of the two years that I was involved in the regulatory investigations was seeing that Bob Healy and Dave Kraslow were highly successful in using the same basic techniques that I had been using in research of records and in

cooperating with honest congressmen and staff members. Together
we had forced an unwilling chairman to do his job.

STUDENT WORK PROJECT SUGGESTION

1. From the most recent *U.S. Government Organizational
   Manual* obtain the history and functions of the Federal
   Communications Commission (FCC), the Civil Aero-
   nautics Board (CAB), the Securities and Exchange
   Commission (SEC), and the Interstate Commerce Com-
   mission (ICC).

2. From *Congress and the Nation* for the 1945–64 period
   obtain a brief resume of the investigation of Bernard
   Goldfine and the investigation of Sherman Adams.
   Explain the key issues in those investigations. Examine
   the most recent GAO investigation on the regulatory
   agency that has the most impact in your local community.
   What are the followup story possibilities from a local
   standpoint and from a national standpoint?

27 THE AGRICULTURE DEPARTMENT AND BILLIE SOL ESTES

The reporters and editors who concern themselves with the coverage of agriculture or economics usually concentrate their efforts on broad matters of policy and politics and pay relatively little attention to the nuts and bolts of how the laws are administered and enforced. Corruption, conflicts of interest, political dealings, and cruel personnel practices often go unnoticed or at least unreported. Inside informants can be cultivated to help expose such wrongdoing and to suggest reform measures. Persistent follow through is vital.

The bureaucratic chain of command often misleads the cabinet officer and the president on essential details where they might be charged with personal responsibility for corruption or mismanagement in government. It is uncomfortable and embarrassing for the president or other high officials to admit to serious error because of reliance upon subordinates, and there is a natural tendency to want to hide evidence of error. Hiding evidence of a crime is a crime in itself—the crime of obstruction of justice.

In this instance the officials of a self-styled liberal administration were involved in police state tactics to crush a truthful dissenter. Those tactics included an illegal retaliation against N. Battle Hales and a brutal and unjustified incarceration of his secretary in a mental institution. To put this story together in its entirety required extensive careful reading of press releases from the Agriculture Department and the contradictory statements made by a variety of high officials in a public press conference, extensive interviewing of all of the officials, and tough and precise questioning of Agriculture Secretary Freeman and President Kennedy in press conferences.

FRAUD IN UNLIKELY PLACES

On the surface the Department of Agriculture would appear the least likely place for fruitful investigative reporting. Because that department is considered of interest to only the newspapers from the farm areas, it is very poorly covered except for the specialists who are interested in legislation, rule making, and policy decisions involving one or two products. Like the reporters who cover the regulatory agencies, these specialists are not inclined to be boat rockers.

Because I came from a farm background and had many friends who were Iowa farmers, I was interested in agricultural matters, particularly corn and soybeans and cattle and hogs. I was fortunate that my interests coincided with those of the *Des Moines Register,* which prided itself on being the outstanding agricultural newspaper in the United States. During the 28 years I was a Washington reporter for the *Des Moines Register,* I was involved with investigations of minor and major corruption and mismanagement in the various agencies in the Department of Agriculture.

Cozy Relationships in Agriculture Committees

The agriculture committees of the House and Senate were usually lax in their policing of the Agriculture Department agencies because of cozy relationships that developed between the members and the officials in the Department of Agriculture. It was necessary for the press and Senator John J. Williams, a Delaware Republican, to prod them in order to launch any investigations, and even after the investigations were started the committee members were usually interested in avoiding embarrassment to the Secretary of Agriculture.

I followed those investigations closely over a period of several years, developing Iowa and Minnesota angles that appeared frequently in the investigation of anything dealing with corn, soybeans, wheat, or other grains. In this way I became acquainted with the General Accounting Office (GAO) investigations directed by Comptroller General Lindsay C. Warren and with the authority the GAO findings had with Congress and with the press. When the GAO made its report the facts could not be dodged as the political work of a congressional committee or the superficial study of a newspaper reporter. The cabinet officers and the president had to accept adverse findings as fact or be prepared for a showdown with tough but fair Lindsay Warren.

The Ladejinsky security case (see Reading 13) in 1955 had established the incompetence and bungling at the top level in the Agriculture Department in the illegal firing of a highly qualified land reform expert. My next expose' involved the purchase of millions of dollars worth of faulty steel grain bins. The Department of Agriculture was being ripped off by contracts for bins and bin construction where bins collapsed. Efforts to get the Agriculture Committee to do a thorough investigation of this scandal were only half successful, and it was necessary to go to the Senate Permanent Investigations Subcommittee where that investigation was completed by LaVern J. Duffy, of Independence, Iowa, who was one of the most thorough investigators in the Congress.

A Good Contact

Another Government Operations Subcommittee that did consistently fine work on the Agriculture Department corruption and mismanagement was headed by Representative L. H. Fountain, a North Carolina Democrat. This subcommittee on intergovernmental relations had specific jurisdiction over the Agriculture Department and dug into scandalous "windfall profits" in connection with selling government agricultural surplus commodities. The key staff man on these investigations and hearings was Subcommittee Counsel James Naughton, who made it his business to keep abreast of all "conflicts of interest" and "windfall profits" in the Agriculture Department programs. He was from Sioux City, Iowa, and a graduate of Drake University Law School.

Naughton would often call me and suggest that I might want to inquire about some possible irregularity in a program in which he knew I was interested. In the spring of 1962, Naughton was starting an investigation of the shady activities of Tino DeAngelis, the salad oil king, for Chairman L. H. Fountain's Government Operations Subcommittee. He alerted me, but my interest in following up the DeAngelis irregularities was distracted by the Billie Sol Estes case, which erupted as a major scandal for the Kennedy administration and specifically for Agriculture Secretary Orville Freeman. Senator Williams and House Subcommittee Chairman Fountain were also deeply involved in the investigation of the Billie Sol Estes case.

A GIANT SCANDAL

Small Beginnings

The Billie Sol Estes case was broken initially by the meticulous record research of Oscar Griffin, Jr., a young reporter for the *Pecos*

(Texas) *Independent* and *Enterprise.* Griffin's stories dealt with the record of Estes' mortgages on more than 33,000 mobile fertilizer storage tanks in 11 counties, and his acquisition of more than $33 million through these mortgages.

That was enough capacity for anhydrous ammonia fertilizer to take care of the whole state of Texas and was as clear an indication of fraud as the purchase of 346 tires and 401 tubes for seven Polk County welfare department cars in 18 months. Griffin consulted people familiar with normal fertilizer requirements and was told that 300 or 400 tanks would take care of all the anhydrous ammonia fertilizer needs for West Texas.

The reaction to the stories in the *Independent* and *Enterprise* was not immediately explosive, for it was a small newspaper with few readers outside of Pecos. Also, the low-key stories made no accusation of wrongdoing against government officials or against Billie Sol. However, those simple factual stories did set the stage for further investigations by local, state, and federal officials. Local farmers and businessmen became concerned. The financial institution that had lent millions of dollars to Estes became uneasy about their security, but there was no panic. The lenders had mortgages on specific liquid-fertilizer tanks. If there was some problem, they believed it could be handled with a quiet and sensible investigation. The representatives of the financial houses from New York to Los Angeles, eager to retain Billie Sol's good will, approached the whole investigation gingerly and diplomatically.

The Story Grows

The Billie Sol Estes case burst on the national scene when Texas Attorney General Will Wilson conducted an investigation and accused the Kennedy-Johnson administration of political favoritism for Estes. Estes had been named a member of the National Cotton Advisory Committee a few months earlier, despite irregularities in his grain-storage facilities and charges in government reports that he had engaged in the "illegal" purchases of cotton allotment from other farmers.

Earl Mazo, an aggressive and experienced Washington reporter for the *New York Herald Tribune,* made a trip to Texas, talked with Attorney General Wilson, and wrote the stories that escalated the *Pecos Independent* and *Enterprise* stories into a major embarrassment for the Kennedy administration.

President Kennedy, angry and uninformed of the details of the budding scandal in his Agriculture Department, was critical of Mazo and impetuously stopped the White House subscription to the *Herald Tribune.* Secretary of Agriculture Orville Freeman voiced the opinion that the Billie Sol Estes case was "ballooned out of proportion" by Republican critics and the Republican press. He had advised President Kennedy that he believed there was no favoritism for Billie Sol. Kennedy accepted that assurance.

Freeman's denials were accompanied by an effort to hide the records from Senator John J. Williams, the House Government Operations Subcommittee, the Senate Permanent Investigations Subcommittee and the press, and to protect officials in the department who were responsible for the decisions that had resulted in Estes' appointment as a member of the National Cotton Advisory Committee.

My interest was aroused by the evidence of an attempted coverup of the first serious scandal in the Kennedy administration. A review of Oscar Griffin's stories in the *Pecos Independent* and *Enterprise* and Earl Mazo's coverage of the Texas Attorney General's investigation established serious frauds, and I told Bob Kennedy so. He told me my view was contrary to the assurances he had received from Secretary Freeman. I replied that he should not accept the Agriculture Department's investigation of itself because the past track record was notoriously bad under all administrations. Then I went to work to learn the details of the evidence as a first step to proving the false statements by the Agriculture Department officials in their malicious coverup.

Evidence of Coverup

The most obvious evidence of the coverup was the shoddy treatment Secretary Freeman and other top officials of the Agriculture Department gave to N. Battle Hales, a career lawyer in the Agriculture Stabilization and Conservation Service. Hales believed that his superiors, Emery (Red) Jacobs and Horace Godfrey, had let political favoritism influence their decision dealing with Billie Sol Estes on cotton allotment matters.

Battle Hales was particularly suspicious of Red Jacobs, his immediate superior, who seemed proud of his contacts with Billie Sol. It also seemed to Hales that Godfrey, the administrator of the Agriculture Stabilization Conservation Service (ASCS) and Undersecretary of Agriculture Charles S. Murphy, were overly solicitous in regard to the Estes cotton allotment purchases. His suspicions had first been aroused in late 1961 by the actions of Jacobs, Godfrey, and others in meetings he attended. As the first stories started breaking in April 1962, Battle Hales decided he would take his evidence and his suspicions right to Secretary Freeman and avoid the chain of command that was so cluttered with those he felt were Billie Sol's friends.

Persecution and Violation of Civil Rights

On April 20th, Hales went to Freeman's office but was side-tracked to Tom Hughes, Freeman's administrative assistant. Hughes had first indicated Hales might talk to Freeman, but changed his opinion of Hales and started to treat him as a culprit rather than an employee who was volunteering to tell the truth about the cotton allotment decisions and other matters.

Although Hughes said he would arrange for Hales to talk with FBI agents who were investigating the Estes case, Hales found that orders had been issued by the office of the Secretary of Agriculture barring him from access to his own office and office files. Hales had said he needed certain reports from his files to corroborate his charge of favoritism for Estes. The department refused to let him go through his own files—even with FBI agents present. Then the Department of Agriculture engaged in a series of actions to take custody of Hales' files, an action one would expect in a Communist police state and not in a department of government headed by a self-proclaimed liberal Democrat.

On April 24, Hales talked with his secretary, Mary Kimbrough Jones, a 51-year old woman who had been an employee of the department for 25 years. He confided to her the troubles he was having about his office files since he had voiced his suspicions to Secretary Freeman's aide. The next day, when some of Freeman's staff members went to Hales' office to take custody of the files containing the Estes reports, Miss Jones protested loudly and tried to block removal of the files. Following a confusing altercation, she was forcibly removed from the office and taken to the office of Dr. Lee K. Buchanan, chief of the department's health division. She was locked in his office, and a short time later was taken to the District of Columbia General Hospital and confined in a mental ward.

On May 3, Secretary Freeman held a press conference declaring that "There has not yet been evidence of one bit of favoritism and special privilege to Billie Sol Estes." Secretary Freeman, of course, made no reference to the still unpublicized offers of Battle Hales to document the frauds and favoritism. And, he made no mention of the hospitalization of Mary Jones a week earlier when she tried to protect the files in Hales' office.

After the press conference, Hales sat down with *Dallas Morning News* reporter Robert E. Baskin and said he had information he believed proved "favoritism" on the part of Agriculture officials toward Billie Sol. Hales did not tell Baskin of the seizure of his files, but he did say he had been barred from his office and shifted to another job after he tried to tell Secretary Freeman about Billie

Sol. Baskin's story stated that Hales had recommended strict action against Estes in connection with the illegal transfers of cotton allotments. He quoted Hales as naming Murphy, Godfrey, and Jacobs as the officials who took part in the decisions to circumvent the stiff criminal and civil actions Hales proposed.

I contacted Hales who told me his files had been seized and his secretary had been sent to a hospital because she had tried to protect his files and that she was still there. He was clear and precise on what he knew but, as a careful lawyer, knew he needed the access to his files to make his claim stand up against the opposition at the top of the Agriculture Department.

Then the Agriculture Department engaged in one of the dirtiest power plays I have seen in Washington. They called a press conference to try to humiliate and discredit Hales. Hales was summoned to the press conference to face the accusations of Murphy, Godfrey, Hughes, and other officials. Under questioning by reporters, Hughes, the Secretary's aide, admitted Hales tried to see Freeman. He said he had told Hales it would be "better" for him to talk to the FBI, and admitted that Hales was barred from his office and files. He said this was simply because Hales was suddenly transferred to another job.

Although Hughes and the others tried to discredit Hales, he refused to be cowed by the open antagonism of superiors who could make or break his career. While those superiors listened, Hales repeated his charges for the benefit of the newsmen who were present at the Agriculture Department press conference. He refused to be confused by frequent interruptions and comments of derogation, and he kept his comments reasonable and logical in the face of insults that were intended to anger him. Slowly and logically he covered the cotton allotment controversy and led into the story of the strange death of Henry Marshall, a Department of Agriculture representative in Pecos. To this day, the cause of Marshall's death has not been clearly established, and specifically whether it was a suicide or murder.

Hales related that he had attended a meeting in the office of Horace Godfrey on November 14, 1961. "At the time of the meeting," he said, "the individuals present . . . expressed the opinion that Billie Sol Estes' cotton-pool agreements were illegal and that penalties should be assessed on his 1961 production allotment. Godfrey actively objected to it on the grounds that the only witness who could conclusively state that Estes did not receive (proper) approval from the Texas ASCS office was now dead—that's Henry Marshall." Hales added that Godfrey had said the penalty against Estes in connection with the 1961 crop should not be assessed because of a technicality in the regulations, that Godfrey then declared he "knew Mr. Estes," that he had worked with him on the Advisory Committee, and that he considered him "a very fine man" who "would not intentionally do anything wrong."

Godfrey interrupted angrily, and later denied that he had ever met Estes.

Hales read from a summary report of a meeting at which he and others present advised Godfrey that another government witness had been present at a key meeting between the late Henry Marshall and an attorney for Estes. This man was available to support the government position. Hales said a signed statement by the named witness was among government records submitted to Godfrey.

"With the exception of Godfrey, all of the individuals present at this meeting agreed that Allen's signed statement was sufficient evidence to cause cancellation of Estes' cotton allotment," Hales continued. Several days after the meeting Hales said he was advised that Godfrey, Jacobs, and Undersecretary Murphy had made a decision not to cancel the 1961 Estes cotton allotment and that no action should be taken on the 1962 allotments until further meetings were held.

This was, in fact, approval of the cotton allotment transfers that were a violation of the law, and it was done in November 1961—a month before Estes was made a member of the National Cotton Advisory Committee.

The Story Begins to Unfold

After the press conference, I talked to Battle Hales at length and found no flaws in his story. In particular I felt deep concern over the fate of his secretary. I talked to Senator Williams about the Billie Sol Estes case and about the plight of Mary Kimbrough Jones. He, too, was more concerned about the apparent disregard for the rights of Miss Jones by a self-proclaimed liberal Cabinet officer in an administration that prided itself on its concern for human rights.

Senator Williams started his own investigation into the jailing of Miss Jones, and his prodding resulted in her release from the mental hospital where she had spent five days in a locked and padded cell. On May 17, 1962, Senator Williams charged that the Agriculture Department had "railroaded" Miss Jones to a mental ward. He declared that the department's medical chief had "arbitrarily" ordered her hospitalized without consulting her personal physician or members of her family.

"Never have I seen . . . the rights of an individual . . . so seriously violated," Senator Williams told the Senate. "She was placed in a mental institution on April 25. But there is no record anywhere . . . (that) any doctor signed the proper commitment papers until two days later . . . I venture to say that if some of the rest of us had been confined in such a cell, sleeping, as she did, on a mattress on the floor, we would not be quite normal."

Senator Williams noted that government regulations require the family be notified before any person is committed to a mental institution, but this was not done in this case. He pointed out that not even Dr. Buchanan signed a statement to commit Miss Jones that day, but left the matter in the policeman's hands. The Delaware Republican went on to state that if Miss Jones had been in a private home, legal procedures would have required the sworn statements of two citizens and two doctors to commit her to a mental institution.

"However, from a public building," the Senator said, "a person can be sent off to a mental institution . . . without certification or examination of any doctor or anyone except the police officer. Once the patient is committed to the institution, she has this 'mental observation' charge on her record and from that moment on it is up to her to prove her sanity."

Senator Williams had talked to Miss Jones' personal physicians and was told there was nothing in her medical history to warrant commitment to a mental institution, yet she was committed on the signature of a District of Columbia policeman, who had seen her for only a few minutes. The department's explanation was that Miss Jones had hit Dr. Buchanan with a shoe, and Senator Williams said that she hit Dr. Buchanan only after he carried her from her office and told her "she was going to be sent to a psychiatric ward."

"So, in the struggle, she hit him with a shoe," Senator Williams said. He added that if he had been in Miss Jones' place, Dr. Buchanan "would be fortunate if it were only a shoe he was hit with!"

To justify its actions, the Agriculture officials noted that the same report that pronounced Miss Jones as sane had said she was ill and needed medical care. Senator Williams attacked that rationalization of the cruel and illegal act committed on Miss Jones: "I say to you, Senators, if your wife, your sister, or your daughter were put in a cell for 12 days, I think you would find that she would be sick too. . . . That was a horrible experience, and to further try to discredit . . . [Miss Jones] now, after what she has gone through, is even more reprehensible" He declared that the whole affair was particularly disgusting because Miss Jones, a secretary with not a single blemish on her record and with a very high efficiency rating, was concerned because Hales had been locked out of the office and his files were being ransacked.

A Real Investigation is Begun

I wrote stories detailing the police state methods used by the Department of Agriculture in this coverup for those responsible for glossing over Billie Sol's fraud. I also went to the Justice Department to talk to Bob Kennedy. At first he was defensive of Freeman's action, and accused me of "falling for Republican political crap." He had bought Freeman's line that Battle Hales was an incompetent lawyer who was opportunistic in trying to blow the whistle on some transactions he had been a part of initially.

It was apparent that Attorney General Kennedy, like so many of his predecessors in that job, did not understand the facts or the law and was going to permit the Kennedy administration to bungle its way into serious trouble. I spelled out the hard facts and law, as I had researched it, and told him he had better pay attention to the criticism from Senator Williams, even if Williams was a Republican. I punctuated that point by noting that Senator Williams, a Republican, had been a major critic of the Eisenhower administration on the Adams-Goldfine case. Then I jarred him with the statement that he was acting just like Eisenhower defending Air Secretary Harold Talbott or like Jimmy Hoffa defending Johnny Dioguardi, Babe Triscaro or Joey Glimco.

"Get Jack Miller (Criminal Division head Herbert "Jack" Miller) into it," I said. "The Agriculture Department's legal office is involved in a coverup."

It was only at that point that Kennedy finally realized how serious the Estes case might be, for he had seen the Eisenhower administration get itself into serious trouble on the Dixon-Yates case and the Adams-Goldfine case. He had been a Senate Committee Counsel on the investigation of Air Secretary Harold Talbott's conflict of interest, and had seen President Eisenhower defend the case and tolerate an attempted coverup long after the evidence of questionable activity was on the table.

In a short time Assistant Attorney Jack Miller confirmed my view on the seriousness of the Estes matter, the incompetency of the Agriculture Department investigation, and the factual errors the department was making in the case it was trying to palm off on the public. The Criminal Division stepped up its investigation of Estes and took the decision making out of Freeman's hands.

While Miller was trying to get Freeman straighted out on the facts and the law in the case, some of Freeman's top aides were reviewing all of the correspondence between the Agriculture

Department and two Republican members of the Senate Permanent Investigations Subcommittee. Senators Curtis and Mundt said it was an effort to intimidate them by getting something on them to tone down their questioning on the Estes case. Tom Hughes, administrative aide to Secretary Freeman, faced with affidavits admitted that he had initiated the "unusual project" but denied any intimidation purpose. He insisted he was interested in past views of the two Republican senators relative to the grain storage issues involved in the Estes case.

THE SCANDAL DIES WITH A WHIMPER

Although the investigations by the Justice Department resulted in indictments and conviction of several officials, most were allowed to resign without further penalty. Because most of the press did not follow the details of the responsibility for the corruption, mismanagement, and coverup, Freeman was able to defend and retain Under Secretary Charles Murphy and Horace Godfrey who were linked with positive "favoritism" for Estes.

For example, Murphy had overruled an adverse report on Estes and had approved appointment of Estes to the National Cotton Advisory Committee. He did it with two highly critical reports on his desk involving Billie Sol's wheeling and dealing in cotton allotments and an FBI report that gave clear leads into other Estes frauds. Freeman admitted Murphy made a "mistake" in approving the appointment. But Freeman accepted Murphy's explanation that he did not give sufficient attention to the details of the report because he was working with hundreds of "important problems." Freeman disregarded the testimony of John E. Francis, head of the review and adjudication division, that Murphy had ordered him to "clean up" the derogatory report on Estes.

Although Senator Williams identified Horace Godfrey as "the man who was partly responsible for the coverup in the Estes case," Freeman approved a "Distinguished Service Award" for Godfrey for his administration of the Agriculture Stabilization and Conservation Service in the period Godfrey's division was making decisions favorable to Estes. Ironically, Battle Hales, who had courageously told the truth about the Estes case handling, was denied an in-grade promotion.

Responsibility of the Press

Secretary Freeman got by with these injustices because the Washington press corps did not follow through on what was considered a provincial "farm story," even though Senator Williams, Representative H. R. Gross, Republican of Iowa, Representative Ancher Nelsen, Republican of Minnesota, and Chairman John L. McClellan, an Arkansas Democrat, tried to point up the full importance of fair treatment to truthful employees.

The reason Secretary Freeman was successful to some degree, was that only a handful of reporters followed through on the vicious retaliation against Battle Hales and on the coverup for Freeman's top aides. Although marred by the picture of mismanagement and corruption outlined in the Billie Sol Estes investigations, hearings, and reports, Freeman managed to follow the politician's course of rewarding his friends and punishing the subordinate who, as Senator Williams explained, "committed the unforgivable sin of giving Congress some information about skullduggery in his department."

There were fine examples of investigative reporting beginning with Oscar Griffin's Pulitzer Prize winning work for the *Pecos Independent* and *Enterprise* and continuing with the aggressive follow through by a half dozen Washington based reporters. However, there was noticeable softness on the part of the administration of President John Kennedy and his liberal Secretary of Agriculture who tolerated and excused the ordeal of Mary Kimbrough Jones.

This was only one of a number of cases in which the press failed to follow through on the ordeal of a truthful and courageous whistleblower, and, by that negligence, gave the political corrupters a victory. My efforts to follow up the story and get justice for Battle Hales were futile, and I realized the general truth of Wolf Ladejinsky's belief that most of the press corps was interested in the initial, sensational developments and would not follow through with consistency.

Whether that lack of followup was motivated by political or ideological bias or was a result of superficiality is unimportant. A real investigative reporter must be both persistent and nonpartisan. The general laxity in the press represents a golden opportunity for success for those diligent reporters who are willing to work to understand and follow through on all ramifications of the story situation, including coverage of retaliation efforts against truthful witnesses. It is a violation of federal law for officials to retaliate against a witness who has given truthful testimony to Congress, but it is a law that is more often ignored than enforced.

An important part of dealing squarely with informants includes the responsibility to follow the details of clever retaliation moves that are in fact malicious violations of federal law. The conscientious investigative reporter must have a deep feeling against injustice and a compassion that will not permit him to milk an informant of story material and then abandon that informant for more exciting new story material. A continuing injustice is, in fact, a more important story than any new story out of our scandal-filled federal agencies.

STUDENT WORK PROJECT SUGGESTION

1. Examine the legislative history of the government production control and government price support program for an agricultural product in your state or region. Obtain the last GAO report dealing with administration and enforcement of the laws relative to those control and price support programs. Are these programs administered in an even-handed manner? Are there indications of political favoritism?

2. Find a local critic of these agricultural programs and interview him on his complaints. Do you feel that any or all of his criticisms are valid? What additional steps would you suggest to further test the validity of your judgments?

28 PENTAGON BUNGLING

The multibillion-dollar Pentagon is one of the most poorly covered departments in Washington. No reporter and no small team of reporters can give it the full coverage it deserves. The demand for coverage of routine policy and procurement decisions uses the energy and talents of the handful of reporters who are assigned to military affairs. Those assigned to the Pentagon rarely have time to dig into the complexities of even the major procurement decisions and rarely cover the congressional hearings that deal with controversial military purchases. Perjury, rigged documents, and brutal misuse of power are unreported, though they could easily be documented by any reasonably competent and persistent investigative reporter.

This chapter demonstrates that Pentagon waste and mismanagement can involve anything from contracts for purchases of shoes to the multibillion-dollar weapons systems such as the F-111 warplane. Although "national security" classifications are proper in many cases, there are many instances where such classification is misused as a coverup device for corruption and mismanagement by military or civilian officials. The Pentagon problem has not changed in the last 30 years, and the opportunity for investigative reporters will be essentially the same as long as billions are being spent with no full public accountability at every stage. General Accounting Office (GAO) reports often catch up with the worst mismanagement but seldom go into the political corruption that is at the root of "mistakes" and "errors of judgment."

SIGNS OF BUNGLING OR CORRUPTION

The shocking manner in which the Pentagon cheated Joseph Lawlor of Ames, Iowa, out of an Air Force contract for mobile water demineralizers was my indoctrination into military contract bungling. This was followed in late 1951 by Representative F. Edward Hebert's "Chamber of Horrors" on military spending encompassing Army, Navy, Air Force, and Marine purchases. Representative Hebert and his staff showed that such mundane things as shoes, nuts, bolts, and other standard items could be purchased cheaper in a retail store than by the military in quantity purchases.

Purchase-Price Irregularities

Representative Eddie Hebert, a former crusading city editor for the *New Orleans States,* achieved an impressive record fighting the corruption of the successors of the Huey Long regime in Louisiana. Hebert was good-natured but tough in the manner in which he roasted Pentagon officials. He pointed out that the Marine Corps was paying $7.50 for the same weight canvas cot that the Navy bought for $3.20. The Marines and Army used the same kind of blanket; one cost the taxpayers $2.50 and the other $1.77. The Navy, Air Force, and Marines were all buying the same low-cut shoe from the same manufacturer, but there was a substantial difference in the price paid in the same time period. The Marines paid $5.31 a pair, the Navy, $6.08 and the Air Force, $7.29. Even more perplexing were the prices the Army and Marines paid for heavy rubber-sole combat boots for use in Korea. Both bought the identical boot from the same manufacturer, but the Marines paid $16.80 a pair while the Army paid $24.65 a pair.

Hebert displayed his "chamber of horrors" in the House Armed Services hearing room under a sign stating: "Abandon Hope, All Ye Who Enter Here." As Representative Hebert and his staff tried to place the responsibility for specific "horrors" in purchasing practices, he ran into the usual problem that congressional investigators face: the man who was most responsible had either been transferred, retired, or was otherwise unavailable. It was similar to my problem in trying to force the Pentagon to take effective action against those responsible for cheating Joe Lawlor's firm out of the mobile demineralizer contract.

Chiding military officials about the "Phantom of the Pentagon" as his hearing started, Hebert said, "He's the little man who's responsible for military purchases but always seems to be gone. Whenever I try to get him before the committee, he has either just retired or left on a trip to the Far East."

Inadequacies of Press Coverage

Although Representative Hebert used a touch of humor to draw attention to the ridiculous purchasing practices at the Pentagon, he was deadly serious in his concern over the coverup of scandals and the lack of follow through by Washington newsmen. The Capitol Hill reporters, who covered the congressional hearings on fraud and mismanagement, did not handle the questioning of Pentagon officials. That questioning was left to the reporters based at the Pentagon. They were often uninformed about the details of testimony or were a part of the kept Pentagon press regulars who had a stake in keeping good relations with the top military and civilian Pentagon officials.

Lack of press attention and lack of an effective follow through made it possible for the Pentagon to stonewall the congressional committees, to avoid action against the dishonest culprits, and to quietly and cleverly retaliate against the honest officials who cooperated with Congress.

A SERIES OF FRAUDS

The Harry Lev Hearings

Investigations of the Senate Permanent Investigations Subcommittee in 1954 and 1955 focused on the dishonest dealing of Harry (The Hat) Lev, the eccentric millionaire owner of Mid City Uniform Cap Company of Chicago. Lev, one of the largest military hatmakers in the country, won his military contracts under irregular circumstances. Testimony disclosed that Lev worked diligently to cultivate the goodwill of procurement officials, hired retired, high-ranking officials of the Defense Department, and showered gifts of delicacies on anyone who might be helpful. He paid the hotel bills of procurement officials, entertained them at his home and on his yacht, and bought dresses and other items of clothing for female procurement personnel. There was other testimony about his business arrangements with government officials, bribery, attempted bribery, and stories of Lev's easy access to inside information on multimillion-dollar contracts. Lev's hats were not inspected to assure that contract specifications were met, and he was often delinquent on delivery dates without suffering the penalties.

Lev and several of his employees were convicted of military frauds. Only one Army Captain was convicted and more than a dozen other officials were fired or forced to resign as a result of laxity or corruption disclosed in the Harry Lev hearings. But, Chairman McClellan and Counsel Robert Kennedy faced a reluctant Pentagon that engaged in foot-dragging, stonewalling, and other tactics to obstruct the investigation. There was little indication of a real desire for housecleaning from the top. Within a few months there was the forced resignation of an Assistant Secretary of Defense after the award of an $834,000 contract for the manufacture of Army cotton trousers to a firm headed by his wife.

Harold E. Talbott—Conflict of Interest

The McClellan committee focused attention on the charge of conflict of interest in the Army cotton trousers contract and followed that case by putting a spotlight on a conflict of interest involving Secretary of the Air Force Harold E. Talbott. Air Secretary Talbott had been active in promoting the business of Paul B. Mulligan & Co., in which he was a "special partner." The evidence showed that Talbott had contacted some firms with defense contracts and had used his official Air Force stationery for promoting business of the management and consultant firm.

There was no public attention on the Talbott matter until news stories were written by Charles Bartlett, then a Washington correspondent for the *Chattanooga Times,* and later by William Lawrence, then a correspondent for the *New York Times.* The *New York Times* gave attention to the details of Talbott's business connection, the increases in his profits from that business while Air Secretary, and the tone of the letters he wrote to officials of the Radio Corporation of America on behalf of his management consultant firm.

The details disclosed by Bill Lawrence of the *New York Times* forced President Eisenhower to take cognizance of the serious conflict of interest of Harold Talbott and to disregard Talbott's rationalization that the Paul B. Mulligan Company did not deal directly with the Pentagon. Talbott was caught with erroneous or false testimony on his contacts with some defense contractors. A few days later, President Eisenhower reluctantly asked that his personal friend, Harold Talbott, resign as Air Secretary.

The resignation pill was made less bitter when the Defense Department awarded Talbott the Distinguished Public Service Award and the highest civilian award of the Defense Department, the Medal of Freedom. There was no serious belief that the Justice Department would take any criminal action against Talbott over the erroneous testimony on his communications with the defense contractors on behalf of his management consultant firm.

President Eisenhower, who was expected to be knowledgeable and tough on defense frauds, had been an apologist for Talbott's conduct. This condoning of questionable conduct by the White House was followed, a few months later, by efforts to muzzle

General Accounting Office (GAO) in a review of the research and development programs designed to evaluate the effectiveness of Air Force policies, procedures, and management. President Eisenhower permitted the use of "executive privilege" by the Air Force in refusing to give Comptroller General Joseph Campbell access to the reports by the Inspector General of the Air Force.

It was ironic that President Eisenhower would warn of the danger of the military-industrial complex when leaving office. He and his administration had been responsible for the claims of "executive privilege" that shielded the crooked procurement officers and the crooked businessmen from the investigations of the GAO and the Congress.

THE "McNAMARA MONARCHY"

I was certain that Robert Kennedy's experience with a number of military investigations, including Harry (The Hat) Lev and Air Secretary Talbott, would make him aware of the importance of tight policing of mismanagement and corruption at the Pentagon. I was pleased at the announcement that Robert S. McNamara, short-time president of Ford Motor Company, was going to be the Defense Secretary for the Kennedy administration. The accounts I had read about his background in the newspapers and *Time* magazine made him seem the kind of intelligent, energetic, and tough man the Pentagon needed to clean up the corruption and bring tight administration to military buying.

Secretary McNamara, guided by the astute public relations hand of Assistant Secretary of Defense Arthur Sylvester, maintained the image of a computer-minded genius through the first 18 months. He said all of the right things, and Sylvester, a former Washington newsman, made certain that McNamara saw all of the right military correspondents and newspaper editors for the frank personal discussions in which he was so impressive. As far as the public was concerned, Bob McNamara, product of the Harvard Business School, was the brightest and the best of all the stars on the Kennedy team. Both President Kennedy and Attorney General Kennedy were in awe of his mastery of the Pentagon budget and his control of the military brass.

While he was centralizing control of the Pentagon in the Office of Secretary of Defense, however, he was stepping on the dissenters with a hard foot, and the Pentagon reporters viewed it as putting the professional military men in their place. The press office was centralized under the Office of Defense Secretary, and a broad range of practices were instituted that further tended to crush dissent. There were a few whimpers by some members of the press. Representative John Moss voiced some sharp criticism of McNamara as having done "a gross disservice" to the people of the United States when he suggested that it was proper to distribute untrue propaganda on the success of the Nike-Zeus missile program when it actually was not successful.

Some of the views that McNamara expressed on muzzling of the military were as disturbing to me as they were to Mark Watson, the veteran Pulitzer Prize-winning Pentagon correspondent for the *Baltimore Sun,* and Hanson Baldwin, the distinguished Pulitzer Prize-winning military analyst for the *New York Times.* Baldwin outlined a host of serious Pentagon problems under the "McNamara monarchy." He told me he believed that many of the steps McNamara was taking were probably necessary, but that no one man, or small group of men, could conceivably hold all the wisdom on military planning. He said he thought that McNamara actually believed all the words of praise being written by the Pentagon press corps, and that this was a dangerous thing.

I generally agreed with Mark Watson and Hanson Baldwin, becoming concerned as they were, that McNamara's words were not being matched by his deeds, and that the more restrictive information policies made it more difficult to obtain the views of dissenters. Baldwin, an Annapolis graduate and the dean of the newspaper military analysts, wrote scathingly of "McNamara's monarchy" at the Pentagon:

"Objections or dissent, even to Congress, are discouraged, muted, or, when possible, stifled . . . . Mr. McNamara has pressured the Joint Chief of Staff to sign written statements testifying to Congress that the Administration's defense budget is adequate. He has censored, deleted, and altered statements to Congress by the chiefs of the services and their secretaries. He has downgraded, ignored, bypassed, or overruled the advice of the Joint Chiefs of Staff. . . . Mr. McNamara has not yet succeeded in forcing all of the service to speak, officially or unofficially, with one public voice. But he has come much closer to it than anyone before him, and he is still trying. And the progress he has made carries its own political dangers."

Mr. Baldwin wrote of one of the dangers of concentrated power: "It places more and more power over the military-industrial complex in the hands of a few men in the executive branch of government. . . . The individual services no longer have the final power to contract. The rewarding or cancellation of contracts—

which may make or break companies and affects thousands of workers—is now ultimately controlled by a very few men in the top echelons of the Defense Department."

My first efforts to penetrate the McNamara Pentagon came after the award of the so-called TFX warplane contract in the fall of 1962. The award of the $6.5 billion contract was made to General Dynamics Corporation which resulted in the construction of the F-111 warplane—known as "The Flying Edsel." That contract was awarded by McNamara against the recommendation of the Pentagon Source Selection Board. The Source Selection Board had recommended the award to the Boeing Company on the basis of a much superior design and a price that was lower by $400,000,000.

THE PRESS FAILS IN DEALING WITH THE PENTAGON

Poor or Reluctant Reporting

The TFX case (see Reading 15) was also an indictment of the American press for its venality and superficiality in dealing with top Pentagon officials and awards of major weapons systems. Highly experienced newsmen like Hanson Baldwin, Mark Watson, and Cecil Holland had understood the record in late 1962 and early 1963 even before the hearings in the McClellan Committee had gone more than a few days. Robert Hotz and George Wilson, of *Aviation Week* magazine, had a good understanding of the political influence and mismanagement at about the same time. The reporting of William Prochnau in the *Seattle Times* demonstrated that even a reporter who was inexperienced in covering complex military contracting could do an outstanding job with conscientious work and attention to detail.

The Pentagon press corps, however, compiled a sorry record, even though a few reporters showed understanding and independence from time to time. Most were "lap dogs" for McNamara's deceptions, taking his handouts and his secret briefings and peddling these falsehoods and distortions on the public without attribution.

One Pentagon reporter for a Washington newspaper wrote stories that undercut the solid reporting by a highly competent Capitol Hill colleague, sold his editor on the rightness of McNamara's TFX decision, and then accepted a high-paying Pentagon public relations job from McNamara. Another Pentagon reporter for a large daily newspaper covered the Senate Permanent Investigations Subcommittee hearings on Gilpatric's "conflicts of interest" while his wife attended the hearings with Gilpatric's wife. Needless to say, his stories did not represent an aggressive search for the truth.

Editorial Pressure

Although some of the fault was with the reporters, in a good many cases it was the fault of editors who bought the McNamara image of infallibility as was merchandised by the multimillion-dollar Pentagon public relations office. Some of those editors were wooed in private meetings with McNamara or other top Pentagon brass, others were not perceptive enough in analyzing the facts on the TFX award.

I was fortunate to have particularly perceptive editors in Frank Eyerly and Charles Reynolds of the *Des Moines Register*. Managing Editor Eyerly saw the TFX for what it was when I first started writing on the subject and gave me the kind of space for my stories that is required in pursuing arrogant deceivers with big titles. Eyerly and News Editor Reynolds did not cringe at standing alone on a documented story of waste and mismanagement in government even when criticism of McNamara was not in vogue in the most "trendy" editor circles.

Too Little, Too Late

When the unpopular Vietnam war finally made Pentagon criticism the "trendy" thing for newspapers to do in the late 1960s, the McNamara regime was in its last days. It was too late for reporters to catch up on scandals in the Pentagon spending that had soared from $40 billion to $80 billion a year. Hordes of reporters suddenly descended on the Pentagon with instructions to do "an in-depth series" on the military-industrial complex. The result was a lot of silly, superficial, and ideological reporting by eager young men who did not have the time to get their feet on the ground and were moved by their own biases, or those of their editors, to engage in blunderbuss criticism of any military undertaking.

Despite the handicap of suddenly being tossed into a difficult job, some of the reporters did a useful, if tardy, job of calling public attention to a decade of corruption, mismanagement, and waste in the operation of the Defense Department. Research was not too difficult on the major problems, because books and extensive articles had been written. These spelled out the details of the blundering on the TFX, the X-22 short take-off and landing plane, and the decision of McNamara to make the U.S.S. John F. Kennedy a conventional carrier. The cases of minor blundering and "conflicts of interest" were described in the hearings and reports of congressional committees that a few of us had been writing about for years.

The public and many editors were suddenly hit with the shocking picture of the misuses of the Pentagon's tremendous multibillion-dollar budget. They suddenly realized that regional political favoritism, "conflicts of interest," and cozy dealings with big and little defense contractors can be a drain on the taxpayers and detrimental to the goal of producing the best weapons system for the best price.

But, there was a tendency on the part of many reporters and editors to let an ideological bias against the military take them to absurd extremes in their conclusions. They engaged in sloppy reporting practices that did not distinguish between the corrupters and mismanagers and those who were aggressive opponents of the corrupters.

A Grave Injustice

Even when the press recognized a scandalous situation in the award or management of a contract for a major weapons system, there was a negligence on the followup that played into the hands of the corrupters. Such was the case of the C-5A Galaxy, a jet transport being built by Lockheed, a giant Georgia-based operation that dominated the defense procurement picture.

The Senate Armed Services Committee, under Chairman Richard Russell of Georgia, and the House Armed Services Committee, under Chairman Carl Vinson of Georgia, shied away from spotlighting evidence of irregularities in connection with the Lockheed firm. Senator William Proxmire, a Wisconsin Democrat, was not so reluctant when it involved the jurisdiction of the Joint Economic Subcommittee on Economy in Government. In November 1968, Air Force Cost Analyst A. Ernest Fitzgerald testified on "cost overruns" of nearly $2 billion in the construction of the C-5A. Fitzgerald gave the accurate testimony over the objections of his military superiors as well as Air Force Secretary Harold Brown.

When Fitzgerald returned to the Pentagon, he was called in by Secretary Brown and severely criticized for acting against orders when he testified truthfully. When Fitzgerald was dismissed, Brown called the Pentagon's personnel office to find out how he could fire Fitzgerald, a Deputy for Management Systems in the Air Force Headquarters in the Pentagon. His job was to analyze Air Force programs for waste and seek ways to eliminate it. In his view it was also his duty to testify frankly and truthfully to Congress unless there was some question of national security involved.

Fitzgerald had winced at his instructions from Brown to deceive the Proxmire committee, but he did not volunteer the information on the cost overruns. When Proxmire asked the question he told the truth. His ten-year battle over that truth-telling testimony made him the most famous of the whistle blowers, and, despite the negligence and superficiality of the Washington press corps, he fought off Pentagon efforts to smear him and destroy his career.

The sensational story that he was fired by Air Secretary Robert J. Seamans for having testified truthfully on the $2 billion "cost overrun" on the C-5A program was covered well. *Washington Post* reporter Bernard Nossiter did a particularly outstanding job of exploring all aspects of that vicious and illegal firing of an honest man. It is a violation of law for an official to retaliate against a subordinate who tells the truth to Congress, but the law is ignored by every administration. Attorney General John Mitchell was certainly not likely to initiate an investigation and prosecution against any officials appointed by the then President Richard M. Nixon.

When Bud Nossiter was transferred to London, there was no leadership in the coverage from the *Washington Post,* and neither the *Washington Star* nor the *New York Times* did a competent job of keeping pace with various smears and harassment of the military and civilian officials that continued throughout the Nixon, Ford, and Carter administrations. Evidence of perjured testimony and the harassment of Fitzgerald went virtually unreported in Washington and New York. Articles on these injustices by Indjy Badhwar and Sheila Hershow in the *Federal Times* and my reports in the *Des Moines Register* were considered only minor irritants as the Pentagon steamroller went ahead with promotions of Fitzgerald's persecuters.

The press concentrated on far lesser crimes in Watergate, and it ignored evidence of perjury, rigged documents, and brutal misuse of power in the Justice Department and Civil Service Commission against Fitzgerald. The evidence of these abuses was recorded in the public transcripts of Fitzgerald's litigation in the courts, in the Civil Service Commission hearings, in the Congressional Record, and in the hearings of the various committees of Congress who made brief but abortive attempts to block the appointment and promotion of the liars and falsifiers, both military and civilians.

An Urgent Need

The ineffective and superficial coverage of the Pentagon continues to be the sorriest story in Washington. Despite an occasional fine job, there is an amazing lack of understanding by the press that honest government is not only practical, it is vital to the future of the United States. It is time for the press to eliminate some of the smart cynical attitudes that tolerate corruption and mismanagement. It is time to exhibit some outrage at the dishonest, political administration of the Defense Department and any other agency of government, including the courts.

For every new reporter in Washington there is an opportunity to understand that every story of Defense Department corruption is worth pursuit by the press until the corrupters pay a penalty or the mismanager is exposed. Those who misrepresent, to hide corruption and mismanagement, should be exposed and criticized for specific illegal or improper action or for their role as accomplices in the coverup.

The point must be made that liars and falsifiers cannot be tolerated in high government office, and that the higher the office the higher the price one must pay for falsification. This has not been the case, and the laxity of the press is an opportunity for the new reporter who is willing to work hard, be thorough, honest, and courageous on the follow through to expose the massive corruption that perpetually permeates defense purchasing and management.

Reading 15: The Flying Edsel—TFX-111

My first interest in the TFX contract award to General Dynamics Corporation was a result of conversations with Senator Henry M. Jackson, a Washington Democrat, who was interested in the complaint of the Boeing Company. The company claimed that it lost the award as a result of irregularities in the negotiation procedures. Senator Jackson said that he had avoided any contact with Secretary McNamara and other top decision makers before their decision on the contract. He knew and respected McNamara, and felt the contract would be awarded to the company producing the best plane for the lowest price. He said he had confidence in the ability of the Boeing firm to compete effectively without political clout.

Senator Jackson, an original Kennedy supporter, had good personal and political relations with the president. He had served as Democratic National Chairman in the 1960 campaign. However, the Washington Democrat had practical reasons for wanting to avoid a political tug-of-war over the TFX contract. From a political standpoint, the Texas-New York combination that backed General Dynamics and Grumman (a subcontractor) had a distinct political power advantage. The 24 Texas electoral votes and the 45 New York electoral votes had gone to Kennedy in 1960, whereas Washington's nine electoral votes had gone to the Republican candidate, Richard M. Nixon.

In the late summer of 1962, Senator Jackson said he heard disturbing rumors of Texas political pressure on the TFX contract, specifically that Vice President Lyndon B. Johnson was trying to steer the contract to General Dynamics. Jackson called Deputy Defense Secretary Roswell Gilpatric and asked him about reports that General Dynamics had the contract in the bag. Gilpatric said there was nothing to these reports and that the award would be made "strictly on the merits."

On October 24, 1962, a story in the *Fort Worth Press,* under the by-line of Washington correspondent Seth Kantor, stated: "General Dynamics of Fort Worth will get the multibillion-dollar defense contract to build the supersonic TFX Air Force and Navy fighter plane, 'the press learned today from top government sources.'"

Kantor wrote that he got the story from two "very high echelon people" in the Kennedy administration. For his Fort Worth readers he said it was estimated that the contract would pump up to $6 billion in federal contracts into the Fort Worth area.

Senator Jackson, suspecting that Vice President Johnson was the source, called Gilpatric to ask if it were true. Again Gilpatric assured the Senator that no decision had been made. He confided that the competition between Boeing and General Dynamics was "extremely close." The Washington Democrat, somewhat naively as it turned out, believed Gilpatric and believed that McNamara would make the decision to buy the best plane for the lowest cost.

Even when the Pentagon announced on November 24, 1962, that the TFX contract would be awarded to General Dynamics, Senator Jackson initially believed that Boeing had lost a fair competition. However, just before he talked to me, Senator Jackson had been told the disturbing news that there had been four separate evaluation studies by the services—an unprecedented number for a single plane—and that all of the evaluation studies rated the Boeing version as "superior" to the General Dynamics proposal.

When he talked to me a few days after the award, Senator Jackson still could not believe the reports were accurate. It didn't make sense that Secretary McNamara, a man dedicated to economy in defense spending, would take the second-best plane and pay several hundred million dollars more for it.

On December 2, Jackson again contacted Gilpatric and was assured that the competition had been "very close" and the decision for General Dynamics had been by a narrow margin. Jackson followed up with questions about the reports that the Pentagon Source Selection Board had unanimously recommended Boeing on the basis of price and performance. Gilpatric conceded that Jackson's information was correct, but he explained that the competition was so close that it was immaterial which firm was finally selected. It was at that point that Jackson told Gilpatric he intended to ask Senator John McClellan to have the professional staff of the Permanent Investigation Subcommittee examine the circumstances surrounding the TFX award.

Before the investigation got under way, I made my own inquiries at the Pentagon press office and ran into a stone wall of questionable "national security" claims. When I told Arthur Sylvester, McNamara's top information man, I had the information that four evaluations of the TFX proposals favored Boeing and that the General Dynamics plane would cost from $100 million to $416 million more than the Boeing plane, his reply was: "Clark, you got the facts all wrong. You must not have a very good informant."

When I asked which facts were wrong, and to be given the right facts, Sylvester said I had to understand that the TFX was a super-secret fighter plane and any facts about it were top secret. I replied that I wanted facts on general performance rating and cost differential and was not interested in the speed and other performance figures, which I understood would be properly classified. Sylvester countered that any discussion of the contract decision would have to include specific performance figures to have any meaning. He hinted that it was on the performance rating that General Dynamics was superior to the Boeing proposal.

I noted that I had heard reports that the Pentagon Source Selection Board, composed of top generals and admirals, was unanimous in its findings that the Boeing plane was lower cost and would also perform better. "Was it true that the Pentagon Source Selection Board was unanimous in its recommendation of the Boeing plane?" I asked.

"You know Washington, Clark," Sylvester said in a flip manner. "You can hear almost anything about anyone." He then suggested that I should turn my queries to other aspects of the competition including Senator Jackson's motivation for asking for the investigation. "Everyone knows he's called the Senator from Boeing," he quipped in his characteristic manner.

I had known Arthur Sylvester for years, had worked with him on some aspects of the Dixon-Yates case and on a matter involving a questionable Eisenhower appointment to the Atomic Energy Commission. But now, he was on the other side of the fence. If Art Sylvester had a solid explanation for giving the award to General Dynamics, he would have found a way to get sufficient evidence on the line without breaching national security. The quippy stonewalling was indicative of the weakness in the case for General Dynamics. There was trouble ahead for them on the TFX investigation.

A few days later I talked to the staff of the McClellan Committee. Counsel Jerome Alderman was an old friend and a veteran of the labor racket inquiry where he had served as an assistant to Bob Kennedy. Robert E. Dunne, an able and experienced lawyer-investigator, had been hired by Bob Kennedy. Thomas Nunnally, whom we later called "Tiger Tom," was a GAO accountant who had been borrowed by the subcommittee staff for the TFX investigation.

On a confidential basis, Alderman confirmed that there had been four evaluations that favored Boeing, that the Boeing price was better by at least $100 million—perhaps $400 million—and that the Pentagon Source Selection Board had been unanimous in its finding for Boeing on price and performance. The only document at the Pentagon that supported the General Dynamics plane was a five-page memorandum of justification, dated November 21, 1962. That document was signed by McNamara, Secretary of the Air Force Eugene Zuckert, and Secretary of the Navy Fred Korth. Deputy Secretary of Defense Roswell Gilpatric had not signed the award, but had agreed with it.

That five-page memorandum of justification was loaded with errors, Adlerman confided. It claimed what appeared to be inflated performance ratings for the General Dynamics plane that did not square with figures from the military evaluation. More surprisingly, there were large arithmetical errors that had been uncovered in Tom Nunnally's brief examination of the memorandum. A week or two later Nunnally told me, he had found separate mistakes of $32 million and $22 million in the documents signed by McNamara, Zuckert, and Korth.

This was a hot story already. Even if McNamara was able to pull something out of the secret cabinets of the Pentagon to justify the award, the large mathematical errors on a major weapons system award was an indication of incompetence and blundering at the top level in McNamara's Pentagon. Cecil Holland, the veteran reporter for the *Washington Star* was also doing an analysis of the TFX controversy—probing the Pentagon explanations, and talking with the staff. This was great news to me. Although Holland was tough competition for the news breaks on a story, he was thorough, systematic, and persistent. His work on the tax scandals of the Truman years and his coverage of the McClellan labor racket hearings had been an important factor in the success of those hearings.

It was very important that there be solid, aggressive coverage in the *Washington Star* because many reporters and columnists relied on the *Star* to stimulate their interest as well as to get solid news leads. When a story carried the by-line of Cecil Holland, Jerry O'Leary, Robert Walsh, Ed Prina, George Beveridge, or Miriam Ottenberg, it was solid reporting.

Holland and I compared notes on the TFX contract and concluded that the burden of proof was on McNamara. It was up to him to show that the errors in the memorandum of justification did not improperly influence the award. In addition to the factual errors, the memorandum contained a number of statements that were highly questionable when viewed against the comments of the technical experts and against other key documents. The Pentagon used these highly technical points to confuse the press corps, and to a large extent succeeded with those who did not put the time into studying the evidence on these technical points.

Aware of the ease with which Cabinet officers can confuse and mislead reporters in technical areas, Holland and I decided that we had to be apprised of all aspects of the several disputed points in the Boeing plane that were highlighted in the memorandum of justification.

McNamara and his civilian secretaries opposed the Boeing plan to use a modern "thrust reverser" braking device in the TFX. They said it was a "risky" development that made the plane less acceptable than the General Dynamics plane with its conventional dive brake. Certainly, Holland and I were not expert on braking devices for planes, but we could become expert on what the experts thought about Boeing's "thrust reverser." It might be that Boeing's plan was "risky," even though its engineers had much more experience in building planes than McNamara, Zuckert, or Korth. As we expected, Boeing's spokesman told me the "thrust reverser" was not risky, was in use on other Boeing planes, and was a highly desirable feature. Boeing's spokesman also told me that, as far as they knew, the military engineers in the Air Force and Navy agreed with their assessment, and they knew of no Pentagon technicians or officials who disagreed with their judgments except McNamara, Zuckert, and Korth.

The Pentagon press office declined to discuss the issue of "thrust reversers" except to reiterate McNamara's conclusion that it was "risky," and, when the McClellan Subcommittee staff said they had been unable to find any technicians or engineers who supported McNamara, Holland and I decided that McNamara was probably wrong.

At the same time, we were tackling the evidence on McNamara's claim that the use of titanium in the Boeing plane was risky and might interfere with Boeing's ability to meet the specified delivery dates. I was advised by Boeing—and the subcommittee staff confirmed—that Boeing had been using titanium in the wing structure of planes for nearly a decade. Engineers and metallurgists told the McClellan subcommittee investigators that Boeing's use of titanium in the wing structure was a "conventional use" of the metal. They said it made the plane lighter—the reason the Navy had requested it for use on carriers—and it entailed no unusual risk in the way Boeing was using it.

The Pentagon press office would not name one metallurgist who was supportive of McNamara's judgment that titanium was risky for use in the Boeing plane. Sylvester hinted that the Pentagon would have experts to support McNamara when the hearing was staged, and asked sarcastically if I thought I knew more about engineering than McNamara who had been head of the Ford Motor Company.

"You don't have any expertise on this type of thing," Sylvester snapped. "Go back to playing cops and robbers with Jimmy Hoffa or the Justice Department where you know what you're doing."

I conceded that McNamara had great experience in industry and that I had none, but he had no credentials as an airplane engineer nor in the field of metallurgy. "According to subcommittee sources, his views on titanium are contradicted by the metallurgists and other technicians," I said.

"Do you think Scoop Jackson is an objective source?" Sylvester snapped in erroneously assuming my source was Senator Jackson. He declared that McNamara would be prepared to answer the question "If the hearings ever come off."

I had heard no indication that there would be no hearings, and had assumed that, if the investigation proceeded as it had up to that point, there would be hearings in February 1963. Senator Jackson said he assumed the hearings were going forward, but that the Pentagon and the Kennedy White House were bringing pressure on the subcommittee members and staff to stop the hearings "on a phoney national security claim." He said that officials of the Boeing Company had been subjected to some pressures and had asked him to withdraw his request for hearings.

Boeing officials were concerned about how they might be treated on future contracts with the McNamara Pentagon and had been given some broad hints that they might receive favored treatment if they were successful in getting the hearings stopped. Senator Jackson did not go into details on these pressures, but said he had told Boeing that he had asked McClellan for the investigation on the belief that it was an irregular contract award. He did not feel he should ask McClellan to halt the probe now that the staff had established worse irregularities than initially imagined.

Senator Jackson suggested that I talk to Senator McClellan and the staff if I wanted more details on the kind of tactics that were being used to block the hearings. McClellan said he had received a call from Bob Kennedy with a request to call off the investigation.

McClellan said he considered it "an improper" effort to interfere with the investigation, but did not go into detail, even on a confidential basis. He said that Bob Kennedy had also called Jerry Adlerman and had used "questionable tactics" to end the TFX investigation.

Adlerman, on a confidential basis, related that Bob Kennedy had called and in an angry voice charged that the staff was "trying to destroy Bob McNamara" whom he characterized as "an honest man" and perhaps the best member of the Kennedy Cabinet. He pictured McNamara as the "victim" of the military brass who were grasping at technicalities to make him look bad. Adlerman said that Bob Kennedy had been misled by McNamara's abbreviated and distorted version, but Kennedy would not take the time to listen to the explanation Adlerman tried to give him and hung up in a rage when Adlerman would not give ground. Adlerman said he worked for Senator McClellan and not Kennedy.

To meet the Pentagon claim of national security secrets, McClellan arranged closed hearings starting on February 26, 1963, with daily transcripts available to the press. This cut much of the impact that would have come from public hearings, because there were only a few of us who would wait for the transcripts and read them carefully for the kind of detailed corroboration that is essential to determine which witnesses are being truthful and which are hedging.

Cecil Holland's stories were great and made up for the mediocre coverage that the *New York Times* and the *Washington Post* were receiving from their military reporters. Holland had considerable experience with investigations and managed to sort out the issues, but it was refreshing to see William Prochnau, a new reporter in town for the *Seattle Times,* follow the same path that Dave Kraslow and Bob Healy had followed in the investigations of the Federal Communications Commission. He was a former sports writer and general feature writer and had little experience in covering governmental affairs when he was assigned to Washington. His managing editor, Henry McLeod, whom I knew through the investigations of Dave Beck, told him to drop in to see me for general guidance on Washington coverage.

It was a happy coincidence that Bill Prochnau came to see me when I was deeply involved in the TFX investigation with the Boeing angles that were so vital to the interests and the economy of Seattle. Ed Guthman, who had worked with me on the Beck investigation, was one of Prochnau's heroes, and I discussed the similarities of the opportunities when an investigation of national importance had major local significance.

Senator Jackson had informed him of the general issues, and he had read some of my stories as well as those written by Cecil Holland. In a nutshell I explained the importance of the errors that were found in the five-page memorandum of justification and in the technical issues, as Holland and I had sorted them out and analyzed them. I told Prochnau that from that point on it was important to study the details of the daily transcripts of the hearings, to talk with the subcommittee staff for guidance on technical problems he did not understand, to be wary of falsifications and distortions from the Pentagon, and to come to me if he had any difficulties sorting things out. He was intelligent, he spent long hours with the transcripts of testimony, and he had a story that was getting big play in the *Seattle Times*.

Although Prochnau asked a few questions about the background of participants or the evidence supporting a technical point, he soon became well versed on the details of the testimony and confident of his own ability to sort things out on one of the most complicated weapons system decisions that could be imagined. His understanding of the TFX investigation and his detailed study of the record was a contrast to sloppy work and superficial study reflected in columns written by a number of distinguished journalists, who were used by McNamara in an effort to counter the bad image. One of those used by the Kennedy White House was Walter Lippmann, usually one of the most perceptive thinkers and writers.

Whether Lippmann sought the interview with McNamara on the TFX or whether the Pentagon sought him out, I did not learn, but the result was a column that I am sure Lippmann regretted writing if he followed the history of the TFX investigation and the disastrous record of the F-111 warplane. The column demonstrated that McNamara deliberately confused him on technical questions of the "thrust reversers" and the use of "titanium" in the Boeing plane. McNamara had given Lippmann the Pentagon's distorted argument on cost and had ignored the unanimity of the recommendations by the Air Force, Navy, and the Pentagon Source Selection Board.

The message of the Lippmann column was that decision making on modern weapons systems is highly complicated and requires the analysis of experts. Lippmann admitted his own inability to come to grips with those decisions in his discussions with McNamara, and concluded that, whether we like it or not, we must leave such decisions to the qualified men who are appointed to assume those responsibilities. Lippmann judged McNamara to be an honest, intelligent and well-qualified man, and reasoned that there was no alternative but to accept his decision and get on with the business of running the country.

The reasoning was logical, but the facts in the TFX case did not square with what he had been told. This was not a case of the Air Force and Navy being at odds over whether Boeing had the best price and performance. It wasn't a strong Defense Secretary stepping in to make a decision for the squabbling military. The choice was that of an authoritarian man, either because he was ill-informed or motivated by politics, who made an arbitrary decision that General Dynamics was going to receive the contract regardless of its second-rate plane and a $400,000,000 higher price tag.

There was no question in my mind about McNamara's being of superior intelligence. He was a Phi Beta Kappa graduate of the University of California and received a Master's Degree in business administration at Harvard in 1939. He was an assistant professor of business administration at Harvard from 1940 through 1943, and from 1943 to 1946 was a lieutenant colonel in an Air Force group that specialized in the study of military organizations. In 1946, he was one of the small group of bright young men who went to work for Ford Motor Company. He rose from controller to assistant general manager to vice president and eventually to president.

However, in the TFX case, and in a few others that I learned about later, he had permitted political pressures to influence his decisions on a multibillion-dollar contract. It made him appear an incompetent as the hearings documented the TFX story.

As shocking as was the choice of a second-rate plane and the potential waste of hundreds of millions of dollars, the fact that McNamara tolerated serious conflicts of interest on the part of Deputy Defense Secretary Roswell Gilpatric and Navy Secretary Fred Korth was even worse. Gilpatric, a former lawyer for General Dynamics, should have had no role in any award that went to his former employer and a firm that still employed his former law firm. Yet Gilpatric was given a key coordinating role in the award.

Fred Korth, a Texas banker, was the former president of Continental National Bank of Fort Worth, Texas. He had replaced the Kennedy administration's first Secretary of the Navy, John B. Connally, who had resigned to run for Governor of Texas. His bank had participated in loan arrangements with General Dynamics, whose General Dynamics-Convair plant was in Fort Worth. This made General Dynamics one of the very best customers of Korth's bank, and Korth numbered the General Dynamics officials among his close friends. Although Korth had stepped down as president of Continental National Bank, he retained more than $160,000 in stock.

Although those "conflicts of interest" facts as well as other facts were finally spelled out by the McClellan subcommittee, it was like pulling teeth for me or other reporters to get any information from the McNamara Pentagon, Gilpatric, or Korth on their relations with General Dynamics. McNamara defended these relationships all the way, even when Korth was finally forced to resign as Navy Secretary and Gilpatric was eased out of the Number Two Pentagon job.

McNamara stuck with General Dynamics even in the face of more revelations of scandalous attempts to force military men to write reports and testify falsely that they supported General Dynamics. This became the classic case of abuse and misuse of Pentagon power to support a political deal. The nine-year record of the TFX was spelled out in the final report of the Senate subcommittee on December 15, 1970. The report said: "Aside from the serious impact which the TFX program has had upon our national security and aside from the obvious waste of scarce resources, the TFX case also has affected public confidence in our defense establishment. As this report makes clear, the primary cause of the TFX fiasco was mismanagement. A series of mismanagement blunders, made for various reasons, compounded errors with more errors and caused the failure of the program. The management blunders were made at the highest echelons of the government. Top presidential appointees in the Department of Defense during the McNamara era overrode expert advice to impose personal judgments on complex matters beyond their expertise. These same officials then made extraordinary efforts to conceal the results of their errors in the TFX case. These efforts included deliberate attempts to deceive the Congress, the press, and the American people. Understandably, this sorry record has done nothing to enhance public confidence in the integrity and competence of the people who are charged with preserving the national security. Nor has it improved the public image of the Department of Defense."

STUDENT WORK PROJECT SUGGESTION

1. Examine the GAO reports made within the last year indicating that Defense contracts and operations are still plagued by the bureaucratic problems and conflicts of interest that existed in the 1950s and 1960s. Write a paper explaining how Cecil Holland, who had no technical expertise in aircraft production, was able to gain sufficient information to challenge technical decisions by Defense Secretary Robert S. McNamara.

2. Why is the experience of Bill Prochnau important as an example to the reporter who is inexperienced in dealing

with the Pentagon problems? What are the lessons this chapter teaches you about your own ability to report effectively upon major Defense Department programs and policies?

29 EXPOSING BOBBY BAKER AND LBJ

There will always be many news stories exploring the financial affairs of senators, congressmen, and the congressional staff members who abuse and misuse their authority. They do it by amendments and by minor modifications in the federal laws where small, and seemingly insignificant, changes can mean millions to business groups. Lobbyists are willing to pay handsomely to political funds or to politically influential law firms for those small changes. Most of the time the cash payoffs to officials are well concealed, but sometimes evidence of sudden affluence can be found in acquisitions of real estate and in sudden dramatic changes in the style of living.

Nepotism is now a violation of the law, and payrolls of the Senate and House members are public so only a fool would have his wife or son on his own payroll. However, there are new twists in which the son or daughter of a congressman or senator is placed on the payroll of a colleague and the colleague's relatives are put on a committee staff controlled by an accommodating associate. Close scrutiny of property acquisitions, living style, and payrolls will consistently turn up minor and major abuses of congressional authority.

Reading 16: Too Much Money

The nuts and bolts of Bobby Baker's wheeling and dealing through stock deals and legislative manipulations held little attraction for much of the press until after sex emerged in the person of a German party girl. Until the Elly Rometch story broke, many prestigious publications had been unwilling to make commitments of manpower, money, and space to a significant story of congressional corruption linked to the then Vice President Lyndon B. Johnson.

I was so preoccupied with other stories that I overlooked the tips I was receiving from my 12-year-old son, Ray. Robert G. (Bobby) Baker, Secretary to the Democratic majority in the Senate, was my neighbor and an acquaintance from Capitol Hill. Although Bobby was regarded by many political writers as one of the best news sources on Capitol Hill, I had only talked with him at the Senate on a few occasions.

Bobby Baker's knowledge was legend on Capitol Hill, where he had started work as a 15-year-old page boy and had progressed up the ladder to be named by Lyndon Johnson as Secretary to the Democrats in 1955 when he was only 27 years old. I knew of his connection with Johnson and Senator Bob Kerr, but he had always been pleasant and accommodating. On a few occasions I had talked with him at the LaFayette grade school playground where his boys, Bobby and Jimmy, were active with Ray in kids' basketball, football, and softball games and in Boy Scouts.

In the late spring of 1963, Ray made the comment that "Bobby Baker's daddy sure is rich." I discounted it as the youthful boasting of Bobby and Jimmy Baker and explained to Ray that Baker had "a very responsible job" at the Senate, but that the $19,000-a-year salary would hardly classify him as rich.

"But, what about the Cadillac he drives?" Ray asked. In fatherly tones I said that the car went with his job in the Senate and that he should not be confused by such symbols of wealth.

"I don't mean the black Cadillac," Ray responded. "He has a pink one with Illinois license plates, and Bobby (Jr.) and Jimmy's mother drive it all the time." Before I could respond, Ray added that Baker was building a new motel at Ocean City, Maryland, but I was so intent on explaining that Bobby Baker was not really "rich" that I told him it was probably "some part interest in the motel that represented a relatively small investment." At some point, Ray got in the comment that Bobby and Jimmy had told him that their father made a lot of money from some vending machines, but I again discounted that as being "probably a small interest in a company."

Although I made a mental note at that time to take a closer look at the affairs of my neighbor in land record books, I was already working on the TFX story and the aftermath of the Billie Sol Estes case. There just was not enough time in a seven-day week to squeeze in a half day for the land record and mortgage research I would have to do before I even approached Bobby Baker on the suspicions based on the conversations of teenage boys.

I even missed the first public indications of Baker's wealth in the announcement that he was a part owner of a new million-dollar

motel at Ocean City, Maryland. The Carousel Motel was built by
Baker, Mr. and Mrs. Alfred S. Novak, and Mr. and Mrs. Donald J.
Novak. The Novaks were in the construction business, and, if I had
noticed the item on the society pages of the Washington newspapers,
I would probably have minimized Baker's financial interest and
marked his role as that of public relations because he had been able
to bring Vice President Lyndon B. Johnson and Lady Bird Johnson
to the grand opening of the "High-style hideaway for the Advise and
Consent set."

I was jarred into action by a *Washington Post* news story that
Ralph L. Hill, president of the Capitol Vending Company had filed a
$300,000 damage suit against Bobby Baker, the Serv-U Corporation,
Ernest C. Tucker, listed as vice president and secretary of Serv-U
vending company, and Fred B. Black, a Washington public relations
consultant for North American Aviation Corporation.

Ralph Hill, a former friend of Bobby Baker from South Carolina,
contended that in 1962 Bobby Baker had put in a good word for him
with Melpar, Inc., a Falls Church, Virginia aerospace subcontractor,
that resulted in his receiving a lucrative vending contract with the
defense industry. Hill said he paid Baker $250 a month from April
1962 through March 1963, and that Baker than stepped up the
demand to $650 a month until August 1963 when he balked at
Baker's demand for a still larger sum. Hill charged that, at this point,
Baker and others created Serv-U vending to buy him out. When he
wouldn't sell, Hill said, Melpar cancelled his contract.

The story on Hill's damage suit by *Washington Post* court
reporter Jack Landau ignited my interest. I went to the courthouse,
read the petition and then contacted Ralph Hill. Hill said that,
because of his pending litigation, he could not comment on the
record beyond what was in his petition for publication, but I
received considerably more personal information on Bobby Baker,
including the details of a conversation in which Baker told his former
friend he couldn't make a damage suit stick and that he could "ruin"
Hill if he filed the suit.

I called Don Reynolds a Maryland insurance man who had been
a close friend of Bobby Baker, who said he would be very happy to
talk to me "on a background basis" because "these are powerful
people we're dealing with and they can destroy you." Reynolds
agreed to see me immediately because he knew that I was a friend of
Bob Kennedy. He also knew that Bob Kennedy disliked Bobby Baker
and Lyndon Johnson and might be encouraged to do the full
investigation and prosecution that was needed. Reynolds became my

most valuable informant, and a key figure in the subsequent Senate investigations.

I talked to Baker, calling him off the Senate floor, and asked him about Hill's law suit. Still the suave con man, Baker said he would like to answer all my questions, but he had been advised by his lawyer, Abe Fortas, that it might interfere with the litigation. He said he could tell me that he had absolutely no interest in Serv-U, and that Hill was a liar who had lost a contract. Hill was threatening to destroy him because he had rejected the proposal that he use political pressure to save Hill's contract.

Bobby Baker's explanation was smooth, and he rejected all questions on grounds of his lawyer's advice. "When it's all over with, you'll be able to see why I couldn't say anything now," Bobby confided. He said he was sure I understood his position.

Vend Magazine, a trade publication distributed from Chicago, carried a story that stated Baker *did* have an interest in the fast-growing Serv-U Corporation—a firm that had become the talk of the industry. This vending firm, starting with nothing, had, in an eight-month period, acquired franchises that would result in gross receipts of more than $3.5 million a year. Most of the sales were reported to be in the Southern California aerospace plants.

At the same time, Lawrence Stern and Jack Landau, reporters for the *Washington Post,* reported that public records in Worcester County, Maryland, disclosed that Baker had engaged in a series of transactions with the Serv-U Corporation. Mr. and Mrs. Bobby Baker and their partners, the Novaks, had sold the Carousel Motel to Serv-U for $1.2 million.

I wondered why Abe Fortas, Democratic stalwart and long-time friend and confidant of Lyndon Johnson, was counsel of record in the defense of the $300,000 damage suit. To me it was an indication that Johnson was interested in protecting Bobby Baker, and I went back for a second interview. Baker was at his most sincere, addressing me by my first name and saying, "I would like to sit right down and explain the whole thing. In the end, I know that you'll see that Hill has been spreading a pack of lies. I do have to be loyal to my attorney and follow his instructions. Some of these stories are so outlandish that I wouldn't believe them about anyone," Baker added, skillfully avoiding any answer. "I've made my enemies around here, and they're busy peddling a lot of filthy rumors. I hope that some of them get in print, because I'll sue."

He did, however, volunteer some information, on a subject I had not touched upon, relative to how "lucky" he had been to be able to buy some of the so-called "MAGIC" stock in the Mortgage Guaranty Insurance Corporation of Milwaukee. That was what had made him his money, he said, telling me that he had bought stock at $2 and $3 a share and that it had gone as high as $51 a share at one time.

I did not understand why Baker had volunteered information on the "MAGIC stock" until some time later when I read a story on the big profits by Julian Morrison, in the *Washington Daily News*. Morrison had done a great job of investigating Bobby Baker's involvement with Mortgage Guaranty Insurance Corporation in a series of articles that made a highly complicated situation quite simple and demonstrated its relationship to legislation that was pending in the Senate.

Vice President Johnson was in Europe when the $300,000 damage suit was filed and the first rash of news stories appeared. The vice president cut his trip short by a day and hurried back to Washington. It was reported by his friends that the Baker problem was on his mind, and the appearance of Fortas as Baker's lawyer supported that thesis.

Despite the continuing stories, Bobby Baker seemed confident he could ride it out. Senator Everett Dirksen, the Republican leader, seemed to be a part of the coverup when he responded to questions about "the Bobby Baker scandal." In his most resonant tone, the Wizard of Ooze said he hadn't seen "evidence of any scandal," that he knew Bobby Baker, and was not going to jump to the conclusion that he should be subject to an investigation on the basis "of charges in some newspaper stories." Dirksen said that as he saw it there was "little public interest in the Bobby Baker case . . . and that, out on the cobblestones, out in the boondocks, they look at it as a little internal problem for the Senate Democrats."

Republican Leader Dirksen's efforts to pour cold water on the idea of an investigation of Baker was also evidence of Johnson's clever touch. If the Republicans didn't complain, the story would die for want of attention, for certainly there was little inclination on the Democratic side to launch an investigation of the Secretary to the Democratic majority. Baker's close friendship with Senator George Smathers of Florida was a plus for him. Majority Whip Hubert H. Humphrey of Minnesota was reported to be working feverishly to stop any Democratic or Republican initiative on an investigation of Bobby Baker.

I contacted several senators who I had been told had been approached by Smathers or Humphrey and asked about the accuracy of the reports. On an off-the-record basis they confirmed that Humphrey had talked to them on behalf of Vice President Johnson to get them lined up early in the event there was any effort to launch an investigation. Smathers' efforts had been less direct, although they assumed he was seeking the same kind of commitment.

For several days I tried to get in touch with the usually very available Senator Humphrey. By the time I caught up with him the Baker case had several new developments, and I put the questions to him bluntly. He admitted some conversations with the senator I had interviewed, and that "the Bobby Baker thing" might have come up in the conversations. But, he declared he wasn't "any stooge for Lyndon Johnson" and he wasn't "going to be a part of any coverup for Bobby Baker."

I pointed out that his story did not quite jibe with what I had been told by several senators and that I had some more checking to do and would be back to talk to him further before writing the story for the *Minneapolis Tribune.* That was the last I heard of Humphrey taking any initiative to kill the Baker investigation, but I heard reports some time later that he had infuriated Johnson by saying he was afraid he would be the subject of unfavorable stories if he contacted anyone else on the Baker probe.

On the plus side, Senator John Williams had become interested in the Bobby Baker case and, on his own, had arranged to talk to Maryland insurance man Don Reynolds. Also, the Justice Department and the Internal Revenue Service had launched full investigations of Baker after completing a preliminary survey of his activities. Attorney General Kennedy also directed that the Baker investigation be conducted with full vigor. He instructed that no punches be pulled, even if the investigation covered matters that might embarrass Vice President Johnson. Johnson was informed that there was to be a full-scale investigation of Baker by the FBI, but he was not asked if he approved or objected.

The signs were ominous for Baker and for Vice President Johnson. The vice president was treated courteously but coolly by the Kennedy White House. It was known that many in the Kennedy inner circle—which didn't include Lyndon—considered the Texan expendable in 1964. Bobby Kennedy was one who held that view, and Johnson knew that, if he was kept on the ticket, his political assets would have to outweigh his liabilities in some clearly demonstrable fashion.

To Johnson's supporters the Bobby Baker case was one more big problem on top of a lot of other problems, and, at presidential press conferences, questions were raised about how President Kennedy felt about "dump Lyndon" rumors. President Kennedy's answers were support, but were far from a pledge to Johnson.

While Johnson was trying to put out the fire of the Bobby Baker investigation, Senator John Williams, a tireless investigator of wrong-doing, was following through on talks with Ralph Hill, who was very cooperative. He knew Senator Williams' reputation and had confidence in him. He knew of Baker's connection with Vice President Johnson and the late Senator Robert Kerr, and knew he would need all the help he could get in his dispute with Baker. He spelled out the details of the delivery of $5600 in cash to Baker over a period of months. He said Baker had insisted that it be in cash, in small bills, and placed in a plain white envelope.

However, Hill indicated that the $5600 Baker got from him was only a drop in the bucket in the entire Bobby Baker operation. He spelled out his knowledge of how the former page boy, now a $19,600-a-year Secretary to the Senate Majority, could claim a net worth of more than a million dollars. He told of the tremendous profits Baker had made on special purchases of the so-called "MAGIC" stock at a time when that firm had two or three problems before federal agencies. He related that Baker had purchased a $125,000 home in the fashionable Spring Valley section of Washington just a block away from Vice President Johnson's home and just around the corner from the home of Fred B. Black, the North American Aviation Company lobbyist.

In addition, Hill directed Senator Williams to Mrs. Gertrude (Trudy) Novak, widow of one of Baker's business partners. Mrs. Novak had specific knowledge of some of Baker's operations in large cash sums. Hill believed that Trudy Novak would be helpful because she felt she had been treated unfairly by Baker in the sale of the Carousel to Serv-U Corporation and in the handling of her husband's estate by Baker's law associates.

Hill also gave Senator Williams the name of another key witness, Don Reynolds, the Maryland insurance agent. Senator Williams telephoned Reynolds to ask him to come by the office to talk. Reynolds did not know Senator Williams except by reputation, and he indicated he might drop by the office "just to get acquainted."

Ralph Hill gave me essentially the same information he was giving Senator Williams, and I also made the contacts with Trudy Novak, whom I knew as a secretary for the Senate Small Business Committee. I talked to Trudy Novak and Don Reynolds on a confidential basis in the same period that they were talking to Senator Williams. Both Hill and Reynolds were from South Carolina and had a long relationship with Baker in business and social-political dealings.

Hill had admitted using his relationship with Baker to get the vending contract with Melpar, had willingly delivered monthly cash payments to Bobby Baker's office in the Capitol, and balked only when Baker boosted the price beyond his means and squeezed him out.

Ralph Hill told me he did not like to do business that way, but that it was essentially the only way to get the lucrative vending contracts from those who did business with the federal government. Hill resented the fact that Baker had tried to push him around and had arrogantly threatened to "destroy" him if he made a public fuss. Although he was not directly involved in Bobby Baker's other deals, Hill was an astute observer of evidence of devious political transactions. He hinted at the breadth of Bobby Baker's political chicanery and the use of easy sex for senators as a political tool.

Hill had done his homework on the relationship between Bobby Baker and Fred B. Black, of North American Aviation, and the award of the multibillion-dollar Apollo contract to North American. He knew of Baker and Black's financial relationship with two Las Vegas gambling figures. Hill did not purport to have direct evidence of these ties and relationships, but he was confident that all the facts could be documented by depositions in his own law suit and through the work of Senator Williams and a few aggressive investigative reporters.

Don Reynolds was more knowledgeable about Bobby Baker's wheeling and dealing in political sex, cash, and legislative actions. He was less precise in telling the story, but a good deal more colorful. Reynolds had been on the inside of the operations. He had joint business dealings with Bobby Baker, had sold large insurance policies to Lyndon Johnson with an illegal kickback arrangement, and had taken a vigorous part in the wild partying and sex.

The story that Don Reynolds told me of dirty dealings in high places in the Senate was nearly incredible. It was such a sordid story of abuse and misuse of power, of blackmail and sex, and corruption of the legislative process that I could hardly believe it. Initially, I didn't believe it was any more than about half true, but after extensive investigation, I came to the conclusion that it was probably about 99 per cent true. However, I was certain that no more than half of it could be proved even with the subpoena power of a Senate committee and with an aggressive chief counsel and chairman. Everything was there: cash payments, clandestine sex rendezvous, and conspiratorial conversations involving two or three people, but the stories would be difficult or impossible to prove.

What was remarkable to me in the long run was the fact that within two years of my conversations with Reynolds in the fall of 1963, about 80 or 90 per cent of what he had told me had been printed in newspapers or magazines. Those stories, usually well documented, were written and published despite the efforts of Bobby Baker's friends to use their power and pressure to stop the investigations. I was able to authenticate a story involving an exotic 27-year-old German woman who had been a part of the Bobby Baker entourage prior to her sudden deportation in August 1963.

Don Reynolds had told me of the woman, Mrs. Elly Rometsch, and identified her as a "party girl" who had visited the Baker-Tyler town house and had made several trips with Baker and one of his business associates. Reynolds told me that Attorney General Robert Kennedy had directed an investigation of Mrs. Rometsch by the FBI. That investigation established her relationship with a number of important government officials and she was returned to Germany because of her "personal misbehavior."

Mrs. Rometsch had come to the United States as the wife of a West German Army sergeant, entering on a diplomatic visa. Her husband was attached to the military mission at the West German Embassy. Reynolds and Ralph Hill related reports that Mrs. Rometsch had been married to a high-ranking military officer in East Germany, then moved to West Germany, and, within a brief period of time, married a West German Army sergeant who was in the process of making plans to come to Washington for assignment at the West German Embassy.

I confirmed with Justice Department sources that there had been a hurried investigation of Mrs. Rometsch by the FBI in the summer of 1963, and that there was some potential "security problem" that was a factor in her deportation. At the German Embassy press office, it was possible to confirm only that Sergeant and Mrs. Rometsch had come to the United States in April 1961, and had left on August 21, 1963, at the request of the State Department. Through Justice Department sources and Capitol Hill sources, I was able to confirm that Mrs. Rometsch knew some high officials of the Kennedy administration, including President Kennedy, and that the possible embarrassment to the Kennedy administration was a factor in the swift deportation action.

Senator Williams told me that he too had been able to confirm information about Mrs. Rometsch and her relations with Baker, and intended to call it to the attention of the Senate Rules Committee the next week. At this point it was only one of a dozen aspects of Baker's activities, financial and otherwise, that Senator Williams believed merited a thorough investigation.

On Friday, October 25, 1963, I wrote a copyrighted story for the *Des Moines Register* and the *Minneapolis Tribune* on Bobby Baker's mysterious "party girl," her hurried deportation, and her reported connection with high officials of the Kennedy administration. The story appeared on a Saturday morning, October 26, and it caused a sensation that expanded the interest beyond the small group of reporters who had been piecing together complicated financial transactions and political relationships. On Saturday and Sunday I received calls from newsmen in London, Paris, Rome, and various points in Germany, who wanted to learn all they could about the details of my story that had not been in the segment circulated by the Associated Press.

Publications in the United States that had been cool to the Bobby Baker story were suddenly willing to make commitments of manpower, money, and space to a story that had been regarded as too complicated and lacking in public appeal. *Life* magazine assigned a crew of several investigative reporters to do the job of rounding up the total picture of Bobby Baker's Washington, complete with photographs of his "party girls" and his role as Lyndon Johnson's "strong right arm" in the Senate.

The Kennedy White House denied that anyone in the White House even knew Elly Rometsch, and we carried those denials without challenge because we did not want to reveal the confidential sources who had specifically identified two White House officials as friends of Mrs. Rometsch. (Bobby Baker in his book *Wheeling and Dealing* admitted that he knew Elly Rometsch, scoffed at the idea that she was a security risk, identified her as a "German lady-about-town" and said that, at President Kennedy's request, he had arranged for Mrs. Rometsch to meet the President.")

Now the Democratic majority could be prodded by Senator Williams to do a thorough job, and a full investigation was also likely to be encouraged by Attorney General Robert Kennedy from his position of influence in the Justice Department. Bob Kennedy disliked Lyndon Johnson and Bobby Baker and would take no chances with the embarrassment of a coverup of any of their improper or illegal actions. It looked like the major work of the investigative reporters was done on the Bobby Baker case, and now the major job would be to report on the testimony of key witnesses and on the contents of important documents relative to Bobby Baker's use of his Senate position to become a wealthy man.

But that situation changed radically on November 22, 1963, with the assassination of President Kennedy in Dallas, Texas. Lee Harvey Oswald's bullet put Bobby Baker's friend in the White House with control over the awesome power of the Executive Branch and its levers over the Congress.

REPORTING ON THE BOBBY BAKER STORY

The Need for Confidentiality

For a considerable time, I was the only reporter with whom Senator Williams was talking frankly. He was wary of being burned by some of the other Capitol Hill reporters who were friends and buddies of Bobby Baker and Lyndon Johnson. I didn't write about what Senator Williams was doing, nor did I tell other reporters as so many do. I leaned over backwards to protect him. An aggressively honest senator was a rare commodity and, I believed, should be preserved to continue his work as "the conscience of the Senate."

Later, Senator Williams developed the same kind of relationship with a handful of other reporters he learned to trust. They included John Barron and Paul Hope of the *Washington Star,* who worked the Bobby Baker story almost full time. Jack Steele, who had formerly worked with Senator Williams from time to time, renewed the relationship and became a working reporter as well as bureau manager for the Scripps-Howard newspapers on the Bobby Baker story.

Steele bolstered and encouraged Julian Morrison, who worked on Bobby Baker's big profits from the "MAGIC" stock at the same time that the Mortgage Guarantee Insurance Corporation had problems before several government agencies. Also, he was interested in legislation that was under the jurisdiction of Baker's friends in the Senate. Steele worked with Dan Thomasson, then a junior member of the Scripps-Howard bureau, on a story involving delivery of $100,000 in cash to Baker in connection with a favorable Senate action on legislation. That $100,000 was said to have been "a political contribution" to be delivered to Senator Robert Kerr, the Oklahoma Democrat. It was eventually one of the key issues in the criminal trial of Baker for larceny or embezzlement because he used that political cash contribution to finance his Carousel Motel.

"Hot" Stories Need Special Care

To keep pace with the rumors and authoritative tips that whirled around Washington, it took all of the talents of Steele, Thomasson and Morrison at Scripps-Howard, Les Whitten at the Hearst Washington bureau, and Wallace Turner, then a West Coast reporter for the *Times* and the *New York Times* Washington bureau. In addition to Reynolds, Hill, and Trudy Novak, there were offerings of information on a confidential basis from a wide range of senators, Senate staffers, businessmen, and labor leaders who said they had information on the political deals of Baker, Lyndon Johnson, the late Senator Kerr and others. Much of it was true, but some of it was made of half-truths, exaggerations, and distortions. The stories came from sources that included public spirited men and women who had been caught in the fringe of the corrupt operations. The informants also included those who wished to curry favor with reporters before they too were caught. There were a few who were maliciously spreading wild tales that simply added to the confusion.

For the investigative reporter working the case, there was no lack of tips and leads. It was a matter of making judgments as to which leads might be productive if followed through with interviews and checks of public records. Most of the record checking included: examining the reports filed by business firms at the Securities and Exchange Commission (SEC), examining land records and mortgage records, and meticulously following the history of legislation in the Senate and the House.

Experienced investigative reporters view it as a danger signal when the land records, the mortgage records, or the legislative history on an alleged political deal do not conform to the story told by an informant. It means that the informant is making something up for malicious reasons, is planting the information to cause confusion, or has unwisely taken known facts and embellished them with his interpretation.

Most of the handful of reporters working the Bobby Baker case used sound tactics in corroborating informants, although there were a few cases where the competitive drive to be first on a story resulted in inaccurate reporting. A majority of the reporters covering the Baker case thought instinctively in terms of obtaining public or private records to substantiate stories of Baker's activity, so they did not have to use any quotations from the informant or even indicate that they had a confidential informant.

The best informant is one whose story can be substantiated on every major point by a public record, and one who can deliver private documents. and correspondence to fill in the gaps and establish guilty intent. Since Bobby Baker and Lyndon Johnson were skillful at hiding their trail and rarely wrote notes (they both used the telephone and usually dealt in cash), it was difficult for a newsman to trace their actions.

Handling a Specially Lively Informant

My best informants on the Bobby Baker case were Ralph Hill and Don (Buck) Reynolds, but Reynolds was a particularly lively raconteur. In telling his gaudy tales, Reynolds used a mixture of what he knew directly, what he had been told by the parties involved, what others had told him, and what he and others had speculated might have taken place. It was necessary to stop him constantly to ask for clarification as to whether he was a direct witness, was reporting information from those who had witnessed transactions, or was merely reporting what someone else had told him.

When he was asked specifically, Reynolds would usually break it down between what he had observed as a direct witness and what he had been told by others. Understandably, there were times when he could not remember if he had actually overheard a Baker conversation or had heard it from someone else at a later time. I stressed over and over that he should try to be more precise because it would be easy for a reporter or investigator to get the impression that he had first-hand knowledge of all the events he related. "Unless you are precisely correct and have the documentation to prove it, every effort will be made to use mistakes to destroy your credibility," I explained.

Many "Exclusives" Exist Within One Story

It was not one newspaperman who did the job nor one newspaper. As is true in most such cases, it was the force of the stories of many reporters and many newspapers following up the leads on a dozen different fronts, and it was having one strong senator, John J. Williams of Delaware taking that accumulation of facts and leads and forcing the Senate to authorize an investigation that it did not want to do.

The *New York Times* developed stories on Bobby Baker's business ties with Las Vegas gambling figures, and some questionable political business dealings in Haiti.

Seth Kantor, of the *Fort Worth Press*, wrote that Baker had admitted that $50 a month was improperly withheld from the salary of a teen-age Senate employee and that the money was paid to another Senate employee who worked under Baker. The young man, Boyd Richie, was a former beau of Lynda Bird Johnson. He complained to Vice President Johnson about the $50 deductions, and they were stopped. It was significant that Vice President Johnson did not initiate any other action against Baker as a result of his direct knowledge of this incident.

Julian Morrison, of the *Washington Daily*, used reports of the Mortgage Guarantee Insurance Corporation filed at the SEC, and the legislative history of bills before the Senate Banking Committee to put together the story of how Bobby Baker netted a $38,000 windfall profit from an insider tip on a stock purchase. Other reporters followed up Morrison's lead, and shed more light on

Baker's profits from those stock transactions, which eventually totalled more than $100,000.

Erwin Knoll and Theodor Schuchat, writing for the Newhouse newspaper chain, reported that Baker had purchased a new town house near the Capitol at 308 N Street, S.W. It was occupied by Miss Nancy Carole Tyler, a one-time Tennessee beauty-contest winner, who was Baker's private secretary at the Senate. Knoll and Schuchat had used records of the Federal Housing Authority, which was involved in the financing of the redevelopment project, as the source of some of the hard facts in linking Baker's name to the town house. The records showed that Baker had made a $1,600 down payment on the four-bedroom town house. He had apparently violated the occupancy rules in listing Miss Tyler as his "cousin" on the application for the town house, which was part of a cooperative housing development. Occupancy was restricted to owners or relatives of the purchaser, and Miss Tyler was not Baker's cousin.

The Elly Rometsch story, which I broke on October 26, 1963, made Bobby Baker a cover boy on *Life, Time,* and other national magazines. I commented to Senator Williams that it was amazing how a little sex angle could stimulate the interests of the nation's great editors in good government! The Bobby Baker case had suddenly taken fire by mid-November 1963, and it seemed certain that the Rules Committee would be compelled to do a thorough investigation of the entire Bobby Baker operation, including those aspects that involved Vice President Lyndon B. Johnson.

However, from the moment of President Kennedy's assassination in Dallas, everything changed. From that moment on, the major role of the little band of investigative reporters was to keep posted on all of the clever moves that Johnson would take to cripple or kill the investigation.

STUDENT WORK PROJECT SUGGESTION

Write a paper on the senators or congressmen from your state exploring wealth, family, and living style. Are the sons or daughters or other relatives on the congressional payroll, or have they been accommodated on the payroll of some executive branch agency? Are they qualified for the jobs they hold? Is there evidence that political influence was a major factor in the hiring? If they are in private employment, is the work related to lobbying on subjects related to the official responsibility of the legislator? This work project can be aimed at one senator or congressman or can be fashioned to cover the entire delegation from the state.

30 COPING WITH LBJ'S COVERUP

Press interest in the Bobby Baker case lagged when the assassination of President Kennedy put Lyndon Johnson in the White House where he was in position to use the power of the presidency to influence the press and the prosecutors. Keeping pace with President Johnson's coverup efforts was more difficult than establishing the "gross improprieties" of Bobby Baker. This demonstrates that from the courthouse to the White House the major problem in getting effective prosecution of government fraud is the misuse of power in efforts to obstruct justice.

President Johnson's administration actively sought to sidetrack the investigation and prosecution of Bobby Baker by harassment of Don B. Reynolds, a key witness, Senator John J. Williams, and others who were actively pushing for a full investigation. The techniques included attempts to bribe and intimidate the special prosecution team, and Republican and Democratic members of the Senate Rules Committee were subjected to subtle and occasionally not-so-subtle patterns of bribery and coercion.

Also, the Johnson White House used direct methods in efforts (some successful and some unsuccessful) to intimidate or bribe publishers, editors, and reporters for the few newspapers who were exhibiting any aggressiveness on the Baker affair. Among other things White House officials linked complaints about aggressive coverage of the Baker case with hints of retaliation against television licenses. President Johnson made personal demands on two publishing executives that a reporter be fired, and suggested that other reporters who cooperated would be rewarded with special White House news breaks.

A DRAMATIC CHANGE

On November 21, 1963, Senator John Williams told me he had decided to retire from politics, and that he would not run for reelection in 1964. He felt that the Bobby Baker investigation was underway and would move forward smoothly. He did not wish to remain in Washington and become "another professional politician."

That story was printed in the *Des Moines Register* and in the *Minneapolis Tribune* on the morning of November 22, 1963. It was the morning that Don B. Reynolds, the Maryland insurance man, was to meet with the Senate Rules Committee staff to produce the documents proving that Vice President Lyndon B. Johnson had been the recipient of illegal kickbacks on two insurance policies written on his life by Reynolds. That was only one important aspect of the story Reynolds was to tell about his dealings with Bobby Baker, Lyndon Johnson, and Johnson's administrative assistant Walter Jenkins.

It was a few minutes before 10 A.M. when Reynolds and his lawyer, James F. Fitzgerald, were escorted to Room 312, of the Senate Office Building to meet with a GAO accountant and with Burkett Van Kirk, a young lawyer from Lincoln, Nebraska, who was serving as Republican minority counsel. For two hours Reynolds told his tale of abuse and misuse of power and money at the Capitol—of Elly Rometsch, the German party girl; of the use of "call girls" by defense contractors to entertain government officials; of business deals involving Baker; and loans arranged from Teamsters Union funds with the help of Teamsters President James R. Hoffa.

At about 1:30 P.M. (Washington time) Reynolds was relating the details and explaining the documentation on the kickbacks to Johnson. The complicated documentation took about an hour, and all of the documents were on the table. Shortly after 2:30 P.M., Washington time, as Reynolds and his attorney were preparing to leave, a woman secretary burst into the room sobbing. While Reynolds and the others looked on, the hysterical woman cried, "President Kennedy has been killed!"

At first they thought it was a joke—a bad joke. Then, as they saw the woman's tears and genuine distress, it was suddenly apparent it was no joke. Reynolds was stunned. If President Kennedy was dead, then Lyndon Johnson, the man about whom he had been testifying, was President of the United States. Reynolds reached for the documents on the committee table, which confirmed his story of the gift stereo set to Johnson and of the television advertising contracts on the Johnson television station in Austin, Texas. He slowly pulled the documents toward him.

"I guess you won't need these," Reynolds said quietly to the Rules Committee staff members. "Giving testimony involving the vice president is one thing, but when it involves the president himself, that is something else. You can just forget that I ever said anything if you want to."

Counsel Van Kirk, recognizing that the situation had changed radically, replied that Reynolds should not concern himself with the problem of what should be done with the evidence.

"The documents on this matter are now the records of the Rules Committee," Van Kirk said. "The decision on whether we will use them is a matter that the Committee will have to decide. None of us can do anything about it."

At 3:39 P.M., Washington time (2:39 P.M. in Dallas), Lyndon Johnson was sworn in as the thirty-sixth President of the United States. A disturbed Don Reynolds returned to his insurance office and tried, unsuccessfully, to work. He had been motivated by a belief that Attorney General Kennedy would conduct a thorough investigation of Bobby Baker's activities regardless of whether Lyndon Johnson was involved. Now Lyndon Johnson had the power to remove Robert Kennedy and anyone else who was a Robert Kennedy man. He also had the power to use the money and power of the executive branch to woo and coerce the members of the Senate Rules Committee. Reynolds knew Johnson would use those powers on him if he dared to take that chance with public opinion. Later that day Reynolds called me to tell me what was troubling him, and he called Senator Williams to get his assessment of the matter.

Senator Williams said that the facts and the documents had the same relevance they had 24 hours earlier. He said he believed everything was so confused at that moment that it would be impossible to predict the course of the Bobby Baker investigation. "But I don't intend to let it drop, if I can help it," the Delaware Republican declared. It was at that point that Don Reynolds knew he had passed the point of no return. He had no choice but to stand firm with Senator Williams.

About a week later, Senator Williams said he was holding up posting the letters announcing he would not seek reelection in 1964 and would make a firm decision later. He told me that he did not see how he could retire to Delaware knowing what he did about the corruption of President Lyndon Johnson. He was aware that efforts would be made to stop the Baker investigation and to end any possibility of any prosecutions.

ATTEMPTS TO PROTECT THE BAKER INVESTIGATION

In the immediate wake of the assassination of President Kennedy, even Lyndon B. Johnson could not have fired Bob

Kennedy from the post of Attorney General nor have directly tampered with the criminal division under Assistant Attorney General Herbert J. (Jack) Miller. That would have caused even a worse uproar than President Nixon caused a decade later in firing Special Watergate Prosecutor Archibald Cox, and Lyndon Johnson was a more astute political operator than Richard Nixon.

As a barrier against later tampering with the investigations and prosecution of the Bobby Baker case, Miller arranged to have William O. Bittman and a small aggressive prosecution team assigned to the investigation under a court order that would bar tampering through routine personnel shifts. Bittman, a tough and independent 35-year-old Chicago lawyer, had a record of 70 straight convictions, including Teamster Boss James R. Hoffa and other major under-world figures.

Kennedy, Miller, and Bittman knew they were dealing with a clever and ruthless adversary in President Lyndon Johnson, and they were not disappointed. Robert Kennedy was still in a state of shock in the first months after the assassination of his brother, so Miller and Bittman took the precautionary steps to insulate the Bobby Baker investigation from expected White House tampering. Independently, I had discussions with both Miller and Bittman about fears that the Baker investigation would be sabotaged, and they were both aware that I was relaying their concern to Senator John Williams at the Capitol and to Representative H. R. Gross, an outspoken Iowa Republican.

If Johnson's efforts to stop the Baker investigation ever became ruthless, Senator Williams and Representative Gross could make appropriate comments on the floor of the Senate or House, so there would be public knowledge of the abuse of power in a public forum that even a president could not control. For the first time in my reporting career, I fully understood and appreciated the importance of the provisions of the United States Constitution which guarantee that senators and congressmen can speak freely in the Senate and House on any subject without being held accountable for criminal prosecution or civil damage actions. A few of us who observed Johnson's use of flattery, bribery, and coercion to force senators and congressmen into line knew that he would not have stopped there if he could have muzzled Senator Williams, Representative Gross, or other critics.

JOHNSON MOVES AGAINST THE INVESTIGATION

Baker's financial associates in Serv-U vending included Fred Black and a host of Las Vegas gambling figures, including Edward

Levinson and Benjamin Siegelbaum. A Justice Department wiretap on Black's suite at the Carlton Hotel in Washington had disclosed Baker's relationship with a wide range of Las Vegas figures, as well as the outline of the political deals that accompanied NASA's award of the multibillion-dollar Apollo contract to North American Aviation.

Some of the tapes of Black's and Baker's conversations included comments about Lyndon Johnson. Although the comments were for the most part vague, they could have been embarrassing to Johnson. Johnson requested copies of the transcripts from the FBI so he could personally review them. From the day he took office as president, Johnson was worried that Attorney General Kennedy had obtained recordings of conversations that might prove a political impediment to him, so he launched his own private campaign to discredit even legal wiretapping.

The Problems of the Press

From the time Lyndon Johnson became president the problem of the Washington reporters changed radically, and I discussed this periodically with John Barron and Paul Hope of the *Washington Star,* Julian Morrison of the *Washington Daily News,* Dan Thomasson of the Scripps-Howard newspapers, and William Lambert of the *Life* magazine investigative team. It was now vital that some of us keep posted on every bit of evidence that showed Lyndon Johnson might be undercutting the Bobby Baker investigation by subverting the Senate Rules Committee, by cutting into the independence of Bittman's prosecution effort, and by using various government powers to threaten and discredit such key witnesses as Don Reynolds.

Although I did not advise the others of my specific role as a transmission belt of information between Bittman and Senator Williams, a handful of my press colleagues knew I had reliable information because of the direct comments that Senator Williams and Representative Gross would make from time to time.

My relationship with John Barron of the *Washington Star* was particularly close in early 1964, and the stories that he and Paul Hope did for the *Star* were vital to keeping the Bobby Baker investigation moving. During this period the interests of some publications seemed to wane, on the assumption that President Johnson would succeed in blocking the prosecution of Bobby Baker.

It was particularly important that the *Washington Star* remain aggressive because of its tremendous impact in the nation's capitol.

I recognized the reality that my most aggressive efforts could be futile if the information was printed only in Des Moines and Minneapolis. These were remote outposts, from a standpoint of essential day-to-day impact on the machinery of government. I had full confidence in the backing I would receive from Frank Eyerly, managing editor in Des Moines, and from Washington Bureau Chief Richard L. Wilson, as long as I engaged in my aggressive pursuit with a systematic caution and accuracy.

I, too, feared that Johnson's efforts to kill the Baker probe might be successful—in part, because of the lack of aggressive press coverage—but I was determined to do what I could to frustrate his coverup effort, as was John Barron and a few other reporters. It was vital that a few of us keep every subtle and ruthless Johnson move under scrutiny.

President Eisenhower, a close personal friend of my publishers, John and Mike Cowles, had been unsuccessful in his efforts to get the Cowles brothers to curb my aggressive style. However, President Eisenhower was basically a decent and direct person, whereas Lyndon Johnson was possessed of neither of these qualities, as I learned in the midst of the Bobby Baker investigation.

The Dangers of Being "Up Front"

Although the distance from Des Moines to Washington muted much of the potential impact of my stories, the repercussions were still too strong for Lyndon Johnson. He believed he had an effective way to stop me, because the Cowles were involved in the purchase and sale of television stations which were under the jurisdiction of the Federal Communications Commission (FCC). Such transfers could be handled routinely, or barriers could be erected that could cost millions of dollars.

As a start, I received an unusual call from James Milloy, a vice president of the Cowles-owned *Look* magazine. Milloy asked me to join him for breakfast at his suite at the Carlton Hotel the next morning, and to say nothing to Bureau Chief Dick Wilson about it. It was a request I could not turn down because he was a vice president of *Look* and also the head of Eastern Enterprises, Inc., the corporation that sent us our paychecks.

Although Jimmy Milloy was usually friendly with me, I suspected that at times he did some questionable wire pulling on tax legislation and FCC problems that occasionally fell below the lofty ethical standards of our editorial pages. Milloy was a highly paid advertising executive, and his connections at the Capitol included top people in both parties. Whatever he did, he did it so smoothly that I never ran into any hard evidence of impropriety, although I was constantly aware that it might happen.

At breakfast, Milloy started off with a statement of "total agreement" with what I had been doing on Lyndon Johnson and the Bobby Baker case. He got in a few licks of his own about what a corrupt figure Lyndon Johnson was—how ruthless, and how clever in his abuse of power. It was nice to have such endorsement of my work from a company vice president, but I knew this was not the reason he had asked me to breakfast. Finally, he got down to the request that I not "be so far out in front on the Bobby Baker story." He said he wasn't suggesting that I not cover the Baker story, but that I avoid breaking new ground in a manner that would be obvious to the White House.

He said that Mike and John Cowles were concerned that my coverage had antagonized President Johnson to the point that he might take some unusual steps to interfere with what should be a routine switch of television licenses. Milloy claimed he had been contacted by someone from the Johnson White House and that the president's displeasure with my work on the Baker case had been linked with a discussion of the Cowles television licenses. Also, someone from the White House, perhaps even President Johnson, had made some comment to either Mike or John Cowles that they had interpreted in the same manner.

Milloy hurried to assure me that, although he had talked with Mike and John Cowles about the problem, neither of them had asked him to talk to me. He said that, on his own, he had decided to talk to me rather than go through Dick Wilson or Kenneth MacDonald, the editor in Des Moines. I had no way of knowing the accuracy of his statements, or of even checking them, without causing the kind of turmoil that would be destructive to any effort in pushing the Bobby Baker case.

Milloy reviewed the potential of millions in legal fees and delays on the television transactions, and made reference to the support they had given me in the fights with the Teamsters Union and in my fusses with President Eisenhower. "We don't want you to stop writing the Baker story," Milloy said. "That would be too obvious. Just don't push it personally at press conferences, and don't be so far in front."

He left me in a tough spot, and I'm sure he knew it. However, it wasn't as tough a spot as if he had told me I should abandon the Bobby Baker case, or as if he had suggested or directed that I write stories favorable to President Johnson or apologetic of Johnson's involvement in the Bobby Baker affair. I thought about the waning interest in the Baker investigation on so many papers, and wondered how many others had been subjected to Johnson's famous arm-twisting techniques. There was no newspaper I could think of that would have been more courageous on many of my past crusades than the *Des Moines Register,* and I could think of none other except the *Washington Star* and the Scripps-Howard organization that was continuing to hammer on the Bobby Baker case now that Lyndon Johnson was president.

Many Ways to Skin a Cat

I made no commitment to Milloy, but did say I would try to take his comments into consideration as various stories developed and to handle them in a manner that would be least likely to cause trouble for my publishers. I had no intention of abandoning my crusade, only of getting fewer "exclusives." Because I was working closely with a number of reporters, it was possible to be more cooperative than usual in sharing information and less competitive in my drive for exclusive stories. There only needed to be a slight modification of my overly aggressive pursuit of news stories and more spreading of information. I continued to keep my inside track between Bittman and Senator Williams, and I was prepared to become more competitively aggressive at any point it appeared that the Baker prosecution might be killed.

I never heard any more from Jimmy Milloy, and I assumed he had no more suggestions to make about my coverage of the Baker case. However, Fletcher Knebel, a member of the Cowles Washington bureau, told me much later that President Johnson had spent nearly two hours one evening trying to get John and Mike Cowles to fire me. Knebel, then serving as president of the Gridiron Club (the elite Washington press club), had overheard the conversation between Johnson and the Cowles brothers. He was seated at the head table with President Johnson on one side, and they were flanked by John and Mike Cowles. According to Knebel, President Johnson spent nearly the whole evening in his efforts to get me fired. Neither Mike nor John Cowles said anything to me about it at that time, but later acknowledged it to George Mills, who was writing a history of the *Des Moines Register* and *Tribune* company.

It was weeks after the Gridiron Dinner that Knebel related the incident to me with the comment that "you would be mighty proud of our bosses if you had heard what I heard at the Gridiron Dinner. Old Lyndon spent the whole evening trying to get them to fire you, and they never gave him a tumble," Knebel said. I didn't tell him of my breakfast with Milloy until years later.

Pressure on Investigators and Legislators

Johnson made similar efforts to pressure and to woo other newspaper publishers, editors, and reporters to inaction on the Bobby Baker case. However, he did not restrict his efforts to the press. In various and devious ways he bribed and seduced the Democratic members of the Senate Rules Committee to get them to limit the investigation sharply.

Through his connections with Minority Leader Everett Dirksen of Illinois, President Johnson tried to obtain information from Senator Williams. Johnson wanted to use Dirksen to discover the extent of proof Senator Williams had on some facets of the Bobby Baker case. Also, it was obvious that the Johnson White House was coordinating a vicious smear effort against Senator Williams to destroy his reputation and credibility on the Baker investigation. The smear effort was unsuccessful, because the young woman Senator Williams had breakfast with at a Maryland motel was his granddaughter. They had stopped on an early morning drive from his home in Millsboro, Delaware, to Washington, D.C.

William O. Bittman and the members of his prosecution team were faced with almost constant harassment, alternating with offers of other lucrative employment that would necessitate their leaving the Baker prosecution. Bittman found it difficult to keep his team working with any enthusiasm in the face of press reports that President Johnson was cool to the prosecution of Baker.

Charles Shaffer became fed up working in a Johnson-directed Justice Department where it was impossible to send reports "upstairs" without fearing how they would be mishandled. He resigned and set up a law practice in Rockville, Maryland. Don Page Moore, also discouraged at the duplicity within the Justice Department, joined a Chicago law firm. Austin Mittler, a bright young law graduate employed at roughly $12,000 a year, was offered a much higher salary to become a law clerk for a Democratic judge in New York. Disheartened about the prospects of a successful Baker prosecution, Mittler accepted the law clerk offer only to reject it later when Bittman pleaded that he had to have someone with him he could trust.

Bittman, then a $16,000-a-year trial lawyer, was the man holding the prosecution together under the special court order that made it difficult for the Johnson administration to remove him from that responsibility. Over the months, he was harassed by the lack of adequate secretarial help and quarters. He was plagued by the assignment of men to his staff under circumstances that caused him to suspect efforts to sabotage the Baker prosecution. Then, in the midst of his preparation for Baker's trial, Bittman was offered a promotion with a substantial increase in pay, either as Special Assistant to Attorney General Ramsey Clark or as United States Attorney in Chicago. There was only one condition—he would have to leave the Baker case.

A PARTIAL SUCCESS

Bittman rejected the offers of advancement and continued with the case until January 29, 1967, when Baker was found guilty of income tax evasion, theft, and conspiracy to defraud the United States government. That successful prosecution by Bittman would not have been possible if some pressmen had not followed the attempted coverup efforts and reported enough to protect the young prosecutor from even more blatant pressures. Senator Williams and Representative Gross also helped by making periodic floor speeches that were critical of the Johnson administration for its efforts to bribe or coerce the prosecutors and for the harassment of various key witnesses against Baker, including Don Reynolds.

But, the conviction and eventual incarceration of Bobby Baker at Lewisburg federal penitentiary was far removed from the full investigation and prosecution we had sought. Bobby Baker was a small sacrifice for President Johnson to make when faced with the alternatives he had between 1963 and the Baker conviction in January 1967. During that period of time Senator Williams watched every move Johnson made on the prosecution. Robert Kennedy was elected as a Senator from New York, and proved to be a sharp and effective Johnson critic within the Democratic Party.

Keeping on top of Johnson's various coverup efforts in the Baker case was a more difficult assignment than digging out the initial crimes and "gross improprieties" of Bobby Baker. It was an escalated version of the efforts of the Republican organization in Polk County, Iowa, to coerce, bribe, and generally undermine the Polk County fraud prosecutions. Johnson's obstruction of justice in the Baker case was so subtle and clever that only a few of the reporters who were watching every development in the case were certain enough of the facts to be able to write about it forcefully.

STUDENT WORK PROJECT SUGGESTION

List the various tactics used by the Johnson administration to impede the investigation and prosecution of Bobby Baker.

Find the parallels for these tactics of misuse of government authority in the Nixon administration's efforts to block or limit the Watergate investigation. Do you believe the successful prosecution of Bobby Baker represented a complete triumph for justice? Explain.

31 PROBING COMMODITY MARKET SCANDALS— A CLASSIC INVESTIGATION

Using a General Accounting Office (GAO) report as an authoritative starting point, it is possible for a small team of reporters to come to grips with basic problems of corruption and mismanagement in such a highly technical field as the operation and policing of the commodity markets. A depth follow through on a complicated matter, such as the Bernhard Rosee case, is more enlightening than months of study of the theories and history of commodity trading and can create a strong pressure for reform.

The Rosee case demonstrates how exploration of one charge of injustice and the malfunctioning of government can lead to other evidence of injustices and bad government if pursued systematically. This chapter demonstrates how exploration of congressional appropriations hearings, the use of GAO reports, and the judicious use of inside informants can expose wrongdoing and initiate reform legislation.

A DIFFERENT KIND OF INVESTIGATION

I resigned as Special Counsel to President Nixon in July 1970, to become Washington Bureau Chief for the *Des Moines Register* and *Tribune*. This gave me the opportunity to direct a newspaper investigation of a federal agency. For years I had inquiries from other Washington correspondents, from local reporters, and from editors asking advice on large and small investigations.

From time to time I had worked in cooperation with other reporters, but it had not been a true team effort. Within the Cowles publications Washington bureau each of us had gone his own way following story leads with little or no consultation or direction from Dick Wilson and only occasionally helping each other out on some aspect of a story. For the most part, I believed that it was best for a reporter to work on his own story, to plan his own strategy, to do his own document research, and to interview his own witnesses, but I recognized that there were some large, complicated investigations where a team effort was more desirable and could be more effective.

At the proper time and with the proper project, I wanted to try my hand at planning and directing a team investigation of an agency from the bottom up. The opportunity presented itself within a few months after I left the Nixon White House. That team effort developed into a project lasting more than five years. The result was the establishment of a new five-member regulatory agency to police the multibillion-dollar commodity markets. It might have been possible to have moved the project faster if George Anthan, James Risser, and I had not been involved in investigations of other aspects of the operation of the Agriculture and other departments at the same time.

Accusations of Dishonesty

The project started when Bernhard Rosee, an elderly commodity trader from Chicago, came to my office with a story of outrageous injustices that, he said, were perpetrated by the Chicago Board of Trade abetted by the active aid or the gross negligence of Agriculture Department officials at the highest levels.

The story that Rosee told me was filled with such charges of financial dishonesty and arrogant misuse of power by the Chicago Board of Trade that I had difficulty believing it was true. He said he had made his complaints with no results to the officials of the Commodity Exchange Authority (CEA)—the regulatory agency with jurisdiction over the commodity market and the commodity exchanges.

Rosee started his story in a carefully controlled voice and with some precision, but within a few minutes the wiry old commodity trader was consumed with anger and became unrestrained, characterizing the Chicago Board of Trade officials as "crooks" and "thieves." He was equally derogatory in his comments about officials of the CEA and the Secretary of Agriculture, who, he said, were involved in collusion with "a crooked commission house" and the Chicago Board of Trade.

The Austria-born commodity trader spoke with a heavy accent in the jargon of the commodity exchanges and with frequent references to the numbers of the code sections in the commodity laws that his tormentors had violated. At some points in his tirade, the strained voice, the Austrian accent, the jargon of the commodity market and the unrestrained name-calling gave the impression that he was another of the raving crackpots who come to see me from time to time.

Getting Facts from an Excited Informant

After a few minutes I interrupted his passionate recitation to tell him I did not understand the jargon of the commodity market and that I was unfamiliar with the sections of the commodity law. I insisted he would have to slow down and give me the opportunity to ask questions to clarify the fact situation and the law. I suggested that it would be easier for me to understand if he was less emotional and more dispassionate in his explanations, and that I could not accept his characterization of anyone as a "crook."

"You will have to explain slowly why the transactions are dishonest, and you will have to give me an opportunity to ask questions about the technicalities of record requirements of the commodity laws and regulations," I said.

Rosee apologized and promised to proceed at a slower pace. I started questioning him systematically to get a clearer understanding on two or three points. I intended to pin Rosee down on those points of his story that I could check in official records of the Department of Agriculture or the Commodity Exchange Authority. He had told me that the commission house, which he claimed had defrauded him of at least $100,000, had been guilty of being under-segregated in its funds. If this was true, it would establish that he was not making a wild accusation of dishonesty against a respectable commission house.

Also, if Rosee had made complaints about his problem with that firm to CEA officials, there should be a written record of that complaint at the Agriculture Department. I knew Agriculture Department records should reveal any finding that had been made against the Baggot and Morrison commission house that Rosee said had defrauded him in his account.

An Initial Quick Checkup

With Rosee in the office, I called Alex Caldwell, the administrator of the CEA, to ask him a few questions that would give me some idea if the old commodity trader was on sound ground on some basic facts. I did not tell Caldwell that Rosee was in my office nor give any indication of my viewpoint or purpose in asking if Bernhard Rosee, a Chicago commodity trader, had made a complaint to the CEA that he had been defrauded by the Baggot and Morrison firm.

Caldwell admitted there had been complaints made over a long period of time and that it was a very old case.

Had the Agriculture Department or the CEA made some finding that the Baggot and Morrison firm had been undersegregated in their customers' accounts? I then asked.

Caldwell replied that he believed there had been some adverse ruling against Baggot and Morrison, but that he did not have the details at his fingertips. He said he would call me back, and I asked him if he would look at the Rosee case file and give me a brief comment about the conclusion of the investigation that Rosee had requested. (The Arbitration hearing had resulted in Rosee's ouster from the Chicago Board of Trade.)

Later, Caldwell confirmed that there had been an adverse finding against the Baggot and Morrison commission house for being consistently undersegregated in funds in the customers' accounts. This irregularity was in the same time period that Rosee claimed the firm had shorted his account by about $100,000.

The Problem of the Trading Cards

Rosee explained the intricacies of how Baggot and Morrison officials had not credited his account with large profitable trades in soybeans. Instead they had used his trading account to pay for losses on trades he had not authorized. He explained that the records of the Chicago Board of Trade and the Baggot and Morrison firm would prove that he was right, but that he had been barred from reconstructing these transactions by the refusal of Baggot and Morrison to produce the original trading cards of his account.

Unfamiliar with the legal requirements on the trading cards or the legal requirements that Baggot and Morrison and the Chicago Board of Trade keep certain daily settlement sheets, I was unable to draw even a tentative conclusion as to whether their records would, in fact, prove Rosee's contention that he had been cheated. However, I now viewed Rosee, not a crackpot, but as a man who was obsessed with a drive to right what he considered to be a serious injustice.

I learned at that early stage that the law required the commission houses and the commodity exchanges to keep records of each trade for the purpose of protecting the public from frauds in the fast moving commodity markets. The law required that the original trading cards and other records, including the daily clearing house sheets, be kept so it would be possible to reconstruct the entire trading record if a dispute should arise between a commodity trader and the commission house that handled his account. The laws and regulations required that there be a settlement every day in line with the balances reflected in the daily clearing house sheets.

Rosee, in 40 years as a commodity trader, was familiar with the details of the records required by law and had submitted his dispute with Baggot and Morrison to arbitration on the belief and assurance that all of the records would be made available. However, after Rosee had agreed, the Baggot and Morrison officials refused to produce the daily trading cards—the original records of their trades for Rosee. Instead, Baggot and Morrison submitted their own summary of what they said Rosee's trades had been and argued that he still owed them $28,000.

The chairman of the Chicago Board of Trade arbitration committee initially said he would require Baggot and Morrison to produce the original records and that he would not accept the commission house's summary as a substitute. However, when Baggot and Morrison's officials continued to balk at producing the original trading cards, the chairman of the arbitration committee permitted them to substitute a summary of Rosee's account. Rosee protested vehemently that he was entitled to "the best evidence," which was the original trading cards, and that Baggot and Morrison should not be permitted to use its summary of his account as evidence.

I could not believe that the Chicago Board of Trade's arbitration committee would permit Baggot and Morrison, a firm already guilty of irregularities in its customers' accounts, to submit a summary of the Rosee trades and refuse to produce the trading cards. I asked CEA Administrator Caldwell if it was true, and he replied that he did not know, but that it was none of his business because the CEA permitted the various exchanges to establish their own rules and to conduct their own hearings without any interference. As the weeks and months went by, I learned even more shocking information about the CEA and the open intention of its officials to keep hands off the Chicago Board of Trade and the other commodity exchanges.

A Clear Denial of Due Process

Although I was unfamiliar with the technicalities of the laws and regulations on commodity trading, I understood better than Rosee that he had been denied basic due process of law in the Chicago Board of Trade arbitration hearing. However, he understood fully that the proceedings were not fair. After Rosee had agreed to submit his dispute to arbitration, he was forced into a closed hearing. He was not permitted to have a lawyer, although Baggot and Morrison was represented by a highly skilled commodity lawyer who was a member of the board of directors of the Chicago Board of Trade.

The arbitration committee chairman would not permit Rosee to have access to the records that the Agriculture Department required be kept for the specific purpose of avoiding frauds. He would not permit Rosee to cross-examine James Baggot or Donald Morrison or other officials of the firm about the authenticity of the questionable summary, which indicated Rosee owed the commission house $28,000. I might be unsure of the mathematics in commodity trading, but I was certain that the Chicago Board of Trade hearing was devoid of due process of law by any reasonable judicial standard. Clearly there was a collusive effort with the Baggot and Morrison commission house against the outspoken Rosee.

I went to Alex Caldwell to discuss the lack of due process of law in the Chicago Board of Trade arbitration hearing and to find out if there was any argument with my interpretation of the record. Caldwell did not dispute me on the lack of due process but said that the CEA did not have the authority to inquire into the manner in which arbitration hearings were conducted. I also found that CEA officials, including Caldwell, had accepted the self-serving declarations of Baggot and Morrison without examining the original trading cards, and had, either through negligence or collusion, permitted the commission house to use what a Chicago court later called "false" and "fabricated" records.

Satisfactory Conclusion

Months went by as I dug deeper and deeper into the complicated story of Rosee's litigation that had been in the federal courts and on administrative appeal in the Agriculture Department. Then, in 1972 I received a call from Bernhard Rosee. Illinois Superior Court Judge Nathan Cohen had given him a judgment of $750,000 against the Baggot and Morrison commission house and James Baggot and Donald Morrison. I then asked for and later received Judge Cohen's written opinion on the decision.

Although Judge Cohen ruled that the Chicago Board of Trade arbitration hearing was "a sham" and devoid of due process of law, he said that there was insufficient evidence to establish that they were in collusion with the dishonest officials of the Baggot and Morrison commission house. Also, he found that CEA officials were negligent and incompetent in permitting Baggot and Morrison to use a summary of Rosee's trading record to perpetrate frauds. However, he repeated that there was insufficient evidence to establish that the federal government officials were involved in a conspiracy with Baggot and Morrison.

When Baggot and Morrison officials said they had lost Rosee's original trading cards and had to rely upon the summary, Judge Cohen declared that he believed they were testifying falsely because of their admissions of destruction of some records. Rosee and one of his lawyers had related to me how they caught the Baggot and Morrison office manager in the act of destroying records of commodity trading for the crucial time period. Although I believed Rosee and his lawyer, Melvin Brandt, I knew they were both parties of interest and that the office manager might deny the record destruction.

In the trial in Judge Cohen's court, the office manager admitted he was in the Baggot and Morrison office on Veterans Day, 1963, when Rosee and Mel Brandt walked into an inner office and found him cutting the pages from one of the permanent record books on commodity trades. Under oath in court, he had no choice but to admit the mutilation of those records required to be kept intact ᵧy federal government regulations and the regulations of the Chicago Board of Trade. The office manager said he cut 90 onion skin pages from one of the hundreds of books "to save space in the office." His explanation was described, in Judge Cohen's opinion, as "ludicrous" when he denied it was part of a scheme to rig a false summary of Rosee's trading.

Judge Cohen told him to his face that he believed he was giving false testimony and that Baggot and Morrison's failure to produce the original trading cards for Rosee's account justified a decision for Rosee. It was the judge's belief that the firm had stolen at least $100,000 from Rosee's account, and probably a lot more, and that Rosee had been wrongfully removed from his seat on the Chicago Board of Trade. He awarded Rosee a judgment of loss and actual damages of more than $500,000. The interest and other damages brought the total judgment to about $750,000.

That forceful opinion by Judge Cohen made it easier to write the Rosee story within the framework of an 800-word to 1500-word news story. It pointed up the perjured testimony, false documents, and lack of due process of law in the Chicago Board of Trade arbitration committee.

A TEAM EFFORT

The Useless Regulatory Agency

After months of unsatisfactory dealings with Caldwell, I had concluded it was hopeless to try to get him to correct obvious injustices. He was either protecting his own past bad decisions on the Rosee case, or he was afraid to challenge the Chicago Board of Trade or the big Chicago law firm that was advising officials of the Chicago Board of Trade. It was a sad commentary on the regulatory agency when the regulation of (at that time) about $100 billion a year in commodity trading was in the hands of a frightened GS-17 bureaucrat on about the fourth level down in the Department of Agriculture with a salary of about $36,000 a year. I finally concluded that the CEA was useless, or nearly useless, as a protector of the public from the financial wolves in the commodity markets and the big commission houses and that there was neither the will nor the competence to do an effective investigation on whether the markets were rigged.

This sham of commodity regulation was worse than no regulatory agency, for the public and the Congress were given the impression that there was strict regulation while the financial pirates were permitted to stage star chamber hearings with arbitrary rules. I talked with friends who dealt in the commodity markets and found they concurred with my conclusions. They had accepted the injustices of the exchanges, the fact that the CEA was not going to do anything about it, and the failure of any Secretary of Agriculture to do anything effective to stop the injustices.

The Soviet Wheat Deal Opens the Way

Other investigations and several months of illness in early 1972 delayed my planning for a depth series on the CEA until July of 1972, when the Nixon administration's bungling of the sale of wheat, corn, and soy beans to the Soviet Union focused national attention on the possibility of rigging the commodity markets. The Soviet wheat deal came under investigation by House and Senate Committees. This gave George Anthan the opportunity to dig deeply into the combinations of bureaucratic bungling and conflicts of interest in that multimillion-dollar fiasco.

The House Agriculture Committee did a superficial investigation of the possible conflicts of interest, profiteering, and general bungling by the Agriculture Department in the Soviet wheat deal. It was worse than no investigation, for it gave the public and the press the impression that there had been a depth inquiry. There was no effort by the House Agriculture Committee to resolve sharply conflicting stories on crucial issues, or to send the transcript to the Justice Department to follow up for possible perjury prosecution.

There was virtually no possibility that the Senate Agriculture Committee, headed by Senator Herman Talmadge, the Georgia Democrat, would do any really searching inquiry into either corruption or mismanagement. Chairman Talmadge was not interested in aggressively pursuing evidence of either corruption or mismanagement in any administration, for the administration might retaliate with a searching inquiry into his dealings.

I went to Senator Henry M. Jackson, chairman of the Senate Permanent Investigations Subcommittee, as the best possibility for the kind of investigation and follow through that was needed. Senator Jackson had not initiated an investigation of the Soviet wheat deal, because he believed that the House Agriculture Committee had taken jurisdiction. He did not want to duplicate their effort, nor did he want hastily to move in on the investigative jurisdiction of Chairman Talmadge. He had read only generally of the House hearings, and the news coverage in Washington was superficial, as it frequently was on Agricultural matters.

It was a surprise to Jackson when I told him that the House Agriculture Committee had not done a staff investigation prior to calling witnesses from the Agriculture Department and from the big international grain companies. I also told him there was no inclination on the part of either the committee or the staff to follow through on contradictory statements and that the House committee had not put the witnesses under oath. When I explained the inadequacy of the investigation, and specifically that House witnesses were not put under oath, Senator Jackson instructed his staff to bring him a memorandum of the facts and a recommendation for action with some cooperation from the Senate Agriculture Committee staff.

The excellent staff of the Senate Permanent Investigations Subcommittee did a more thorough investigation—put witnesses under oath, wrote a stinging report, and sent the transcript of the testimony to the Justice Department with recommendations for prosecution for perjury.

Obtaining Congressional Sponsors

The political explosiveness of the mismanagement, bungling, and conflicts of interest in the Soviet wheat deal made it possible to get public attention on the general inadequacy of commodity regulation under the CEA. In the aftermath of the 1972 election, I planned a team investigation to force continued congressional attention on the evidence of corruption and mismanagement in the regulation of the commodity markets.

Representative Neal Smith, an Iowa Democrat, headed a House Small Business Subcommittee with a claim to some jurisdiction on investigations of irregularities in the commodity market. Representative Smith owned a farm near Des Moines, had followed agricultural legislation for years, and had a good general understanding of the laxity in the policing of the commodity markets.

Representative Smith was quick to see the commodity regulation problems, as illustrated by the manner in which Rosee was cheated by a commission house and was denied due process of law by the Chicago Board of Trade. He also recognized the grave implications of the CEA officials standing idly by in the face of such gross injustices. Smith was a reliable investigator and one with bulldog persistence. He had the ability to articulate a firm position in the face of objections from the Agriculture Department and the commodity industry lobbyists.

On the Senate side, newly elected Senator Dick Clark, an Iowa Democrat, was the most likely leader. He was elected in November 1972 and, even before he took office, I arranged to have dinner with him at the National Press Club in Washington to explain the commodity regulation problem. At that point Dick Clark had no knowledge of the operations of the commodity markets, and only the most general ideas about what was wrong with the policing of the commodity markets. As I ran through the Rosee case with him, he quickly grasped the unfairness of the arbitration hearing and understood why the original trading cards were the key to reconstructing the record.

I also went through the mechanics of the Soviet wheat deals and explained why the CEA did not have the competency to make an adequate investigation of a rigged commodity market. To cap it off, I gave him copies of some of my stories and columns on the Rosee case and a copy of a GAO report that had been published in 1965 on the operation of the CEA.

Although the report was seven years old at the time, it was an outline of the GAO findings on the weaknesses in the regulation of the commodity market at the time of the multimillion-dollar salad oil scandal involving Tino DeAngelis. I had read the report several times and had gone over it with congressional investigators and experts on the commodity market. I knew that Alex Caldwell had not followed many of the recommendations that the GAO had made in 1965 for tightening the policing of the commodity markets.

Clark was going to ask for assignment to the Senate Agriculture Committee and that was ideal for my purposes. I explained that Chairman Talmadge was not an aggressive investigator of government wrongdoing but that he would permit other members of the Argiculture Committee to have a free hand in pursuing their interests. Although many senators will listen attentively and indicate that they intend to initiate action, most of them do not follow through. Thus,

I was pleased to hear from Senator Clark a few days later and to learn that he had read and digested the GAO report and the columns I had given him. He was ready to launch the action any time I was ready.

Confronting the Agency Director

I had explained to Senator Clark that I had given copies of the same GAO report on the commodity market regulation to George Anthan and Jim Risser, fellow reporters at the Cowles Washington bureau, and that, when they had digested it thoroughly and had completed some investigations in Kansas City and Chicago, we would question Caldwell, the administrator of the CEA, on that report. Now I had to say we were not ready yet because the investigations were not complete and the series was not written. I suggested that he should try to familiarize himself with the House hearings and the Senate Permanent Investigations Subcommittee hearings on the Soviet wheat deal.

After Anthan and Risser read the GAO report, made trips to Kansas City and Chicago, talked with Rosee and other informants on the commodity market scandals, we were ready to talk to Caldwell. Because I was interested in all three of us being advised on the general problems and, particularly, the responses of government officials on key interviews, we went together to Caldwell's office. Using the GAO report as my authoritative guide as to what was wrong with the operations of the CEA, I led the general questioning. Anthan and Risser, by this time well-schooled on the commodity problem, fired questions at Caldwell on specific items about trading frauds and market-rigging allegations they had studied.

Caldwell admitted he had not followed the recommendations of the GAO in a dozen areas, and excused his lack of action by deprecating the GAO's understanding of commodity market regulation. He also stated that the recommendations were outdated. I asked him if there were any more recent investigative reports by the GAO or by the Department of Agriculture, and he declared there had been no recent investigations. However, from a congressional source and from an Agriculture Department source, I knew there had been a recent investigation by the Agriculture Department's Office of Inspector General. I was told that the conclusions of that investigation were precisely in line with what the GAO had recommended earlier.

When confronted by this, Caldwell suddenly remembered there had been a recent investigation. He then tried the old dodge of claiming it was "a secret report" and that he could not disclose or confirm its contents. I told him I knew what was in the report and that the conclusion of the Agriculture Department's own investigators had been precisely in line with the GAO on crucial points. An embarrassed Caldwell reluctantly admitted that his inaction had been recently criticized by the department's investigators.

Armed with specific knowledge of Caldwell's admissions and his positions on a wide range of controversial issues, Anthan and Risser went back to the investigation with greater confidence. They felt they understood the complicated commodity regulations or knew people who could be trusted to give them expert advice when needed.

Results

The series of articles we did for the *Des Moines Register* in February 1973 led to more hearings in 1973 and the passage of legislation in 1974 that established a new independent five-member Commodity Futures Trading Commission (CFTC), which gave greater authority to the policing of the commodity markets. Our followup stories on the commodity trading, and information I received on the cancellation by the Japanese of a huge corn purchase, led us to unearthing a scandalous situation in which dirty and substandard grain was being shipped to foreign markets as a result of deceptive practices by some of the big international grain trading firms.

Jim Risser pursued the dirty grain series, which won him a Pulitzer Prize in 1956. George Anthan and I followed through on scandals in the meat packing industry, which brought about the first major revision in the Packers and Stockyard Act in 50 years. On each of these investigations we followed the same basic system, after scrutiny of routine story situations indicated that there were serious basic weaknesses or corruption in the functioning of federal agencies.

LOOKING FOR CLUES AND FOLLOWING THEM

The GAO reports on the agencies gave us an authoritative starting point. Close examination of the hearings of the appropriations and legislative subcommittees of Congress gave excellent documentations of some long-standing problems and leads into other bad situations that committees did not pursue. Reading past investigative hearings provided a guide to some of the things that had gone wrong and could go wrong again. We used the Freedom of Information Act to obtain records in the Rosee case, the Soviet wheat deals, the dirty grain scandals, and the weakness and irregularities in the enforcement and administration of the Packers and Stockyards Act of 1921.

In order to gain a perspective on contemporary enforcement and administration of the law, we studied the history of investigations and the conditions that caused Congress to pass the Packers and Stockyards Act in 1921. In each case we did a comprehensive series of stories dealing with essentially every major aspect of the problem of regulating of trading in grain and the sale of livestock.

We did not drop the story when the series had run, nor did we expect Congress automatically to pass reform legislation against all the pressure of the vested interests that would oppose any change. Our basic philosophy was: If the initial mismanagement and corruption was worth the work of developing a series of stories, then it was worth pursuing until the officials took action to reform the laws or properly enforce or administer existing laws.

When the five-year work ordeal of investigating and reforming the regulation of trading in grain and livestock was over, I felt that the *Des Moines Register* Washington bureau team had given a good demonstration of what one newspaper and a small aggressive team of reporters could do to reform any area. Although most big investigations I had formerly worked on required the impact of many newspapers and many reporters, we were virtually alone in pursuing these investigations and legislative reforms. Our success was even more encouraging because we were competing with the Watergate scandals and the impeachment hearings that forced the resignation of President Richard M. Nixon.

The press concentration on Watergate meant that less attention was paid to the major scandals in the commodity and livestock markets. However, it permitted the *Des Moines Register* team to control the pace of its investigative effort and to avoid the kind of confusion and superficiality that often accompanies wild and destructive fights for newsbreaks.

STUDENT WORK PROJECT SUGGESTION

Select a GAO report on a subject in which you have an interest. Preferably the GAO report should be more than two years old and should be highly critical of a government agency in several areas of operation. List the recommendations made by the GAO, and then seek to determine whether the GAO recommendations for reform were followed. If any of the recommendations have not been followed, the class members should seek an explanation as to why the recommendations were ignored or were intentionally rejected.

32 WATERGATE AND THE AFTERMATH

It took the combined efforts of many experienced investigative reporters using the best police- and court-reporting techniques to create the climate for the government investigations that forced President Nixon out of office. The best work of many experienced reporters could have been frustrated by the power of the office of the president, if there had been a serious weakness or a lack of integrity in either Chairman Sam Ervin or United States District Judge John J. Sirica. The importance of the press role was not in digging up new evidence but in creating a climate in which honest government investigators could do their job in the face of massive efforts to obstruct justice.

It is a disservice to the cause of the press and to the *Washington Post* to overemphasize or distort in any manner the importance of the "Deep Throat" source. The greatest contribution by the *Washington Post* was thorough record research and systematic followup with interviews and aggressive stories. Even as explained in *All The President's Men* by Bob Woodward and Carl Bernstein the "Deep Throat" source was not a good corroborative witness to any single transaction.

THE ROLE OF THE PRESS

Watergate was a police story that shook Richard Nixon out of the White House. From time to time reporters turned up evidence that government investigators and prosecutors had not uncovered; however, careful analysis of the development of the case against Richard Nixon and his White House gang will demonstrate that the vital role of the press was in publicizing evidence already in the hands of government investigators and prosecutors so it could not be covered up by Nixon or his political appointees.

It is a disservice to the cause of sound investigative reporting to do anything to perpetrate the myth that either inexperienced reporters or experienced reporters "dug up" new evidence that the FBI or other government investigators had overlooked. Such a superficial analysis tends to glamorize relatively unimportant developments and to downplay the vital and indispensable role of focusing public attention on arrogant misuse of White House power to obstruct justice.

The Known Facts

From the time I read of the arrest of five men in the Democratic headquarters on June 17, 1972, it was apparent that the Nixon political organization was involved in the affair and that the major problem was to get the police and the Justice Department fully to explore that involvement. These were the hard facts available to any reporter at that time:

1. The five burglars arrested at 2:30 A.M. in the office of Democratic Chairman Lawrence O'Brien were well-financed. The transportation of four Miamians to Washington was an expensive venture and could not be justified on a cost-effective basis on cash or equipment they might steal from the Watergate headquarters.

2. The fact that James McCord was a former employee of the Central Intelligence Agency (CIA) and was then on the payroll of the Nixon reelection committee (CREP) established in my mind that there was some political motivation behind this extraordinary burglary.

3. Police found more than $5000 in new $100 bills in the possession and on the persons of the burglars. These new bills had consecutive numbers, and normal investigation by the FBI of the source of those bills could produce strong leads on the vital question of identifying those who financed the burglary effort. Simply following the dollar trail in a routine manner would inevitably lead to those who had financed the burglars.

4. On the Monday following the Watergate burglary, Senator William Proxmire, the Wisconsin Democrat, has his investigating staff initiate inquiries of the Federal Reserve Board on this highly vulnerable point—the traceable $100 bills found on the burglars and in their hotel rooms. He was demanding that the Federal Reserve System and the Justice Department

make a report to him on the results of their investigations of this mysterious cash.

5. Representative Wright Patman, chairman of the House Banking Committee, had recognized that tracing the money from the Watergate burglars back to the source could produce significant evidence on the financing of the unusual burglary at Watergate headquarters. The wily Texas Democrat suggested that his staff director, Joseph C. (Jake) Lewis, send investigators out immediately to interview possible witnesses, to obtain documents, and, most of all, to try to keep the Justice Department honest in its inquiry. Chairman Patman wisely did not seek a special authority or appropriation from the House Banking Committee, for that would have created an early political confrontation with the Nixon administration before he had firm evidence.

6. Howard E. Shuman, Proxmire's administrative assistant, and Richard A. Wegman, his legislative aide, were given the job of following through and coordinating their efforts with Patman's quietly aggressive staff investigators.

Strengths and Weaknesses of the FBI

In that first week of the investigation, I had conversations with Proxmire, Patman, Lewis, Shuman, and Wegman. There was general agreement that the burglars were financed directly or indirectly by money from the Nixon presidential campaign committee. There was a consensus that a thorough investigation by the Justice Department and the FBI would inevitably establish the link between the burglars and the committee to reelect the president (CREP). We were all aware of the strengths and the weaknesses of the FBI. The major strength was that it was a highly professional organization and that, if it was permitted to do its job properly, the individual FBI agents would run down all leads and turn up every scrap of evidence that was relevant to any federal crime.

However, a major weakness was that the FBI was seldom given a free hand on investigations involving politically sensitive matters touching the White House, members of Congress, or labor organizations or officials. Even when that organization was headed by J. Edgar Hoover, the attorneys general and various presidents gave secret orders that sharply restricted the inquiries made by the individual agents.

In June 1972, the FBI was particularly sensitive to political influences from the White House. L. Patrick Gray, III, was the acting director of the FBI. This Nixon political crony was ambitious to be appointed as the permanent director of the huge and prestigious federal investigative body. I had some contact with Gray when he was an assistant secretary of HEW under Secretary Robert Finch. He was known to be a wishy-washy bureaucrat and totally susceptible to the dictates of White House Chief of Staff H. R. (Bob) Haldeman and Special Assistant John Ehrlichman. I expected Gray to be putty in the hands of Haldeman, Ehrlichman, or Attorney General Richard Kleindienst, who had been confirmed on June 8, 1972—nine days before the Watergate burglary.

The understanding I had of the internal workings of the White House and the relationships of the various members of that staff was important in my early analysis of the Watergate matter. For example, I knew that Jeb Magruder, a former White House staffer who was deputy director of CREP, was likely to be Haldeman's puppet. If CREP had financed the burglary, it was likely it had the approval of Haldeman. From my position as special counsel on the White House staff, I had observed Haldeman's use of Magruder to undercut Communications Director Herb Klein and take over direction of Klein's staff. Only a few days before the Watergate burglary, I visited Magruder at his CREP office and was told that he had actually been running CREP from the deputy director spot before John Mitchell had resigned as Attorney General to take over the director's job. I knew that Magruder, ambitious and eager to please Haldeman, was clearing all but routine matters with Haldeman personally.

Reading 17: Reporter's View

On Sunday, June 18, when the Associated Press first identified James McCord as a "security coordinator" for the committee to re-elect the president, the picture was clear to me. He had worked for the FBI from 1948 to 1951 and for the CIA from 1951 to 1970 and had operated his own consulting firm in Rockville, Maryland. He had been on the CREP regular payroll at $1200 a month from January 1972, according to reports filed under the new federal election law.

The *Washington Post* carried its first story on the Watergate burglary under the byline of Alfred E. Lewis, a veteran police reporter, with a note that there had been contributions by eight reporters: Bob Woodward, Carl Bernstein, Bart Barnes, Kirk Schafenberg, Martin Weil, Claudia Levy, Abbott Combes, and Tim O'Brien. That excellent story reported the details of the police report on the burglary. It included the burglars' possession of a walkie-talkie receiver that could pick up police calls, two 35mm cameras with 40 rolls of unexposed film, and some sophisticated bugging devices. The burglars were wearing surgical gloves when captured inside Democratic headquarters and were reported to have $2400 in $100 bills in their possession. The United States Attorney's office entered the hotel rooms of the arrested men and found another $4200 in cash, also in $100 bills, with the serial numbers in the same sequence as the money taken from the arrested men.

Most important, the *Washington Post* had used a lot of manpower to get this story and was, at least for the moment, concentrating on the kind of detailed coverage necessary to produce results in situations involving government corruption or political conniving. Bob Woodward's contribution to the story was particularly significant because it dealt with the circumstances under which Douglas Caddy, a Washington corporation lawyer, had come into the case at 3:00 A.M.

Although Caddy was at that time reluctant to engage in public discussion of his role, Woodward had pried from him the explanation that he had showed up at the police station at that early hour as a result of a call from the wife of Bernard L. Barker, one of the three Cuban-Americans, who lived in Miami, Florida. It was unlikely that a routine request for legal advice would rout a Washington corporation lawyer out of bed in the early morning hours to go to a police station to arrange bail for a burglar suspect he had met only casually over cocktails at the Army-Navy Club in Washington. Also, it was significant to me that Caddy would not answer the *Post* reporter's questions as to why he had brought an experienced criminal lawyer, Joseph A. Rafferty, Jr., into the case to represent all of the burglars.

Caddy's explanation was, "She [Mrs. Barker] said that her husband had told her to call me if he hadn't called her by 3:30 A.M., that it might mean he was in trouble." If the five men were arrested at 2:30 A.M., why would the signal for the trouble be set in motion automatically at 3:00 A.M.? The only possible explanation, other than Republican intrigue, was that a group of erratic and irresponsible Cuban-Americans had chosen to try to do President Nixon a political favor in the hope that the administration would be more amenable to their aspirations for United States government assistance in an invasion of Fidel Castro's Cuba.

It was of special interest to me that a former Iowa congressman, Deputy Democratic Chairman Stanley Greigg, was called to Democratic headquarters to coordinate facts on the burglary-bugging attempt. Greigg told the *Post* that it was "obviously important" that several of the suspects came from Miami and Miami Beach, where the Democratic Convention was to be convened on July 10.

On Sunday, I tried unsuccessfully to get some tangible evidence of Haldeman's knowledge of the burglary-bugging from my friends and former associates at the White House and at the reelection committee. Panicky, they did not want it known that they were talking to me. They were fearful I might write a story critical of Haldeman and that they might be identified or suspected of being the source. Although they didn't say it to me, it was apparent they were fearful of Haldeman's White House spy system, which included a good many secretaries and others who kept lists of all incoming and outgoing telephone calls and visitors. They had the same feeling I had—that Haldeman's insatiable curiosity for reliable inside information on what everyone was doing and planning had led him to approve political bugging and wire-tapping.

I tried to reach Stan Greigg on Sunday to get a first-hand account of his participation in events at Democratic headquarters and to inquire into his precise role in the developing events. I finally made contact with him on Monday. Since Greigg was a former mayor of Sioux City, Iowa, and a former Iowa congressman, I knew I could develop a story of considerable local interest to readers of the *Des Moines Register* even if he had no new information.

It would have been difficult to find a better source of information than this 41-year-old deputy chairman. He had been the first man on the scene on June 17, and he had been designated by Democratic Chairman Larry O'Brien to provide liaison with the Secret Service, the FBI, and the Metropolitan Police in the District of Columbia. Although I did not expect to obtain confidential information from Greigg, he was an infallible source for checking the accuracy of information in the newspapers, on the wire services, and the hundreds of rumors that were afloat. And, indeed, it was mutually beneficial to discuss the hard evidence and to speculate where it could lead. It was Greigg's job to keep on top of all facts and to prevent a whitewash. This included trying to make some educated guesses on the involvement of White House figures and the countermoves that could be expected.

It was my judgment, after sifting the evidence and making my own projections, that the former Iowa congressman was sitting "on top of the biggest potential political bonanza the Democrats have had in the effort to unseat President Nixon in 1972." I wrote it precisely that way for the *Des Moines Register*. Greigg told me that initially he had thought of political espionage as the reason for the break-in, but had dismissed the idea as too far out until he learned the true identity of McCord and his connection with the reelection committee. I told Greigg it was my view that Haldeman controlled the reelection committee through Magruder, and that Magruder would not have initiated such a burglary on his own. I reviewed the manner in which Haldeman used Magruder to undercut Klein and Haldeman's White House spy system. I expressed the opinion that the motivation for the burglary and bugging was likely to be as simple as Haldeman's insatiable curiosity about "the enemy's game plan." I warned Greigg that proof would be hard to develop because of Haldeman's extreme caution about putting his own views or instructions in writing. Magruder, however, might have carelessly left big tracks showing his involvement, and, if Magruder was involved, it had to be on either direct or indirect approval from Haldeman.

In my story written on Friday, June 24, for use in the *Des Moines Register* that weekend, I set out the hard evidence and the real danger of a Nixon administration coverup in this five-point summary:

1. McCord, one of the five arrested in the Democratic headquarters officer at Watergate, has now admitted to being a top security man for two major Republican organizations dedicated to the reelection of President Nixon.

2. McCord held a federal license for use of walkie-talkies and other use of air waves for "security activity" on behalf of the Republican National Committee.

3. Mitchell, head of the Committee for the Reelection of the President, is recognized as one of the men closest to Mr. Nixon, and until recently was Attorney General Richard Kleindienst's boss.

4. The acting director of the FBI is L. Patrick Gray, who served as an assistant attorney general under Mitchell and had been nominated as deputy attorney general by Mr. Nixon with approval by Mitchell just prior to being named to the FBI post on the death of former Director J. Edgar Hoover.

5. The Justice Department, now responsible for the investigation of the Watergate burglary and bugging, is headed by Kleindienst.

In that story I noted that Democratic Chairman Larry O'Brien and Joseph Califano, the lawyer in O'Brien's $1 million damage suit against the Nixon committee, could question witnesses under oath in pre-trial depositions, and that this broad discovery power in the civil suit was one check on a Justice Department cover-up.

It was obvious from those facts that someone with money and considerable authority in the Nixon political structure had put together the Watergate bugging-burglary and that there would be a strong temptation for President Nixon to try to use the power of the presidency to obstruct justice in order to protect Haldeman or any other White House officials who might be involved. I knew of no evidence linking President Nixon to advance knowledge of the burglary. I also knew that Haldeman frequently embarked upon ridiculous ventures that might have been sidetracked by the politically wary Nixon.

The use of the FBI, the CIA, and the Justice Department to cover up Haldeman's responsibility was a clear possibility. However, there were a few counter forces at work. The civil damage suit depositions were one of the forces that could not be controlled by the White House, and the Congress was under Democratic control. Although some of the Democratic committee chairmen could be bribed or conned by a coldly cynical White House, there was virtually no chance of keeping the lid on all Democrats. To me, it was clear that political common sense, as well as the political desire to be regarded as honest, dictated that President Nixon should accept the fact that he had to make an honest investigation of the Watergate affair or risk serious political consequences later. The only safe course for President Nixon was a bipartisan commission headed by honest men of stature. I made the suggestion in a "Watch on Washington" column written on Monday, June 26—nine days after the burglary—and published on July 2, 1972.

To demonstrate how easy it was to analyze the full importance of Watergate within the first two weeks, that "Watch on Washington" follows:

The potential for damaging political fall-out from the burglary and "bugging" of National Democratic Party headquarters is so great that only forceful action by President Nixon can save the Republican Party from serious consequences in the November election.

To date, the most damaging fact is the arrest of the top security man for two Republican Party organizations along with four others at gunpoint at Democratic headquarters on June 17.

So far, there are only hints of lines of responsibility that point to the White House. However, the hints are strong enough that the president should waste no time in taking a leaf from President Calvin Coolidge's book when he set up a bipartisan special counsel to handle the investigation and prosecution of the infamous Teapot Dome scandals.

It was a precarious step for President Coolidge to take, but it was necessary to avoid political blame in the 1924 election for the crimes of the Harding administration. Eminent men, one a Republican and one a Democrat, were named to head the investigation independent of the Justice Department. The then attorney general, Harry Daugherty, was involved in improprieties on the fringe of the Teapot Dome scandals.

The fact that Coolidge won the 1924 election by a substantial margin is some indication of the worth of the bipartisan special committee's decision absolving him from blame.

President Nixon could take a long step up the credibility ladder by naming similar men of recognized integrity to investigate the Democratic headquarters burglary independent of the Justice Department.

Former Senator John J. Williams of Delaware, whose aggressive pursuit of dishonesty and unethical conduct in both parties was the hallmark of his 24 years in the Senate, would be the type of Republican who should be named.

Former Senator Paul Douglas, a liberal Democrat from Illinois, is the type of man who would have the confidence of most liberal Democrats.

The fact that there have been so many questions of credibility raised around Kleindienst's confirmation is one of the reasons the public may have grave doubts about how thoroughly the Justice Department, headed by Kleindienst, will handle the investigation promised on the alleged robbery and "bugging" caper.

This is particularly sticky because the Committee for the Re-election of the President is headed by former Attorney General John N. Mitchell, Kleindienst's former boss.

Also, the acting director of the FBI is Patrick Gray, who had served as an assistant attorney general under Mitchell and had been nominated as deputy attorney general by Mitchell and Nixon prior to being named to the FBI post upon J. Edgar Hoover's death.

President Nixon cannot afford to leave unanswered questions in the investigation of the burglary at Democratic headquarters, and it is unlikely that any investigation under the direction of Kleindienst and Patrick Gray will be sufficient to stifle doubts of the Democrats as well as many Republicans.

Many Democratic political figures have taken advantage of the political bonanza, and O'Brien has moved into an enviable strategic position. His $1 million damage suit can be milked for $100 million worth of publicity in the months between now and the election.

The case is in the hands of two clever lawyers—Edward Bennett Williams and Joseph Califano. This civil damage suit permits the calling and swearing of relevant witnesses in the pre-trial depositions.

There are essentially no limits on the use of the procedure, and almost anyone in the White House or the Republican National Committee or the Committee for the Reelection of the President who had dealings with McCord, would be subject to questioning.

Democrats are free to stage the depositions and time them for maximum political benefit, with full newspaper and television coverage.

Implications of "political espionage" by White House personnel is a fascinating bit of business, and even if there are very few lines to the White House, the Democrats will savor every morsel before the television cameras or in the nation's press.

Democrats control the committees of the House and Senate and many chairmen are bold and eager to get into the big act of 1972—even if only on the fringe and on a most limited jurisdictional basis.

The president, a man with considerable experience in investigations, should be the first to recognize the potential dangers in the months ahead. He also should recognize the advantages inherent in following the Coolidge pattern of seizing the initiative soon and selecting a believable bipartisan committee to look into the entire burglary and "bugging" incident.

At the time I wrote that column I did not know that *Washington Post* night police reporter Eugene Backinski had been informed that address books found on two of the Miami men contained the name and phone number of a E. Howard Hunt, with the notation "W. House" and "W. H." Bob Woodward had followed up that informant lead with some innovative calls to the White House to determine if Howard Hunt had some official position. A series of calls established that Hunt had worked as a "consultant" to Special Counsel Charles W. Colson and had some writing job at the Washington public-relations firm of Robert R. Mullen and Company.

The FBI was already on the trail of Hunt and Liddy, both former White House aides. It was not until several days later that *Newsday* published its first stories that G. Gordon Liddy, a former White House and Treasury Department lawyer, had resigned from the position as a lawyer for the reelection committee after refusing to cooperate in the FBI investigation of the Watergate burglary. *Newsday* identified Liddy as a lawyer for the Finance Committee at CREP, a former FBI agent, and an unsuccessful candidate for the Republican nomination for a New York congressional seat in 1970.

John Mitchell had also resigned as director of CREP on July 1, with the explanation that it was "for personal reasons" related to Martha Mitchell's dislike of Washington and politics.

At that time no one knew that Richard Nixon was already trying to use the CIA and FBI to obstruct inquiries on the involvement of the two former White House aides in planning and execution of the Watergate burglary-bugging. In my innocence, I called White House speech-writer Pat Buchanan and told him of my column suggesting a bipartisan commission to investigate Watergate. I suggested that he might want to call it to President Nixon's attention and offered to send him a copy. Pat was deeply concerned about the possible implication of the White House in the Watergate affair or in an attempted coverup.

Equally ignorant, Buchanan agreed that a bipartisan commission would prevent Haldeman from involving President Nixon in an unwise defense of Charles W. Colson, who by that time had been identified by the *Washington Post* as one of Hunt's White House contacts. At that point, the only tangible evidence of a White House connection was a story by Woodward, which disclosed that two Watergate burglars carried address books containing the notations "W. House" and "W. H." and the information on the home telephone number of E. Howard Hunt, a $100-a-day White House consultant.

Buchanan said he knew nothing about Hunt and didn't want to know anything about him. He was mainly concerned with "keeping the Old Man (Nixon) out of it." I knew that Buchanan was not one who was close to Haldeman, Ehrlichman, or Colson and would not have been told of any plans to burglarize or bug the Democratic headquarters. He complained mildly that the *Washington Post* story headline "White House Consultant Linked to Bugging Suspect" was the kind of "guilty by association" that the *Post* usually deplored.

I disagreed with Buchanan on the complaint of unfair coverage by the *Post*. I approved of the kind of aggressive job of follow through that the *Post* had failed to do on a number of other stories involving White House improprieties. I told Buchanan that the Nixon White House could not register a legitimate complaint until it was completely open and honest with regard to the facts on Hunt's employment and Colson's role.

"The hard fact is that Watergate is going to come unwound at some point, and the President should get on top of it," I warned. "The Democrats control the committees of Congress, and some of those Democrats are going to force this investigation because it is to their political advantage to do so. And you know, as well as I do, that the press and the television networks are not going to help a Nixon administration cover up anything. This is the time for the president to stand back from the investigation and not become tarred with a coverup."

Buchanan agreed that the president's problem was to avoid involvement. He said he thought that Senator John Williams would make a good member of an investigation commission, remarked that Senator Paul Douglas was "too liberal" but believed he would be honest, and said he would "take it up with the powers."

It was late July before Pat Buchanan got back to me with a response on the suggested bipartisan Watergate investigation commission after getting a reaction from Haldeman and Ehrlichman. "The powers reject it," he said. "They want no part of Senator Williams."

"Doesn't the president understand that in the long run an independent straight investigation will be for his protection?" I asked.

Buchanan said that he did not know President Nixon's precise view on this point but that Haldeman and Ehrlichman "don't want John Williams in there prying around under any circumstances. The powers feel more comfortable with (White House Counsel) John Dean handling it." While Buchanan continued to show concern over Watergate, he was euphoric about the way the "game plan" was shaping up for the 1972 election. Nixon was certain to name Vice President Spiro Agnew as his running mate, and the Miami Beach convention would be presented on prime-time television so that its efficiency and control could be contrasted with the chaotic brouhaha staged by the Democrats when they nominated Senator George McGovern, the ultraliberal South Dakotan, as their standard bearer.

Another significant news break in July was the story in the *Washington Star-News* by reporters Joseph Volz and Patrick Collins on the resignation of Hugh W. Sloan, Jr., from his post as treasurer of CREP at about the same time he was being questioned by a federal grand jury on the Watergate affair. Sloan was quoted as saying he resigned for "purely personal reasons," which was obviously a cover story. I had known Sloan when I was on the White House staff and regarded him as a serious and dedicated young man who would never knowingly have done a dishonest thing. To me he seemed to possess an integrity, a competency, and a seriousness that went beyond the polite, well-groomed superficiality that were the characteristics of so many others on Haldeman's staff.

I called Sloan to verify the *Star-News* story. He said the Watergate affair was upsetting to his wife who was expecting a baby in September. He told me he had cooperated with the FBI but declined to discuss that testimony or what it might mean relative to the involvement of CREP officials. He said that he had returned my call because he regarded me as a friend from the White House. I remarked that he was treasurer of the Nixon reelection committee, which made him the legally responsible official for campaign reports filed with the Office of Federations at the GAO. He said he had been proud when he was given the title and responsibility, but now agreed with my observation that he may have been set up as a fall guy in case anything went wrong. He assured me he had handled his duties properly and legally. I said I was sure he had, but he was noncommittal as to whether others at CREP had handled their responsibilities in a legal and proper manner. "It is under investigation by the grand jury," he said, and I knew he was deeply troubled. Because he had principles, he was out of a job and was unlikely to find one in the administration. He had demonstrated that his loyalty could not be relied upon when it came into conflict with his conscience.

The story by Volz and Collins was important because it demonstrated that there were some honest people at the Nixon reelection committee who were going to be honest in the grand jury even if it meant losing a valuable political job. To me it was heartening to learn that the FBI was pursuing all such potential witnesses as Sloan, Liddy, and Hunt.

In July, unknown to the press, the House Banking and Currency Committee had linked two highly questionable financial transactions to the bank account of Bernard L. Barker. One was a $25,000 certified check deposited in Barker's bank account. Kenneth H. Dahlberg, a Minneapolis business executive, had delivered the check to Maurice Stans on April 11 as a campaign contribution from wealthy financier and commodity trader Dwayne Andreas. It was he who had put big cash contributions behind Democratic Senator Hubert Humphrey and Richard Nixon.

Barker's Miami bank account had also been the depository for four cashier's checks totalling $89,000, issued by the Banco International in Mexico City to Manuel Ogarrio Daguerre, a prominent lawyer. The cashier's checks had been deposited in Barker's account on April 20—less than two months before the Watergate burglary-bugging. Richard E. Gerstein, a local prosecutor and state's attorney for Dade County, Florida, Representative Patman's investigators, and the FBI were all following those money trails on the Watergate story.

Walter Rugaber of the *New York Times,* following the leads of Gerstein's office in Miami, had gone on to Mexico City on the trail of the details of "the Mexican laundry" for the campaign cash. Rugaber broke the first stories on "Cash in Capitol Raid Traced to Mexico" in the *New York Times* on the day that *Washington Post* reporter Carl Bernstein flew to Miami to take up the money trail. Although he was following several days in Rugaber's wake, he hoped to catch up on another aspect that the local prosecutor knew about.

Gerstein said he did not have details on the investigation of the money trail, that he had been unable to get much cooperation from the FBI on what its agents had found, and told Bernstein that Martin Dardis, an assistant in his office, was the man most knowledgeable on the case. Dardis let Bernstein examine bank records and the Manuel Ogarrio and Kenneth Dahlberg checks, and said he had not yet been able to determine who Dahlberg was.

Bernstein called Woodward with the details on the Kenneth Dahlberg check. Woodward asked the *Washington Post* librarian to check the clipping files for anything on a Kenneth Dahlberg. That produced nothing. Editor Barry Sussman asked for a check of the picture file, and received a picture of Senator Hubert Humphrey with a small man identified as Kenneth H. Dahlberg. Woodward called information in Minneapolis, obtained Dahlberg's number, placed a call, and confirmed that Dahlberg was the same Dahlberg who had a winter home in Florida.

Then Woodward asked the direct question about the $25,000 check deposited in the bank account of Barker, one of the Watergate burglars. The initial silence was followed by the hesitating, reluctant comment by Dahlberg that he didn't know what had happened to the money after he turned it over to the Nixon reelection committee. He avoided the questions regarding Dwayne Andreas as the source of the contribution, but said he had turned it over to "the treasurer of the committee (Hugh W. Sloan, Jr.) or to Maurice Stans himself."

By fast work on the telephone and skillful questioning, Woodward was able to get admissions from Dahlberg for a significant story—a $25,000 cashier's check, apparently earmarked for the campaign chest of President Nixon, was deposited in the bank account of one of the Watergate burglars nearly two months before the burglary. This technique allowed Woodward and Bernstein to break that story at least a day before Rugaber and the *New York Times* would have been prepared to handle it because of a slower and less daring approach.

The publication of the *New York Times* story on the Mexican laundry for CREP funds and the *Washington Post* story on the Dahlberg check opened the way for Philip S. Hughes, director of the new Federal Election Division of the GAO, to announce publicly that he was investigating the circumstances of the questionable campaign contributions to CREP that might constitute a violation or evasion of the new election laws.

House Banking and Currency Committee investigators were already deeply involved in tracing the Dahlberg check and the Mexican checks when the *Washington Post* story broke. They were pleased to see the story in print because it would put pressure on the Office of Federal Elections, the FBI, and the Justice Department to conduct the thorough investigations needed and to set the stage for public hearings before the House committee that Chairman Wright Patman hoped to schedule in September.

It was apparent at this point that the Justice Department was not going to be able to limit indictments to the five men caught in the Democratic headquarters at Watergate. Republican congressional sources and White House spokesmen were making statements that there would be "no coverup" and that "some people with White House connections" would be included among those indicted. The "game plan" was apparent to me. There would be the addition of some minor figures with White House connections indicted to give the impression of a forthright investigation, but even those indictments would be a part of an obstruction of justice unless they included Magruder, Haldeman, and Stans.

By mid-August, my conversations with Republicans in the White House and in Congress convinced me that E. Howard Hunt and G. Gordon Liddy would be sacrificed to keep the lid on the scandal. It was conceivable that Jeb Magruder might be numbered among the indicted. The evidence was firm as to the involvement of CREP officials and Hunt, but the word was being spread that a group of irresponsible people and adventurers had engaged in a "caper" and were acting without benefit of approval from the White House.

The White House plan was to time these indictments early enough to put a muzzle on further comments, but late enough so the trial could not be held before the November election. The return of the indictments could be used, as it often was, as an argument for refusal to cooperate with congressional investigators. However, as I saw it at that point, there was no way the Justice Department could impose a muzzle on the deposition being taken in the civil suit brought by Democrat Lawrence O'Brien against the Nixon reelection committee and its officials. Also, there seemed to be no way that Chairman Patman could be barred from making public the reports of his staff investigators on the campaign funds collected through Kenneth Dahlberg and those that had been channeled from Texas oil interests through the Mexican bank.

By this time, Dan Thomasson of the Scripps-Howard newspapers and James Squires of the *Chicago Tribune* had written important stories on reports about the contents of E. Howard Hunt's White House safe and about the questionable handling of Hunt's records. Also, Thomasson and I had obtained the information from government sources, including two independent reports from FBI sources, that CREP officials had kept a cash slush fund in excess of $300,000 in the offices of the Nixon reelection committee.

I had made a request to interview Maurice Stans, chairman of the CREP finance committee, in July but had been stalled throughout August. I had little hope of success when I renewed my request in September. Suddenly, on September 12, I was called and told that Stans would be able to see me within a few days. It couldn't have come at a better time, for I had just obtained a copy of the still-secret House Banking and Currency Committee's 80-page staff report on the $89,000 traced to Barker's account through the "Mexican laundry" and the $25,000 Kenneth Dahlberg check that had originated in a cash contribution from Dwayne Andreas.

My appointment with Stans, set for 8:00 A.M. on Wednesday, September 14, was postponed until that afternoon. This gave me more time to peruse the well-documented Patman report on the important details of questionable cash contributions Stans had accepted. At the last minute, Stans and Dick Moore, a White House public relations man, insisted that the interview be on a background basis and that there be no quotations attributed directly to Stans because he was involved in litigation and might be called before the Patman committee. I reluctantly agreed; there was no other way to get this important interview.

The series of stories from that interview with Stans in mid-September revealed these important points:

1. White House Counsel John Dean, heading a White House investigation of Watergate at President Nixon's request, was providing legal opinions to Stans and others at CREP who were responsible for irregular and perhaps illegal handling of huge amounts of cash.

2. President Nixon had consulted with Stans, had some knowledge of the Mexican laundry maneuver, and had expressed no criticism of Stans or of the manner in which the reelection committee was being run.

3. Stans and the Nixon White House hoped to end the Watergate inquiry with the indictment of the five men arrested at

Democratic headquarters and a few others—probably Hunt
and Liddy. Stans would not be indicted.

4. United States District Judge Charles Richey, a Nixon appointee,
had wrapped the depositions in the civil suit in a secrecy that
would limit the use of that information on the sworn statements by key Republicans.

5. The White House and Stans had confidence that the House
Republican leadership (specifically House Republican Leader
Gerald Ford and Representative Garry Brown, both of Michigan) could block Chairman Patman from obtaining subpoena
power for any effective hearings until after the November
election.

6. The White House hoped to block the effectiveness of the
Office of Federal Election and the GAO until after the
election because the GAO did not have subpoena power and
would "have to go through the Justice Department."

7. The White House would have the cooperation of Attorney
General Kleindienst to restrict and control the FBI and the
United States District Attorney until after the election when
Nixon would have "four more years."

Neither Stans nor Dick Moore realized that their admissions of
facts, their expressions of confidence, and their admissions of
contracts with President Nixon and others had revealed the clearest
outline of the Watergate coverup—a criminal obstruction of justice.
Because I wrote the series on the Stans interview without quotations,
it was ignored by the wire services, and, although I sent the stories
to the *Washington Post,* they were not used. The day after my Stans
interview, on September 15, indictments were returned against the
five Watergate burglars and Hunt and Liddy. It was an important
step for the coverup.

As a result of the Stans interview, I now knew that Richard
Nixon was involved in planning and directing a coverup that was
being executed by John Dean in the White House. I also knew that
the Republican White House believed it had pulled the teeth of the
civil suit through Judge Richey's imposition of secrecy on depositions. President Nixon and his associates believed Chairman Wright
Patman was the only serious hurdle to get over before the November
election.

I recognized the importance of the Patman committee, because
Stans had told me that House Republican Leader Gerald Ford and
Representative Gary Brown, whom he had mentioned, were key men
in the plan to kill Patman's investigation by denying him subpoena

power. The House Banking and Currency Committee should have been the scene of the important fight over whether John Dean, Maurice Stans, Jeb Magruder, and John Mitchell would be required to testify in public before the election. But, most of the press was off chasing all kinds of "new angles" on Watergate that were unrelated to the vital story of the coverup. The Republican maneuvering in the Patman committee had no more than routine coverage by the wire services or by most newspapers, including the *Washington Post* and *New York Times.* In Congress Patman was accused of being engaged in "a political witch hunt," and Representative Garry Brown, then proud of his role in the White House move to stop Patman, and Gerald Ford succeeded in persuading the Republicans to stick together and to win the support of a few Democratic committee members. By a vote of 20 to 14, with six Democrats joining the Republicans, Patman's attempt to uncover the truth was blocked.

The *Los Angeles Times,* with ace investigators Jack Nelson, Ron Ostrow, and Bob Jackson, did some of the most consistent work on the Watergate story from the outset. In September and October, the *Los Angeles Times* helped to thwart the Nixon administration's coverup efforts.

Following the return of the Watergate indictments on September 15, 1972, Nelson noted the name of Alfred C. Baldwin, III, a former FBI agent, as key witness. Nelson's taped interviews with Baldwin gave the public the first detailed, inside account of the Watergate burglary. The stories on how Baldwin had been hired by Jim McCord to monitor telephone conversations from Democratic headquarters sparked new interests in Watergate.

The story dramatized the fact that the Watergate burglary was not "the caper" of some irresponsibles, which the White House contended it was. Baldwin had monitored the telephones at the Democratic headquarters from Room 723 of the Howard Johnson Motor Lodge, across the street from Watergate. His employment by McCord had been cleared with Fred LaRue, then an assistant to campaign director John Mitchell. Baldwin's interview revealed that he had dealt with McCord and Liddy, and that there had been discussions of burglary and bugging of McGovern's campaign headquarters. The former FBI agent revealed that he had overheard about 200 telephone conversations. He typed logs describing the conversations and passed them to McCord. He said he had destroyed his own handwritten notes on those conversations and did not know what McCord had done with the logs. On one occasion, Baldwin said, he had been instructed to deliver a report on the conversations to a guard at the Nixon reelection committee, but could not remember the name of the man.

Nelson's stories on Baldwin—a story the Justice Department and the White House wanted to suppress—were the most important factor in keeping the Watergate problem alive through the election and in making it impossible to bury the other details in plea bargains. There were moves by the Nixon administration to kill further probing on Watergate and to take quiet pleas of guilty. Those moves, however, were stopped by United States District Judge John Sirica. Judge Sirica, a man of integrity and courage, blocked those moves by criticizing the prosecution and by insisting upon a tough followup on the evidence that Jeb Magruder and some other witnesses had engaged in willful perjury as a part of the White House coverup.

From early in 1973, the initiative for uncovering the coverup came from Judge Sirica and from Senator Sam Ervin, the outspoken critic of executive privilege claims that were the heart of the coverup. From that point on it was only necessary for the press to do a competent job of covering the Senate hearings and the various court proceedings to keep the pressure on the administration and to detect evidence of what was by that time generally recognized as a White House-directed obstruction of justice.

Close analysis demonstrates that no one newspaper and no small group of reporters uncovered the Watergate coverup that forced Richard Nixon out of office. It took the combined efforts of 40 or more reporters working in cooperation with honest government investigators and in opposition to the dishonest coverup. Those reporters were dependent in varying degrees at the outset upon the honest conscientious work of FBI agents, investigators and officials of the Federal Office of Elections, and the aggressive thrusts of Senator William Proxmire and Representative Wright Patman.

Any realistic analysis must conclude that all of the work of the government investigators and newsmen would have been futile if it had not been for the firmness and courage of Chairman Sam Ervin, the Senate Watergate Committee staff, and the nonpartisan integrity of United States District Judge John J. Sirica. It took all of the news media force to create a public awareness that a serious situation existed that required the House Judiciary Committee to initiate impeachment proceedings against Richard Nixon.

Although most of the reporters worked with some confidential informants from inside the governmental structure, the forward movement of the Watergate case was not contingent upon any "Deep Throat" informant as much as it was on the solid record search and interview techniques that have paid off from the time of Lincoln Steffens and Ida Tarbell to the award-winning work on Watergate by Frank G. Wright of the *Minneapolis Tribune,* Jean

Heller and D. Brooks Jackson of the Associated Press, Jerry Landauer of the *Wall Street Journal,* James R. Polk of the *Washington Star-News,* and Carl Bernstein and Robert Woodward of the *Washington Post.*

Other reporters who made equally great contributions to the success of the Watergate probe included Harry J. Kelly and James Squires of the *Chicago Tribune;* Jack Nelson, Robert Jackson, and Ronald J. Ostrow of the *Los Angeles Times;** Joe Volz and James G. Wieghart of the *New York Daily News;* Seymour M. Hersh, James M. Naughton, Anthony Ripley, Walter Rugaber, and Wallace Turner of the *New York Times;* Robert Greene, Martin J. Schram, Russell Sackett, and Anthony Marro of *Newsday;* Nicholas Horrock of *Newsweek;* Dan K. Thomasson of Scripps-Howard; Hays Gorey and Sandy Smith of Time, Inc.; Helen Thomas and Jane Denison of United Press International; Jack Anderson, Brit Hume, Joe Spear, and Leslie H. Whitten, of *Washington Merry-Go-Round;* and Ronald Kessler, George Lardner, Morton Mintz, Spencer Rich, Lawrence M. Stern, and Barry Sussman of the *Washington Post.*

The full accurate coverage of the hearings by the wire services, the *Washington Post,* the *Washington Star-News,* and the *New York Times* was vital in keeping the entire press corps and the television networks apprised of all important new developments on the many facets of the story. The use of legal specialists by the networks was a great contribution to Watergate coverage, making it possible for the networks to avoid the superficiality that so often marred previous coverage on such issues. Carl Stern, the lawyer-reporter for NBC, and Fred Graham, a lawyer-reporter for CBS, were permitted to do a careful analysis of legal issues that avoided oversimplification and mere grasping for a catchy news peg.

For the Washington newsmen, Watergate was an extension of the same techniques of competition, cooperation, and coverage that exposed the tax scandals of the Truman administration, the regulatory agency scandals of the Eisenhower administration, the Billie Sol Estes case in the Kennedy administration, and forced the Johnson administration to prosecute Bobby Baker.

It entailed careful research of government records, skillful, confidential dealing with government investigators, systematic interviewing of all potential witnesses, and a constant awareness of

---

*A strong argument could be made that the *Los Angeles Times* Washinton bureau did the best overall coverage of Watergate but did not gain recognition because the stories were not printed in Washington.

the possibility that government officials will misuse their power to hide the crimes of their friends and political associates.

STUDENT WORK PROJECT SUGGESTION

Read *All the President's Men* and do a careful analysis of the contributions of the "Deep Throat" figure and the importance of this contribution to moving the investigation forward.

33 THE ARIZONA PROJECT

The team reporting project under the direction of Robert W. Greene provides a blueprint for sound investigations of complicated subjects and a sophisticated plan for giving complete protection for confidential news sources with a minimum of danger to the newsmen involved. The premature criticism of this IRE project resulted in Greene taking additional steps to insure that the team's series was not vulnerable on points raised by critics.

It is possible for an experienced editor to weld an effective investigation team together with a handful of experienced reporters and a large number of relatively inexperienced volunteers. Planning is the key to success, and the team director must give great attention to detail to avoid the serious mistakes that can come from lack of proper coordination.

FOUNDING THE INVESTIGATIVE REPORTERS AND EDITORS (IRE) GROUP

Watergate stimulated a great interest in investigative reporting in the public, the press, and the academic world. Suddenly even the most skeptical recognized that persistent pushing for truth in governmental affairs was indeed different from superficial routine reporting of government and politics, which is the dominant fare in most newspapers. There was a realization that a simple report of statements by the president or other government officials was little different from handout collecting, unless there was a systematic and determined effort to test the official utterances against documents and all available records.

Paul N. Williams, a professor of journalism at Ohio State University and a Pulitzer Prize-winning reporter, understood the need for getting behind pious official statements to uncover hidden frauds and mismanagement. His effective investigative work for the Sun Newspapers of Omaha had cracked the facade at Boys Town in Nebraska and exposed the misrepresentations and frauds that permeated that religious undertaking. It was the first time a weekly newspaper had been awarded a Pulitzer Prize.

In 1974, Paul Williams set out on a systematic search for the views of the nation's best known investigative reporters and editors. He wanted to analyze their experiences for a textbook system on investigative reporting. I was among the first reporters he interviewed on his project. As we talked about the constant patterns of corruption in city, county, state, and federal agencies, Williams said he believed it would be helpful if reporters and editors with an interest in investigative reporting had an organization or center for the exchange of information on fraud patterns.

I informed him that, in 1950, a group of less than 20 crime reporters had formed an informal organization that had been important in the success of the Kefauver Crime Committee, and that I also had been the informal coordinator of a similar group of like-minded reporters on a number of investigations, including the successful labor racket inquiries of 1957, 1958, and 1959. There were other instances when groups had cooperated, and the Associated Press had established an excellent investigative team for certain special projects. However, by and large, most of the work of the wire services was pretty routine and totally inadequate for coming to grips with the realities of the political world or the underworld.

Several months later, I received a call from Williams who was taking time out from his book project to establish an organization for investigative reporters and editors. I could not attend the first meeting in Reston, but agreed to speak at the first convention of the Investigative Reporters and Editors group in June 1976. It was being held in Indianapolis, Indiana, because of the leadership role that Richard E. Cady, Myrta Pulliam, and others on the *Indianapolis Star* had taken in the organization of IRE.

FIRST PROJECT OF THE IRE

On June 2, 1976, the bomb attack on Don Bolles, an investigative reporter for the *Arizona Republic*, shocked the journalistic world and particularly those of us in the field of investigative reporting. For years we had proceeded about our business ignoring threats to our lives and our job, more or less assuming that the bosses of organized crime and politics would "be too smart" to kill a reporter or editor and stir up the whole journalistic community. I had expressed that view in any number of speeches, and had actually been prepared to reiterate the idea in a speech I was preparing for delivery at the final luncheon of the IRE convention on June 20.

That speech on "The Precarious Profession" of investigative reporting was aimed at illuminating the *subtle* hazards involved in stepping on the toes of powerful political and business leaders. Prior to the bombing death of Don Bolles in 1976, I could not recall one incident of a reporter being an assassination target of organized crime since the blinding of Victor Riesel in April 1956. The last murder of a reporter investigating organized crime that I could recall was the shooting of Donald Mellett in the 1930s. When Don Bolles, an IRE member, died on June 12, it was inevitable that the first IRE convention would be dominated by the discussion of his death and the deeply felt desire to demonstrate that the murder of an investigative reporter would not end the inquiry into corruption but would intensify it.

Choice of Team Leader

The resolutions to take up the Arizona investigation were passed unanimously, and it was left to the Board of Directors to decide the framework and to name a leader. Under incompetent or weak leadership such a project could be disastrous. Robert W. Greene, an editor for *Newsday* and a member of the Board of Directors of IRE, was the natural selection to head the team effort on the Arizona project. Greene was recognized as one of the top ten investigative reporters in the nation. He had more experience with team investigation than anyone, except possibly George Bliss of the *Chicago Tribune.* Greene originated and refined the concept of a permanent investigative team in 1967 and functioned as the chief of the team's daily operations in addition to reporting and writing with fellow team members. Between 1969 and 1975 his *Newsday* team won more professional awards than any other similar unit in the history of American journalism, including the 1974 Pulitzer Prize Gold Medal for Distinguished Public Service.

Greene knew public records at city, county, state, and federal levels and had worked with law enforcement officials at all levels as well as with state legislative committees and with congressional committees. He knew the benefits to be derived from working with honest government officials at all levels and the hazards of careless involvement with devious and dishonest law enforcement officials or prosecutors. An English major at Fordham University, Greene sharpened his natural investigative talents as a senior staff investigator with the New York Anti-Crime Committee between 1950 and 1955 before joining the *Newsday* staff. In 1957, he took a one-year leave of absence from *Newsday* to serve on the staff of the Senate Labor Rackets Committee. At Bob Kennedy's request he headed a staff of investigators working on the ties between organized crime and the Teamsters Union in New York City, northern New Jersey, and Long Island—the areas he knew best.

Greene's work with the New York Anti-Crime Committee and with the Senate Labor Racket Committee gave him a familiarity with systematic record keeping required by city and state police and the FBI. It also taught him how to weigh evidence like a real professional, how to obtain affidavits, and how to preserve evidence for use in trials and congressional hearings.

All of these talents were needed to put together an effective investigation of the pervasive corruption of city, county, state, and federal officials in Arizona that Don Bolles had been trying to expose with varying degrees of success. Wisely, Bob Greene arranged to make a comprehensive survey of the Arizona scene before becoming committed to the project. After some effective undercover work by Tom Renner, *Newsday's* organized crime expert, and Greene's own overall assessment of what already had been printed and what leads could be followed, Greene took charge of the Arizona project.

Opposition and Cooperation

Greene undertook the project amid warnings from a number of editors and publishers that it would fail. There was outright opposition from such men as Benjamin Bradlee, executive editor of the *Washington Post,* and A. M. Rosenthal, managing editor of the *New York Times.* Bradlee commented caustically that investigative reporters were too egotistical to work together and that it was arrogant for a group of outside reporters to believe that they could do a better job in Arizona than the local press. Rosenthal viewed the joint investigation project as a questionable move because it would encroach upon "the diversity and competitiveness" that has been "the great strengths of the American press." Rosenthal said, "We shouldn't be getting together; if a story is worth investigating, we should do it ourselves. If you do it on this story, why not on other stories? Why doesn't everybody get together and investigate everything; you'd soon have one big press and no diversity."

Normally a meticulous investigator, Bob Greene reacted to the protests and criticism from Bradlee, Rosenthal, and others by taking additional precautions to avoid mistakes in handling the investigation. The premature criticism may have been a blessing in disguise as it increased Greene's resolve to bring off a successful investigation. He actually used the comments of critics to enhance the spirit of the more than 35 editors and reporters who worked on the Arizona project for varying degrees of time.

The call for volunteers had resulted in 21 publishers, one local radio station (CBS-Boston) and one small TV station agreeing to supply reporters and pay their expenses for periods ranging from eight days to six months. In addition to *Newsday* staffers, the volunteers came from the *Boston Globe, Miami Herald, Detroit News, Kansas City Star, Indianapolis Star, Chicago Tribune, Denver Post, Eugene Register-Guard, Arizona Star,* and other smaller papers with a long tradition of public service.

Strategy

Bob Greene mapped the Arizona project strategy with varying degrees of help from the most experienced of the dozen reporters and editors among the volunteers. Vital to the ultimate success of the project, Greene had the total support of *Newsday* publisher William Atwood as well as others in top management of *Newsday.* They supported the project philosophically and financially and gave generously of the services of Greene, Tom Renner, and Anthony Insolia, the team's story editor. The step by step development by the big team that worked the complicated Arizona project was as thorough and comprehensive as my three-man projects on the irregularities and frauds in grain and livestock marketing.

The plan that Bob Greene followed on the Arizona project was totally consistent with the principles in my lectures on the Checklist for Investigative Reporters (see Appendix) at the American Press Institute and with the "roadmap" system that Paul Williams developed as a reporter for the *Omaha Sun* and as a professor of journalism at Ohio State. It was largely a newspaper adaptation of the best techniques used by any well-run congressional investigating committee or by the GAO in a depth survey of any governmental program.

Praise and Criticism

While there was criticism of the 32-part series of articles that finally emerged from the Arizona project, most of it was the kind of personal quibbling over writing style or the depth proof behind some of the general conclusions of the articles. The question of writing style is always subject to the whim of the individual, and much of the criticism was based on just such whims and arbitrary opinions of editors who often had some other, less noble, reason for not wanting to run the Arizona series.

There were some critics who said that the research was not up to some imaginary high standard that the editor had set for his newspaper. The proof of the soundness of the series was the fact that the handful of unsuccessful libel suits filed were obviously attempts at harassment by the corrupt, the corrupters, and the compromised.

The Society of Professional Journalists, Sigma Delta Chi, gave its 1977 Public Service Award to the Arizona project, and Bob Greene was the recipient of the University of Arizona's prestigious John Peter Zenger Award for Freedom of the Press and the People's Right to Know. Greene and the IRE team were also the recipients of a large number of other major journalism awards, including the American Society of Authors and Journalists Conscience in the Media Gold Medal Award. The American Society of Authors and Journalists called the Arizona project "the finest hour in American journalism." The praise by the press overwhelmed the scattered criticism.

In the wake of the Arizona project, Colby College gave its prestigious Elija Parish Lovejoy Fellowship posthumously to Don Bolles. Bob Greene delivered the tribute to Bolles portraying him as a martyr to the cause of "responsible, persistent, and courageous" public service reporting in the face of inadequate support and local apathy. Melvin Mencher, Professor of Journalism at Columbia University's graduate school, was unstinting in praise of the Arizona project and Bob Greene's leadership in a comprehensive article of analysis in the *Columbia Journalism Review*.

While a few cynics continued to cast stones at the Arizona project even after it was established as a successful venture in public service reporting, there was nothing but praise from honest law enforcement officials and legislators in Arizona. Attorney General Bruce Babbitt (later governor of Arizona) told me that the mere presence of the team of outside investigative reporters made it possible for him to focus the attention of the citizens of Arizona on the organized crime problem in a way that would not have been possible otherwise. In addition, Babbitt said Bob Greene and his investigators had developed new evidence and leads and public pressure that were vital in bringing Bolles' killers to justice as well as for taking new initatives against organized crime and its political allies.

LESSONS FROM THE ARIZONA PROJECT

Study of the Arizona project series can be helpful to anyone seeking a deeper understanding of how old, festering problems of corruption and compromise of public officials can be pursued. An intelligent research of public records is necessary and that research must be carefully meshed with systematic team interviews with all key figures, including police, prosecutors, and judges. At some point in the study, research of almost every type of public records was made, including birth rolls, marriage records, divorce records, death records, bankruptcy court records, probate records, and a wide range of records dealing with civil and criminal litigation.

Research Counts

Although the overall planning and execution of the Arizona project took all of the experience and skill that Bob Greene had accumulated in more than 25 years in the investigating business, most of the individual parts of the project could be put together by reporters with little experience on investigations through systematic research of records and common sense follow-through interviews. If the local records of city hall, police stations, and county court-houses are reviewed until they are fully mastered, the reporter has taken the first vital step to becoming a fully competent investigative reporter. The rest is a constant growing process. Systematically one learns about more records and court processes and knows to weigh the evidence and the credibility of witnesses as any law enforcement officer or lawyer must learn. Some reporters and editors can grasp these techniques in a few years; others spend an entire career in the newspaper business and never learn to sort out the difference between established facts and allegations by a party of interest.*

The Arizona project demonstrated how the local police, court, and land records must be the base for effective investigative reporting that touches the city, county, state, or federal institutions. It illustrates varying degrees of corruption and compromise in the ranks of police, prosecutors, and in the state and federal judiciary. That corruption and compromise was traced to both political parties. It showed how organized crime uses political contributions as well as outright bribes to purchase favoritism. Those practices in Phoenix

---

*Jack Taylor, skilled investigator for the (Tulsa) *Daily Oklahoman,* recommends that investigative reporters keep available a copy of *Where's What,* a book on sources of information for federal investigators, prepared by Harry J. Murphy, Office of Security, Central Intelligence Agency (CIA). This book on record research was prepared under a Brookings Institution fellowship and is published by Warner Books. It contains samples of standard city, county, and state records as well as explanations of the records kept by all of the federal agencies of government and the manner in which copies of those records can be obtained or examined. It also contains a list of other standard reference books on every conceivable subject, as well as trade association information sources and basic reliable sources of information on other nations.

extended from the office of a venal local prosecutor, who paraded as a liberal Democrat, to the office of an arbitrary conservative federal judge, who arrogantly upset a jury conviction involving the son of a Mafia boss.

Weakness of the Press

The Phoenix press was not blameless. Robert Greene's IRE team established that the negligence and the compromises of the local press were responsible for the corruption and compromise that permeated local law enforcement, prosecution, and judicial decisions. Decisions above the level of reporter and city editor resulted in a lack of follow through on evidence of serious obstruction of justice. Organized crime was able to use its connections in the banking, legal, and general business communities to influence the same kind of "selective law enforcement" I had seen in city, county, and state government in Iowa.

Although its reporter, Don Bolles, was assassinated because of his persistent inquiry into corrupting influences in Arizona politics, the *Arizona Republic's* top management balked at printing the IRE series. Rather than infuriate the powerful corrupt forces in politics and business, the *Arizona Republic's* top decision makers accepted the chastisement and scorn of the nation's press by publishing a mild and modified Associated Press version of the IRE series. This gave the newspaper's top management the opportunity to straddle the fence on the subject of corruption that had cost the life of its reporter, Don Bolles. On the one hand, it could explain to compromised and corrupt friends in the business and political world that it opposed the IRE investigator's findings and conclusions by only carrying a routine report by the Associated Press. On the other hand, without being specific, it could explain to critics that it had cooperated with IRE's investigators, but disagreed with its conclusions.

Some of its top editors acknowledged privately that this was a less than noble and courageous way to react to the assassination of Don Bolles. Nonetheless, they argued that a Phoenix newspaper had to face the reality of the power of the corrupt forces in the community, and it could not afford the luxury of the courageous and idealistic standards of other newspapers that ran the entire series. There was a natural unwillingness of the *Arizona Republic* to muckrake its own past record. Steps were taken, however, to shuffle its top staff in order to reduce the possibility of repeating the mistakes that led to its compromised position in dealing with conditions that led to the murder of Don Bolles.

The lack of follow through by the Phoenix newspapers on stories of corruption in government encouraged major and minor obstructions of justice—the ultimate corruption in the prosecution and judicial process. My own experience indicated that the combination of laxity and compromise by the Phoenix newspapers was a widespread weakness that afflicted many of the best newspapers in the nation to some degree. Even some newspapers that did consistent initial investigative work did not follow up aggressively in the coverage of prosecutions and reforms. Often pockets of half-exposed corruption continued to fester and spread their poison through the investigative, prosecution, and judicial machinery.

Because of a lack of intelligent follow through by the press, the public is often lulled into a belief that the criminals have been prosecuted and reform started. In fact, usually only the minor crooks are penalized; the major crooks are soon back in business using their power to persecute the honest whistle blowers.

Reading 18: Blueprint for Investigation

Although many contributed to the success of IRE's Arizona project, it was Bob Greene's experience and leadership in planning and execution that made the project an excellent blueprint for any newspaper investigation. If that blueprint is followed intelligently by reasonably experienced reporters and editors, it will bring success on any minor or major investigation. The following numbered paragraphs represent the accumulated wisdom of successful investigative reporters from Lincoln Steffens and Ida Tarbell through Paul Y. Anderson, Ted Link, George Mills, and George Bliss. The blueprint can be used as a guide by an individual reporter, can be used by an editor to check the thoroughness of a reporter, or can be used by a team.

1. *Read all the news stories directly related to the subject of the investigation.* Greene read all of Don Bolles stories from the *Arizona Republic* and all related stories in the *Arizona Republic* and the afternoon sister paper, the *Phoenix Gazette.*

2. *Talk with other reporters and editors who have dealt with the subject, and read all governmental reports and books that may deal with the subject.* Greene contacted the *Arizona Star* in Tucson, talked with the editors and reporters who had knowledge of organized crime activities, and reviewed 13 pounds of unpublished memorandums as well as the newspaper clippings related to the inquiry. Greene also contacted members of IRE, including Jack Anderson and Les Whitten, for all information that might in any way be related to the operations of organized crime and politics in

Arizona. Anderson and Whitten supplied a huge package of research as well as unexplored leads on organized crime in Arizona. House and Senate crime committee files were reviewed for Arizona activities, and books were studied for information on Arizona's relation to the crime syndicate.

3. *Interview law enforcement and prosecution officials at all levels who have responsibility or knowledge on the subject, and assess their knowledge and their reliability.* With *Newsday's* crime expert, Tom Renner, working undercover, Greene explored the reliability and honesty of various law enforcement and prosecution officials at local, state, and federal levels. He concluded that many of the local law enforcement, prosecution, and judicial officials were corrupt or were compromised to a sufficient degree to raise serious questions about their reliability. The list of those with total reliability included Arizona Attorney General Bruce Babbitt, the members of a small intelligence unit on the Phoenix police department, the Arizona state narcotics strike force, the top officials in a recently reorganized Arizona Department of Public Safety, two sheriff's offices, and the FBI. The office of the United States Attorney was a question mark as far as Greene was concerned, as were the Phoenix police department, many sheriffs, and nearly all local prosecutors.

4. *Enlist help and cooperation from all institutions—academic, business, or otherwise—that may have a natural interest in a thorough examination of the targeted area.* Greene contacted the departments of journalism at the University of Arizona and at Arizona State University to make arrangements for each school to assign six of the best students to the investigation with college credit for the work done on the project. He also arranged financial assistance from the Arizona Association of Industries without relinquishing the independence of the investigation.

5. *Analyze the problem and try to break it down into a series of manageable projects. Try to distinguish between those projects that are certain to develop and those that are long shots.* Greene in consultation with the staff, laid out a dozen areas for new investigations or for further investigations where it appeared that there were unexplored leads that might provide useful information. As the project moved forward, each segment was under constant analysis. Some projects were abandoned because they were long shots or because the detailed work required for success was beyond the capacity of the IRE team due to the practical time limitations on the investigation.

6. *Write memoranda on key interviews, and keep copies of public records or reliable condensations of relevant information*

from documents complete with dates and docket numbers. Greene required written memoranda each day from experienced and inexperienced investigative reporters that gave the substance of interviews and the substance of documents examined. Copies of documents were attached in some instances. When the information was from a confidential informant, the name of the informant was coded in the reports and only Greene and the reporter who obtained the information knew the identity of the informant.

7. *Engage in a constant review of the information with others on the project, with an editor, or with someone who is knowledgeable on the law or the facts.* It is easy to become so involved with one facet of an investigation that an obvious connection or lead is overlooked. Greene scheduled a meeting at 8 A.M. each day for a review of the memoranda that had been given to him the previous evening and for a detailed discussion of what each reporter planned to do in the way of record examination and interviews during the next day. This permitted the combined wisdom of all of the reporters to focus on the names and patterns in all parts of the project. Greene, with the total overview, was available for consultation with all reporters on the strategy and timing of interviews for the best results. He was also available for consultation with the least experienced reporters on the methods of verifying informant testimony through city, county, state, or federal records. These records were meshed with interviews of others who might corroborate all or any part of an informant's account.

8. *Have an experienced editor analyze the first draft of the work to see if it needs amplification or clarification to have maximum impact on the average reader.* Greene subjected his own work as well as the work of even the most experienced reporters on the project to revamping and rewriting by such experienced editors as Tony Insolia and Jack Driscoll of the *Boston Globe.* He then had it scrutinized and reworded by the project lawyers and the lawyers for a number of newspapers that planned to run the series.

STUDENT WORK PROJECT SUGGESTION

Read the 32-part series on "The Arizona Story" as printed by *Newsday* and other newspapers in March 1977. Read Robert W. Green's speech "Not in Vengeance, But to Inform" given at the John Peter Zenger Award ceremony on January 21, 1978. Write a brief analysis of each of the articles from a standpoint of the soundness of the documentation.

34 THE CONTINUING PROBLEM AND OPPORTUNITY

The continuing problems of government provide the press with great opportunities for responsible public service reporting. The "seven rules" for sound investigative reporting provide guidelines for fairness that will minimize the chances of serious error and, if adhered to in a conscientious manner, could do much to restore press credibility.

THE PRESS—FAULTS, VIRTUES, AND OPPORTUNITIES

Aggressive press coverage in the wake of Watergate forced Congressional investigations of the Federal Bureau of Investigation (FBI) and the Central Intelligence Agency (CIA). Because of the exposure of the tactics of Richard Nixon and the other Watergate coverup conspirators, there was wide concern about how the FBI and CIA could be used to obstruct the proper administration of justice for political goals. There was little inclination for the press to muckrake itself and to demonstrate how its naivete, its venality, its laxity, and its lack of follow through had contributed to the FBI and CIA abuses of power over a period of decades.

With Regard to Government Investigative Organizations

Past laxity of the press with regard to the abuse of power by the FBI and CIA presented an opportunity for a whole new group of investigative reporters, led by Seymour Hersh, who had the audacity to suggest that generals, admirals, cabinet, and subcabinet level officials gave false testimony and fabricated documents for use in court or before congressional committees.

From time to time, the crusaders against the arrogance of the FBI and CIA were too indiscriminate, arrogant, or illogical in their criticisms and did their own cause a disservice. Some of the press coverage of the abuses, as well as imagined abuses, of power by the FBI and CIA was shrill, out of perspective, and irresponsible to the point of interfering with proper legal functions of those important organizations. But, most of those damaged by the unjust criticism or questionable prosecutions were in fact, guilty of other serious crimes of obstruction of justice for which the statute of limitations or other technical problems barred prosecution. In general, it was a good thing that the unaccountability of the untouchables at the FBI and CIA was brought to an end.

The major harm done by press excesses in the FBI and CIA investigations was to its own image when reporting or comments were not sound and in a balanced perspective. Errors and unjust criticism provided even the guilty government officials with an excuse to lash out at the press and win a measure of public sympathy. There was wide public understanding that an effective government must have an FBI, or similar organization, or face internal chaos, and that the reality of international conditions requires the maintenance of a reasonably efficient espionage organization to counter the Soviet KGB and the intelligence agencies of other potential adversaries.

It is the responsibility of the investigative reporter and Congress to keep a constant surveillance on these organizations for evidence that they are violating the law or otherwise overstepping the bounds of their charters. Over more than 30 years, evidence of abuses of power and outright law violations by the FBI and the CIA had surfaced periodically in civil and criminal court suits, in civil service hearings, and in congressional hearings. But, little attention was given to the complaints of former CIA officials, like Hans Tofte, who complained of burglaries or other illegal actions by the CIA and obstruction of justice by the FBI. In 1966, Senator Eugene McCarthy, the Minnesota Democrat, found it impossible to arouse the Congress or the Washington press corps with hard evidence that the CIA was using its secrecy to hide law violations in burglarizing Tofte's Georgetown home.

With Respect to Major Departments in Government

Likewise, the Washington press was superficial in treating major defense scandals and thoroughly negligent in failing to follow through on such continuing outrages as the TFX contract and the C-5A scandal. The press consistently permitted stories to be handled by the Pentagon reporters who had a built-in conflict of interest. Their editors required that they stay on good terms with the corrupt and compromised bosses of the military establishment. It was naive to expect that reporters, who must depend upon the Pentagon brass for the bulk of their stories, would feel free to pursue aggressively evidence of either corruption or mismanagement. It is easier to accept a press handout without question, even though the official response was written to deceive or cloud the issue of responsibility for manipulated contracts or false testimony.

Although there have been some major exceptions, the general pattern of press coverage at the Pentagon and the State Department has been one of cozy relationships and a total disinterest in pursuing any evidence of mismanagement or fraud. This laxity persisted through the Truman, Eisenhower, Kennedy, Johnson, Nixon, Ford, and Carter administrations, and I have reason to believe that there will be no substantial change now or in the future. For the young reporter this negligence at the Pentagon is an ever-present opportunity for vigorous investigative reporting comparable to the opportunity that Lincoln Steffens found in the police station in New York City before the turn of the century. The opportunity that exists at the Defense Department also exists at the State Department where the diplomatic correspondents are part of the foreign service establishment and are even more protective of the so-called statesmen who "leak" them the routine on a confidential basis.

The scandals at the General Services Administration (GSA) that emerged in 1978 and 1979 are typical of the kinds of festering corruption that can be found in essentially any agency of government by any reasonably intelligent investigative reporter. It is now well recognized that the GSA, an agency created in 1949 to reform government buying practices, started to go wrong within a few months after it was established to centralize the purchase of government supplies and real estate.

RECENT SOFTNESS IN INVESTIGATIVE REPORTING

Because the Washington press corps concentrated its efforts on Watergate-related investigation, such as the abuses of power at the FBI and CIA, evidence of serious corruption and mismanagement in other programs was virtually ignored. Such crimes were regarded as too mundane or as too complicated and uninteresting to have much impact upon editors or on the general public. There were a number of attitudes expressed by editors and reporters that influenced this post-Watergate laxity.

First and foremost, the two-year press crusade that led to the resignation of President Nixon was a hard act to follow. The pilfering of a few thousand dollars or a few million seemed like petty larceny by comparison, even though cumulative measurable dollar loss to the taxpayers was often far in excess of that of Watergate.

Second, many of the nation's editors decided that their readers and the institutions of democracy could not stand further shock waves so they did not publish scandal stories. They printed only sharply edited and meaningless accounts of serious scandals in nearly all the departments of the federal government.

Third, Washington reporters, frustrated and discouraged by the lack of editorial attention to serious problems of corruption and mismanagement below the cabinet and subcabinet level, failed to follow through aggressively on evidence of maladministration of medicare and medicaid programs. They soft-pedalled million-dollar ripoffs in meat purchases by the military and by the Agriculture Department and serious retaliation against honest whistle-blowers in the departments of Defense, State, Treasury, HUD, HEW, Agriculture, Labor, Interior, Transportation, Commerce, the Civil Service Commission and the General Services Administration.

Fourth, the members of congressional investigating committees and the staffs of those committees became discouraged by the lack of press attention to serious problems of mismanagement and corruption, or the arrogant actions of executive branch officials when asked to produce records by the General Accounting Office (GAO), or by congressional committees with oversight responsibility. Senate and House investigations of serious mismanagement and corruption in health and educational programs were virtually ignored by every news organization except the Scripps-Howard Washington bureau. The coverage by harried reporters for the Associated Press and United Press were often superficial and scanty, and stories were treated as local issues rather than as a significant part of a national problem.

Fifth, because of the lack of press attention, there was no effective follow through by most congressional committees, so the corruption took deeper roots. The crooks and mismanagers dug in and retaliated against those who had given forthright testimony on the involvement of superiors in falsification of documents, perjury, and obstruction of justice. The classic case was the ordeal of A. Ernest Fitzgerald, the Air Force cost analyst, who engaged in a seven-year fight to regain his defense department job while those who were responsible for mismanagement, falsification of documents, and perjury were promoted to higher positions. For the most part, press coverage was superficial in dealing with the fully documented outrages against Fitzgerald and the arrogance of the Air Force bureaucracy.

Although the case of Ernie Fitzgerald became the classic case of subtle and not so subtle persecution of an honest government employee who had the audacity to tell Congress the truth, there were others. Dozens of officials in the Indian Health Service, the Office of Education, the meat grading service in the Agriculture Department, the Internal Revenue Service, and in the GSA suffered similar indignities and persecution with even less attention to their plight.

The multibillion-dollar GSA scandals, estimated by many to be the worst dollar scandals in American history, did not surface for most of the press and the public until the *Washington Post* gave them priority attention in 1978. By that time, one of the *Post's* most able investigative reporters, Ron Kessler, had been working on evidence of GSA mismanagement and corruption for more than five years. Over the years many of us had written about parts of the GSA corruption with varying degrees of success, but we were distracted from the depth investigation that was needed by other, more pressing stories.

The combination of Ron Kessler's meticulous investigative reporting and the clout of the *Washington Post* was needed to get proper national attention for the hundreds of major and minor frauds that give the GSA scandals the potential for being the worst frauds in the history of the nation. As the pattern of false billings for services and for equipment never delivered was noted in the stories by Kessler and others and in the indictments returned against GSA officials, I was reminded of the Polk County fraud trials, except that the false billing frauds were measured in millions of dollars rather than in thousands.

THE NEED FOR AN HONEST, DEDICATED, AND RESPECTED PRESS

On every hand it was apparent that frauds and mismanagement were draining billions of dollars from every government agency, from programs for the underprivileged, and even from the major defense weapon systems. Primary responsibility to expose and eradicate these debilitating frauds is on the executive branch of the government and on the oversight committees of Congress. But, realistically, the public cannot count upon any administration to do a strict job of policing itself, nor can it count on even-handed policing by the politically partisan investigating committees of Congress.

In the end, the public is dependent upon the objectivity, the accuracy, and the balance of the newsmen who report on political and governmental affairs. Thus, the press is the lifeline of democracy in reporting upon the use, misuse, and abuse of power by those entrusted with the responsibility for spending more than $600 billion a year.

It is a big job. It may be too big a job for the American press to handle effectively, but it certainly cannot handle it competently in the haphazard, venal, superficial, and partisan style that has dominated the past. Publishers, editors, and reporters must develop a professionalism with consistent high standards in dealing with governmental affairs and politics. Newspapers and television must resist the temptation to permit the entertainment value of exaggerations, distortions, and oversimplifications to destroy the credibility of serious news accounts.

What Can be Done

The low public opinion of the press is obvious on every hand. It has been registered in public opinion polls, including the 1973 polls by Louis Harris and George Gallup in which the newspapers ranked far down the line among public and business institutions on questions of respect and credibility. Robert P. Clark, Executive Editor of the *Louisville Courier-Journal* and *Times,* while speaking in 1978 at Washington and Lee University, declared the institution of the press had developed some "grave problems" in credibility.

"Many journalists seem unable to see the flaws," Clark said. "Or if they do, they refuse to recognize them. It is the public which, more and more, is holding the cracks up for examination. And the public, after all—in the democracy we cherish—will hold the upper hand, the opinions of journalists notwithstanding. . . . What I am talking about is our credibility, our believability. Newspapers are in trouble, not only because their content is no longer of interest to many, or because people no longer have time for us, or because our readers have 'already seen it on TV'. . . . We are in trouble also because people do not trust us as much as they used to. Our image is tarnishing."

Charles Seib, the press ombudsman for the *Washington Post,* wrote in 1977 that the public has "a pervasive distrust of the press. . . . Many readers feel like the media generally, newspapers and broadcasters alike, are on a destructive rampage. They feel that the zeal that exposed Watergate is being directed toward all public institutions (except the press), and they find it frightening." Seib concluded, "One way to reduce this distrust is for the press to examine some of the present practices and to be more responsive to its public and more open about its operations and its failings. If public scrutiny is healthy for the other institutions of society, it should be healthy for the press itself."

Robert W. Greene, speaking in the same ethics forum at Washington and Lee University, declared in 1978 that "the American media have finally risen to the ethical level of a Times Square pimp hustling 12-year-old girls." Greene, Suffolk Editor for *Newsday*, was speaking for his more than 25 years of experience in the front line of solid investigative reporting and in the wake of his directing of the Arizona project. "In this broadside," Greene explained, "I do not describe all journalists. There is an insistent minority that adheres to a standard of mother's-knee ethic in both personal and professional life. And we are infinitely improved as a craft over the era when we universally accepted bribes, free trips, and free meals as a matter of course."

Greene spoke of the need for high ethical standards in the area of investigative reporting. He disagreed sharply with a *New York Times* reporter who had been quoted in *More* magazine as saying he would "lie, cheat, and steal" to get a good story. Greene said that it was against his own personal ethical standards to do any of those things for a story. He could conceive of some rare occasions when he might use deceptive or illegal tactics if the story itself met "the test of compelling public urgency." In discussing and analyzing thoughtfully the tough ethical questions that the investigative reporter must face, Greene said ethics in media is not a problem confined to investigative reporting.

"What of the newspaper publishers and other media moguls who ignore their public service responsibilities because stenographic reporting—mere reporting of form—is less controversial and far more profitable? And what about the publishers, editors, and reporters who suppress unfavorable news about their friends and protectors but ruthlessly pursue others? ... Even more insidious is the publisher, editor, or reporter so convinced that he possesses the right view that he dedicates himself or herself to the absolute erasure of opposing views," Greene declared.

A Growing Danger

More than 50 years ago, Walter Lippmann warned that "increasingly angry disillusionment about the press" should not be disregarded by wise publishers, or Congress might some day "in a fit of temper, egged on by an outraged public opinion," put the axe to freedom of the press. It is this continuing and growing danger of government action encroaching upon the free press that makes it essential for the press to establish sound investigative techniques and standards of fair play that are consistently applied without political partisanship or bias.

The press must not for one moment let up on its aggressive policing of the actions of government agencies, but it must demonstrate that it can be fair, that it can be nonpartisan, and that it can be responsible in the handling of its heavy responsibility in public service reporting. Although the press has struggled mightily to establish workable ethical standards, it has not been able to reconcile any system of discipline or control with the concept of a truly free press. The results have been generalized codes about searching for "truth" that are, in fact, meaningless. However, there are various procedural rules in story development that can be general guides to sound investigative reporting.

THE SEVEN BASIC RULES

Rule One: Avoid political partisanship

You will cut off 50 per cent of your effectiveness if you investigate only one political party or even have a special leaning toward investigations of one political party. Such an attitude will hurt your credibility. There are as many Republican crooks as there are Democratic crooks and vice versa. And, if you haven't noticed it, there are a large number of *bipartisan* crooks, who have figured how to get a hand in the government treasury regardless of whether Democrats or Republicans are in power.

Rule Two: In seeking facts and answers make a conscientious and determined effort to be equally aggressive whether the public officials involved are men you admire or distrust

You will do your friend a favor by asking him tough, direct questions because you will be demonstrating that he will be held accountable. This will prod him to be a better public official than he might be if you are too indulgent in excusing him or disregard his errors. Equally, it is wise to give those you dislike or distrust the benefit of the doubt as you embark on your investigation. This is your protection against jumping to an unwarranted conclusion that can undermine the soundness of your whole investigation.

Remind yourself constantly that, if the case against the public official is really there, it will emerge eventually and his deceptions and falsehoods will weigh doubly against him. This is as true in an investigation of a mayor, a county commissioner, a sheriff, a governor, or a congressman as it was in the case of Richard Nixon who told various falsehoods about Watergate.

Leaning overboard to be fair is never harmful to your investigative efforts. It protects you against libel. It makes you more credible. Above all, common decency and fair play are as basic as due process of law. This is particularly important in those areas of the country, or in those localities, where there is only one newspaper or where there are two or more newspapers under one control.

Rule Three: Know your subject, whether it is a problem of city, county, state, or federal government, or whether it involves big labor or big business

In preparing for an important interview, do your homework on the facts, the laws, and the individuals involved in your study. (This does not mean that you know only enough to parrot a few wise questions fed by a politically partisan opponent. Nor is it enough simply to read the clipping file and jot off a quick note or two that may or may not be in context.) If the subject is important enough for you to seek a serious interview, it is important enough to consult the law, to study the history of the agency, and to have a reasonably full grasp of the background and general motivations of the persons involved.

The rule of knowing your subject cannot be overemphasized. If you are in a highly technical area or are dealing with a complicated fact situation, you may make unintentional mistakes simply because you did not understand what you heard. It is also possible that you will not recognize violations of the law. The poorly informed or half-informed reporter is a sitting duck for a snow job.

Rule Four: Don't exaggerate or distort the facts or the law

There is enough wrong in our society that you don't have to fabricate or exaggerate anything. This is particularly true of the operations of any of the agencies of the federal government. If you do a proper job of investigating and follow through on virtually any federal agency or department, the truth will be more shocking than any fiction you might dream up. Watergate and the investigations that followed dealing with the CIA and the FBI should have driven this point home so it will not be forgotten.

Remember, efforts to sensationalize will discredit your investigation in the long run.

When in doubt, leave it out.

Rule Five: Deal straight across the board with your sources and investigation subjects alike

Ask straightforward questions that go to the heart of the problem, and do it in a serious manner. Don't use tricks or pretense to get people off guard. Don't use a false name or identity, and particularly do not impersonate a law enforcement official.

If you promise to keep a confidence, keep your word even if it means personal jeopardy. Above all, don't go around blabbing to your press colleagues the identity of a confidential informant. If you deal straight with the subjects of your investigation, it is quite likely that they will be your best sources of inside information at some future time. Respect and trust will encourage further confidences.

Rule Six: Do not violate the law unless you are prepared to take the consequences

Any time you violate the law to obtain information you develop a vulnerability that can destroy your credibility as well as the story you are pursuing. Such behavior gives errant public officials an opportunity to get the spotlight off of their corruption and mismanagement and to focus instead on excesses of the press. If you give the problem sufficient study, there is usually a legal way to obtain information, although it may require more patience than a burglary. Learn how to use the Freedom of Information Act. Know government records. Know information policies and procedures—information is your business.

If you do not know basic information tools, you are as lacking in competence as a doctor who does not know basic anatomy or a lawyer who does not understand basic rules of evidence.

Rule Seven: Use direct evidence when writing a story that reflects adversely upon anyone and give that person an opportunity for a full response to the questions raised

Direct testimony is often unreliable, even when the witness has no personal interest, and chances for error increase geometrically as your source is removed one, two, or three steps from the event. Do not use hearsay, double hearsay, or triple hearsay evidence to reflect adversely upon anyone just because some reporters have used such evidence and got by with it. Woodward and Bernstein got by with double and triple hearsay in *The Final Days* only because Richard Nixon, as a thoroughly discredited former president, was libel proof.

Although interviewing second and third hearsay witnesses may be the best, or even only, avenue open as to what took place, it does not constitute proof of the events or even admissible evidence. It is not sound investigative journalism to go into print with such information, and this is particularly true when it comes from sources you cannot disclose. No story is worth that risk to your credibility and to your reputation.

THE PROFITS IN ETHICAL PRACTICE

If you follow the seven rules given, you will have been accurate, you will have been fair, and you will not be vulnerable to inevitable counterattacks. Nothing I have said here is intended to discourage anyone from aggressive pursuit of the truth that will establish responsibility for corruption and mismanagement. It is simply a warning to test all the facts and the law and then proceed with a firm aggressiveness.

The reporter and editor who adhere strictly to the seven rules in the pursuit, the writing, and the display of a news story will always be on sound ethical grounds. Violation of the rules does not automatically constitute unethical conduct; however, it does open an area of vulnerability that the reporter or editor must be aware exists. Publishers and top editors have the responsibility of creating the kind of nonpartisan atmosphere of freedom in which reporters can use the techniques, traits, and talents of investigative reporting.

The continuing problems of government and the press are ever-present opportunities for those in the press who have the techniques and talents for effective public service journalism. There can never be too much sound investigative reporting. However, there is always too much irresponsible writing that passes itself off as "investigative reporting" and is a discredit to the whole profession. Only a few cases of serious error will permit the corrupters to portray the press as irresponsible and can undermine the work of dozens of sound investigative reporters.

Even sound investigative reporting has enough hazards because it confronts powerful men in labor, business, or politics. You can ride out the storms of protest if you—and in the clutch it has to be you alone—can sustain your case with evidence that is admissible in court.

Effective investigative reporting should not be a slam bang all-out effort "to get" someone, and you should avoid that motivation at all cost even when it becomes bitterly frustrating to deal with deceptions, stonewalling, and outright lies. Effective investigative reporting entails hard work and patient, persistent, pushing forward to obtain documents, to get answers to questions, and to pin the responsibility on the proper officials.

CHECKLIST FOR INVESTIGATIVE REPORTERS

THE COUNTY OR CITY BOARD OF SUPERVISORS, COMMISSIONERS, OR COUNCILMEN

The Budget-Making Process

What is the budget-making process? Usually there is a provision calling for the heads of various departments and offices to submit budget requests to the governing body, and there is a requirement for public notice and a hearing. The supervisors or commissioners compare the budget request with tax income and determine whether to grant the request or cut it. Sometimes budget requests come in lump sums or in several sets of round figures that give no indication of how the money is to be spent. Department heads like to be able to count on a surplus or an overage for an "emergency." This may mean money to hire some political pal for a commissioner—or it could mean actual fraud. Look for corners under which a department head can tuck money away. Make him account for it.

1. What are the checks available on budget requests?
2. Are there public hearings?
3. Do citizens ever bother to question or protest expenditures?
4. Is there a taxpayers association at the local level to make an objective study of budget approvals and tax income? Who heads this group? Is he so close to politics that he is no more than a rubber stamp for the politicians or special interest groups?
5. Laws usually provide for a number of checks to be made on the supervisors and departments. Are these laws being observed?

Conflicts of Interest

What are the side business interests of the commissioners or supervisors? What business are their friends and relatives in? Are commissioners or department heads using their positions in government to give contracts, insurance business, equipment purchases, and so on, to businesses in which they or their close friends or relatives have a financial interest?

1. What is the system in the various departments for purchasing equipment and property and awarding contracts and other business? Are sealed bids required in every department? Is the low bidder too frequently ignored and the contracts made with certain favored business interests?

2. If a few firms have cornered all the business, what are the ties with the commissioners or department heads who are in charge of awarding the business?

3. Are the laws governing the system being observed?

4. If all bids are identical, this is an indication that competitors are conspiring to get a high price and are dividing the pie. If commissioners and department heads accept identical bids, it is an indication that somebody in government may be getting a piece of the pie.

5. Check specification requirements. Specifications, if they are rigged, can throw business in the lap of a favored company and rule out competing companies.

6. How about the system for approving bills for purchases made by the various departments? Is there any loophole in the system to allow false billing? Are dozens or hundreds of bills approved by the commissioners or councilmen by voice vote, without a close, or even occasional spot check on what is being paid for? Is the responsibility for approving bills clearly established?

7. If the commissioners have split up the responsibility among themselves by appointing each other to "committees"—is this practice a legal one?

8. Is the system for approving bills so tight that a criminal case could be brought against a commissioner or a department head found guilty of false billing? Short of that, can you show negligence in the bill-approving procedures?

Liquor and Beer Licenses

What is the system for approving and issuing these licenses? Is a particular councilman or supervisor or commissioner given the right to issue licenses for all bars and taverns and package stores in his district or ward? Are the commissioners ignoring the provisions that prohibit persons with criminal records from operating these establishments? Is there always a public hearing before the licenses are issued so that other businesses and property interests can be heard on whatever objections they may have?

1. Who sells insurance to these establishments? Does the approving commissioner have any connection with the firms which get this insurance business?

2. Who is furnishing juke boxes and pin ball machines and other coin operated devices to these establishments? The coin machine industry is a big one. There are all sorts of possibilities here for shakedown and kickbacks. If the industry in your community is controlled by one or two distributors, it probably means there is a pipeline to the courthouse. Remember this: the tavern or bar cannot operate without the approval of the licensing authority.

SOME COMMON EVILS FOUND IN
LOCAL GOVERNMENT

1. *Payroll padding.* Are the officials charged with setting your departmental budgets using the budgeting process to get political jobs for relatives, friends, or for political hacks? Check the various departments that submit budget requests. Look closely at their payrolls. Who are they employing? Is there anyone closely connected with the commissioners or councilmen who will approve the department budget? When there is a substantial budget increase for a department and it is not explainable, check to see who this particular office recently hired. Does each employee in each office have a function? Are many killing time at taxpayer's expense? Do some have outside jobs at which they work on government time?

2. *Personnel: Hiring and qualifications.* Is there civil service status? If there isn't, these employees are nothing more than campaign workers at election time—and this includes sheriff's deputies and police officers. What is the method of promotion? What is the pay and background of those holding key jobs? Is there adequate protection of the local government retirement fund? Is there a provision to block the hiring of persons advanced in age who will be eligible to retire without making a substantial contribution to the retirement fund? Is there a provision to block phony medical retirements for employees who plan to draw their retirement and go into other work?

3. *Vacations, sick leave, and work time.* Is this centrally supervised and controlled or does each office take care of its own workers without answering to anyone? Is there any possibility that your county or city is paying "dummy" or nonexistent employees hired by the department head who is pocketing the money? The auditor's office is the logical place for central control.

4. *Property management and inventory control.* What special services (such as automobiles) are furnished by the various offices, and what services are bought or paid for? Who gets the business and why? Responsibility for property management should be lodged in the office of the county or city recorder. Any system for pinning down responsibility for property delivered to various offices can be perverted until it is meaningless or until it is completely disregarded. This is a weakness that may encourage false billing.

5. *False billing.* This is a common practice for hiding the misuses of funds in government. Auditing systems won't usually catch it. A false bill accounts for each disbursement so that no shortage shows up in records. The only way to pin this down is for a reporter to make a direct check of all questionable items.

6. *Expenses: Travel per diem, and so on.* Here is where padding can and does frequently occur. It is a simple matter to examine bills of officials when they turn them in after junkets or, in the case of police officers, after returning prisoners or serving warrants. Often there is a stipulated agreement for county or city employees traveling on government business to pick up a stipulated amount for mileage, and this in no way relates to the actual miles traveled.

THE CITY OR COUNTY AUDITOR

1. *Records.* Under most systems records helpful in uncovering some of the "common evils" mentioned above will be found in this office. For instance, this office houses records applying to property management, false billing, travel expense padding, and, certain personnel records. In checking billings, look at bills for long distance toll calls. This may tell a story about whom the office is talking to out of town and out of state. This office may also be helpful in furnishing data pertaining to conflicts of interest on the part of local government officials. Beer bond and cigarette bond records will be recorded here, for example, and may reflect that a company in which a local government offical has an interest on the side, is getting this business because of his position with the county or city.

2. *Accounting for cash fees.* What is the accounting setup on cash fees paid for dog licenses, automobile inspections, and so on?

Is this a mere journal entry, which can be doctored—or ignored? Or is there a cash receipt book and cash register with numbered licenses or stickers handed out to each person who pays money? Will the system permit an employee to pocket fees occasionally—or frequently at license renewal time—without having it show up in some book-balancing procedure?

3. *Financial checks.* Since the employees in this department play a vital role in checking on the finances of other departments, it might be well to take a close look at the outside business interests of the key personnel in this office. Check *them* for possible conflicts of interest.

4. *Assessments.* The county assessment function is often lodged in the office of auditor.

5. *Election machinery.* Examine fraud possibilities in the county election machinery in this office. In some cases, the League of Women Voters may offer a means of assistance in exposing voting irregularities.

THE SHERIFF'S OFFICE AND POLICE DEPARTMENT

1. *Sheriff's fees.* Is the sheriff on salary, or does he receive a salary and fees? What are the possibilities for rackets to increase these fees?

2. *Illegal liquor seizures.* Does the system make it possible for seized and condemned liquor to get back in circulation? This takes a check of records from the time of seizure by law enforcement officials through the court condemnation to the actual destruction with witnesses. A basic question is this: Is seized property identified by serial number or otherwise at the original time of seizure?

3. *Illegal gambling equipment.* Apply the same standards of checks on the system of seizure and final condemnation. Are the serial numbers on slot machines or other gambling equipment recorded at the seizure and on the condemnation order?

4. *Jail practices.* How free are the prisoners in the jail? Can a trusty go home for the night? Can a trusty roam the streets or hold a job? Are there any other special accommodations for special prisoners with political pull? These things do happen.

OFFICE OF THE CLERK OF COURT

1. *Probate records.* Obtain all the blanks on information required to be filed in connection with the settlement of estates. Here is precise information on inheritances. (The Governor Hanley

case came from these records as well as a fraud in the welfare department real estate division.)

2. *Divorce records.* There is much financial detail available in doing a complete job of examining the petitions and testimony in divorce cases. Run the dockets. Get the original petitions and testimony. Get the names of the witnesses who may have further information. Don't rely on old clippings.

3. *Marriage records.* Obtain the marriage blanks for the information required on a marriage record. What books are kept?

4. *Criminal indictments and past grand jury reports.* Run the docket for disposition of indictments. Examine original indictments for details on the crime charged, the witnesses before the grand jury, and other similar data including attorneys of record and the judge. Review testimony. Past grand jury reports may show long-standing evils and corruption that have been ignored or have been exposed and corrected but have been creeping back in.

5. *Warrant handling.* Are cases being dismissed in court because warrants are disappearing or because warrants are being made out improperly through ignorance, inefficiency, or through intentional mistakes? Are warrants being dismissed in court because the clerk fails properly to issue subpoenas for witnesses or fails to notify police officers who are prosecuting witnesses of the date of trial? Are John Doe warrants or fictitious names being used as a gimmick to keep names of prominent or notorious figures with courthouse "pull" off criminal files and out of newspapers?

6. *Bail bonds.* Check the property listed as surety for professional bonding companies to make certain that it has true value. Make regular checks of forfeitures to make certain that the clerk and the courts are making bondsmen pay up on their forfeitures. Are certain bondsmen favored by the clerk in awarding big bonds? This indicates a possible kickback.

7. *Witness fees.* Police officers, deputies, and constables may be collecting witness fee money for cases that are settled by defense attorneys without trial by plea of guilt. If officers are collecting witness fees for cases settled on "cop-out day" there probably is a kickback to somebody in the clerk's office who makes out checks and vouchers. Check the list of subpoenaed witnesses against checks or vouchers issued to witnesses to make sure the clerk or one of his deputies isn't inventing "dummy" witnesses. Then check subpoenaed witnesses against witnesses who actually showed up at certain trials to make sure that the clerk's office isn't issuing dummy subpoenas to cover dummy witnesses.

8. *Jury selection.* In most systems, the clerk of the court has the responsibility of keeping jury lists up to date and furnishing lists to

the court. There is always a danger of a stacked panel of veniremen if the person in charge of this function is susceptible to pressure or corruption. Your local prosecuting attorney is not always above being a party to this stacking. If a case is important enough and time available, run a quick check of the criminal records of all jurors. In some jurisdictions it is commonplace for a gambler to get on gambling-case juries and a strong union man to get on labor case juries.

9. *Civil suits.* Run the docket for any civil disputes. Nearly any kind of a damage suit or other litigation will include some material of importance. It may contain financial detail that, at the time, seemed uninteresting. It may include a cross examination of the person in question that will produce some leads.

THE RECORDER'S OFFICE

1. *Filing fees.* These represent about the only possibility for unjust enrichment in this office. Examine the fee recording system for the normal loopholes.

2. *Service fees.* Such fees, as for photostatic copies of records, may be loosely handled. In some states there is no statutory regulation on fees for photostatic copies but the charge is at the discretion of the recorder. Examine this for control of supplies paid for by the taxpayers. Also determine what kinds of records are kept on the income. Are there any business firms that are making a good thing out of having the county do the work for them?

3. *Corporate records.* In some states these records are in the office of the secretary of state. In other states there may be a provision for filing corporate papers with the county recorder or in some other county office. Check the system. Obtain the law on the general information that is required from corporations.

4. *Personal property mortgage records.* The recorder's office is usually the place for filing such mortgage records as those on automobiles. Here is an opportunity for an excellent index to the financial status of any public official. When did he buy his car? What did he trade on it? How big a mortgage did he take on? Can he handle it on his salary as set under the law? How much cash did he have?

5. *Real estate mortgage records.* Here is another excellent index on the financial status of public officials or others. The tax stamps can be overbought, but they will usually give a rough idea of the cost of real estate. These records can also give you details on any sale of a prior home from which an official may have received funds

for making a down payment. Pieced together, these facts should give you a pretty good idea of whether there were any large amounts of cash involved in the transaction. The schedule for payment on the mortgage is often included, or can be figured with reasonable accuracy. This can be balanced against the office holder's salary. Is it a reasonable payment under the circumstances?

6. *Veterans discharge papers.* In some states a war veteran can record his discharge papers and can obtain photostatic copies of the discharge through the county recorder. This is an excellent source of background material on the service record, and it may include other material you want.

THE SCHOOL SYSTEM

1. *Building contracts.* Who builds your schools? How are the contracts awarded—by sealed bids or by random selection of the board? Is the low bidder frequently overlooked and a favored builder selected? Does the school board give the board member in whose district the school is built the say-so about who builds the school—or about who teaches in the school? And how are the architects selected?

2. *Purchasing.* Who sells your county its equipment and supplies for the schools? Check out everything from school buses to stationery. Are sealed bids required for such purchasing? Does the business office of the school system make the decision? If purchasing in the school system is a closed operation find out why.

THE HIGHWAY DEPARTMENT

1. Where does this department buy its equipment? There is room for graft and kickbacks in everything from building machinery and gravel to center-line paint.

2. Find out where the road-building machinery is operating. You may find out that it is being used to pave driveways for county supervisors or the county highway department officials.

THE TAX ASSESSOR

Check out property owned by county officials and influential political figures. Are they getting special considerations in the way of rock-bottom assessments?

CITY OR COUNTY HEALTH DEPARTMENT

In most cases the health departments have charge of maintaining standards in city and county hospitals. Sometimes in public hospitals these standards are a joke. Sometimes they exist only on paper. The health departments also have the responsibility of rating restaurants, hotels, and motels and making them maintain standards of sanitation. If you have sufficient evidence (particularly pictures) that sanitary conditions in local restaurants are below par and can put enough pressure on the city government, it can request the U.S. Public Health Service (USPHS) to get an official investigation as the basis for writing a new restaurant sanitation code. In such a survey, USPHS will rate local restaurants against its own scale, will name names, and cite specific details.

A FULL PERSONNEL PROBE

1. *Birth records* at the bureau of vital statistics. Authentic records of birth are a necessary *starting point.* The names of father and mother can be used to run mortgage records on their *economic status,* and for examination of probate records if they are deceased.
2. *Marriage records* at the office of the clerk of court.
3. *Divorce records* at the office of the clerk of court.
4. *Criminal record* in the docket of the municipal court or state court.
5. *Civil court disputes* in the office of municipal court or state court.
6. *War veterans discharge* in the office of the county recorder.
7. *Former work records,* if available.
8. *Personal property mortgages* in the office of the county recorder.
9. *Real estate mortgages* in the office of the county recorder.
10. *Tax liens* in the office of the county recorder.
11. *Bankruptcy action* in the office of the clerk of federal court.
12. *Federal tax disputes* of civil nature in federal court or U.S. Tax Court.
13. *Automobile registration and driver licenses* in the office of the county treasurer.
14. *Property assessments* in the office of the county treasurer with more detail in the office of the county assessor.
15. *Corporation records* in the office of the secretary of state or the office of the county recorder.

In certain cases, the following additional checks may be indicated:

1. *House Committee on Un-American Activities* reports.

2. *Kefauver Committee* reports.

3. *Immigration records* through nearest district director, Immigration and Naturalization Service, Department of Justice.

4. *Election records* in the office of the county recorder and federal election office.

5. *Credit rating* through your own front office.

6. *State Department Passport Division.*

7. *McClellan Committee Reports,* especially with regard to Portland, Oregon; Scranton, Pennsylvania; Gary, Indiana; Chicago; Tennessee; Michigan. These hearings and reports are indexed.

Suggested Reading List

Anderson, Jack, with James Boyd. *Confessions of a Muckraker.* New York: Random House, Inc., 1979.

Baker, Ray Stannard. *American Chronicle: The Autobiography of Ray Stannard Baker.* New York: Charles Scribner's Sons, 1945.

Behrens, John C. *Typewriter Guerrillas.* Chicago: Nelson-Hall, Inc., 1977.

Bernstein, Carl, and Bob Woodward. *All the President's Men.* New York: Simon & Schuster, Inc., 1974.

Bolch, Judith, and Kay Miller. *Investigative and In-Depth Reporting.* New York: Hastings House Publishers, 1978.

Borkin, Joseph. *The Corrupt Judge: An Inquiry into Bribery and Other High Crimes and Misdemeanors in the Federal Courts.* New York: Carlson N. Potter, Inc., 1962.

Crouse, Timothy. *The Boys on the Bus.* New York: Random House, Inc., 1972.

Downie, Leonard, Jr. *The New Muckrakers.* Washington, D.C.: The New Republic Book Company, Inc., 1976.

Duscha, Julius. *Taxpayers' Hayride.* Boston: Little Brown and Company, 1964.

Dygert, James H. *The Investigative Journalist: Folk Heroes of a New Era.* Englewood Cliffs, N.J.: Prentice-Hall, Inc., 1976.

Fitzgerald, A. Ernest. *The High Priests of Waste (The C-5A Scandal).* New York: W. W. Norton & Company, Inc., 1972.

Hohenberg, John. *The Pulitzer Prize Story.* New York: Columbia University Press, 1959.

Kwitny, Jonathan. *Vicious Circles.* New York: W. W. Norton & Company, Inc., 1979.

Lyons, Louis M. (ed.). *Reporting The News: Selections From Neiman Report.* Cambridge Mass.: The Belknap Press of Harvard University Press, 1965.

Miller, Norman C. *The Great Salad Oil Scandal.* New York: Coward McCann & Geohegan, Inc., 1965.

Mintz, Morton, and Jerry S. Cohen. *Power, Inc.* New York: The Viking Press, Inc., 1976; Bantam edition, 1977.

Mitford, Jessie. *Poison Penmanship.* New York: Alfred A. Knopf, 1979.

Mollenhoff, Clark R. *Washington Cover-Up.* New York: Doubleday & Company, Inc., 1962.

Mollenhoff, Clark R. *Despoilers of Democracy.* New York: Doubleday & Company, Inc., 1965.

Mollenhoff, Clark R. *Tentacles of Power: The Story of Jimmy Hoffa.* Cleveland and New York: The World Publishing Company, 1965.

Mollenhoff, Clark R. *The Pentagon.* New York: G. P. Putnam's Sons, 1967; Pinnacle Books, 1972.

Mollenhoff, Clark R. *Strike Force.* Englewood Cliffs, N.J.: Prentice-Hall, Inc., 1972.

Mollenhoff, Clark R. *Game Plan For Disaster.* New York: W. W. Norton & Company, Inc., 1976.

Mollenhoff, Clark R. *The Man Who Pardoned Nixon.* New York: St. Martin's Press, Inc., 1976.

Mollenhoff, Clark R. *The President Who Failed.* New York: Macmillan Publishing Co., 1980.

Murphy, Harry J. *Where's What: Sources of Information For Federal Investigators.* New York: Warner Books, Inc., 1976.

Nader, Ralph, Peter Petkas, and Kate Blackwell. *Whistle Blowing.* New York: Grossman Publishers, Inc., 1972; Bantam edition, 1972.

Nelson, Jack, and Jack Bass. *The Orangeburg Massacre.* Cleveland and New York: The World Publishing Company, 1970.

Ryther, Philip I. *Who's Watching The Airways?* Garden City, N.Y.: Doubleday & Company, Inc., 1972.

Schwartz, Bernard. *The Professor and The Commissions.* New York: Alfred A. Knopf, Inc., 1959.

Seigenthaler, John. *A Search for Justice.* Nashville/London: Aurora Publishers, Inc. 1971.

Semonche, John E. *Ray Stannard Baker: A Quest For Democracy in Modern America, 1870–1918.* Chapel Hill, N.C.: University of North Carolina Press, 1969.

Steffens, J. Lincoln. *The Autobiography of Lincoln Steffens.* 2 vols. New York: Harcourt, Brace & World, Inc., 1931.

Sullivan, Mark. *Our Times.* (Vol. I) "The Turn of the Century." New York: Charles Scribner's Sons, 1926.

Sullivan, Mark. *Our Times.* (Vol. II) "America Finding Herself." New York: Charles Scribner's Sons, 1927.

Sullivan, Mark. *Our Times.* (Vol. III) "Pre-War America." New York: Charles Scribner's Sons, 1930.

Sullivan, Mark. *Our Times.* (Vol. VI) "The Twenties." New York: Charles Scribner's Sons, 1935.

Tarbell, Ida M. *All in The Day's Work*. New York: The Macmillan Company, 1939.

Theim, George. *The Hodge Scandal*. New York: St. Martin's Press, Inc., 1963.

Vaughn, Robert G. *The Spoiled System: A Call For Civil Service Reform*. New York: Charterhouse, 1975.

Wendland, Michael F. *The Arizona Project*. Kansas City: Sheed Andrews & McMell, Inc., Subsidiary of Universal Press Syndicate, 1977.

Werner, M. R., and John Star. *Teapot Dome*. New York: The Viking Press, Inc., 1959.

Williams, Paul N. *Investigative Reporting and Editing*. Englewood Cliffs, N.J.: Prentice-Hall, Inc., 1978.

INDEX

Adams, Sherman, 235, 236, 238–44, 255
Agriculture Department, Billie Sol Estes scandal involving, 246–58
  commodity market scandals and, 306, 307, 312–16
  security risk claim by, 205–15
  Soviet wheat deal and, 312, 313
Air Force investigation, 162–66. *See also* Pentagon
Akers, Chester B., 71, 110
Alcohol Tax Unit (ATU), 138–42, 151–52, 179–81
Alderman, Jerome, 271–72, 275
American Lithofold Corporation, 179–80
Anderson, C. Elmer, 198
Anderson, Jack, 241, 347–48
Anderson, Paul Y., 59, 226
Andrews, Bert, 149, 150
Anthan, George, 315, 316
Antifreeze case, 142–45, 158
Arizona project, 339–49
Arrest records, 13, 14, 23
Assessments, irregularities in and revaluations, 129–35, 368
Auditor, city or county, checklist for, 364–65
Automobiles. *See also* Welfare department fraud
  black market, story on, 61–63, 72
  war surplus, fraud involving, 108–11

Backinski, Eugene, 327
Badhwar, Inderjit, 268
Baggot and Morrison firm, 308–11
Baillie, J. F., 65, 118, 122

Baker, Bobby, case involving, 280–304
Baldwin, Hanson, 264, 265
Barnes, Bart, 321
Barron, John, 290, 298
Bartlett, Charles, 262
Beardsley, William S., 118, 137, 140
Beck, Dave, 198, 201, 219–22, 226, 227
Bender, George, 202, 220
Bennett, Myron J., 114, 115–17
Benson, Ezra Taft, 205, 206, 207, 209–14
Benton, William, 168, 169, 170
Beveridge, George, 272
Bernstein, Carl, 5, 331, 359
Billing, false and double, 120–24
Bittman, William O., 297, 298, 301, 302, 303
Blair, William, 213, 240
Bliss, George, 341, 347
Bliss, William L., 111, 112
Blue, Robert D., 106, 107, 108, 110, 118
Board of supervisors, checklist for dealing with, 361–63
Bolich, Daniel, 179
Bolles, Don, 16, 340–41, 342, 344, 346
Boyle, William M., Jr., 179
Bradlee, Benjamin, 342
Brennan, Sidney L., 196–99, 203, 219, 221, 222
Bribes. *See* Favors; Payoffs
Bricker, John, 200
Bridges, Styles, 207, 208
Brislin, John Harold, 227
Brown, Harold, 267
Buchanan, Lee K., 251, 254

Buchanan, Pat, 328, 329
Budget-making process, checklist
 on, 361
Bureau of Internal Revenue, in-
 vestigation of, 175–82
in Truman administration tax
Butz, Earl, 206–207
Byrd, Harry F., 177

Cady, Richard E., 340
Caldwell, Alex, 307–10, 311,
 314–16
Carlson, Frank, 214
Cars. *See* Automobiles; Welfare
 department fraud
Caudle, T. LaMar, 180, 190, 191
Celler, Emanuel, 191
Central Intelligence Agency (CIA),
 350–51
Chelf, Frank, 191
Chotiner, Murray, 237, 239, 242
Civil Aeronautics Board (CAB),
 232, 234–36
 reading on, 239–43
Clark, Dick, 314, 315
Clark, Robert P., 355
Clark, Tom, 190
Clerk of Court, 21, 23, 24
 checklist on, 365–67
Cohen, Nathan, 310–11
Collins, Patrick, 329, 330
Colson, Charles W., 327, 328
Combes, Abbott, 321
Commissioners, checklist for dealing
 with, 361–63
Commodities market scandals,
 305–17
Communists, fear of, 206, 208–15
Condon, Lester P., 200, 218
Confidential sources, pitfalls of, 5–6
 protection of, 290
Conflict of interest checklist on, 362
 examples of, 124–25, 133–34, 230,
  233, 239, 262–63, 266–67, 277
Congress, follow through on investi-
 gations of, 174–84
 McClelland committee of, 223–27,
  271, 273, 277
 news of, of local interest, 168–75
 reporting on, 147–67
 Senator Kefauver Crime Committee
  of, 150–55

sources in, 156–62, 290
Conkling, Mark, 121, 124, 127, 128
Connelly, Gerald P., 197, 198, 203,
 219, 221–23
Coolidge, Calvin, 325–26
Corroboration, 88–91, 103
Corruption, 40–50. *See also* Fraud;
 Labor rackets; Payoffs
 exposure of, 59–70, 78–80
 officials involved in, 92–98
 in regulatory agencies, 230–45
 spreading of, 55–57
Cotton, W.H., 85–90, 101, 102,
 111, 112, 124
Councilmen, checklist for dealing
 with, 361–63
Court(s). *See also* Grand jury;
 Prosecutor
 Clerk of, 21, 23, 24, 365–67
 coverage of, 73–74, 40–45
 records of, use of, 21–39
 routines of, 51–54
 state, influence of, on prosecution,
  106–109
 understanding of, necessary for
  reporter, 9–11
Cowles, John, 299, 300, 301
Cowles, Mike, 299, 300, 301
Credibility, of witnesses, 88–89
Crime. *See also* Labor rackets;
 Mobsters felony, flow chart on,
 42–43
 investigation of, 17–18
Crime Committee, Kefauver, 150–55
Crime laws, victimless, 40–49
Criminal cases, effect of politics on
 prosecution of, 114–19
 fixing, 22
Croft, Elmer G., favoritism case and,
 93–95, 98
 fraud by, 62–69, 71–77, 118,
  121, 123
 interview with, 74–77
 lessons from, 100–105
 politics of prosecution and, 107,
  108, 109, 111, 112
Cunningham, Paul, 159

Dahlberg, Kenneth H., 330–33
Dean, John, 329, 333, 334
Defense contracts, reading on
 bungling of, 162–66

Defense Department. *See* Pentagon
Denison, Jane, 337
Department of Justice, on investi-
    gations and prosecutions, 185–93
Dewey, Ben B., 101, 124, 131
Dirksen, Everett, 284, 302
Dockets, public, 21–24, 52, 54
Dolliver, James, 159–60
Dolliver, Jonathan P., 160
Douglas, Paul, 223
Driscoll, Jack, 349
Drunken driving fix, as example of
    investigative reporting, 25–39
Duffy, LaVern, 226, 248
Dulles, John Foster, 208, 211, 212
Dunlap, John B., 181–82
Durfee, James R., 235

Ehrlichman, John, 321, 328, 329
Eisenhower, Dwight D., Ladejinsky
    case and, 205–208, 210–15
    Pentagon and, 262–63
    regulatory agencies and, 233–35,
        239, 242–44, 255
Ervin, Sam, 336
Estes, Billie Sol, 246–58
Ethics, press, 4–5, 11–12, 55–57, 360
Evidence, from witnesses, 87–91
Exclusives, 292–93
Executive privilege, Air Force use of,
    263
    regulatory agency corruption and,
        233–37, 243, 244
Eyerly, Frank, 31, 44, 45, 136, 142,
    154, 201, 266

Farm Bureau, property assessment
    and, 130–32
Farrell, Lew, 55–57, 67, 151–54,
    176, 180, 182
    reading on, 138–42
Favoritism, in Billie Sol Estes case,
    256
    evidence of, 94–95, 98
    in regulatory agencies, 230, 233
Favors, for reporters, 56–58
Federal Bureau of Investigation
    (FBI), 63, 350–51
Federal Communications Commis-
    sion (FCC), 236–39
Felonies, flow chart for, 42–43
    investigation of, 17–18

Files, on printed stories, 187–88
Finletter, Thomas K., 164
Fitzgerald, A. Ernest, 267, 268,
    353–54
Fixing, 22
    drunk driving, case in, example of,
        25–39
Flanders, Ralph, 171–72
Ford, Gerald, 334–35
Fortas, Abe, 227, 283, 285
Fountain, L. H., 248
Fratto, Luigi. *See* Farrell, Lew
Fraud. *See also* Estes, Billie Sol
    in billing, 120–25
    in Polk County, 71–91
        follow through on report on,
            78–83
        report on, 71–77
        trials for, 84–91
    outside Polk County, 103–105
    welfare department, 64, 65, 68–69,
        71–73, 85–90, 102
Freedom of Information Laws, 9
Freeman, Orville, 246, 248–52,
    255–57

General Accounting Office (GAO),
    on Agriculture Department, 247
    analysis by, 160, 231, 234
    commodity market scandals and,
        305, 314–16
    familiarity with, necessary for
        reporter, 10
    Pentagon bungling and, 259, 263
    records by, 353
General Services Administration
    scandals, 352, 354
Gill, John P., 27–28, 61
Gillette, Guy, 161–66, 168–71
Gilpatric, Roswell, 269–70, 272,
    277, 278
Godfrey, Horace, 250, 252–53, 256
Goldfine, Bernard, 238, 243, 244,
    255
Gorey, Hays, 337
Government. *See also* Courts; Names
    of departments; Regulatory
    agencies
    history of scandals involving, 10
    investigative organizations of,
        350–51

Government (*cont.*):
  local, checklist for common evils
    in, 363–64
  Polk County lesson on, 120–28
  press offices of, 3
  property of, management of, 120–24
  scandals involving departments of,
    351–52. *See also* Agriculture
    Department
  state, and investigation at Iowa
    capital, 136–46
  understanding of, necessary for
    reporter, 9–10
Graham, Fred, 337
Grand jury, dishonest member of,
    80–81
  in drunken driving case, 27, 31,
    33–35, 38
  on laxity for special prisoners, 98
  in politics of prosecution, 109–11
  selection of, 79–80
  teamsters' rigging of, 197
Gray, L. Patrick, III, 320, 321, 324,
    326
Greene, Robert W., 16, 229, 339,
    341–49, 356
Greigg, Stanley, 322–24
Griffin, Oscar, Jr., 248–50, 257
Grimes, John M., 110
Gross, H.R., 160, 184, 297, 298, 303
Grossnickle, Basil, 64, 66–68, 96–98
Grothe, Jens, 108, 109
Grund, Harry B., 116
Guthman, Ed, 218–20, 224, 225, 227

Hagerty, James, 214, 243
Haldeman, H.R., 321–25, 328, 329
Hales, N. Battle, 246, 250–53, 255–57
Hardy, Porter, 159, 184
Harris, Oren, 241
Hartzer, Floyd, 54–55, 57, 58
Harvey, Sid, 115, 116
Hayden, Carl, 171
Health department, city or county,
    368
Healy, Robert, 230, 237–39, 243,
    244, 275
Hebert, F. Edward, 159, 260
Heller, Jean, 337
Hersh, Seymour M., 337, 350
Hershow, Sheila, 268
Hickenlooper, Burt, 161

Highway department, 368
Hild, Roy J., 90–91, 101, 102, 113,
    124
Hill, James T., 165, 166
Hill, Ralph L., 282, 286–88, 291
Hiss, Alger, 208
Hodge, Orville, 120
Hoeven, Charles B., 159
Hoffa, James R., 197, 200, 201, 219,
    221, 223, 226, 227
  interview with, 221–23
Hoffman, Clare, 200, 202
Holland, Cecil, 186–89, 265, 272–73,
    275, 276
Holmes, Oliver Wendell, 232
Hope, Paul, 290, 298
Hoschar, Al, 30, 31, 69, 136, 143
Hotz, Bob, 264
Hughes, Charles Evans, 201
Hughes, Tom, 251, 252, 256
Hume, Brit, 337
Humphrey, Hubert, 198–99, 284–85
Hunn, Hiram, 133–34
Hunt, E. Howard, 327, 328, 332, 333
Hunt, Lester, 154

Income tax investigations, 175–82
Informants. *See also* Witnesses
  dealing with, 100–103
  excited, getting facts from, 307
  handling lively, 291–92
  information from, 125
Insolia, Anthony, 343, 349
Interviews, adversary, value of, 72–73
  "hard," 71–72
  techniques for, 13, 18–19
Inventory systems, fraud in, 122–23
Investigations, *See also* Records;
    Research
  blueprint for, 347–49
  government, dealing with, 19
  income tax, 175–82
Investigative reporter(ing), blueprint
    for, 137–38
  checklist for, 361–70
  continuing problems and oppor-
    tunities in, 350–60
  in Washington, D.C., 147–50,
    188–89
  Mollenhoff primer on, 13–20
  pitfalls in, 4–7
  purpose of, 2–4

recent softness in, 352–54
seven basic rules in, 357–60
talents, techniques and traits of,
    8–20
violent attacks on, 340–41
Investigative Reporters and Editors
    (IRE), 16, 339–44
Ives, Irving M., 220

Jackson, D. Brooks, 337
Jackson, Henry M., 269–71, 274,
    276, 313
Jackson, Robert (Bob), 335
Jacobs, Emery, 250, 252, 253
Jail, Polk County, 92–99
Jensen, Ben, 157–58
Johnson, Lyndon B., 269, 270,
    280–304
Jones, Mary Kimbrough, 251, 253,
    254, 257
Judd, Walter, 205–206, 208, 209, 212
Judge, choice of, 81–82
Jury. *See* Grand jury
Jury board, role of, 79–80
Jury commission, role of, 79–80
Justice Department, on investi-
    gations and prosecutions, 185–93

Kantor, Seth, 272, 292
Keating, Kenneth, 191
Kefauver, Estes, 150–55, 174, 175,
    180, 181, 195
Kefauver Crime Committee, 150–55
Kelly, Harry, 337
Kelly, Herb, 30, 31, 44, 45
Kennedy, John, Billie Sol Estes case
    and, 246, 249, 250, 257
    Bobby Baker case and, 287–89, 295
    labor rackets and, 223, 226
    Pentagon and, 263, 269, 270
Kennedy, Robert, Billie Sol Estes
    case and, 255
    Bobby Baker case and, 282, 285,
        288, 289, 296, 297
    labor rackets and, 220, 223–27
    Pentagon and, 261, 263, 274–75
Kerr, Robert, 290, 291
Kessler, Ron, 354
King, Cecil, 186, 187, 190
Kleindienst, Richard, 321, 326
Knebel, Fletcher, 154, 301
Knoll, Erwin, 293

Korth, Fred, 272, 273, 277, 278
Kraslow, David, 230, 237–39, 244
Krock, Arthur, 148
Kuble, Francis, 26, 31–35, 65

Labor rackets, 194–203, 217–29
Ladejinsky case, 205–15
    reading on, 209–15
Lainson, Percy A., 103, 104
Lambert, Williams, 217–18, 224, 227
Land transfer research, 13
Landau, Jack, 283
Landauer, Jerry, 337
Landrum-Griffin labor reform act,
    226
Lardner, George, 337
Larson, Robert L., 107, 108
Law(s), understanding of, necessary
    for reporter, 9–11
    victimless crime, 40–49
Law enforcement, selective, 44–45
Law enforcement officials. *See also*
    Jail; Police
    dealing with, 19
Law practice, of U.S. attorneys, 192
Lawlor, Joseph P., 162–66
Lawrence, Bill, 262
Lawson, Alfred, 182
LeCompte, Karl, 158
Leece, William, 218, 224
Lev, Harry, 261
Levy, Claudia, 321
Lewis, Alfred E., 321
Liddy, G. Gordon, 327, 332
Lilienthal, David, 161
Link, Ted, 176, 177, 179, 180, 185,
    225, 226
Linn, Harry, 110
Lippmann, Walter, 276, 356
Liquor and beer licenses, checklist
    on, 362–63
Liquor control, investigation in-
    volving, 137–42
Liquor laws, in example of payoffs,
    43–49

MacArthur, Douglas, 206, 208
Marro, Anthony, 337
McCabe, Edward, 220, 224
McCarthy, Joseph, 168–72, 178,
    208, 210, 213, 224

McClellan, John L., 220, 223, 224, 257, 261, 262, 274–75
McClellan committee investigations, 223–27, 271, 273, 277
McCone, John A., 164
McConnell, Sam, 219–20
McCord, James, 319, 321–24, 327, 335
McGranery, James P., 191, 192
McGrath, J. Howard, 180, 190, 191
McLeod, Henry, 275
Mack, Richard A., 236–39
MacKinnon, George, 203
McLeod, R.W. Scott, 207–209, 211
McNamara, Robert S., 263–65, 269, 270, 272–78
Magruder, Jeb, 321–24, 332, 336
Marks, Joseph A., 117, 140
Marshall, Henry, 252
Martin, Thomas E., 158–59, 175, 176
Mashburn, Lloyd, 201
Mazo, Earl, 249, 250
Meany, George, 221
Mellett, Donald, 341
Military. *See* Pentagon
Miller, Herbert J., 255, 297
Milloy, James, 299–301
Mills, George, 136, 145
Milne, Edward J., 169–72, 185, 189, 190
Mintz, Morton, 337
Misdemeanors, flow chart for, 42–43
  indictable, flow chart for, 42–43
Mitchell, John, 268, 324, 326, 328
Mobsters, 151–55, 175–76, 181
  See also Farrell
Mollenhoff primer, 13–20
Moore, C. Edwin, 101, 102, 109, 116, 117, 139, 140
Morrison, Julian, 284, 290, 292
Morse, Wayne, 241, 242
Moss, John, 184, 234
Moulder, Morgan, 233
Murphy, Charles S., 250, 252, 254, 256

Naughton, James, 248, 337
Nelson, Jack, 335, 337
Nepotism, example of, 280
Nixon, Richard M., 5, 237, 268, 305, 318–38
Nossiter, Bernard, 268
Nunnally, Thomas, 272

O'Brien, Lawrence, 319, 323, 324, 326, 332
O'Brien, Tim, 321
Office of Price Administration (OPA), 61–63
O'Leary, Jerry, 186, 272
Oliphant, Charles, 175, 176, 179, 181
Olson, James B.E., 179
Oosterhout, Martin Van, 102, 103
Ostrow, Ron, 335, 337
Ottenberg, Miriam, 272
Overturff, Vane B., 62, 64–65, 68, 70, 93, 101, 131, 134

P-60 scandal, 142–45, 158
Packers and Stockyards Act, 316, 317
Parkhurst, Charles, 59, 60
Parmenter, Charles, 88, 90, 101, 102
Patman, Wright, 332–35
Payoffs, 40–50. *See also* Favors
  in drunken driving cases, 25
  probe of, 114–19
Pearson, Drew, 241, 243
Pentagon, waste and mismanagement at, 259–79
Personnel management, in county government, 123–24
Personnel probe, checklist for full, 369–70
Plant, Francis X., 198, 202, 203, 218, 224
Polk, James, 337
Police departments. *See also* Jail; Law enforcement officials
  checklist on, 365
  corruption in, 54–55, 57–58, 60
  court reporting and, 40–45
  records and procedures of, use of, 21–39
  routines in, 51–58
Political parties, Congressional reporting and, 157–58
  criminal prosecution and, 114–19
  favoritism and, 98–99
  informants and, 101, 103, 104
  powerful, and corruption, 59–60, 65, 70, 79–83
  prosecution and, 106–13
  TFX case and, 269
Pope, James S., 182, 234
Potter, Chester, 177, 180, 185
Potter, Phil, 213

Powers, B.J., 112
Press, free, 1–7
Press agent, 178–79
Press officers, government, 3
Primer, Mollenhoff, 13–20
Prina, Ed, 272
Printed stories, saving, copying, and
    using, 187–88
Prochnau, William, 275, 276
Property, assessments of, 129–35
    government, management of,
        120–24
    reading on, 125–28
    records on transfer of, 13
Prosecution. See also Trials
    criminal, effect of politics on,
        114–19
    politics of, 106–13
Prosecutor, choice of, 82
    dealing with, 19
Proxmire, William, 267
Pulliam, Myrta, 340

Rackets. See Labor rackets
Rand, Peter A., 95–98, 101
Rayburn, Sam, 186, 232
Real estate. See also Property
    reading on, 125–28
Record(s), arrest, 13, 14, 23
    checking of and research of, 13–16,
        23, 51–53, 291, 345–46
    of Clerk of Court, 21, 23, 24,
        365–67
    drawbacks to use of, 55
    on investigation, 16
    land transfer, 13
    police and court, use of, 21–39
    on printed stories, 187–88
    routine, 15–16
Recorder's office, checklist on,
    367–68
Reece, Ben, 225
References. See also Records
    on printed stories, 187–88
Reformers, 64–70
Reforms, analysis of, 2–3
Regulatory agencies, 230–45. See also
    Commodities market scandals
Renner, Tom, 343
Reporters. See Investigative reporter
Reppert, Howard, 70, 86, 87, 93–98,
    118, 134

Republican party machine, 59–60,
    65, 70, 79–83. See also Political
    parties
Research, importance of, 345–46.
    See also Records
Revolving door syndrome, 232–33
Reynolds, Charles, 266
Reynolds, Don, 285–88, 291–92,
    294–96, 303
Rice, Downey, 152–53, 181, 195,
    196, 198, 200–203, 218, 224
Rich, Spencer, 337
Riesel, Victor, 223, 341
Riis, Jacob, 41, 52, 59
Ripley, Anthony, 337
Risser, Jim, 315, 316
Rodino, Peter A., 191
Romer, Sam, 196
Rometsch, Elly, 280, 288–89, 295
Roosevelt, Theodore, 40–42, 58, 60
Rosee, Bernhard, case involving,
    305–12, 314
Rosenthal, A.M., 342
Ross, Heck, 115, 116
Rubber stamp incident, 121–22
Rugaber, Walter, 330, 331, 337
Russell, Richard, 267
Ruther, Walter J., 108
Ryan, Earl, 31–34

Sackett, Russell, 337
Schafenberg, Kirk, 321
Schneider, Harry, 178–79
Schoeneman, George L., 175, 176,
    178, 179, 181
School system, checklist on, 368
Schoolfield, Raulston, 226
Schram, Martin, J., 337
Schuchat, Theodor, 293
Schwartz, Bernard, 233–42
Seamans, Robert J., 268. See also
    Security risk
Secrecy.
    in Congress, provisions for, 174–84
    on property assessment, 131–33
    reading on attack on, 180–82
Security risk, claim of, 204–16
Seib, Charles, 4, 355
Seigenthaler, John, 218, 225–27
Seymour, Gideon, 194, 196, 199,
    200, 202, 203
Sheriff(s), checklist on, 365

Sheriff(s), checklist on (*cont.*):
example of careless, 92–99
Sinclair, Upton, 195
Sirica, John, 336
Sloan, Hugh W., Jr., 329–30
Smathers, George, 284–85
Smith, Milan D., 210, 211, 213
Smith, Neal, 313–14
Smith, Sandy, 337
Smith, Wint, 200
Snyder, John M., 178, 189, 190
Sources. *See also* Informants
members of Congress as, 156–62
Soviet wheat deals, 312–13
Spear, Joe, 337
Spry, Clyde, 137, 142–45, 157
Spry, Dick, 25, 26
Squires, James, 333, 337
Stans, Maurice, 333, 334
Stassen, Harold, 213
State courts. *See* Courts
State government. *See* Government
Steele, Jack, 149, 150, 155, 290
Steffens, Lincoln, 14, 16, 41, 42, 52, 58–60, 195
Stern, Carl, 337
Stern, Lawrence, 283, 337
Stories, "hot," 290–91
printed, saving, copying, and using, 187–88
Strohmeyer, John, 177, 180, 185, 225
Sussman, Barry, 331, 337
Switzer, Carroll, 70, 80–83, 86, 87, 90, 94, 98, 101–18, 122, 123, 127, 128, 139, 140
Sylvester, Arthur, 263, 271, 274

Taft-Hartley Law, 195–96, 201, 203, 222
Talbott, Harold E., 255, 262–63
Talle, Henry O., 160
Talmadge, Herman, 312–14
Tax assessor, 368
Tax scandals, 175–82, 185–93
Taylor, Jack, 17, 227–28
Teamsters Union, 195–203, 217–18
Teapot Dome scandals, 59, 226, 325–26
TFX case, 265–66, 269–78
Thayer, Edwin S., 82, 87, 89, 101–103, 108–12, 114–18, 121, 133, 134

Theim, George, 120
Thomas, Helen, 337
Thompson, H. H., 86–88, 101–104, 106, 113, 126–27
Thomasson, Dan, 290, 333, 337
Thomson, James C., Jr., 4–5
Tobey, Charles W., 154, 195, 198–200
Trade publication reporters, 239
Treasury Department, tax scandal involving, 185, 189
Trials. *See also* Prosecution
fraud, in Polk County, 84–91
Truman administration tax scandals, 185–93
reading on, 189–93
Turner, Wallace, 217–18, 224, 227, 337

Uhl, Raymond, 133

Van Kirk, Burkett, 295
Velie, Lester, 223
Vice, 40–50
Vinson, Carl, 267
Volz, Joseph, 329, 330, 337

Walsh, Robert, 272
Walters, Paul, 64–70, 73, 79, 81, 82, 85, 87, 89, 93–98, 103, 104, 107, 108, 112, 113, 117, 118, 121
War surplus cars fraud, 108–11
Watergate scandal, 5, 318–38
Watson, Mark, 264, 265
Weighart, James, G., 337
Weil, Martin, 321
Welfare department fraud, 64, 65, 68–69, 71–73, 85–90, 102
Welker, Herman, 171
Wennerstrum, W.F., 111–13
Wheat deals, Soviet, 312–13
Whitten, Les, 290, 337, 347–48
Williams, John J., 177–80, 183, 184, 186, 240–42, 244, 247, 248, 250, 253–57, 285–98, 301–303, 326, 329
Williams, Paul N., 339, 340, 343
Wilson, Charles E., 163
Wilson, George, 264
Wilson, Mike, 29, 30, 34–36
Wilson, Richard, 148, 149, 194, 205
Wilson, Will, 249

Winegardner, Jack, 126–28
Winegardner, Robert, 125–27
Winship, Tom, 238
Witnesses, cooperating, 88
  credibility of, 88–89
  evidence from, 87–91

"friendly," informant as, 100–103
  hostile, 87–88
Woodward, Bob, 5, 6, 322, 327,
  328, 331, 359
Wright, Frank, 336

p 361